JOHN BIFFEN
SEMI-DETACHED
WITH A FOREWORD BY MATTHEW PARRIS

Biteback Publishing

First published in Great Britain in 2013 by
Biteback Publishing Ltd
Westminster Tower
3 Albert Embankment
London SE1 7SP
Copyright © The Estate of John Biffen 2013

Cartoon by 'Marc', Mark Boxer. Reproduced by kind permission of Mark Amory.

ISBN 978-1-84954-239-5

A CIP catalogue record for this book is available from the British Library.

Set in Baskerville

Printed and bound in Great Britain by
CPI Group (UK) Ltd, Croydon CR0 4YY

MIX
Paper from
responsible sources
FSC® C020471

CONTENTS

FOREWORD BY MATTHEW PARRIS

Asked by John Biffen's widow, Sarah, if I would write a short foreword to *Semi-Detached*, my immediate response was one of pleasure. I respected John enough – tremendously – to want to accept this honour. I liked him enough too: I liked him enormously.

But did I know him enough? Surely there would be old colleagues who knew him better: confidants, comrades-in-arms, people he'd knocked around with more, members of his gang?

But a moment's reflection suggested this was unlikely. John didn't have a gang. Anyone Sarah had asked would have responded similarly: 'I'd love to, but surely someone knew him better.' Little as I felt I ever really knew John, I have a strong impression that almost nobody else in politics did either. There are perhaps scores of us in England individually convinced that somebody must have known John well, but that it wasn't us.

These are the memoirs of a man who had hardly an enemy in the world, but none of whose many friends really knew him. The thing to say about John – everybody said it – was 'lovely chap, but of course he's desperately shy'. I don't think he was shy. He was intensely private but in no sense guarded: he could be shockingly honest. In some sense this quiet privateness sprang, I suspect, not from nervousness but from confidence.

I don't think – though this was often suggested – that John was particularly lonely. I do think he needed looking after. And in the end, and happily, there was Sarah to look after him.

John didn't carouse, confide, chat or endlessly socialise because he didn't have to and didn't care to. He had an inner life and I suppose a very deep one, but no great compulsion to share it. As these memoirs show, he was always a man of ideas; but I'm very sure he was a man of feelings too, curiously passionate in his way. So confident was he of his ideas that he had on the whole concluded that they were strong enough to stand alone; and so, although he was always ready to set out his thinking, he felt no need to evangelise and very little need even to persuade; I doubt John ever twisted an arm in his life. As to his feelings, you will find in the pages that follow some fascinating hints, but never any wish to wallow.

Above all – and anybody, literally anybody you ask who worked with him, will echo this – there was less pretence about John Biffen than almost any other successful politician we could name. Read these pages and ask yourself whether there is within them a single feigned affection, a single deliberate untruth, a single false claim. This virtue in him is the key to a rather extraordinary quality in the style and content of his prose: it is clear, matter-of-fact, usually low-key, occasionally even a little flat – like a schoolboy's essay … and then, all at once, comes a flash of astonishing honesty: an observation delivered in a matter-of-fact way without fanfare and for no other reason than that it is germane, useful and true.

You always felt with John – this unassuming, understated, contemplative man – just a hint of danger: the thrilling possibility that he might suddenly and quietly upset the applecart. A Eurosceptic when it was brave to be a Eurosceptic, an admirer of Enoch Powell's with the moral and intellectual stature to question Powell's judgement, Biffen was (in my view) Enoch's intellectual superior, but entirely lacking the latter's showmanship, and uncorroded by personal ambition.

I will mention another Biffenite quality: one which distinguished him from Enoch. He was fastidious. Not in the girly sense – a less girly man I never met – but in a steadfast refusal to compromise himself or his own very personal politics. He would have detested (indeed when I last saw him he indicated how much he detested) 21st-century British politics, with its 'messages', focus-groups and soundbites. This fastidiousness was, I believe, born not only of self-respect, but of respect for his countrymen and countrywomen: his belief that they were neither fools nor children, and capable of understanding any important thing in politics if only it was patiently explained. The happily very full chapters in this memoir about his boyhood and rural circumstances – quite unencumbered by nostalgia – give a clear and engaging picture of the England he believed he knew, and in which he placed his trust.

Like many of the greatest, John was really always an outsider. Bullied at school and unable to understand the bullies, he becomes gently and unapologetically (he says) 'a little swot'. A scholarship to study history at Cambridge transports him from rural Somerset and the family dairy to (via Cyprus, Egypt and National Service) the Cambridge University Conservative Association. Here his inherited rural conservatism, formed quietly around an Aga in the Quantocks, solidifies. He surprises himself by unexpectedly being adopted as the Tory candidate for Oswestry.

There or at Cambridge or at Westminster, did he think he ever fitted in? He grew up on a farm, but wasn't really a farmer. He went to Cambridge, but was never assimilated into the smart set. He was amongst the leaders of his political generation when

I knew him at Westminster, but I always set him apart from the rest. Somehow, and always courteously, he set himself apart.

Margaret Thatcher's press secretary, Bernard Ingham, spoke the truth when he called John 'semi-detached', but what Bernard failed to recognise was that the phrase confers upon him the highest possible praise. These are the memoirs of the least-known leading politician of his generation, and of a good and brilliant Englishman.

PREFACE BY SARAH BIFFEN

In a letter to Matthew Parris dated 3 February 2004 my husband wrote this:

> I am near completing my time and life. I never intended to write it, but when I fell seriously ill with total renal failure Sarah suggested I should leave 'some recollections' for her children Nicholas and Lucy.
>
> The book is divided equally between childhood, National Service, Cambridge, working in engineering in Birmingham and then as a business economist in London. The second section consists of about twenty odd 'sketches' on Westminster, including personal sketches of Margaret Thatcher, Edward Heath and Enoch Powell, as well as recollections of the great European debates, the forgotten age of endless arguments over statutory prices and incomes, years as a member of the 1922 Executive and time in the Cabinet.
>
> This section is *not* full of views. It is a somewhat sardonic reflection on a vocation (more than a career) that happily occupied my life.
>
> As an only child I was brought up on a farm in the depths of the country; no mains water or electricity etc. Education was the ladder from the village school to a First at Cambridge.

For over ten years from the mid-1960s to the mid-1970s I had to cope with manic depression which had an influence on my Westminster life. At the time I could not make this public, but I devote a 'sketch' to this and I am so relieved I can put it on record.

‡

In the autumn of 2000 John was diagnosed with complete renal failure. By the time he started dialysis in the New Year he had been ill for several months and was very weak. In an effort to divert him while he lay recovering on the sofa in our Battersea house I suggested that he talk to me about his Somerset childhood and I take notes on my laptop. For many months he reminisced and I typed and printed. As he got stronger he became enthralled and eventually took over the project, expanding it to cover his whole life. It was a major source of interest to him. Over the next few years he checked facts and dates and sorted through photographs and finally started looking for a publisher. Written while John was undergoing several hours of dialysis three times a week, the book is probably different from the one he might have produced at an earlier, healthier stage of his life.

From 1968 until 1990 John kept a diary, of which I have included extracts – particularly from the period of his eight years in the Cabinet. He would write it up each day in an A5 diary, two days to a page. He clearly intended to publish it at some stage as he had edited it up until the mid-1970s, drawing a red line through most of the highly personal material.

I think of John as a brave man. Brave in overcoming terrifying nerves to become first an MP and then a Cabinet minister. Brave to persist until he found the correct treatment to help him cope. Brave to undergo stoically the discomfort and considerable side effects of dialysis for six and a half years. And, on a more personal note, brave to marry for the first time a divorcée with two young children the day before his 49th birthday. We were married for just short of twenty-eight years.

The 1980s were a turbulent time of extreme pressure, hard work and drama. But things settled down in the 1990s. John was a tremendous House of Commons man. He was devoted to its history and traditions and spent hours of his many years as an MP sitting in the Chamber, watching and listening. He could be a brilliant public speaker. His speeches, whether in the House of Commons, the constituency or elsewhere, were famous for their sheer quality and thoughtfulness. The Chamber of the House of Commons would fill when his name flashed up on the television monitor. I tried to be in the gallery for all his important speeches and particularly when he had to take Question Time. He used to glance up to see if I was there. He would start hesitantly and as he got into his stride would rock on his feet with an occasional, almost balletic bounce. He had a gift for the off-the-cuff witty remark. This man, while being deeply engaged in the world, was an acute and sometimes amused observer of it.

Leaving the Commons in 1997 was a wrench but he soon became attached to the House of Lords and a regular attendee until a couple of weeks before he died.

John was very much a family man. He loved being at home in our house on the Welsh Borders. He was very proud of his stepchildren and they became his main topic of conversation at political functions. Wives of visiting statesmen would tell me how much they had enjoyed hearing all about my children. He adored his cat, Miss Puss, who lived to be seventeen and has a hand-inscribed slate memorial under a walnut tree.

A methodical man, he would set the kitchen timer for twenty minutes and go down on his hands and knees and weed the cobbled yard. Another twenty minutes would be spent filing in the attic and then perhaps twenty minutes writing his diary or stoning plums.

The publication of this book would have been an immense source of pride and pleasure to John.

EARLY CHILDHOOD

I was Somerset born and Somerset descended. It really is remarkable that for over two hundred years my forebears seemed to have dwelt not only in Somerset but within a twenty-mile radius of the Levels and the Mendips. Theirs was a truly rural lifestyle: the Biffens mostly tenant farmers, the Bennetts on my mother's side occasionally owner occupiers. Some were agricultural labourers; none were ever squires.

I was born in the Mary Stanley Nursing Home on 3 November 1930. It was a difficult birth; my mother nearly died in the process and was advised not to have any more children. I think that must have been a factor in the close relationship I had with both my parents and particularly my mother.

Hill Farm, which my father tenanted, was equidistant between the villages of Otterhampton and Combwich. It seemed a very big place to me with an enormous garden, of which I was the only occupant. When I was small my mother used to put me in a playpen out on the front lawn whilst she ran the house – no mean task given the size and lack of amenities. Once she tried putting Flossie the farm dog in the pen with me to keep me company. I must have poked her in the ear or disturbed her in some way as she turned round and bit me. Everyone agreed it was my fault but that I had acted out of ignorance. Anyway it had a lasting consequence. My fear of dogs dates from this episode and it was the last time my mother tried that method of babysitting. Later on she put me in the corner of the dairy whilst she got on with her work.

With no brothers and sisters or neighbouring children to play with, the animals were my playmates and the farm my playground. We didn't have any domestic animals in the house as the dogs and cats all lived outside. My first special friend when I was very young was a pet rabbit kept in a wooden hutch. He was white with a few black spots and I announced he was to be called Peter. The fact that subsequently he turned out to be a doe rabbit was something I ignored. He was particularly fond of milk thistles and I used to go out into the hedgerows and pick great bunches for him. On special occasions he was allowed into the kitchen, where he hopped around. I was very fond of him and he lived to a venerable old age and died in his sleep. I was never encouraged to replace him with another domestic pet. My parents' view was that they had enough on their hands without having animals in the house.

There were masses of cats on the farm to keep me company. They were kept firmly out of the house and made their home underneath the big hay loft. They were mostly very wild and bred prodigiously. A particular friend was a black cat with touches of ginger called Prince. He was tamer than the others and would follow me about when I was playing in the yard. Many years later we had a highly domesticated ginger cat. With no originality he was called Ginger and, breaking the family rule, was allowed into the house where, like most cats, he ruled the establishment.

From a very early age I recollect being strongly tied to farm and family. I did not relish change or adventure. Once we had a neighbour to tea and she commented to my mother, 'Your John has a double crown. That means he will travel.' Apparently my face creased and tears began to form. 'I don't want to leave you,' I said. I suppose it was an early sign of the insularity which I have never quite lost.

With the number of animals we kept there was muck everywhere. From time to time it was cleared up and put in the central midden by the stables, where it was a very prominent feature of farm life. One day when I was quite small I decided to go off exploring on my own. My mother's sister Ruth was living with us at the time and she thought I was with my mother whilst my mother thought I was with her. I traipsed off down towards the farm gate. For some reason instead of going out onto the road I turned left and fell head first into the muck heap. It was no joke and I would have suffocated if Wiggy, a farm worker, hadn't come to the rescue and pulled me out. This incident became part of folklore and had a bizarre consequence. Wiggy's son Brian became an employee at Gatwick airport. He was checking the baggage of Tristan Garel-Jones and noticed he was an MP. 'My Dad knew John Biffen and saved him from the manure heap,' he said. Garel-Jones, then a whip and a Euro loyalist, shared the Whips' Office view that I had been in the fertiliser, or something more basic, ever since.

HILL FARM: HOUSE AND YARD

Hill Farm was a substantial building that had seen better days. In the 1930s it was decidedly shabby. The house stood apart from the outbuildings, but it had the most unprepossessing entrance, covered by a corrugated iron roof. The house was a classical E-shape and probably dated from the sixteenth century. The theory was that it was not built as a farmhouse but had once been the local 'big house', occupied by a squire rather than a tenant farmer. It pre-dated Hill House, which had been the substantial home of the Everards, the local 'big family', and which became a girls' private school in 1939.

The farmhouse was deceptive. Despite its size it did not contain many rooms. They were all large and seemed to be called by the wrong name. The kitchen took no part in food preparation and was really the dining room. It was a square room with wooden beams and a large window with a fixed window seat against which stood a table. At the beginning of the war this room was the scene of a great drama. My father had removed the old range and installed a brick fireplace with a very effective fire. Unknown to him a beam had been left bricked up in the chimney. Over a period of time it began to slowly smoulder and eventually a most terrible acrid smoke broke through into the room one night. All the stored food was affected and the place was smoked out. As a result the entire chimney had to be rebuilt. Because of the war my parents felt obliged to eat up all the tainted food, a sad process which seemed to last weeks.

Despite the mishap the 'kitchen' became the centre of our wartime lives. All our meals were eaten there; my father had a huge roll-top desk where he stored his papers. The radio provided the news and the table was used for endless games of cards. It remained so for thirty years or so until my father retired.

The room where my mother cooked led off the 'kitchen' and was known as the 'scullery', a large all-purpose room lined with cupboards for the crockery and a food store. Until the war she coped with a primitive Florence oil cooker. But early in the war this was replaced by an Aga which transformed the place. It was also a sign that farming was doing better after the hardships of the 1930s.

Opposite the kitchen there had been a huge room with no passage. This had been altered by the erection of a flimsy wooden partition which created a passage and two small rooms. We huddled in one of these rooms during the winter before the kitchen was gentrified. With scant imagination it was known as the 'little room'. The second room was used as a store for my mother's lethal home-made wine; dandelion was the family favourite.

The prize room was at the end of the house. It was called the 'top room' and had a fine westerly view of the Quantock Hills; it was by far the most pleasant room in the house and, paradoxically, not much used. It was the room that had the date marking of 1666 over the fireplace, with beautiful plastered ceilings and a wall frieze that covered the timbers. I was not much aware of these virtues. For me the top room meant space and freedom from adults. Alone I invented battles and races, with cigarette cards where I was able to determine the winners and losers. We always went there after lunch on Sundays and my father would read *The People* until it was time to do the milking. Special visitors were welcomed there. In November 1938 Patrick Heathcoat-Amory, the luckless Conservative candidate in the Bridgwater by-election, was taken there and given White Horse whisky. It was one of my first political memories.

Attached to the rear of the farmhouse was a small brick room which had been built fairly recently. It was known as the 'back-house'. Its tiny space contained a blackleaded fireplace which heated a side oven. It was extensively used until the arrival of the Aga. It required intuitive cooking skills and no tears were shed when it fell into disuse. The 'backhouse' also contained an old-fashioned boiler, again heated by a coal fire, which was used for the family laundry, and also a sink (with the only tap in the house) for washing up. I came to know it well. From an early age I was conscripted to do the drying whilst my mother and her sister Ruth would put the crockery away in all corners of the house. It was about as unplanned an arrangement as you could imagine.

The top floor of Hill Farm was spacious and gave some idea of its age. Originally all the bedrooms led from one directly to the other. Subsequently a wooden partition was erected, which formed a passage. There were five bedrooms, all rather large. One had fallen into disuse, and its floor was largely used to store fruit and vegetables. In 1949 it was adapted to provide the bathroom, a development with no architectural imagination.

My parents had a very large bedroom with a south-facing window seat. I remember my mother sitting in the window seat in the early summer mornings, at around 5 a.m., listening to the dawn chorus from the neighbouring coverts. There was also a guest bedroom and the capacious west-facing room that was used as a cheese store, and my own bedroom, which looked over the farmyard.

We always slept with the windows open and in the summer bats would fly in and out. They lived in the tumbledown 'potato house' wing of the house. Although a nervous child, I got used to their visits and rather enjoyed them. Guests tended to feel otherwise.

The garden at Hill Farm was extremely large, even after discounting the plot that was attached to the cottage that formed a wing of the house. A gravel path ran from the roadside gate to the front door. There was lawn on either side of the porch and three pairs of trees including a couple of arbutus trees. They were quite distinguished, but the overall impression was that the garden had seen far better days.

The vegetable garden had once occupied over two-thirds of the total space but now only half was in use. My mother was a devoted gardener. Although my father did little gardening he was generous in allowing his employees to help my mother. I was encouraged to take an interest and given a plot where I tended cos and dwarf lettuces. The enthusiasm soon waned, never to be renewed.

In retrospect it was very pleasant to have lived in an Elizabethan farmhouse. However, the facilities were primitive to the extreme. I can just remember the days when there was no mains water. It came from a well in the field called Well Close, which had been in use for generations. It was carried in by a yoke and two great pails. The water was then poured into a huge pitcher which we dipped into as we needed. We were connected to a mains supply in the early 1930s and then had only one tap in the farmhouse. The farm buildings did rather better.

We had no mains electricity until 1949, by which time I had left home. There was never any question of having a generator to provide our own electricity, so throughout the time I lived at home we managed with oil lamps. We still had some old-fashioned lamps inherited from my grandmother but the main source of light was from an Aladdin lamp. It gave out a beautiful soft light and was immensely superior to the other oil lamps. We used to carry it from room to room but it was very temperamental. The mantle would often soot up and catch fire and the slightest movement would disturb it. Knowing this you might wonder why anyone would venture to thump the table. However, my family of inveterate card players was always thumping the table. My father was a very successful card player. If he had a trump which would take a decisive trick, he would bang the cards down on the table with a shout of triumph, at which moment the Aladdin lamp would go on the blink. My mother was always mournfully saying, 'It gives out a beautiful light but it's very temperamental.'

Throughout my school career I did my homework by oil lamp. At bedtime the Aladdin was turned down and blown out and we went upstairs by candlelight. Of course there was no heating upstairs. It was spartan. When I was very small I had a night light in the bedroom. In the winter we used to undress at night and get up in the morning by candlelight. As I got older I would read in bed by candlelight, which worried my mother because of the possible effect on my eyes.

During the war life was transformed by the arrival of the Tilley lamp. This was much more robust with a pressure pump and gave a harsh but reliable light. When the Air Force came to the camp in the neighbouring village they introduced us to hurricane lamps. They were like portable Tilleys and could be used in the farmyard. We were edging into the twentieth century, but not, alas, with the loo.

We had an outdoor privy at least thirty yards away from the farmhouse. Situated down a beaten earth path it became a hazardous expedition in rain and frost. It was a modest brick building with a wooden seat and earth closet. There was no light so one had to take a torch or a lantern at night; and it was provided with ample discarded copies of the *Daily Mail* and *The People* newspapers. The worst job on the farm was cleaning it out, and every so often one of the employees dug it out and spread the contents over an unused part of the garden. My mother absolutely hated it and it was one of the least attractive aspects of farm life.

Early in the 1930s the local authority sent round the health inspector. First he was shown round the farm buildings. Then he looked at the house and tramped down the garden path to inspect the lavatory. My mother was very crestfallen when he said, 'Oh that's all right. It's a long distance from the house.' She had hoped that it would be banned and she could get a 'proper' lavatory. Both her sister Keturah and my father's sister, Millicent, had houses with up-to-date plumbing. However, my poor mother had to wait until 1948 before a bathroom and indoor loo were installed on the top landing.

Bathing as a child meant a galvanised tin bath. There were several sizes and they lived suspended on the wall of the backhouse. Every Friday night I would be washed in one of the small tin baths. The boiler in the backhouse would be heated up and hot water poured into the bath where I would sit and be given a very good scrub by my mother. One of the diversions was when a farmer calling to deliver produce would come in and throw a penny at me which would plop into the water and circle round until it came to rest on my stomach. I was always ready to perform my role: money before decorum.

The sink in the backhouse served for both personal toilet and washing up. Every morning my father would stand there in his shirtsleeves shaving. By the time I was old enough to be an audience he had given up his cut-throat razor and was using a safety one. He used to sing in an amiably tuneless way 'Goodbye

Dolly Gray' and songs from *The Maid of the Mountains* and *The Quaker Girl.*

Despite the lack of facilities, standards of cleanliness were maintained and my father never brought the farm into the house. At the end of the day's work he would strip to the waist and have a good wash at the sink. He was meticulous about his hands and nails. He had a lovely bone-handled pocket knife; razor sharp, it was used for everything from cutting out foot rot to manicuring his own nails. I was amazed at the skill and dexterity with which he achieved a perfect result.

The family wash also took place in the backhouse. It was all pretty basic. We hardly ever used the Bridgwater Steam Laundry and almost everything was washed at home, usually mid-week when my father was at Bridgwater market. It was all put into the copper bath and boiled up together and then rinsed in one of the tin baths. I suppose there was a 'white wash'. It was then put through a formidable ancient wooden mangle. This was eventually replaced in the mid-1930s by a Jiffy with rubber rollers, which was a great improvement, even though it would not take the really big things. It was all put out to dry on a massive clothes line in the paddock. The bushes and privet hedge were put into service and things would be spread over them to dry.

It was a huge performance and when I was small I would hold the pegs whilst my mother hung up the clothes. These were a mixture of small wooden ones with metal springs and large hand-carved wooden ones sold to us by travelling gypsies. Proximity to the Bristol Channel meant there was lots of wind where we lived, so life would be punctuated by a fair number of alarms when we had to rush out and get the clothes in before they blew all over the farmyard.

The farmhouse was matched by a fine set of old farm buildings of varying ages up to two hundred years old. Subsequently they were converted into several houses without much care to preserve their character. The centrepiece was a two-storey brick barn in which hay was kept in the loft and sacks of animal feed, fertiliser and nitrogen on the floor below. In summer the hay would be loaded into the loft by a creaking mechanical elevator. Subsequently it would be fed to the beef cattle. These were housed in the Round House, a semi-circular stone building with a tiled roof adjoining a partly covered yard. At the far end of the yard was a shippen for around thirty-five dairy cows. It was a mean wooden shed where the hand milking took place twice a day. I thought it was dreadfully smelly and I kept away. We also had solid stone mushrooms on which to pile the ricks of hay and corn, mostly wheat and barley.

There was also a large steel open-sided Dutch barn, which must have been a fairly recent addition to the farmyard. It stored the harvested wheat and barley; in the winter it ceased to be a store and became a battleground. A huge threshing machine would arrive, steam powered and belt driven. It made a horrendous din. I would watch this spectacle from as great a distance as I could manage. The threshing disturbed the nesting rats, and the threshers pursued the rats with stones and pitchforks. It was crude hunting accompanied by much bad language which I did not then understand. I was a fascinated but frightened spectator.

In contrast to this drama there was a stone building with feeding troughs and a superb studded door. It seemed ageless and usually housed pigs or calves. Hill Farm was about 120 acres with a remarkable range of buildings, in size and age. Unaware of its history, it was my childhood playground, reasonably adventurous but close to my parents.

3

FARMING AND CHRISTMAS

My father inherited the tenancy of the farm from his parents. They had moved to Otterhampton from the Polden Hills just after the First World War. Granny Biffen used to deplore the dreadful state of the farm under the previous tenant: ditches overgrown and carcass bones left in the fields. The landlord, Oliver Leigh, lived near Axbridge. He made only infrequent visits and I was always spruced up for the occasion. I think my father was a responsible tenant. He realised his landlord shared the generally poor circumstances of farming after the First World War. He only sought improvements and renovations for the farm buildings. The Elizabethan house continued to decay gently and my mother stoically accepted the earth closet and the pervading dampness.

Although beef cattle were my father's pride there was plenty of other stock. He always had a modest number of sheep, often Dorset Downs. He bought his lambs from the sheep sales on the Brendon Hills. I can remember accompanying him when he went to sales at Cutcombe and Raleigh's Cross. The sheep fair lasted most of the day. It was a wonderful family outing. My father enjoyed the bargaining and my mother and I would go for walks on the hillside amidst the pens of sheep. There were dogs everywhere but I just managed to suppress my fear. My mother packed a picnic, invariably hard-boiled eggs, which we ate together whilst my father would go to the village inn to promote convivial relations with the dealers. He loved it. Hill Farm was some fifteen miles from the Brendon and Exmoor sheep fairs, but up to the Second World War the purchased sheep were driven home on foot. Later we used road hauliers.

My father did quite a trade in pigs as a result of the cheese-making. He reared them and also fattened store pigs on barley meal and whey. They were Wessex Saddlebacks and my father tended to sell direct to local butchers. I particularly remember Bill (Porky) Hatcher from Highbridge. His grandson became a distinguished Shrewsbury solicitor.

The dairy herd was always fairly modest; in my mind it must have been around thirty or forty cows and followers. The replacements were bred from the herd and the anguished bawling of cows deprived of their calves is a potent memory. The dairy herd was a mixture of breeds, including shorthorns, but with hardly a trace of Friesian. I suspect it reflected on my father's general lack of enthusiasm for retail dairying, but the herd, whatever its mixed progeny, certainly enabled my mother to make good cheese. Dairy cows were the core of mid-Somerset farming. All my immediate family who farmed kept cows and usually made cheese.

Of course we kept hens. They were all over the place and strutted around the yard as if they owned it. My mother would feed them, scattering corn from a bucket. I liked going with her and chasing the hens. It was on one of these occasions that I tripped over and fell on the bucket, cutting open my nose. I wasn't taken to the doctor but to Mrs Kidner, a neighbouring farmer's wife, and my mother patched me up. The result was that I bear this childhood scar across my nose to this day. My father was indulgent about the hens: 'I pay for the feed and your mother collects the egg money.' It was true; but the hens never made money. They were farmyard ornaments. Some thirty-five years later Enoch Powell was visiting Bridgwater and I told him of this poor investment. He strode up to her and said, 'You're John Biffen's mother, and you keep chickens and they don't pay.' Unabashed by this reproach from the high priest of monetarism, she continued her uneconomic husbandry until my father gave up farming and subsidising chickens.

We also had a handful of ducks, originally Khaki Campbells, and latterly Aylesburys. They ended up as Sunday lunch, and replacement ducklings were purchased from other farmers or Bridgwater market. The ducks had use of a huge pond immediately adjacent to the farm buildings. It contained a deep subterranean well that had probably been a spring. This part of the pond was fenced with rickety tubular railings. It would have been a nightmare for modern health and safety standards. In the twenty years I was at Hill Farm it never claimed a victim, not even a stray animal. Wisely I only played at the far end of the pond. My favourite pastime was floating empty sardine tins, the consequences of a Sunday tea delicacy, and sinking them with a shower of small stones. In my mind they were the Italian navy.

No livestock farm in the 1930s would have been complete without horses. Hill Farm was no exception. I was particularly fond of the horses. The oldest was Jack, a First World War veteran. He had been a draught horse in France and the men on the farm would talk about him affectionately. It was said that he would 'get the shivers', which was a sign that he had been affected by gas or other traumas relating to his distinguished war service.

Colonel and Duke were much younger and did all the work. Bay horses with huge white socks and enormous long manes hanging down their necks, they seemed mountainous to me. They operated as a pair, pulling the plough and the wagons.

Roger, a sturdy roan, was smaller and remained on the farm during the war. The demise of Colonel and Duke coincided with the purchase of our first tractor in 1938. A bright orange Allis-Chalmers, it was a spectacular addition to the farm and my father was immensely proud of it. Whilst not being the only tractor in the locality it was certainly one of the first and it was a clear indication that he was something of an innovator, making 'a go' of farming.

It was used mainly for ploughing and at first my father guarded it protectively, allowing no one else to drive it. Eventually as time went by and the novelty wore off, Wiggy, the most senior of the farm workers, was allowed at the wheel. My father was very sensible and wouldn't have me near it or any of the other farm machinery.

I find it extraordinary that my father's 120 acres not only supported a wide range of livestock but also enabled him to do arable farming. From earliest childhood I can remember him growing wheat, barley and oats. He had never received any formal training in agriculture but had acquired a flair for judging seed corn. I would watch him get out the well-honed pocket knife and slice a single grain and judge whether it would make good quality seed. He could sift through a sample and, hawk eyed, spot weeds. Over thirty years later he did the same on the farm of a Shropshire neighbour, John Gittins at Ruyton-XI-Towns. He had not lost his touch: 'Here,' said John, 'you've been doing this before.' During the Second World War he had to put more land under the plough and grew clover and sugar beet. The latter was not a success but I remember his delight on having a bumper clover crop which he sold for seed. He was finally making money after the lean years.

Our expenditure at home was limited. We never went on holidays and there were only a few outings. The family occasionally went to Taunton to watch Somerset play cricket but that stopped with the war. In the 1930s farming was coming out of a deep recession, and we tended to live off the farm. There was always masses of meat and vegetables. Sunday lunch, or dinner as it was called, was always a joint of meat or fowl. The vegetable garden provided more than we needed. There were a few treats bought from a family grocer, Horniman, in Bridgwater. I remember the spices purchased at Christmas. One delicacy was Camp coffee, with the memorable label of an Indian bearer serving a kilted Army officer. During the war we had a poor substitute called Bev. I never tasted 'real' coffee until after the war.

The only books in the house were the few that my father had won at Sunday school. In the winter of 1939 my mother bought a bookcase complete with books. Thereafter I began to stock the house, always asking for books for my birthday and Christmas and sometimes working at hay-making and harvesting to be rewarded with a book.

As a child I was not really aware of family finances. We always ate very well but very simply. The middle class symbols of car and telephone were always needed for the business. Our first car was a small four-door Wolseley, registration AYC 99. We bought our cars from Walter Challice, who had a garage in the neighbouring village of Cannington. He had served in Mesopotamia in the First World War and had been at Kut-al-Amara. I loved listening to his stories. He was a family friend and looked after my parents well. His care and attention were much valued during the war. We then had an ageing Austin, and it was constantly needing repairs. Walter Challice and his assistant Cyril Hunt were past masters of improvisation. On one memorable occasion going with my father to a sheep fair in the Brendons the car broke down on a steep hill, Elworthy Boroughs. The pipe connecting the radiator had punctured. It was very dramatic. The engine boiled and there was steam everywhere. Elworthy was isolated and the Challice garage was nearly twenty miles away. A local farmer allowed us to use his telephone and Cyril Hunt rescued us. All ended well but the breakdown took the edge off the day.

I think my father's financial fortunes began to turn in the mid-1930s. There had been several difficult years after his marriage to my mother in 1929. The arrival of the Milk Marketing Board gave some much-needed stability and cheese was more profitable than milk. When I gained a scholarship to Dr Morgan's School in 1941 my father had to pay a fee on account of his income.

At about this time the tenancy of Putnell Farm became available. It was in the neighbouring parish of Cannington, rather larger than Hill Farm but with less scope for crops. Like Hill Farm it was owned by the Leigh family. My father was given the tenancy. For a dreadful moment I thought I was going to be uprooted from Hill Farm. There was a much happier outcome. The cows were sent to Putnell. Wiggy and his family moved to the farmhouse, which became a growing part of my father's business. He drove from Hill Farm to Putnell every day. Just after the war he purchased thirty acres of grazing land near Putnell and for the last twenty years of his life farmed around 300 acres, a considerable size for mid-Somerset.

There was an established routine that we would spend Christmas and Boxing Day with my Aunt Millicent and Uncle Leonard at Causeway Farm, Woolavington. It was a proper family Christmas. Granny Biffen was then living with Millicent. Uncle Harold, the oldest Biffen son, and Aunt Winifred came down from Bristol with their two children, Reg and Joan. They were over ten years older than me, as were Millicent's children, Maurice and Phyllis. In effect I was a small child amidst grown-ups. Causeway Farm, although not imposing, was a listed building and had a lovely walled garden. These refinements

meant little to me. I remember that the house had the great
virtue of an upstairs bathroom complete with bath and flush
lavatory in sharp contrast to the lack of facilities at Hill Farm.
We always sat down to an enormous midday Christmas dinner.
Invariably it was turkey and a Christmas pudding laced with
silver threepenny pieces. Aunt Millicent always ensured that I
got one. There was always plenty of beer but in the 1930s wine
was not merely a rarity in the household, it was quite unknown.
The dining room was dominated by huge photographs of
Uncle Seward and Granny Biffen when she was young and
strikingly handsome.

Once the huge meal was over there was no pause for a diges-
tive break or a walk in the village; the family instantly played
cards. This went on until tea time when we struggled with
an immensely rich Christmas cake. Cards were then resumed,
and at around eight o'clock there was a supper of cold
ham and tongue followed by trifle. Every year it was the same.
The final card session could last until midnight or beyond.
Nap was the favourite game. It did not require as much
application as solo whist, also a favourite. Everyone shouted
– a Biffen characteristic. There was the noise of triumph,
the noise of inquest and occasional noise of recrimination.
The games were always for money but for small sums. Uncle
Harold, the eldest sibling, was amusing and quick witted. He
did not have an easy life. He had served in the trenches in the
1914–18 war and disliked the Belgians more than the Germans.
I liked him. Millicent's husband, Uncle Leonard, was quiet
and my father and Uncle Harold used to 'rag' him. He stoically allowed the waves of banter to break over him. There
was not much small talk once card-playing had begun, but
inevitably some reference was made to the state of farming.
There were also mildly risqué jokes, usually made by Uncle

Harold, but they were tempered by the puritanical presence of
Granny Biffen.

I hated Christmas. When I was very small I would play around
under the table or by the fireplace. But it was a lonely occasion
for me. I wanted to stay at home in the familiar surroundings of
Hill Farm. I didn't want to be bundled into the car and driven to
the other side of the county.

There wasn't a lot of church-going. Granny would go to
church in the morning but none of the menfolk would go.
Come 27 December we would get in the car and drive back to
Otterhampton. The whole thing would be repeated at New Year
when most of them would come to Hill Farm. Everything was
almost exactly the same except we had goose instead of turkey. I
found this more manageable because it was at home and I could
run around and escape.

The performance went on year after year up to and including the war. Increasingly I resented being in a noisy uncongenial
atmosphere. My genuine dislike of Christmas dates from this time.

By contrast, in the early days at Combwich School I quite
enjoyed the preparation for Christmas. Connie Sayer, the
teacher, would tell us the story of the birth of Jesus and about
Joseph, Mary and the Angels. We would make cut-outs which
were pinned up on the wall and were made to feel that it was a
very special occasion. It was then that I became aware that I was
better off than most. Whilst I had a Christmas stocking many of
the other children in the class did not. I would take to school the
presents I had received and show them around and then realise
that some of the others hadn't received any presents.

The village school was quite ambitious with a modest
Christmas play put on by the seniors. Striking was Sheila Stone,
a junior who had a walk-on part, whose only words were 'hark'.
She was very pretty.

From the earliest days we always had two or three workers on the farm. But the two who were with us longest and formed a central part of our lives were Wiggy Haggett and Buster Stone. Wiggy had been with us for ages and had worked for my grandmother. I do not know how he obtained the nickname 'Wiggy', but its use was universal. His Christian name was Evelyn, the same as that of his wife. They lived in the cottage which comprised a wing of Hill Farm. A primitive method of communication evolved, banging on our scullery wall if he was needed. The wall was immensely thick but my father's ham-like fists could do the trick.

Wiggy was the senior farm worker and would be left to run the farm whilst my father was away. His wife came from London and, although she fitted in well, she always maintained an urban outlook on life. Her brother Lou was a policeman in London whose views were frequently quoted as an authority. When the abdication crisis came, Evelyn was heard to say, 'Lou says in London they are all for Edward as King'. The abdication came when I was six and was a great event even in Somerset life. My family were much relieved when Edward abdicated and were very strong supporters of King George VI.

Buster came from Stockland, Bristol and was the son of a farm worker. A hardworking conscientious man, he had a lisp. His Christian name was Stanley but he was slightly portly – hence the nickname. He first came to work for us in the mid-1930s but had to join the Army in 1940. After the war he returned with a wife, Barbara, and eventually left to run a smallholding. They were strong supporters of the church and became good family friends.

Others came and went but Wiggy and Buster were the two mainstays of the farm. They played a large part in my life. The farm was a very cheerful place with lots of laughter, though it was more relaxed when my father wasn't there. My father was clearly 'the boss' but life was immensely informal, with no strict employer–employee relationship. After they retired both Wiggy and Buster maintained the friendship with my parents and visited us regularly for the rest of their lives. Many years later Barbara Stone, then a widow, considered donating a kidney so that I could have a transplant. It was a wonderful gesture.

4

CHEESE-MAKING AND MARKETS

Early in the 1930s my father decided to start cheese-making. Hitherto the milk had been sold to Stanley Norris, who had a milk round at Wembdon near Bridgwater. Demand was variable. Some days he wanted the milk and some days he didn't. Dairy farmers were over a barrel because there was nowhere else to sell milk on the days he didn't want it. It just had to be taken home and thrown down the drain or fed to the cattle.

Cheese-making was a more reliable way of using up the milk on a dependable basis and the equipment was already in place on the farm because my grandmother Biffen had made cheese. My mother's family had also made cheese and as a child she had to row the cheese down the River Brue to the market in Highbridge.

From the early 1930s onwards cheese-making became a very dominant part of farm work. This meant that we had to keep pigs to dispose of the whey, which was a by-product of cheese-making. My father was very traditional in his farming methods. Not for him the modern Large White Landrace pigs, he chose Wessex Saddlebacks. They lived in a low farm building with a beautiful studded door and a stone trough. Their noisy mealtime manners are an abiding memory.

Every evening my father would put me on his shoulders and

take me round the farmyard to look at the animals. My mother said that I used to be terribly excited and would shout 'More! More!' as we went from pen to pen looking at the pigs. I showed no such enthusiasm about cows.

I believe that my mother made quite good cheese. The whole thing was taken very seriously and from time to time she would go to the Somerset Farm Institute at Cannington and take refresher courses. She did this despite the fact that she had been making cheese since she was a child.

It was a mammoth task for one person with little help. She started immediately after breakfast using that morning's milk together with the milk stored from the previous evening. In between cheese-making she would dash into the kitchen and prepare lunch and before I was old enough to go to the village school I would be 'parked' in 'the dairy' and got used to picture books.

My mother was greatly helped after Aunt Ruth came to live with us in 1936. Cheese-making prospered and in 1940 we employed a cheese maker. Sheila Peel was a great asset. Her mother and siblings had been evacuated from London. She finished her education at the nearby 'big house', which had become St Hilda's School for Girls. She was an excellent horse-woman and a valued young companion for my mother.

Initially my mother made Cheddar cheese, the natural Somerset territorial product. Then she switched to making Caerphilly. This sold well to the mining communities in South Wales. It was a bold step to take and it was a tribute to my mother's skill at cheese-making and my father's business acumen that it proved such a success.

Hill Farm had plenty of space for storing cheese whilst it matured. In the 1930s this required several weeks and my parents used the best upstairs room in the house as a store. It had its own staircase leading from the 'top room', and had a wonderful sunset view of the Quantock Hills. Its use for cheese storage was another example of Farm before Family. I frequently used the room as a playground. I savoured the pungency of maturing cheese but refused to eat it. This foolishness lasted until 1954, when I saw the light in Florence and succumbed to Bel Paese rather than my mother's Cheddar. But I quickly learned, late in the day, to like English cheeses.

My mother had inherited antiquated cheese-making machinery which had served a couple of generations. In the early 1940s my father bought a boiler which was installed adjacent to the cheese vat. A fearsome contraption, hissing a great deal and generating steam, it was known as 'the donkey'. The circular copper cheese vat was thrown out and replaced by a modern rectangular job with hollow sides which were steam heated from the donkey.

There was a sad epitaph. A Bridgwater dealer rescued the discarded vat from the farmyard. It changed hands for a few bob. About fifty years later my wife, Sarah, and I took my mother to lunch at Raleigh's Cross in the Brendon Hills, of sheep fair fame. There Sarah espied a superb burnished copper vat used to store logs. 'Look, look,' she exclaimed, 'isn't that copper log-container fantastic?' 'Yes,' replied my mother with a touch of nostalgia, 'I used to make cheese in it.'

My father relished the challenge of selling the cheese. Every Monday he would set off for Highbridge. Selling cheese was very different from selling livestock but my father revelled in the process. Buyers from South Wales armed with cheese bores would arrive and negotiate. Though not as grand as wine-tasting, it was a skilled business which they undertook with great seriousness as they sniffed, tasted and compared the cheese. One buyer, Mr Rees Thomas, stuck in my mind because of Mr

Morse, his agent in Bridgwater, known to all as Cheesy Morse. It was easy to see what other farmers were getting for their cheese and on his return home my father would regale us with how we had done better than our neighbours. I am sorry we never entered any competition. However, I do have a silver pepper grinder in the form of an old-fashioned milk churn which my paternal grandfather had won at a Somerset cheese fair in the early 1900s.

Many years later in the 1970s, continuing the family tradition, I renewed my interest in farmhouse cheese-making. I made friends with David and Jill Hutchinson Smith, who farmed at Hinton, near Whitchurch, and were constituents. Jill pioneered a 'Blue Cheshire cheese'. She had been very innovative but production was always limited to milk from neighbouring farms. I was modestly connected with the enterprise and loved visiting the farm and watching the making and maturing of the cheese. It had no equal. I believe Shropshire Blue was made by one of the Scottish milk marketing boards. I say no more. Alas the making of Blue Cheshire had none of the dramas of my father at Highbridge market. It was conducted with solemn young supermarket executives. My visits to Hinton were enlivened by Jill's parents, Maurice and Jessica Alsop. They were dedicated country folk who regarded themselves as trustees for the countryside and its values. Jessica provided the only humorous incident during the fearful foot and mouth scourge in 1968. A bearded Ministry of Agriculture official arrived at the Hinton farm gate. He was challenged by Jessica. 'Young man, have you disinfected that beard?' Confused and nervous, he retreated and the Hinton herd escaped the virulent disease.

The Somerset farm was our whole life. Our main travelling was to visit relatives and other farmers. Uncle Jack and Aunt Keturah Case, my mother's oldest sister, farmed at Huntspill and

Aunt Rosa helped her sister, as Ruth helped my mother. The Sunday trip united four Bennett sisters.

Uncle Leonard and Aunt Millicent, my father's sister, farmed at Woolavington. As ever the conversation would be about local grass sales and what barren cows had made at Bridgwater market.

We made regular visits to a farming neighbour, Ernie Heal. He was a widower with a rather angular Welsh housekeeper, Miss Watts. A visit to King's Farm was a real excursion; it started with the men rough shooting and after supper the grown-ups would settle down to cards. Not much of a party for a six-year-old. I remember causing my mother great irritation by refusing a brown boiled egg for tea as I insisted on having a white one 'like I have at home'. Miss Watts understood; peace was easily bought, but the incident was long remembered and was often told against me.

There was one occasional non-farming visit favoured by my father – county cricket. The trips to the Taunton County Ground were instantaneous rather than planned. 'Tish,' my father would say, 'clean up the cheese things as quickly as you can and we'll watch some cricket.' It meant we would get to Taunton for about two or three hours at the end of play. I loved it. My Somerset heroes, inevitably, were Harold Gimblett and Arthur Wellard. They both featured in my cigarette cards.

My father's main recreation was to go to market. It was the highlight of the week. On Wednesdays he would take livestock to Bridgwater to sell, and buy store cattle or calves to bring home. It was always very social and entailed going to the Clarence Hotel or some other farmers' hostelry afterwards. Occasionally my mother would go in and do the shopping and meet him at the pub.

My father always dressed for market. He would wear his best suit. My mother always made him a buttonhole. She would pick violets or a rose from the garden. I am sure he felt the better for his smart market clothes and maybe they helped him to be the successful bargainer that he was.

Sometimes I would be taken along but usually I would remain at home in the care of Aunt Ruth. When I was left behind my mother would always bring me back a lead soldier. I had a modest collection and spent a vast amount of time enacting battles on the floor around the house. My father coming back on Wednesday and, seeing me add yet another soldier to my army, would say, 'With all those lead soldiers I could buy a decent cow.' I was never quite sure whether or not the words were spoken in jest. 'Butter before Guns' neatly reversed Goering's dictum.

5

PARENTS AND FAMILY

The farmhouse and its buildings were my playground and provided a happy childhood. In retrospect the sun was usually shining, a nonsense of course, but the true contentment was the happy relations with my parents.

My father's family had always been farmers based on the Mendips and the Somerset Levels. Granny Biffen had been a Miss Middle from a well-established family of tenant farmers. She was a forbidding person with a mass of snow-white hair which was piled high. When she went to bed she would take out all the pins and comb it at considerable length. Always dressed in black, she had a severe countenance and was very austere in her manner. To the very end she commanded respect from the family. She was a devout Anglican who knew her Bible and Prayer Book well.

My father was born at Burtle in 1896, the youngest of three sons and a daughter. The elder siblings were Harold, Seward and Millicent. Sadly Seward, the middle brother, died as a result of a cricket accident. He was hit on the head by a cricket ball and subsequently died of a blood clot. My father always said that his mother never recovered from his death. He was clearly a very handsome man and a large photograph of him hung in the living room of my Aunt Millicent's farmhouse.

My father was educated at Dr Morgan's School, then a small independent establishment founded in 1723. It was the school to which I got a county scholarship and which became a grammar school under Butler's Education Act in 1944. My father's education was cut short, but not before he had been taught beautiful handwriting.

Tragedy struck just before the First World War. My grandfather had a serious accident catching his arm in a farm machine, which left him permanently disabled and unable to run the farm. He lived on for some while as an invalid and was still alive when the family left Woolavington and moved to Otterhampton some ten miles to the west on the far side of Bridgwater. He died on Christmas Day 1923. My father, barely out of his teens then, together with Granny Biffen had the task of running the farm. This fell to him because his eldest brother, Harold, was married and in the Army.

Growing up on the farm my father had to learn his skills 'on the job'. He never received formal tuition, but learned a great deal from Uncle Fred, a very successful cattle dealer in Wiltshire. It was not just husbandry; he stripped my father of innocence and explained how a 'dealer's ring' operated and should be avoided. Running the farm with Granny was a huge task with the collapse of farm prices after the First World War.

However, it wasn't all hard work. When my father was in his teens he took up dancing. He would set off, pinning the tails of his tail-coat so they were clear of the spokes, and cycle to Burnham-on-Sea for dancing classes. Given the basic style and profitability of the farm, I find it intriguing that his wardrobe included tails and a black silk topper which he wore at his brother Seward's funeral.

He was very dapper in appearance but with time lost his hair and put on weight. He always went to Williams & Bevan in Bridgwater for his suits. Granny used to say 'the young man likes to have his suits tailor made'. Later he developed a taste for striking trilby hats. Made of felt with a subdued feather in the band, they were a source of fascination to my stepson, Nicholas.

He must have been a competent farmer and it says much for my father's skill that unlike many others he was able to keep going during the depression. By contrast his older brother, Harold, who had returned to farming after serving in the Somerset Light Infantry in the war, couldn't farm profitably and moved his family to Bristol where he went to work for a road haulage company. My mother's family was also deeply affected by the depression; her father had to give up his own farm and ended his days as a farm worker.

My father was canny and well respected as a farmer. His strong point was buying stock and as a child I would stand beside him whilst he bargained. In the early 1950s a friend from Cambridge, John Halton, came to stay at Hill Farm. A mathematical genius, he had a Cambridge Major Scholarship and eventually became a professor at the University of Wisconsin. He was also very reckless. My father said, 'I'm hoping to buy some yearlings, would you two lads like to come?' Soon John and I were witnessing my father in action. It was almost a bazaar with offer and counter-offer, the prices were traded on a per head basis and alternatively for a grand sum for the herd. At last my father pulled a sad face and said 'Charley, that was my last word. We'll never deal.' John Halton was listening intently; a Londoner to his fingertips, this was a new world.

The mathematician's clock had been ticking. He intervened, 'Mr Willis, if Mr Biffen won't buy them I will.' He had calculated that in the bargaining they had got confused between the headage price and the herd price. My father and the vendor were aghast. Using the principles of quick wit and mental arithmetic they had accurately calculated bid and counter-bid. The gap that John perceived was a mirage, despite his formidable academic mathematical qualifications. He was told to keep his skills at Cambridge. My father would often say of dealing, 'the sharps live off the flats'. The non-deal was celebrated by a visit to the village inn and John's short career as a dealer was toasted and became folklore.

My father was a very honest person with strong standards of financial probity. He didn't have a very good grasp of accountancy. He valued farming more by a traditional sense of husbandry than by profit. I learned this when I helped him with his accounts in the late 1950s.

Cattle-rearing was a vocation as well as a livelihood. He tended his livestock as if they were children. In the evening he would drive around his fields counting the cattle and checking that all was well. He often took my mother and me with him. We usually ended up at the Anchor in Combwich.

His skills as a stockman were recognised after the war when he was appointed a 'farmer grader' by the Ministry of Agriculture. Each week with a 'butcher grader' he would go to the market and, on the hoof, assess the grade of cattle. He loved it and on days when the stock was below quality he would compensate by drinking champagne with Eddie Rogers, the butcher from North Petherton. 'A good market will toast itself; but this one needs some help.' Post-war farming was certainly a far cry from the 1930s.

One year my father won the champion prize at the Bridgwater Christmas Fatstock Show. He was much moved. At the dinner that evening he made a short speech: 'The three things that have made me most proud are winning this prize, getting married and having a son.' He didn't specify the order.

As the years went by he played an active part in the community. He was chairman of the parish council, a member of the

Bridgwater Rural District Council and chairman of the Water Committee, and also chairman of the governors of Combwich Village School. Inevitably he was chairman of the Coronation Committee. His great achievement was when he was made a member of the Somerset War Agricultural Executive Committee. This was an appointment made by the Ministry of Agriculture and intended to be a link between the ministry and the rural community, to which I refer in Chapter Seven.

He was also very pleased to be chairman of the Rural District Water Committee. An impressive new reservoir had been built at Durleigh, close to Dr Morgan's School, and my father was always proclaiming the cheapness of water. He also thought it should be used sparingly. In 1960 we had a charming American girl to stay, Robin Sabin from Roanoke, Virginia. She took a bath every morning. My father belonged to the 'once a week' school. 'Missy,' he said, 'I'm chairman of the Water and I must say you do use rather a lot.' Of course it was spoken in jest, but not entirely so. I had forgotten the incident but Robin recently reminded me. She had been vastly amused.

My relationship with my father was coloured by my closeness to my mother. To me my father was a noise. He would stand in the yard or, indeed, in the house and shout to get attention. A boisterous man, he seemed very extrovert to the world outside. I look back upon him as being strident but concealing uncertainty. Having said this he could fight. The county council decided that the children of Combwich and of Stockland Bristol schools, whose numbers were much increased by evacuees, should be reallocated to take account of the increase. It meant I would be snatched from Combwich and transferred to Stockland. I was horrified that I was to be torn from the world I knew. I dreaded the thought of leaving the comfort of Connie Sayer, the infants' teacher at Combwich, and my friends and going to the unknown quantity of Stockland. My father fought a vigorous battle and in the end the Somerset county authority climbed down and agreed that all the evacuee children would go to Stockland and we locals could stay at Combwich. To the school planners at Taunton it seemed like a triumph of educational apartheid. Miss Sayer told us the county inspector did a site visit to help calm the storm and in bureaucratic exasperation said, 'Who is this man Biffen?' For me he was seven feet tall.

Although my father was noisy he was not at all violent. He did not approve of chastising but was happy if the school used the cane. He hated guns although in his early life he did some rough shooting with fellow farmers. For most of my years on the farm the 12-bore shotgun was put away under the stairs.

His leisure activities were decidedly sedentary. I have mentioned the Biffen preoccupation with cards. This went beyond the circle of family and farmers. In the 1940s he joined a poker club of local businessmen and went to the Enmore Golf Club every Saturday evening, leaving my mother and me listening to the radio at home. It was hardly surprising I felt closer to my mother than to him. He enjoyed watching cricket and was a loyal Somerset supporter but disapproved of Botham – for all his skills – as he did not come from the county.

He continued farming until he was well over seventy and left little time for a life in retirement. Sadly in his closing years he had little leisure activity other than watching sport on TV.

My mother was the stronger character of the two. Father would get terribly upset by adverse incidents whilst she would remain calm. Once, when I was in my teens, he got into a local row. The accusation was that he had used his influence on the district council to get a council house allocated to a farm worker of his when other residents in the village were ahead in the queue. There was a huge village storm about it. I well remember how nervous my father was before the meeting of the parish council. He did not seem at all like the extrovert figure that he was assumed to be.

My mother was devoted to my father. Looking back it was probably unconscious chauvinism but my father would never have thought of blacking his boots himself. My mother always did it for him. On the other hand my father would never carve the Sunday joint. That was a job always left to my mother.

An extraordinary example of my mother's following of my father was when he had his teeth out shortly after the war. It was a time when the fashion in dentistry was to extract teeth; bridges and crowns were unknown to Bridgwater. My father had bad teeth. His dentist was called Mr Clapp and, when the time came for his teeth to be removed, my mother had hers removed as well to keep him company, and for no compelling dental reason.

My mother was a spirited woman. In the early days of their marriage when my father had not quite shaken off his bachelor ways he went on a boys' outing to Lundy Island. The only present he brought back to her from the day out was a small pebble from the beach, which she promptly threw at him. That said, it was a marriage of mutual affection.

Around 1936 my mother became very ill. She was diagnosed as suffering from a gastric ulcer. She was in bed for weeks on a diet of Benger's mixture. It was a slimy gruel. There was no way that my father could cope with the farm work, the house and me. So he approached my Aunt Ruth, who was living at home in Chiselborough with her parents, convalescing from being badly bitten by a dog. She was delighted to get away from home and moved in straight away. She stayed with us right up until the war started.

Ruth was known to us all as Cookie. She was the ninth child and about eight years younger than my mother. Pretty with dark

hair, she was a very vivacious person. I never resented the arrival
of Ruth. My father liked her very much also and it was a happy
relationship. Her presence made the house more balanced and
eased the triangular situation between my mother, father
and myself.

My mother and Ruth were very close and the house rang with
laughter as they worked together. They took a great interest in
clothes and would dress up for the few outings that took place.
I have a photograph of the three of us at Bristol Zoo. Mother
and Ruth were done up to the nines for the day out. These were
the sunshine days before the war. The two of them seemed to
work together throughout the day. The evenings were often
spent cutting up old clothes and making rag rugs for general
use on the farm. It was remarkable how little use was made of
the radio.

Ruth played a large part in my life and I was very close to her.
She was someone to talk to and show my comics and cigarette
cards. Many years later when I wanted to confide in someone
intimately I wrote to Ruth. I couldn't have written in that candid
way to my mother.

Ruth would come to meet me from school. She would walk
as far as Dame Withycombe's house just by the Otterhampton–
Combwich road whilst I would walk to meet her on the footpath
from school. I enjoyed our journeys and would confide in her the
doings of the school day.

Card-playing had always been a large part in my parents' life.
The arrival of Ruth made things easier and the three of them
would play cards most evenings and when I was old enough I
joined in, starting off with simple games like Newmarket. Cards
were certainly the main entertainment when visitors came from
other farms. Solo whist was a great favourite. They were always
very noisy affairs, particularly the inquest after each hand. My

father was a good card player and above all he liked to win. He could read cards and he excelled in solo whist. Fortunately he was never a gambler but his skill was such that in other circumstances he could have made money at cards.

Towards the end of their lives my father and mother played cribbage every morning immediately after breakfast. It was a firm fixture even if we had guests. Small change passed hands which my mother put in a missionary box. My father decidedly thought charity should start in Otterhampton.

By the time I was in my early teens I was going to the village whist drive on a Friday night. Although at first I found it nerve-racking, I was a competent card player after all the years of practice at home. The whist drive was a very important part of village life both during and immediately after the war and helped combat my nervousness.

My mother was born Edith Annie Bennett. She hated her Christian names and insisted on being called Tish, which was the nickname given to her by her sisters. The Bennetts were farmers and cheese makers, all farming folk from the Somerset Levels or thereabouts. Great-Grandfather Bennett had been a very hardworking and successful farmer, so much so that on his death he was able to leave a farm to each of his children. I am told that he rented Steart Island and used to drive his sheep from the mainland to the island at low tide.

His son, my grandfather Bennett, started out with the great advantage of having a farm of his own. But his story is one of failure. Despite his providential start in life he was not a successful farmer. With a family of thirteen children to support, things were exacerbated by the bad conditions for farming of the 1920s. He eventually went bankrupt and moved to Bristol to run a shop. This venture also failed and he ended life as a farm worker in Chiselborough. My mother and I would visit my grandparents when he was working there and living in a thatched cottage. They ended their days in a council house in West Chinnock.

My mother was the second eldest of the thirteen children. There were eight girls and five boys, all of whom subsequently married and had families of their own. I ended up with well over thirty maternal first cousins, only one of whom went to university. It was quite different by the succeeding generation.

It must have been very difficult for my maternal grandparents to make ends meet. Pictures show that it was a family with hand-me-down clothes. The children were all the product of an intensely rural background and were brought up in a very disciplined manner.

From a very early age the older children had to work on the farm before and after they went to school. It was hard work. My mother had to milk and feed the cows before school. She would be close to tears as she struggled to put the hay in the feeding trough whilst the large cows shifted to and fro pushing against her.

She went to the village school at Huntspill and left at fourteen. Although she was a bright student, there was never any question of continuing with her education. In fact the only one of the thirteen who went to a grammar school was my Aunt Ruth. All spoke with strong Somerset accents, as did I until I went to Dr Morgan's School.

When my grandfather's farming failed and he moved to Bristol, the family was dispersed, which was why my mother left home. Aged nineteen she went to work for my grandmother Biffen at Hill Farm, which is how my parents met. Meanwhile my mother's eldest sister, Keturah, had already left home when a relative offered to take her to live with them. She accepted this with alacrity and eventually inherited their farm. She went on to marry Jack Case, a conscientious farmer who took a great interest in drainage. It was his major topic of conversation. This was wholly appropriate as the farm at Huntspill was on the Levels. He was quiet but rather a character. He asked the local motor dealer if he could buy a Daimler. Farming was not that profitable and the dealer, puzzled, enquired why. 'Oh,' said Jack, 'a Daimler is the only car I know that has enough space in the back to put a milk churn between the seats.'

My mother's early home training stood her in good stead when she started work at Hill Farm. She was a very attractive and vivacious woman. She never wore make-up but just occasionally would put on some California Poppy scent.

One of the first occasions my father took her out was to a Conservative whist drive in the village. Not a very grand social event. My father was slightly taken aback when she wore a red dress and the incident lived on in family memory for many years.

My mother had a winning way with animals. She was always given the task of rescuing runt pigs. When things went wrong the poor little piglets would sit in the warming oven of the Aga whilst she fed them by hand. One pig became very special. She was christened Tilly and would answer to her name even after she had farrowed. My mother would go to the pen and call Tilly. Suddenly there would be a great eruption, the straw would be thrown up and she would emerge snorting and grunting and come running to the door so that my mother could scratch her head. We could never think of her as bacon.

One of the farm chores was rounding up the chickens in the evening. It was a nightly ritual to keep them safe from the foxes. There were chickens everywhere in the farmyard and quite often you would only find them when a whole new batch of chicks emerged from a hiding place. I would help my mother as she ran round after the hens. She would grab them by the feet, whisk them upside down and hand them to me to hold whilst she went after the next one. I hated having to hold the chickens whilst they flapped away as they twisted and turned trying to peck me. It confirmed me early on in the view that I was never going to make a farmer. All our animals were reasonably well treated and both my mother and father were punctilious in their care of the stock.

My mother was a keen horsewoman, having ridden since childhood at Chestnut Farm. In the early days we only had cart horses at Hill Farm. When the war came many people who kept horses for pleasure had to give them up because of the difficulty in feeding them. Living on a farm we did not have such a great problem and took care of a couple of hunters. The first horse was called Cornflower. My mother rode her all around the farm and along the shore at Steart. Poor Cornflower died in tragic circumstances when she was gored by one of the cattle. Later Mother had a mare called Melisha. My father was always very nervous that my mother would have an accident whilst riding. The same anxiety meant he would not allow her to learn how to drive a motor car. This became a sad restriction in later years, but my mother accepted it philosophically.

My parents married in romantic circumstances and were devoted to each other throughout their married life. My mother had not been working long at Hill Farm before she and my father fell in love. My father was twelve years older than her and she swept him off his feet. It was very difficult for Granny Biffen.

My father was a very determined man. Having made up his mind he wasn't going to have a lot of bother; they got married by special licence on 28 October 1929 at 8 a.m. with only a handful of family present and no photographs. They went to Bournemouth for their honeymoon.

This was a terrible blow for my grandmother. In her eyes my mother was not really the sort of person she expected her son to marry. Also she did not expect it to be a hole-in-the-corner affair, particularly as there was no reason for a hurried wedding. Shotgun weddings were common in rural areas and many an elaborate wedding would be followed by the arrival of the first baby a few months later. If you look at the photographs of the weddings of my Uncle Harold and his sister Millicent you realise that a farm wedding was a proper do and a great event in the community.

Matters were made worse when my father decided that they couldn't all live under the same roof, so Granny was despatched to The Myrtles, a house they owned in Cossington, a village on the Polden Hills and near where Millicent and her husband Leonard Waites farmed. This was a source of some acrimony. As a result of this, in the early days of their marriage, not surprisingly there was a certain reserve between my mother and Granny Biffen.

My arrival was the cause of reconciliation. Eventually Granny used to come and stay with us. She would wheel me up and down the lane in my pushchair. I used to insist on picking all the dandelions I passed and wouldn't let her go on until I had done so. She would come back saying that it was quite impossible to take me on a proper walk. She had made for me a tiny chair painted and lacquered black with a little cushion. However, I had already been given a child's chair and ungraciously said, 'I don't want that. I got one.'

Towards the end of her life she left The Myrtles and went to live with Millicent in Causeway Farm. I was taken to see her as she was dying in 1946. It was eerie, but even on her death-bed she had an imposing presence. The funeral was held at Woolavington Church, although her husband had been buried at Otterhampton. After the service I went back to Causeway Farm. It was a traditional male occasion: cold ham for the men in one room whilst the women went to another room and had tea and cake.

6

COMBWICH VILLAGE AND SCHOOL

I had shown signs of being bookish from a very early age. I read everything I could get my hands on, although my parents were not great readers and there were few books in the house. Christmas was the great occasion when I would get my Tiger Tim and Rupert Bear annuals. My maternal grandparents always gave me the *Daily Mail Nipper*.

My mother thought that it would be good for me to go to school early. She decided it would be company for me and let her get on with her work. So, aged four, I was despatched to the local Church of England village school. The school was in the neighbouring village of Combwich. It was quite a long way to walk across several fields. The village lay downhill and as we walked we could hear Ernie Quick the blacksmith hammering away in his smithy and the uncertain sound of the school bell in the distance.

On the first day I set off hand in hand with my mother. I cried like anything when she left me even though I knew she was coming back to collect me at lunch time. On the second day I wanted her to stay so that I could be there the whole day. I quickly adapted to school life and very much enjoyed it and the companionship of the other children.

Eventually I made the journey to school on my own, but the way was full of hazards. My shyness made me frightened of meeting people on my walk to school. So when I saw anyone coming the other way down the footpath I would make great detours to avoid passing them. The path went by a couple of houses alongside the lane, in one of which lived Dr Sheppard, the female half of a brother and sister doctor practice. She owned a German sausage dog called Victoria with a yap quite out of proportion to its size. I was terrified of this dog. I made enormous efforts to avoid it altogether and hurried past the house as quickly as possible, hoping to escape its notice. It was this experience that confirmed my paranoia about dogs.

Combwich School was a standard Church of England school, housed in a solid, ugly, late Victorian building. The lavatories were good old-fashioned earth closets and the asphalt playground was split into two, half for the juniors and half for the seniors. When I was there it took pupils up to the statutory attendance age of fourteen.

The building was equipped with a large bell attached to a chain hanging in the school room. In theory this was to summon the children to school but by the time I arrived the system was so antiquated that it only rang about every fourth pull. This didn't stop us. We vied with each other for the honour of ring-ing the bell, and heaved and strained at the chain until we were rewarded with a dull clang.

The school was heated with two large, black cast-iron stoves surrounded by an enormous fireguard. In wet weather it doubled as a clothes horse and was draped with mounds of steaming clothes. The windows were so high that you couldn't see out. I imagine they were built like that deliberately so as not to distract the pupils. In the infant school we were surrounded by jars of tadpoles, wild flowers and childish drawings on the walls.

However, it was no playgroup and we were given a structured education and taught in a fairly formal fashion.

There was one large school room catering for thirty to forty children and divided in two by a demountable wooden partition. The smaller side was for the infants and the larger for the older children. The infants were presided over by Miss Connie Sayer. A farmer's daughter and a good friend of my parents, she was not a qualified teacher. I was very fond of her with her homely face, horn-rimmed glasses and kindly voice. She had a wonderful cosy way of dealing with children. In my early days at the school she would talk about the First World War and how they were only allowed a limited amount of butter and sugar. In my mind this meant a slab of butter thinly coated with sugar and for a while I held a wild misconception of what war was like.

On the other side of the room were Miss Rimer, who did the intermediate teaching, and Mrs Hunt, the head teacher. Married to Silas, a garage proprietor from North Petherton, the latter was a formidable person. She carried a stick which she rattled around your chair but never actually used, and was given to moments of affection when she would praise you and clasp you to her ample bosom.

In the senior school we sat on the most uncomfortable benches secured to wooden tables. We all shared the messy duty of filling the ink pots. In those days the school provided education and nothing else. No school dinners were served, so all the village children went back home for a meal. I lived too far away, as did Margaret and Peggy Wilkins from Putnell Farm. Arrangements were made for us to have our dinner with Mrs Stockham in the village. Her husband Ernie had a smallholding and a milk round. There we were given a simple meal, and all I can remember is playing outside with Margaret and Peggy in the paved garden. Margaret, a vivid redhead, was older than me. Both girls wore

their hair in long thick plaits, painstakingly done up by their
mother each morning.

The Stockhams had an adopted son, Denis Hepper. He
was older than me but we played French cricket together. Mrs
Stockham's mother, Granny Robinson, was a background presence. Very deaf, she seemed permanently installed in a chair
by the fire, nodding and usually asleep. She died in early 1940
and I was amazed and rather concerned that anyone should
live and die without realising we were at war. Table talk at the
Stockhams was inevitably about school, farming and the minor
dramas of the village.

I enjoyed my time at Combwich and made steady progress.
There was a certain amount of mild bullying because of the
huge age range but on the whole it was what you would expect
from that kind of rural community. The boisterousness mainly
involved the older boys and girls. It was possibly more adoles-
cent horseplay than bullying but in my innocence I would not
have known.

It was primarily a working-class industrial village. The major
employer was the brickyard where kilns, using local clay, made a
range of bricks and tiles. Also there was Combwich and District
Farmers, which made and sold animal feed. Many of the children
from the larger families came in 'pass-me-down clothes'. The
village was predominantly non-conformist and had a Methodist
chapel. At school my father was the only parent who owned a
car. If it was raining he would drive to the school gates to take
me home. This was a great prestige symbol of which I was very
proud. It was an Austin and I remember it vividly, which is more
than I can say of my present car.

In the large school room there was a map of the world with
all the British parts in red. This took on a greater significance
with the Coronation of George VI in May 1937. The wall became

adorned with a series of maps marking the Empire. We used our crayons to colour their products: sheep for Australia, wheat for Canada, tea for India and so on.

At break we ran round the playground in a general mêlée. We played all the usual games such as 'The farmer wants a wife' and 'Bingo La'. In the latter you lined up in two rows and took it in turns to run between the lines whilst everyone tried to hit you with a tennis ball. I entered into all the fun, if sometimes a bit over-enthusiastically. One day I came home and told my mother that when we were playing in the yard I had hit Mary Nurton. I was so pleased with this achievement and was very crestfallen when my mother said I shouldn't have done that and to go and say I was sorry.

Being a Church of England school, the vicar, the Rev. C. W. Hamper, played a prominent part. He was a tall man with rather piercing blue eyes and a shiny pate. In my mind I thought that God must look like that. He used to come and give us scripture lessons and when I was nine I won the prize for learning a chunk of Hebrews: 'Faith is the substance of things hoped for, the evidence of things not seen.' My prize was a good improving book, *Parson John of the Labrador*, which I still have. Over sixty years later I was in hospital. The senior nurse came from the West Indies and was a devout evangelical. She was always quoting the scriptures. One day she started the Hebrews passage 'Faith' and from my bed I capped the text. I got even more tender care.

I was reasonably good at drawing so I was entered into a competition sponsored by Ovaltine. To my amazement I won a tremendous prize. A great big Meccano set. Not having many toys at home this gave me many happy hours of play, particularly as I could do so on my own. But sadly, as time passed, my drawing skills faded.

I had a few special friends. One was Norman Hunt, an only child like me. His father worked in the brickyard and lived in the middle of the village. Occasionally I would bring him home from the village to play. We would go off into the woods, which was very exciting, or use the farm buildings for hide and seek. But mostly I was on my own.

A characteristic of the village was that it consisted of a number of very large families who had been in the area for generations. The Kibbys, the Fears and the Smiths were all large families. Everybody seemed related to everyone else. Connie Sayers reckoned it was her teaching task to know the village genealogy and rivalries.

The rougher end of the village lived in adjacent council houses immediately opposite the school. They were always squabbling amongst themselves, but were a source of endless fascination to me. The Smiths were all daughters and one son. The father, a shady-looking character sporting a couple of days' growth, was called Twister because he was supposed to have done time. Mrs Smith never wore make-up and had ample bosoms and it was said that she and her elder daughters entertained American servicemen.

Although my mother was pleased to have me at school and mixing with other children, she had some reserve about 'those children in the village'. She regarded them as a rough lot and undoubtedly some were. It is arguable that I might have bene-fited from their company, certainly that of the Smith girls. They would have taught me what books never mentioned. All of this gossip was outside my world, but once an American serviceman arrived at Hill Farm enquiring if it was the home of the Smiths. My mother answered icily that it was not.

By contrast the Fears were all sons and one daughter and were rather more settled. One of the boys, Dennis, used to come and help on the farm at weekends.

I had only just started school when we celebrated King George V's Silver Jubilee in 1935. We had a special school sports day and my father, as chairman of the school governors, took a prominent part in the organisation. I was entered into the infants' race and my father was the starter. The idea was to run to a flag a short distance away. We had all been thoroughly rehearsed. The big moment came and my father said, 'Ready! Steady! Go!' Immediately I turned round and ran back to him, causing great merriment all round. However, we were all given prizes and I got a lovely silver pencil.

Later on we had the Coronation of George VI in 1937, which made a huge impact on school life. In the class we coloured in the procession with the coaches and horses. There were more sports, lots of bunting and a Coronation mug for everybody. In the evening there was high tea and a dance for the whole village.

There was no set school homework but I read every evening at home. The A. A. Milne books were great favourites. From about 1937 onwards I became fascinated by stamps and cigarette cards. My stamp collection started because the Stockhams, where I had lunch, were next door to a stamp dealer called Stevens. He interested me in collecting. He would show me stamps and tell me about them. I was given a stamp album when I was around seven. I would buy my stamps from him in penny packets and stick them in my book. Originally I was so ignorant of the whole technique that under the guidance of my mother I pasted them in with flour and water, which was sacrilege. Cousin Barbara used to come and stay with us. I got her interested and she said she would like to buy stamps too. So I went to Mr Stevens. I bought two packets, one for her and one for me. On the way home I opened the packets and transferred from her packet the stamps I did not possess and replaced them with ones I already had. I still feel guilt about the episode but I now know that worse things happen at Sotheby's.

I spent much time studying the stamps; they were a treasure house of history and geography, the subjects I most enjoyed at school. My interest in stamps carried on right through the war. It was a pastime you could indulge, despite rationing and the restrictions on travel. Since my stamp album also listed the capitals of each country I became an authority on that subject, soon remembering that it was Canberra and not Sydney that was the capital of Australia. Eventually I enlarged my collection by buying the entire stamp collection of Maurice Peel, the younger brother of Sheila who helped my mother make cheese. I bought the stamps for a trivial sum, and the deal was that I did not tell a soul because his mother would have been outraged. Sixty years later I still have the stamps and his album.

Cigarette cards were another of my passions. Before the war all the main cigarette companies used to put cards in their packs of cigarettes. My father smoked Players so I had a ready supply. Once it became known that I was collecting, people in the village would give me their cards. It was a thoroughly enjoyable activity for an only child.

There were series, each of fifty cards on endless topics, but predominantly nature, sport, military history and the theatre. In a way they mirrored the prospect of war with a series in 1938/39 on naval warships, and another on civil defence. I would play endless games on my own. In the process I became so knowledgeable of the 1938 Players cricket series that my father had only to show me the hairline of the player and I could recognise him.

My memory of cigarette cards was long lasting. In the mid-1980s I attended a Cabinet meeting devoted to a protracted and technical discussion of no relevance to myself. To help pass the time I started listing the fifty cricketers who made up the Players

1938 series. I managed forty-eight. I felt a twinge of triumph but cravenly decided not to offer the manuscript to Margaret Thatcher for the Prime Ministerial signature. It would have made a good raffle.

Sadly cigarette cards came to an end in 1940. This was a dark day and my Uncle Leslie, whose father ran the King's Arms in Bridgwater, told me that they had had advance warning that cigarette cards were being discontinued. My heart sank and I realised what war was all about. It was a terrible blow, and although I had a large collection I couldn't add to it.

Another source of self-entertainment was playing solo cricket: using a tennis ball and throwing it against the wall of the potato house and hitting it as it returned. A tree provided the stumps and I had the satisfaction that when I bowled myself out at least I had done the bowling even if I had failed at the batting. I would do this for hours at a time. Frequently it ended with the ball in the flower bed. Finally I ruined so many begonias that my mother told me I had to take my bat and ball elsewhere. I transferred to the farmyard and continued my solitary game until I was in my teens.

The culmination of my time at the village school was the scholarship exam for Dr Morgan's Grammar School. My father had been at Dr Morgan's and I knew how important it was to him that I should succeed. I was ten years old and terribly nervous and fearful that I would fail. My parents tried to reassure me that even if I wasn't successful, they would pay for me to go to Dr Morgan's. At that time it was still partly fee-paying and didn't become a full grammar school until 1944. On the day of the exam I was so apprehensive I went to the lavatory at the end of the garden and locked myself in. I said I didn't want to go to school and couldn't bear the thought of it. Eventually I was coaxed back into the house and my father drove me to school.

When I got there and looked at the papers I calmed down immediately because I realised I could do it. Some of the questions were very topical – concerning the measurement of black-out material. It took up most of the day and I heard the result of my scholarship two weeks later. My parents were delighted and gave me a present to mark the occasion. The book I chose was *The Wind in the Willows*.

7

VILLAGE AT WAR

The war was the great Rubicon of my childhood. Before the war were the sunshine days: the village school, and Ruth coming to live with us. Afterwards nothing was the same. The outside world was strange and hostile: evacuees, the rituals of putting up the black-out curtains and life now much more restricted, with few visits beyond Bridgwater.

The war did not come out of the blue; it crept up gradually. I was blissfully unaware of the wider world at the Coronation in May 1937 but I was very much aware of Germany by the Munich Agreement of 1938. Even then I began to take notice of the headlines and the pictures and the maps in the *Daily Mail*. I have a very vivid memory of the Prime Minister, Neville Chamberlain, returning from Munich. Our Philips radio was the prize piece of furniture. It was run on acid batteries which had to be renewed frequently. Typically, the acid was very weak when Chamberlain returned and the wireless was barely audible. My father crouched over the radio with his ear jammed to the loudspeaker whilst he listened to the 'Peace in our Time' speech. My father relayed the news to us; he was immensely relieved. He had not fought in the 1914 war but he was grimly aware of its devastation. His relief was to become conditional. The general mood was soon that war had been postponed and

not avoided. The latest series of cigarette cards were devoted
to 'Civil Defence', ranging from pictures of barrage balloons to
homely advice on how to tape your windows and prevent them
from splintering from blast and how to deal with an incendiary
bomb with the help of a bucket of sand and a spade. Meanwhile
my mother went to Bridgwater and bought 'black-out' material,
which she then sewed into lengths which would fit our windows,
happily not all that large. For some reason, when peace came,
they were used to drape the chicken runs.

So, even though I was only eight years old, in a sense I
was aware of the impending possibility of war. On Sunday
3 September 1939 we were all in the kitchen listening to the radio
for Chamberlain's announcement that the country was at war.
My parents were very solemn – Father more so than my mother
because of his memories of the First World War and the heavy
responsibility he had borne of running his mother's farm. For
my part I was devastated. I ran from the kitchen and up to the
top room and cried and cried. I thought the world was coming
to an end. A door was being shut and bolted and I wasn't sure
what other door would open. My parents followed me up and
tried to comfort me saying that we would all be together and I
would be all right.

Once the war had begun our radio became the hub of the
house. Our neighbours, Dr Irene Shepherd and her friend Miss
Royds, would often visit us to listen to Churchill addressing the
nation. We sat in the kitchen glued to his words. When it was
over the National Anthem was played and to general amazement Miss Royd sprang to her feet and gave a full rendering of
'God Save the King', whilst we all remained loyal but seated.

The first real feeling we had of war was in late 1939 and
early 1940 when the Army installed a searchlight unit in one of
the fields at Putnell Farm. The Germans had started bombing

South Wales and their flight path led over Somerset. This lone searchlight supposedly formed part of our defences. Its beam was colossal. It was a very dramatic sight. Officially we were not encouraged to go near it, but, as it was installed on our own farm, the military couldn't stop my father taking me to have a look.

The main effect of war locally was the big change in village life. Very soon all people of military age were conscripted and went off to fight leaving behind the young and the old and those in reserved occupations. At the start of the war the Local Defence Volunteers (LDV) had been hastily formed wearing only arm bands. With the fall of France in 1940, they were quickly replaced by the Home Guard, who were soon equipped with uniforms and eventually rifles.

In Combwich they were Sunday morning soldiers. The training was novel. John Merrett, a bookkeeper with Combwich and District Farmers, would go ahead across a field; the rest would crawl some way behind. From time to time John Merrett would suddenly turn around and see if he could catch anyone moving. I suppose it was a test of reflexes, but happily such training was never put to the test by the Waffen SS. I knew John Merrett rather well. He regularly came to the farm and did my father's accounts. All the material was kept either in my father's memory or in bundles of papers threaded upon farm wire. John was earnest and meticulous and also a strong Labour man. My father accepted that 'working men' might be Labour (especially in Bridgwater) but he could not understand a bookkeeper from the village having such heretical views.

In 1940 the village received a number of evacuees, almost as many children as there were in the village. They came largely from the East End of London. In Bridgwater Dr Morgan's School hosted the Poplar School of Navigation. They remained separate for teaching purposes but shared the school premises. They did not use a cane for discipline but chastised with a small knotted rope – in the naval tradition I assumed. My parents took in an evacuee boy, James (Jimmy) Edgar Biggs. His sister was billeted in the village. They came from Islington, where their father was a policeman. It was a great upheaval for me to share the household and the bedroom with him. In retrospect I think we had a tolerably good relationship and I am certain my parents thought it good for me to have someone of my own age in the house. Jimmy was more interested in the farm than I was and certainly less committed to school and books. We played war games together and my parents were scrupulous in treating us as equals. Like most of the evacuees he and his sister returned to London after eighteen months or so. He was slightly older than me and considerably more sexually alert. I think I got more sex education from him than from any other source, certainly more than from school or my parents. There was no physical homosexuality but Jimmy talked knowledgeably and without inhibition. His interests were moving towards village girls when he returned to Islington and my partial sex education ended. The episode had been pleasurable but I did not feel I could divulge it to my parents. I was left with uncertainty and guilt which persisted for a considerable while. I was glad when he left because I liked the solitude and independence of being the only child with a farm as a playground. We never heard from Jimmy after he returned to Islington.

The immediate effect of the war on our farm was that we lost one of our farmhands and had to employ land girls. Over the period of the war we had three land girls. First there were Irene and Rose, both from Portishead outside Bristol. They had worked in the Wills tobacco factory and life on the farm was a complete novelty to them. Later they were joined by Joan Green from Wigan. All three of them were outstanding workers, very enthusiastic and great fun.

Irene, always known as Rene, was strikingly handsome. She used to ride my mother's horse, Melisha, and eventually married a farmer's son from the neighbouring village. Rosina, always known as Rose, was much more ebullient. Joan was quieter but all three were good company. They lived with the Haggetts at Putnell. Every Thursday night my mother would invite them to come to Hill Farm for supper, and the simple but ample meal was washed down with farmhouse cider from a jug or occasionally a huge three-handled loving cup. I enjoyed those evenings, partly because I was aware that the girls were attractive (I was about thirteen) but more so because I enjoyed listening to grown-up conversation, even though it was mainly about the farm and the village. The evening inevitably ended with cards, Newmarket and nap being the favourite games. My father usually won.

Initially Wiggy, our head farm worker, wasn't as enthusiastic about the land girls as we were. He was intensely conservative. These girls came from industrial Bristol. It was a case of the countryman confronted by people with a wholly urban background and different outlook on life. Coming from factory work, there was a learning curve but they soon mastered the job. They did all the farm work other than the very heavy jobs. They looked after the cattle and did the milking. Of course there was no question of them driving the tractor. My father would have had forty fits at the thought of a woman driving anything.

My mother kept on with the cheese-making during the first half of the war. But later on this was discontinued when animal feed rationing meant that my father couldn't keep enough pigs to use up the whey. Also there was now a guarantee for all the liquid milk so he had a safe market.

Because of the war, farmers were given a price guarantee on

most things but they were also subject to a good deal of direction as to what they should or shouldn't grow.

Early in the war the Ministry of Agriculture set up county-based War Agricultural Executives. They were a talking shop for ministry officials and for farmers and those in related activities such as land agents and feed merchants. The Somerset War Agricultural Executive Committee was under the chairmanship of Lord Waldegrave and my father was very proud to be made a member, not least because his family came from the Mendips – Waldegrave country. I think he felt he had made good, and rightly so. I always thought it meant he could match his cousin, Wilfred Middle, who was rather grand and became master of the Mendip Farmers' Hunt.

My father's ministry work and farming generally entailed a certain amount of travel, so he was given a petrol allowance. Although it was by no means generous it did mean that we had a touch more freedom than if we were dependent on horses and bicycles to get around. We didn't have to go through the whole rigmarole of trying to get hold of black-market petrol like some of our friends and neighbours. With Army and Air Force units scattered around the county it was not impossible to get to know a helpful person and supplies were fairly readily obtainable.

My father's farming took account of wartime conditions. The Ministry of Agriculture encouraged the growth of sugar beet. It was not a great success. The soil wasn't ideal and in those days beet hadn't been developed to the form we now know. The roots were small and gnarled in funny shapes. Farming was a very secure occupation in the war and my father was so relieved to know he could farm and make money and put the memories and uncertainties of the 1920s behind him. However, when Wiggy's son Brian was born, the doctor who had been attending the birth had a word with my father and said, 'Well, Mr Biffen. Farming's doing very well, I suppose.' My father was stung by this and replied, 'Doctor. Why should it take a war to make farming pay?' Silence followed.

However, farming was no sinecure and, if a farmer was not making a success and was negligent, he could be dispossessed by the ministry and the land would be made available to someone else to farm. This threat acted as a background discipline.

It would be wrong to say that my father enjoyed the war but he had a certain sense of achievement. He was forty-three when it started and nearly fifty when it finished. It coincided with him renting the second farm, Putnell. There was always a problem with labour but the land girls bridged this gap.

During the war there was greater emphasis on crops and my father had to plough up more land than hitherto. Apart from sugar beet and clover, he grew wheat, barley, oats and kale. He also grew swedes and turnips for forage. It was an extraordinary range of crops for the three hundred acres that comprised Hill and Putnell Farms.

We were never short of food, but living off the farm meant it was pretty basic. At intervals we killed a pig. The saying that 'we eat everything except the squeal' came true to me. Certain joints like pigs' trotters my father loved. Slaughtering was a great farm occasion but I kept well out of the way. My aversion to violence and blood was well established by then.

The vegetable garden was enlarged but it was so enormous that even at the height of the war it wasn't all utilised. My father, like many farmers, had no great love of gardening, a trait I inherited. My mother was an enthusiast and was assisted by the land girls. The garden yielded a cornucopia of wholesome vegetables: new potatoes, broad beans, peas, carrots and parsnips. My mother persevered with asparagus but not with great success.

8

RAF STEART: VILLAGE IN VICTORY

During the war I followed events very closely indeed. It was almost with a frightening commitment. If, at the age of seventy, I met my fourteen-year-old self, I would have been embarrassed by the intense partisanship I then exhibited. I had a huge map of the world pinned to the wall of the cheese room. I would mark up the progress of the war with pins and crayon. The map was based on Mercator's projection. This meant that as you approached the North Pole everything got bigger and bigger. The British had sent an expedition to Spitsbergen. On the map this was inflated to such a size that it equalled the area of the German occupation of Russia. I would console myself that even though they had got a lot of territory, on *my* map so had we.

Every morning and evening I listened to the news on the radio. I read the paper from cover to cover. Also I followed avidly the news and views of the wide range of people who came to Hill Farm. In 1942 my class at Dr Morgan's had to give a talk about the war. In a most precocious way I gave an overview of events and a comprehensive analysis of strategy. The teacher listened to this with some bewilderment, occasionally interrupting to correct my Somerset syntax. She asked me what paper we took at home. She was none the wiser when I answered that it was the *Daily Mail*.

By contrast with my armchair strategies the real wartime impact upon the village was the establishment of a Royal Air Force station at the little hamlet of Steart. This isolated collection of houses, within the parish of Stockland Bristol, was on the Parrett Estuary. It had a small church and a telephone kiosk. It overlooked mud flats and even by local standards was the end of the world. My parents would often drive there to spend an evening with the Govetts. The family had farmed there for decades. Jimmy Govett was very gruff and did not welcome outsiders. His wife was very protective to my mother, who was many years her junior. I remember her for not allowing flowering may in the house because of ill luck.

Steart was an outpost of a RAF base at Westonzoyland. This was a village near Bridgwater which had been used by the RAF since before the war. It was then used for gunnery practice, with a Westland Lysander aircraft towing a target at slow speed. The trainees hoped to hit the target and not the plane. Once the war started it was decided to make Bridgwater Bay into an area for more advanced training. This meant they wanted a small RAF unit near Bridgwater Bay where the targets would be land based and not flown.

A small unit, of about four Nissen huts, was constructed between Steart and Otterhampton. A team of airmen would call in the fighter planes from the base at Westonzoyland, which would swoop over Bridgwater Bay firing their 303 machine guns at fixed targets on the sea shore bearing huge black crosses on a white background. Steart would then telephone back the score to Westonzoyland. It was a relatively simple operation but quite a noisy one with the chatter of machine guns. The village felt it was a touch nearer 'the real war'.

The RAF recognised that Steart was a 'back of beyond' posting and every Friday they would send an ENSA concert party to entertain the airmen. Selected local people were also invited. It was a somewhat divisive gesture, but the station commander wanted to keep on side with the local establishment and especially the farmers. My parents were obviously included and they took me. These Friday evenings were great events. The concert party numbered four, usually a pianist, a comedian (of sorts), a singer and someone who could play the accordion. A Nissen hut was adapted for the show, with a make-shift stage and rows of utility chairs for the audience. I now realise the performers had more informality than skill but the whole evening was wonderfully relaxed and occasionally boisterous. My parents much enjoyed it; such entertainment had been barely known in their pre-war days, although I can remember them going once to the Bristol Hippodrome.

The station personnel knew my father could take a joke and one evening they arranged for an ample-bosomed singer to leave the stage, visit the audience and sit on his lap. She then sang and planted a lipstick-drenched kiss on his bald pate. It was uproarious and my father took it in good heart.

After the show, which lasted about forty-five minutes to an hour, we had an excellent buffet (or so it seemed in wartime days). Then the hut was cleared for dancing. In deference to the village the pianist and accompanist would play the veleta and the barn dance, then move on to the waltz, quickstep and foxtrot and finally to the conga and jiving. It was a noisy occasion and the hut was gradually enveloped in cigarette smoke. There was plenty of beer on offer. Meanwhile, aged thirteen and the only juvenile on the premises, I would retreat to a corner where I read history books. *A Modern History of Europe* by E. Ketelby was my favourite. I enjoyed the atmosphere, but equally I enjoyed my reading.

We got to know people at the camp very well and they became

friends and visited us at the farm. They would play cards with my father. Padre Scott, based in Westonzoyland, was particularly fond of pontoon. We were so impressed that a vicar could play cards and that, when he turned up the prize card he would say, 'I will turn my collar round.' Other regulars for cider and cards were 'Chiefy' Dawson, a senior NCO at the camp, and an L. A. C. Davis from Liverpool, who had sold Jacob's biscuits before the war. They would come by invitation. Once an officer known to be married brought a girlfriend. My mother was not amused.

One of the people who became a really close friend was Wilfred Turner. He was then a flight lieutenant and in charge of the Steart camp. He came from a mining community in Nottinghamshire and had come up through the ranks. He was particularly fond of my mother, and we all remained great friends for some years.

Years later Wilfred Turner looked after me on my first visit to London and took me to the House of Commons. I was on my way to a week's course on current affairs being held at Ashridge, near Berkhamsted. The visit to the Commons was a huge success. Wilf introduced me to his MP, Harold Neal. He was drinking with a fellow mining MP, Arthur Jenkins, who represented Pontypool and was father of the illustrious Roy, who founded the Social Democratic Party a generation later.

Wilfred Turner went with the advancing Allied forces through Europe at the end of the war and sent me my European stamp album from Brussels which I still use. He was a fascinating man and a role model for me. In the 1930s he had been on the *Eagle*, an aircraft carrier, in the seas off China. He was very knowledge-able on current affairs. I used to sit and listen to him in respectful silence, and value his words. He was rather cryptic and given to longish periods of silence whilst he sucked upon his pipe. I think he enjoyed the informality of Hill Farm and the contrasting personalities of my parents. After the war I did not see very much of him but I was a guest at a mess dance at RAF Amesbury, where he was stationed in the summer of 1953. Alas, all contact was lost by the time I was elected to the Commons. This was sad as he was a decidedly inspirational figure at an important point in my life.

RAF Steart provided an early experience of the hazards of the market economy and demonstrated quite uncharacteristic rashness on my part. What will one do for cash! I was in my mid-teens before I was allowed modest pocket money. Hitherto I had been encouraged to take fallen apples to school and to sell them to my fellow pupils. I then decided that spent RAF cartridges were a better bet than the produce of our rather unkempt orchard. Also the RAF range was so isolated on the Steart flats that no other pupils would cycle the six or seven miles to search for a range that was carefully concealed. I learned the attractions of being a local monopoly supplier. I would cycle as near as I could to the range and then walk across three or four fields and collect my crop of spent 303 brass cartridges and the more imposing 0.45 which were fired by the Mustang fighters. Of course I was well within the forbidden zone but there never seemed to be any risk unless a red flag was flying, particularly as I did the journeys in the evening. I then altered the pattern and went one afternoon. Then my easy assumptions were, literally, shot to pieces. An aircraft swept in from nowhere, the noise was deafening as, I think, all its six guns were firing. I ran like fury back towards the road. My movement attracted the airman in the concrete observation hut who was monitoring the target practice. He then fired a Very light to warn the aircraft to cease firing. I needed no warning. Apart from the noise of gunfire I could hear the bullets, sounding like angry wasps, as they sped to the target. I managed to reach my bicycle and returned to the farm as nonchalantly as I could. My father would have erupted had he known what I had done, but I still console myself that the money I made from my fellow pupils gave me a valuable introduction to 'commercial risk'.

Towards the end of the war we all had a sense of triumph and anticipation. We knew we were winning. From the D-Day landings, on 6 June 1944, I started saving the newspapers. They piled up as I followed the events intensely and eventually in early 1945 I persuaded my parents to change from the *Daily Mail* to *The Times*. I continued saving them. The piles got larger and larger and gradually filled up the room that had been given to me as a study. Finally enough was enough and we gave them to a market gardener in the village. He was delighted to use them for compost. It was entirely appropriate that he should dispose of my wartime collection of newsprint because he had been a courageous member of the Parachute Regiment.

When the great victory day came, the village had a common church service at St Peter's, Combwich, attended by both Methodists and Anglicans. Today this would be a very normal event but it was the first time that this had happened in the village and was quite a memorable occasion. The church was decorated with bunting and home-made flags. The Rev. William Napier Skrine took the service and Mr Venner, a Methodist farmer, read the lesson.

The Rotary Club operated a system to help returning service-men and prisoners-of-war with transport. Louis Palmer, a local auctioneer, was a great friend of my parents. I was with him when the telephone went saying that an ex-POW was arriving and could he meet him at the station and drive him to his home. Louis Palmer asked me if I would like to come along. We picked up the returnee, John Frampton, and drove him home. His family were chicken farmers. The whole village had turned

out and lined the street to greet us. It was a most spontaneous and moving reception. You felt that the war was over and
now our own people were returning. John Frampton was quite
overwhelmed.

There was, alas, an incident that spoiled the memories. On
the night of VJ Day there was much celebration. The Steart
Air Force got into a lorry and whooped it up as they drove to
Bridgwater. They were armed with Very pistols and, as they
drove past the farm, they were firing away. One shot fell into a
rick of hay and set it alight. It burned furiously and the crop was
totally destroyed. It was sad that the driver, a girl called Dorothy,
afterwards said that she had passed the farm earlier in the evening and had then seen smoke. This left some understandable
bitterness with my father. It was an unhappy episode after all the
good times we had shared.

9

DR MORGAN'S SCHOOL: BACKGROUND

Whilst my childhood evolved into teenage years on the farm, in the village there was the parallel development of school. Winning a county scholarship encouraged my natural bookishness, but it was with customary nervousness that I started at Dr Morgan's in the autumn of 1941.

The school was originally founded in 1723 by Dr Morgan as a school for boys, with an emphasis on navigation. Through the years it became recognised locally as a school which catered for the sons of farmers and the professions. My father had been at the school, travelling daily on the Somerset and Dorset Railway from Burtle to Bridgwater. His father, incidentally, had gone to a private boarding school in Weston-super-Mare. The school ceased to be purely a private school when the Somerset County Council started to provide awards to help able pupils to attend. By the time I got my scholarship, two-thirds of the school were funded by the county and one-third were fee payers. Butler's 1944 Education Act resulted in Dr Morgan's being established as a state grammar school and all the fee payers had the good fortune of being converted into state-funded pupils. In my father's day it had been located in the middle of Bridgwater, but just before the Second World War a brand new building was constructed on the outskirts of the town. Together with the

Odeon cinema it was one of the last buildings to be built in the area before the war. When I arrived it had about two hundred pupils with twenty to twenty-five to a class. The school uniform had been immensely conspicuous with a bright red blazer and cap and black emblem. To my relief, because of the war, new school uniforms were not available and I spent all my time there in mufti. The only concession to uniform was a navy cap with a red badge on it representing the school emblem of a pestle and mortar. When I became a prefect I had a blue cap with a red tassel. My parents were very impressed.

As a new building the school had very good facilities for its time with light classrooms and large glass windows. Within the grounds was the caretaker's house and a large part of the gardens was devoted to vegetables. The classrooms took up one side of a grassed quadrangle. Science laboratories, cloakrooms and administration offices occupied the other sides. The school also owned one full-length and one smaller rugby pitch, a fair-sized cricket pitch and a running track.

However, the war put a stop to any replacement of equipment and things began to get run down, particularly the desks. These were wooden with flip-lid tops that became detached, exposing the raw metal hinges. One boy had his jacket torn and there was a tremendous row. His parents were naturally furious because clothing was restricted by wartime rationing. The headmaster came to the classroom. Glowering at us, he personally dismantled the offending hinge. He did not favour parent power.

I was immensely apprehensive about going to my new school even though I had visited it with my parents before the term started. Despite being eleven I was a very nervous boy. From the first day I set off on my own with my satchel and was picked up by the bus just outside the farm. The only other boy from Combwich

School was Eric Charles, who also had got a scholarship. He settled in more easily, being more extrovert. Although we had shared five years of our Dr Morgan's schooling I never felt very much warmth towards him, after a bullying incident which took place in my second year.

On the whole it was a happy school. The boys came from professional families, as well as sons of farmers and trades-people. There was little or no class consciousness.

The school seemed enormous after the village school and it took me a while to get used to it. The teaching was very formal and I had a very deferential attitude to all authority. A particular problem was the food. This was served in the school hall and it didn't take me long to decide that school dinners were a short cut to death. I had always been a difficult child as far as food was concerned. I wouldn't eat cheese, which caused great grief to my cheese-maker mother. I wouldn't eat fat and I wouldn't eat greens. At Hill Farm greens meant home-grown cabbage, kale and broccoli. My mother gave in and made me packed sandwiches. So for the rest of my career at Dr Morgan's I sat at a bench at the back of the hall with a few other boys eating food brought from home. School meals were served and fought over under the wearied eye of the master on dinner duty, trying to bring some order to the chaos. This was a continuation of the fairly lengthy period of my getting more and more neurotic about food. The habit was only blown open by National Service. In my defence, wartime school dinners were a rather grey and dreary proposition.

I started school being very proud to have won my scholarship but apprehensive as to how I would perform in the exams at the end of the first term. In the event I was second in the class, which was the highest I ever came. This initial success was followed by a period of greyness. It covered a time when I had poor health, the weather was bleak and I was being bullied. It was also a time when the war news was bad. It was therefore not wholly fanciful to think that my rather indifferent school performance was as a result of these factors.

The bullying incident took place in my second year. Desperate to do well not least to please my parents, I was anxious to attend all available classes. This provoked for me a crisis. The school bus left in the afternoon at a time when we had to leave the last class five minutes early. The boys from Dr Morgan's and the girls from the adjacent grammar school used the same general service bus. The boys concocted a story that we now had to catch the bus from its starting point in the centre of Bridgwater. This meant they had to miss the entire last period of school. I refused to go along with it and persisted in staying in class. I was trapped! Fearful of sticking out against the majority of the boys, fearful of being found out by the school, and also fearful of what my parents would say.

The other boys accepted that I was a little swot. They ignored me but the girls were different. On the bus I was jeered and hooted by the girls and I was absolutely miserable. It wasn't a situation I felt I could share with anyone. At the time it was very stressful. I liked friendship and good relations and felt that I hadn't done anything wrong to deserve this treatment. This lasted for about a year before it petered out but the memory of the misery still lingers.

10

DR MORGAN'S SCHOOL: STAFF

Up until 1939 the staff had been entirely male. However, the war changed everything. As the younger men left to go to war they were replaced by women and I had the novel experience of unisex staff. Until I reached the sixth form the headmaster was C. M. Trenchard, known to us all as Trout. Slightly built, he was an Oxford graduate of the old school with undoubted presence who inspired a wide measure of awe. A strong disciplinarian, he was not unwilling to use the cane. His great enthusiasm was the Air Training Corps, which had been formed just before the war.

The deputy head, Percy Gillard, doubled as the mathematics teacher. Known as Butch, he was given to natural or calculated fits of agitation which resulted in his neck going purple. These episodes had the most fantastic disciplinary effect on the class. He exercised authority by controlled bursts of rage. I remember him picking up a box of chalk with no lid and hurling it to the ground. We were showered with stub ends.

Harold Storey, known as Staggers, came from London. Middle aged and balding, he never lost his temper, but was a kindly man with an amiable personality. We all liked him. He taught us geography and English by rote rather than inspiration. He did not conceal his conservative social and political attitudes.

However, the master who stood out in my early school days

was Jack Lawrence. His subject was history but he was also the physical training (PT) master. Just as I had a dedication to history I was particularly undistinguished at PT. Eventually he took me to one side and said, 'You are very good at history and I am sure that one day you will be a gold medallist but you must try and do better at PT.' The school had a very modern and well-equipped gym and I struggled at hanging upside-down on the parallel bars and jumping over the horse but I was all fingers and thumbs. It was a mercy I did not injure myself.

One day Jack Lawrence studied us all and drew lines of our shapes. He told me that my body was crooked, as a result of which I was made to lie on the coconut matting for hours during lunch breaks. I don't think it made a lot of difference.

Many years later I was asked by *The Independent* to write an article on 'a hero'. I think they expected me to choose a politician but I decided on Jack Lawrence. He was delighted.

One master who had taught before the war and was unavailable for military service was Gwilym Rees. He was in charge of music, woodwork and metalwork. My uselessness at both wood and metalwork was only matched by my inability to sing. I struggled along in the workshop and made the statutory teapot stand and copper spoon (which surprisingly I still have) but my work was always that bit out of kilter and an indication as to my future lack of dexterity. The real terror, however, was singing. We gathered in the assembly hall for our singing lessons. The repertoire was not very demanding and happily the singing was almost always as a chorus. Occasionally Rees would shriek 'You' and point at some poor boy for a solo performance. I was always terrified that it would be me because I was completely incapable of producing more than a strangled croak.

Gwilym Rees was always exhorting us to greater effort. 'Stop! Stop!' he would cry. 'Put some more effort into it!' On one occasion we were struggling through the hymn 'Lo he comes with clouds descending' when he interrupted us by crying, 'Think of it as a German paratrooper.' Seen through the eyes of a boy aged eleven or twelve it was all very formidable. Years later I returned to the school and was surprised to find that he and his wife were charming and didn't at all fit my memory of the mechanically musical tyrant.

The turnover of our female teachers seemed greater than the men. Winifred Jones taught me French and became a close friend. Always dressed in black, she was a slight figure with beautifully arranged hair. Her natural language was Welsh but she spoke very concise English. She was an effective teacher who dominated the classroom. Alas I didn't have an ear for languages but I was inspired to work conscientiously. I gained a pass in French for the Higher School Certificate.

We corresponded for many years after I had left school and well after I had become a Member of Parliament. She put snatches of French in her letters, doubtless hoping it would encourage me to make amends. It never did and as Trade Secretary I had an interpreter for any French discussions.

Winifred's sister was an enigma. She seemed to have married very well and ended her days living in the Ritz. Winifred died intestate and her administrator contacted me as he had found letters from me amongst her papers.

The second and third forms were taught French and German by Mrs Tucker. During my time with her my German was better than my French but I then went on to Mrs Whittingham, a young and nubile Labour supporter; but she didn't have the same inspirational qualities as Mrs Tucker and my languages suffered.

Amongst the host of female teachers who did their turn during the war was Mrs Richardson, who taught us physics. Her husband had been taken a prisoner-of-war and wasn't released until May 1945. Miss James taught us biology and wore a lot of make-up. I confess that neither my physics nor biology prospered but I cannot blame the teachers.

Mrs Henderson was an Austrian married to an Englishman and taught us French and German. She was hopeless at keeping order. We treated her in the most beastly fashion. On one occasion we chalked up on the blackboard, 'Death to the German hordes,' and underneath, 'Death to the Austrian hordes.' Mr Trenchard, the headmaster, spotted the mayhem going on in the classroom. He stormed in and caned every one of us, including me.

I only began to show qualities of scholastic attainment in my fourth year. It was then clear that I showed promise at history and geography and was reasonably competent at English and mathematics. I still have the Higher School Certificate papers and they strike me as being really quite tough and demanding a lot of interpretive judgement particularly in history.

Such was my enthusiasm for history that, for the Oxford School Certificate, I did Modern English History, but in my own time I studied Modern European History and got top marks in both papers.

The step change was to drop from a class of twenty-five to what was effectively a tutorial in the sixth form. I was growing up and one's mind became more disciplined. Learning became less blotting paper to absorb facts and more a matter of interpretation.

When the Bristol University Higher School Certificate results came out I had achieved a distinction in history and passes in English and French. It was adequate for university entrance but not outstanding. At that point it would never have occurred to me that in a matter of months I would be a successful candidate for a Cambridge open scholarship and go on to get a first class honours degree.

11

DR MORGAN'S SCHOOL: FRIENDS

Because of the war I was totally isolated out at the farm. Unlike the boys living in Bridgwater, I could have no social life after school. My life was the farm. I cocooned myself there, reading my books, doing my homework and tracing the progress of the war with a developing interest. I did not learn to cycle until I was twelve.

Then everything began to turn when I was thirteen. I started coming out of my shell. I concentrated on being good at history and geography and the bullying and teasing crisis abated. I started making friends at school. Adrian Rendall remained a close friend during my time at school. He came from Bridgwater and after leaving school had a career in banking. He was a strong Labour supporter and we shared a great enthusiasm for cricket. We both took a keen interest in the progress of the war. We corresponded for years and sadly he died of cancer in 2003.

Other people with whom I made friends during the school lunch time break included Sheepy Shepherd, whose parents farmed near Muchelny, and John Moore from Highbridge.

The moment I got into the sixth form I worked as part of a group of six and became closer to them than I could lower down the school with a greater number of people. VE Day was May

1945 and I started sixth form in 1946. The war had finished and
everything opened out. I now had an Elswick bicycle and could
visit Bridgwater pretty much at will.

The bicycle was indispensable. I can still recall cycling on a
wonderful moonlit evening on a completely empty road from
Bridgwater to Hill Farm, a distance of five miles. In post-war
Britain the West Somerset roads were practically empty.

The sixth form was a new life – albeit male dominated. Peter
Thorak, Malcolm Chilvers, Roy Gigg, Peter Haggett and Trefor
David were all either in the sixth form as exact contemporaries
or the year behind. At this stage, for all my bookishness, I was
really quite involved in school games as well. When it was an
away rugby game I would go to help out even if I was not playing. So I began to have a weekend social life.

My closest friend was Malcolm Chilvers. He was a year
younger and an extremely good rugby player. His personality
made him a natural school leader. His parents wanted him to do
science and be a doctor. But this was an impractical idea because
they couldn't possibly have financed his studies. After sixth form
he joined an engineering company where he prospered. He
eventually took over a store and post office in Bridgwater until
his retirement. He was an only child like me, and I used to go
to his home where we gossiped a great deal.

I was fanatical about politics. That was tolerated by my friends,
but we used to talk mainly about life at large and endlessly about
women. Talking and speculating was about as far as I got. I was
smitten by a girl who worked in Chants, the greengrocer, but I
could never summon enough courage to order Brussels sprouts,
let alone to ask her name and seek a date.

Roy Gigg was an interesting example of the ladder provided by
a grammar school. His father was a farm worker from the village
of Chedzoy. Roy was an all-round academic who eventually had

a distinguished career with the Medical Research Council. We kept in touch over the years.

Trefor David, Malcolm Chilvers and I went round as a threesome. Trefor was highly articulate and came from a Welsh-speaking family. His father was a school master and Trefor inherited his politics. He was a good radical and fully able to match me in the school debating society. It was a matter of some amusement that he was the only one of my sixth-form friends who gained a National Service commission. He emerged as radical as ever.

Peter Haggett was in many ways the most gifted academically. He was a year behind me and specialised in geography. He came from the village of Pawlett, very much my family territory as my uncle and aunt farmed at Woolavington, the next-door village. He was a serious boy and a Methodist. He was not a games player but a hardworking secretary of various games clubs. We were good friends and corresponded over the years. He went to Cambridge on a scholarship to St Catharine's. Subsequently he taught geography at Bristol University and temporarily stood in when the Vice-Chancellorship fell vacant. He didn't take up the opportunity to fill the vacancy because he preferred academic work to university administration.

Peter Thorak joined us in the sixth form, having come to England after spending the war marooned in Switzerland where he had gone for medical treatment. His was a particularly interesting story. His father Josef Thorak was a gifted sculptor who had known Hitler as a young man. His mother Gilda, although a Roman Catholic, was partly Jewish. When the marriage broke down in the late 1930s her husband and friends helped Peter and her to escape to France. Peter then fell ill and was sent alone to Montreux to convalesce. This coincided with the German invasion of France in 1940. Peter's mother escaped to England

and wasn't reunited with her son until after the war. Eventually she was permitted to work and, in 1946, came to teach at Burnham-on-Sea and sent Peter to Dr Morgan's.

He came straight into the sixth form and made friends very easily. I saw a lot of him. We all made great use of our bicycles and he used to come out to Hill Farm. One day he said he would like to go camping and asked if he could pitch his tent in our field. Could he bring his air gun and hopefully shoot the odd rabbit? My mother said, 'Of course you can but why don't you come and be our guest and sleep in a proper bedroom?' Peter was determined and set up his camp. Of course it rained like fury and fairly quickly his visit was adjusted and he moved indoors. He then became a good friend of the family. My parents liked him no end, particularly my mother. My father couldn't really understand why Mrs Thorak, who didn't seem to have much visible means of support, kept going abroad. She had many friends overseas, particularly the Schmellings; Max had been a heavyweight boxer before the war and fought Joe Louis.

Peter wrote a piece in the school magazine saying how much he had enjoyed coming to Bridgwater, which I reproduce below.

My Impressions of Dr Morgan's School

Everybody will understand that a foreigner is terrified at the idea of coming to a new country, to a new school with a different system, with different views, especially after having heard quite a lot about English national pride and English reserve. However, these fears faded away after my first visit to the school, where I was received with so much friendliness, interest and helpfulness on the part of the headmaster and the teachers. But even more astonishing was the hearty and friendly welcome of the boys. They made me feel at home immediately and accepted me as one of themselves.

I do not think that Swiss boys would have accepted English boys with the same interest and friendliness.

I much appreciate that they never laugh at or make fun of my faulty English, although I cannot help smiling when, as I enter our wind-swept hut, they greet me with an occasional 'Bon matin'.

Feeling very happy in the school I wish to express my gratitude to everybody.

P Thorak, Form VI

Dr Morgan's had a decidedly arm's length relation with the Girls' Grammar School, whose buildings were adjacent. Our common performance was playing hockey against each other. This was a very friendly occasion for which I was the organising secretary. In the sixth form there was a certain amount of cross-teaching. The other link was dancing classes, which I attended with some trepidation at the Girls' Grammar School. The instructress wore an ankle chain, which gave rise to a good deal of intense and ungenerous speculation on the part of the boys.

I hated dancing. I was dumb-struck when confronted by a gaggle of girls. My dancing skills were negligible. My mother had tried to introduce me to dancing. We had an ancient gramophone and records of waltzes. I could do the veleta, the waltz and formation dances. Old-time dancing was very much in vogue after the war and my father was a very good dancer.

At school I was made to do the quickstep, the foxtrot and the tango. I tried all these without much success but I could just about cope with the progressive barn dance. In later years, when Conservative Associations used to put on dances, I would make a deal with the band that they would put on a barn dance and watch me until I had completed the circuit of the room and danced with everyone, and then stop.

12

DEBATING AND POLITICS

The war had the consequence of mothballing all the modest sporting ambitions of the school – rugby excepted. Trips to the municipal baths were discontinued. There was no school tennis but after the war two sub-standard tennis courts were renovated. An uncertain game could be played on the crumbling asphalt surface. Cricket was a wartime casualty because we didn't have the staff to maintain the cricket ground. Rugby, barely maintained during the war, recovered quite soon and the 1st XV were playing twenty games a season with a modest fixture list for the Colts XV.

I went through a period of trying to avoid all sport so that I could read my history books. It wasn't until I was being groomed by the teaching staff to become head of my house and subsequently school captain that even I realised that I would have to show some commitment to games in order to hold down these positions. The school rather pretentiously had a house system based upon where you lived. All the houses were named after Civil War commanders. Wyndham House was for boys living in Bridgwater Town, west of the River Parrett, and Fairfax House was for boys living east of the River Parrett. Cromwell House was for boys living at Highbridge and Burnham-on-Sea, and Hopton for boys from the country areas. The house captain was elected by the house members and the headmaster was anxious that I became head of Hopton. The masters leaned very heavily on the boys to try and get me elected. I just defeated a very ebullient and accomplished rugby player called Jimmy Munn who had recently come to Bridgwater from Paisley. I was an unlikely house captain, but school captain was an appointee of the headmaster. It was then that I started to take an interest in rugby and played lock forward. Although I didn't play with much distinction, I enjoyed it. I confounded myself and everyone else by winning a cross-country race. Actually that was no mean achievement. When I realised I was going to win, I tore off my shirt so that I should run in and break the tape stripped to the waist. It was exhibitionism I would now deplore.

I also took a modest interest in track events and to my utter amazement did the high jump 'western roll', a feat I still cannot believe.

After the war the cricket pitch was restored and although we had very limited and much-used equipment, we started playing. It was my great love, although I was very mediocre. Undeterred I pursued the ambition to be a wicket keeper. I had just enough quickness of reaction to maintain a flicker of hope that did not die until I was at Cambridge. Meanwhile I had the unsought distinction of having half my front tooth knocked out by some-one juggling with the ball so that it bounced into my face. For several years I had a half-crowned tooth. The top half rotted away and I went around a most unprepossessing sight with a decaying brown top and a white crown. Eventually a neighbour approached my mother with friendly advice and said that some-thing should be done about my front tooth. It says something about my lack of concern for personal appearances that I should have accepted the 'half-crown' solution for so long.

My interest in current affairs had been noted. I had already made a mark giving a talk about the progress of the war in 1943. After the war and the general election of May 1945 it was decided to start a debating society. The first chairman of the debating society was Gerald Tout, who was a year ahead of me in the sixth form. At first we had the usual schoolboy debates about hunting and hanging and then we settled for having a school parliament. I was the very vocal spokesman for the Conservatives and with great pomposity issued our own Dr Morgan's Conservative Manifesto, putting some distance between ourselves and the Conservative Party. My major opponent was my good friend Trefor David, who was a highly articulate and a very convinced socialist and remained so throughout his successful career.

We would have our stormy sessions once a week. The gladiatorial battles between David and me had a certain entertainment value, and our meetings were quite well attended. I revelled in every minute of it, enjoying the public speaking, which I found relatively easy. It was always a very vigorous performance. I think I would describe myself at that time as articulate and garrulous. Many years later at school reunions my old colleagues still recalled my performance at the school debating society. Sadly it didn't last long after I left school.

From an early age I was fascinated by politics. It was a trait which became so intense and partisan that I am embarrassed to recall it. At the village school I had shown an interest in history. This flourished whilst I progressed through Dr Morgan's School, and I regarded current affairs as history 'brought up-to-date'. This meant I studied the war intensely, aided by the *Daily Mail* and the BBC Home Service radio. Inevitably, I took a view on politics, and by 1943/44 – aged thirteen – I was well informed but partisan.

I cannot imagine why I chose to be a Conservative, when there was the alternative of Labour or, more adventurous, the

Common Wealth Party. I suppose it was out of deference to my parents. I followed my success of talking in the classroom with an attempt to speak in the open air on the rugby ground during the lunch hour. It was not a success. I had a prayer book thrown at me, which I have kept ever since. I attended my first public meeting in 1944 when W. S. ('Shakes') Morrison, MP for Cirencester and Tewkesbury and later Speaker of the House of Commons, spoke in support of Major Gerald Wills, who was then prospective Conservative candidate for Bridgwater. It was still an age when there were large public meetings, and even in Bridgwater there was some heckling and rowdiness. At school I can recall being very concerned over the Yalta Conference and having great sympathy with the Poles, who were the luckless victims of power politics and the deal struck between Stalin and Roosevelt.

At the age of thirteen/fourteen I was making most precocious judgements. Also I had doubts. I taxed my Aunt Ruth with my problem of supporting coal nationalisation whilst wanting to be a Conservative. She said it was all right. Years later I had no problem about being an elastic Tory. In the 1945 general election, aged fourteen, I was a teller at the Combwich polling station. Shortly afterwards the Young Conservatives were started. Although underage (I was fifteen), I became secretary. It was not much of a success. I was far too intense in my politics and quite unable to handle the branch social programme, which was the main attraction for members. Pompously I announced I was standing down as secretary so I could concentrate on study for my Bristol Higher School Certificate exams. That did not prevent me from having my own personal political programme.

A mark of my political fanaticism was how I studied the *Times Guide to the House of Commons*, published after the 1945 general election. Quite soon I could name some six hundred of the six hundred and forty members. Alas I never matched such omniscience again, even when I was Leader of the House.

In 1946 there were local elections and I was able to devote my political enthusiasm to family use. My father was defending his rural district council seat. The challenge came from Kenneth Haybittle, a relative newcomer to the village, who had set up a bus service at the beginning of the war. He represented 'the new order'. My father was decidedly traditional. Haybittle was for a new village hall, whilst my father felt we had gone for generations without one. The village hall was the litmus test and national politics were never mooted. But there was no shortage of issues. For example Kenneth Haybittle did not run his buses in and around the village. He required passengers to walk; a petrol economy no doubt, but a populist issue.

I was, in effect, my father's agent and we worked very hard. I attended the count in the village school. The turnout was higher than at the preceding general election. My father won handsomely and ironically the village hall went ahead and prospered beyond belief until the social world, with the arrival of modern transport, shifted to the lights of Bridgwater.

My political interest was encouraged by three men. A. G. Edwards was the Conservative agent who guided my enthusiasm, realising I was a misfit in the Young Conservatives. In the school holidays I would do door-to-door canvassing and recruiting for the party. It was an experience for me, but my most treasured memory was calling upon Tom Roman in a 'rough' Bridgwater area, West Street, now demolished. He was the town's leading Communist and he frequently wrote to the *Bridgwater Mercury*. A classic example of a self-educated working-class Marxist, his modest house was book lined. I always enjoyed my visits: not a bid for conversion, just conversation. Secondly, there was Alec Aitkenhead, who was the association chairman. He was a thrusting businessman who had come from London just before the war. He was an evangelist for the market economy and I was anxious to learn from him, and warmed to his infectious enthusiasms. More than anyone he gave me some political beliefs.

Finally John Riggs, a local farmer and village cricketer, used to take me to Labour meetings in the neighbouring villages. We became seasoned hecklers and behaved disgracefully. We managed to break up a meeting in Cannington using the unlikely topic of the trade in Argentinian beef. We were leather lunged and the chairman was polite and weak.

Mr Edwards, the Conservative agent, had put me in touch with the Ashridge Trust, which operated from an imposing country house in Hertfordshire. This house had been made available to become a College for Citizenship in memory of Bonar Law, Conservative Prime Minister following the First World War. After the Second World War the trust had no formal links with the Conservative Party but there was some residual 'Bonar Law money' of which I was a beneficiary.

My week or so there in August 1948 was a tremendous experience. I had to overcome the challenge of travel to London and – horror – of getting from Paddington to Euston. The journey achieved, I immediately sent a postcard to my parents: 'I've made it!'

The Ashridge course was on serious politics with an emphasis on international affairs. In contrast to my travel problems I was ecstatic with the course. At seventeen I was the youngest of the hundred students, of whom ten were from the USA. The others were mostly in their twenties and thirties and included Viscount Keren, the son of Field Marshal Lord Wavell. I had no nervousness about speaking up in the discussion groups and general lectures. I was in *my* political world – a far cry from the Young Conservatives.

Two MPs gave lectures. Martin Lindsay, the Tory from Solihull, talked about Parliament and Christopher Hollis from Devizes talked, memorably, about the 'Spiritual Crisis of Europe'. They were both inspiring, as was Frank Owen, author of *Tempestuous Journey: Lloyd George, his life and times* and one-time editor of the *Daily Mail*.

I returned to Bridgwater with a sharper step. I had negotiated the jungle between Paddington and Euston and I had talked knowledgeably with my elders about contemporary Europe.

Just before doing my National Service I was asked to do the vote of thanks to Lord Winterton when he addressed a three-hundred-strong Conservative meeting at Bridgwater Town Hall. It was a success. Ashridge had done much for me. Aged eighteen, I was not overawed with nerves and managed to speak with wit, emotion and brevity. It was a good send-off to the world of politics I eagerly anticipated at Cambridge.

13

DR MORGAN'S SCHOOL: CHARLES KEY AND CAMBRIDGE

My time in the sixth form coincided with the staff being augmented by a number of men returned from the war. My sixth-form years were much influenced by two teachers, Gareth Vaughan Jones and Jack Lawrence. It was a very small sixth form and we had the most intimate tuition. The first and second years were taught together. There were three arts pupils in my year and three or four in the year ahead. We met in the corner of the school library. Looking back I realise that, although it was not a very distinguished state grammar school, it had sixth-form teaching ratios which would have been the envy of many independent schools.

Jack Lawrence was immensely effective as a traditional teacher of history but Gareth Vaughan Jones was charismatic. He taught me English and Latin. I had to do Latin to get a reasonable chance of university entrance. The school did not teach Latin in the lower school, so I was given a Latin primer and spent quite a bit of my closing months in the fifth form doing Latin by myself. I had the added assistance of the vicar of Otterhampton, the Rev. William Napier Skrine, a kindly and meticulous man.

The first two years of the sixth form were occupied taking

the Bristol University Higher Certificate. I was taking Latin as a subsidiary subject.

Gareth Vaughan Jones took me through my Latin set book, *The Jugurthine War* by Sallust, and he brought it alive for me. He had a most infectious way of teaching. He is still a mystery. He turned up at Dr Morgan's, having had quite an eventful war. I think he was in the Welsh Guards. He had certainly been in the vanguard of those who entered Belsen. It is quite clear that Vaughan Jones would have been much more at home as an Oxbridge don but it was our gain. He would talk to us and bring alive Housman, Browning, Orwell and Waugh. He ranged from topical literary figures to the classics. He was the first person I heard talking about Housman and, above all, Browning. Years later I would occasionally quote Browning in the House of Commons: 'Trust God: see all, nor be afraid' was a handy sentiment.

The possible key to the mystery of why he remained in a small Somerset school was that he had married into a well-established Bristol family, the Hartley Hoddens, who lived in a grand house in the Apsley Road. He was quite prepared to have a split-site marriage and was not unhappy to be teaching in Bridgwater. He would skittle and drink with my father. Paradoxically he was the son of a Congregational minister, which made it even more bizarre.

We took what was called Oxford School Certificate when I was in the fifth form. I did quite well – not brilliantly, but well enough to carry on into the sixth form. The most significant thing was that Mr Trenchard retired as headmaster and was replaced by a rather quiet man called Charles Key. Unlike Trenchard he was not at all formal. The latter was never happier than when he was drilling the school Air Training Corps (ATC) or teaching scripture. Key was unassuming in manner but intellectually quite impressive with a great devotion to learning. Coming from a grammar school in Gloucester, he had been at Selwyn College, Cambridge and had written a text book on geography. He was jointly a historian and a geographer and took a lively interest in the performance of the sixth form.

It was Key's idea that I should sit for an open scholarship to Cambridge. I contested the decision for the genuine reason that I thought it would give my parents expectations which I couldn't conceivably fulfil. There was no tradition at all of the school sending its sixth-form pupils to Oxbridge. Most boys went either to Bristol or Exeter. But Key was insistent. He said that, after I had the result of my Bristol higher, in which I would achieve a distinction in history, he was going to put me in for an open scholarship to Cambridge. The exam was scheduled for the first week of December 1948. In addition to modern history I was put in for the mediaeval history paper. This was a subject that I had never done before. I therefore spent the period between June and November almost exclusively studying mediaeval history. Charles Key gave me a list of books to read. The majority of the study took place during the holiday months of July and August. I used to get up very early in the morning and go to the top room at Hill Farm to read and make notes.

I can still recall that period. The top room was quiet and secluded with a faintly musty smell. I slumped in the ample armchair or sprawled on the floor reading at a measured rather than brisk pace. At this stage I had reformed my handwriting; it was barely legible when I was taking notes in my first sixth-form year.

I cycled to Bridgwater occasionally to discuss my work with Key. I worked then as I have never worked before or since. By the end of November I had got a good smattering of mediaeval history. Of the number of entrants for the examination, which was well into three figures, there were less than half a dozen who did both papers. Looking back I was so grateful to Charles Key, firstly for dragging me into taking the examination, but above all for insisting that I could neglect modern history during the months before the exam and use the time to develop from scratch a knowledge of mediaeval history, thus enabling me to tackle both papers.

For the Cambridge open scholarship the colleges were grouped so when you took the exam you indicated in priority which college you preferred. My headmaster, who knew the score, said it would be far better if I went to a small college. I had no knowledge of the pecking order of the colleges and which I should choose. All I knew was that I wanted to study history.

For the exams I stayed in college and one of the senior undergraduates gave us a talk about life at Cambridge. I was captivated. It really was a view of a far wider world than I had ever experienced scholastically or socially in Bridgwater. I had only once ventured out of Somerset, for a short course at Ashridge Adult College. But that window on the outside world was nothing compared to the feeling I got of how exciting life must be at Cambridge.

The examination took place in a huge hall, packed with candidates, and we were solemnly told that when the invigilator told us to stop writing we had to stop. It was an awesome occasion and yet I wasn't as frightened of it as I had expected. I think I was stimulated by the challenge. It never occurred to me that I would get a scholarship and I thought it was likely that I would get a place at Bristol. The scholarship was the head's idea, whereas I looked upon it largely as a new experience. Possibly this meant that I was calmer in myself than if I had thought I was in with a chance. I think this attitude helped me in the exam.

I was in the school library when the results came through. The headmaster came to see me. He said, 'Biffen, I must congratulate you. You have won a scholarship to Cambridge.' I was elated and asked if I could telephone my parents. I went to the secretary's office and telephoned my mother. She said, 'Oh John, that's wonderful. What would you like for supper?' and I said, 'Baked beans.' They were on points in the rationing system so that they were a bit of a treat.

Everyone was delighted by my success. The headmaster gave the whole school a half-day holiday to celebrate. I went into town and found several colleagues hanging out of the window of the Billiards Club shouting their thanks.

The headmaster was overjoyed. He had only just arrived and was anxious to improve the academic performance of the school, particularly at sixth-form level. It was a tribute to his success as a headmaster that a number of other boys followed me to Cambridge, including the distinguished geographer Peter Haggett, and Ivor Slocombe, a distant maternal relative who became Wiltshire County Chief Educational Officer.

The period from December 1948 until I was called up in April 1949 was an anticlimax. I tried to get my National Service deferred but that failed because of the understanding between the universities and the armed forces that National Service would come first. There was little to do, but I was school captain so I went to school. I did some work renumbering books in the school library and I continued reading history books. It was a curious twilight existence under the shadow of joining the Army.

14

CALL-UP AND EARLY ARMY DAYS

With Dr Morgan's now behind me I awaited the summons to National Service.

Before call-up day I visited Bristol for a Trade Test to find out which regiment I was to be assigned to. There were the usual medical tests of coughing and peeing. Then came the critical moment when I was asked to assemble the pieces of a bicycle pump, pushing my mechanical skills to their limit. The Army sergeant held aloft my assembled pump, which momentarily dangled uncertainly in his hands before disintegrating. This example of mechanical competence ensured that I was assigned to the Royal Engineers.

I was called up in late March 1949 and presented myself at Cove Barracks near Aldershot on 7 April, a date ever stamped on my memory. I then joined Number Three Training Regiment, Royal Engineers.

Those proceeding to university in the autumn of 1950 were deliberately called up in April 1949. This neatly embraced the eighteen months of National Service. The device proved a valuable protection when National Service was extended to two years in response to the Korean crisis. The Army stood by their bargain with the universities and I slipped under the wire six months ahead of my luckless conscript colleagues.

For me, doing National Service was the hurdle before Cambridge University. I really wanted to go to Cambridge first and postpone the unknown and suspected hardships of the Army as long as possible. I had the wholly erroneous belief that service life might be less rigorous after university than straight from school and that there might be a greater chance of either a commission or service in the Royal Army Education Corps. However, it was a general rule that those going to university had to do military service first.

The whole prospect of National Service filled me with apprehension but the one thing that absolutely terrified me was how I would cope with Army food. Back home I certainly hadn't managed school meals. As an only child my mother had indulged me and for my entire school career I always took home-made sandwiches to school.

From the moment of arrival at Cove Barracks the whole thing was traumatic. From the barber to the uniform to the barracks and the food it was a series of shock waves. My treasured hairstyle was reduced to bristles. Ill-fitting Army clothes were thrown at me at random. Time then had to be spent with the Army tailor vainly trying to have the appropriate adjustments made. It was a forlorn task. I had little clothes consciousness before joining the Army. I had none thereafter.

Then there was the food. You went to the cookhouse for your meals. In retrospect I realise it was not unreasonable but given my history of picky eating it seemed profoundly unappetising, although I was soon reconciled to bacon and baked beans (known as bugle fruit) for breakfast. The noise was incredible with the banging of pots and pans and the crashing of mess tins. These were a great shock too. At home I had never eaten off anything but a plate and didn't know there was any other way of eating food. We lined up holding our square tins into which was slopped potato, meat and vegetables. Eventually I got used to Army food but I missed my mother's cooking terribly.

From the moment we were woken the racket began. All the huts (for some reason called spiders) were connected by a Tannoy system. This provided a background of noise; reveille, general commands, and endless current popular music. There was no respite. When reveille was sounded it was known in the barrack room as 'hands off cocks, put on socks'. There was a perpetual chorus of swearing. Everything was linked with oaths. All our actions had to be at the double. Doubling apparently was essential for the work of turning our disparate rabble from the farms, offices and factories into a disciplined military force. Near exhausted, we usually spent the evenings in the barrack rooms. The great favourite over the Tannoy in April–June 1949 was Pee Wee Hunt's 'Twelfth Street Rag'. Doris Day was also a great favourite. She proved more durable than Pee Wee Hunt.

From the moment we arrived we were housed in Nissen huts where you were assigned a bed and a locker. We soon got used to Army bedding. The mattresses consisted of three separate bolsters, strangely known as biscuits. During the day these were piled at the head of the bed along with the olive-green sheets and rough blankets. Sex-dominated barrack-room folklore asserted that the sheets were green to show if you had been masturbating.

The people in the adjacent beds could be crucial. For me, with no previous experience of intimate dormitory life, it was important to have soulmates as immediate neighbours. I was lucky that the Army had grouped together all who were deemed potential officer material. Most of us were going to university and that was a bond in our early and bewildering conscript days.

15

BASIC TRAINING

Each hut had a corporal in charge. We had Corporal Finn. Corporal Fryer and Corporal Holton were in charge of the two other huts. The latter was an outstanding footballer. Even we surly raw recruits held him in awe. He had the subsequent distinction of going on to play for Arsenal. The corporals relished the authority they possessed. They accepted all the bullshit that emanated from the officer hierarchy and were the link in exercising the detailed discipline on us squaddies. They fitted naturally into a chain of unquestioning authority which seemed to form the basis of military order.

The days began very early and proceeded with relentless momentum, starting with the hazards of getting dressed for your first parade. I fumbled my way through.

There was no time for solitude, which I missed very much. We soon got to know our fellow sufferers and were desperate for the sub-culture of friendship uniting us against the Army system.

The main and almost sole topic of conversation was sex. There were infinitely more discussions about sex than all military topics put together. Endless debates went on as to whether 'they' were putting bromide in our tea to reduce our potency which otherwise would have been a threat in this all-male society. After an exhausting day of basic training such a precaution seemed wholly unnecessary. I had a fairly steep and speedy learning curve. I found that everything was conducted to a background of lurid and vainglorious accounts of my colleagues' conquests with their girlfriends. The more promiscuous had a simple philosophy: the four 'Fs': Find, Follow, Fuck and Forget. All this contrasted with my own miserable background of no girlfriend and, as far as I could see, little prospect of one.

There was also much talk about homosexuality. It was a topic hitherto almost unknown to me. We would receive regular lectures about the iniquities of 'two men on a bed'. In retrospect I now realise that homosexuality was much more widespread in the Army than I then realised. Later on at Chatham one of my close friends was gay, but I never knew at the time.

There was endless foul language which echoed through the barracks. Swearing was so ingrained that it ceased to have any meaning. It was like a shrill Greek chorus. Looking back it intro-duced me to a good wide-ranging barrack-room vocabulary, which I don't often use but still sometimes find a tremendous therapy. Interestingly I have never felt terribly inhibited from using bad language and see it as a natural release. My Army experience of foul language was in sharp contrast to life on the farm. There life was punctuated by a flow of good-natured swearing, but of a modest nature. My father was a shouter and had a good line in vigorous language. The cart-horse would be encouraged by cries of 'Move over, you lazy sod', but I never heard him use four-letter words.

My three months' basic training at Cove passed in a flash but various incidents stick out. They illumine my earnest but maladroit efforts to show leadership potential and other qualities which would lead me to the officers' mess.

An inglorious episode was my performance on the rifle range. We had what seems in retrospect rather cursory training on the standard Lee Enfield Army rifle. Eventually the great day arrived when we were taken to Ash Range. It was a glorious summer's day and together with a line of fellow conscripts I lay on the ground nestling my rifle and aiming at the target a hundred yards or so away. After firing the targets were brought forward so that our marksmanship could be assessed by the supervising NCO. Not only had I not scored particularly well, I had in fact managed to shoot my whole magazine into my neighbour's target. Clearly I was not Bisley material.

The rifle was your most valuable possession. You guarded it with your life. When we went away on exercise we always took our rifles with us. Climbing into a lorry we would stack them together at the rear. On one occasion returning to barracks my rifle was lost in the general mêlée of reclaiming our equipment. There was no time to make a methodical search. Our next engagement was immediate, involving some very swish parade of inspection by the colonel. Petrified, I went on parade without my rifle and stood as close as I could to the men beside me so that the loss of my rifle would not be noticed. Along came the colonel, accompanied by a major and the usual entourage of junior officers and NCOs. As every man passed my heart missed a beat. All was well until the very end when the corporal approached, winding up the inspecting party. He suddenly ground to a halt and hissed at me, 'Sapper, where's yer rifle?' All I could whisper lamely was, 'I don't know, Corporal.' I really feared they would whip me off the parade ground and put me in the guardroom. To my amazement and relief the corporal hurried on after the inspection party. Never since have I experienced forty-five seconds of such total terror as I did then. The blessed rifle was awaiting me at the Nissen hut, having been retrieved from one of the trucks used in the exercise.

We all received training in the use of bayonets. Clearly the idea was that these were to be deployed in close hand-to-hand combat as in the First World War. Bayonet practice would start with the sergeant shouting, 'Baaaa-yon-ets.' One then thrust one's hand behind one's back to unsheathe the bayonet from one's belt. To the order 'Fiiix' one desperately tried to attach it to the end of the rifle. Then came the bawled command 'Charge', at which we all ran madly forward shouting, swearing and screaming. At the end of the field was a series of sheaves of corn stalks representing the enemy into which one had to thrust and jab. Standing at the side stood the corporal, urging us on with cries of 'Pretend it's your mother-in-law'. We asked one of the old hands, 'Did you use your bayonet in the war, Sarge?' 'Only as a toasting fork', came the reply.

The conscripts all had to take turns in the kitchens. It was hard work and few of us had any idea how to cook and serve food, but we were under the careful guidance of the regular cooks. Years later I rather fancied my hand at cooking when I shared bachelor flats in Birmingham, but in my Army days I was a fearful novice. The crowning error was when I made the tea in huge two-gallon buckets. Unnoticed by me they had previously been used for peeling onions and had not been washed out. The reaction from my fellow National Servicemen was instant and menacing. I feared the authorities would allow my misdemeanour to be resolved by barrack-room lynch law rather than formal discipline. The whole episode blew over but it did not sustain my supposed ambition to be a leader of men – after all had not Napoleon said that an army marched on its stomach?

Drill was another torture particularly for those of us being considered for a commission. Quite properly it was judged that your skill at marching and commanding a march gave a general idea of your alertness and physical coordination. I was unlikely to shine.

We marched in close order in columns of three. As a conscript who might become an officer, one was sometimes given the doubtful honour of drilling one's fellow squaddies: 'All right, Sapper So-and-so. You take over.' Those who have not done National Service can have no idea of the kind of pressure one was under on parade. You were in a highly exposed situation on the square. All your inadequacies were under the spotlight. One was subject to a continuous barrage of reprimands from those in command. There was, however, a convention of 'no swearing on parade' so the occasion was less colourful on that account.

The key to a good parade is precision and coordination between the movement and the command. Something which I never really mastered. I dreaded the moment when I was called out to take my turn in charge. There was a three-step sequence for marchers to come to a stop. It was essential that the command to halt came exactly as the correct foot hit the ground, two further steps bringing the feet together and the parade to a stop in 'neat order'. I couldn't work this out at all. In the end I reckoned, as only two feet were involved, I could only be 50 per cent wrong so I just shut my eyes and called out 'Halt' at intervals, followed hopefully by 'Squad about turn'. When it was all over and the lads came off the square I anxiously asked one how it had gone. 'We were hoping you would get it right at least once, Biff, but you got it wrong every time.' I fear that this was yet another nail in the coffin of my hopes of a commission.

In the Army nicknames were the order of the day and I was always known as Biff. An inappropriate sobriquet in view of my quiet and unmilitary bearing.

A short part of our three months' basic training was devoted to 'watermanship'. The Royal Engineers had the responsibility of transporting provisions and baggage by water so it was deemed an important part of our training. Here again on Hawley Lake the same problem of coordination I had experienced with drill defeated me. Although in no way were there the same pressures as on the parade ground, it was still disappointing not to do better.

We were trained in cutters, large wooden boats requiring a crew of eight or more and big enough to move a modest amount of cargo. Their weight and size made them particularly difficult to manoeuvre. In any circumstances a trained and coordinated crew was needed to shift them. I was neither trained nor coordinated. What should have been a pleasant escape from the barrack square turned into a week of frustration as my hands blistered, my shoulders ached and I repeatedly caught crabs. Sadly this experience put me off any interest I might have had in rowing or sailing. Having been brought up so close to the sea, I was, ironically, a total stranger to water. I didn't learn to swim until my mid-fifties and have never touched an oar in my life.

What use either bayonet practice or watermanship were ever going to be in my service life I had no idea. At the time it seemed to me to be tokenism. It was as if the authorities had a shopping list off which they struck the items after the briefest amount of training.

Amidst this catalogue of humiliation there were two episodes in which I shone. One was when we had to take it in turns to make a short speech. Here my time in the school debating society and as a Young Conservative gave me a head start over my colleagues, whose performances were on the whole uninspiring. When my turn came I stood up and made an impassioned five-minute speech about Britain and the Empire. Corporal Fryer, the most rough hewn of our three corporals, was in charge. Colleagues later told me that he seemed visibly moved by the unexpected eloquence of this unpromising recruit.

My other moment of slight glory was when we were undergoing 'the jabs'. These were a cocktail of injections designed to ward off all known diseases. One was an anti-diphtheria precaution, a knockout injection, commonly known as the 'schick test'. This was incredibly painful and we were given the afternoon off to recover. The other lads lay on their beds listless and silent but, for some reason, a few of us were unaffected and found ourselves ministering cups of tea to our prone colleagues.

Basic training at Cove Barracks was so frenetic that one had little time for leisurely friendships. This came later. I have only a passing memory of those who dominated my life at this time. Near the top of the military hierarchy was Major Aeneas Perkins. He did not belong to the vociferous tendency and was remembered for his salute which was performed saluting with his fingers spread apart. We knew that none of us could show such individuality on the barrack square – it would imply levity bordering on insubordination.

We had two troop officers of contrasting character. Lieutenant Peacock was a National Serviceman but not a kindred spirit. He relished order and noisy command. After military service he went to Cambridge and, I believe, became an estate agent. Our paths never crossed. Lieutenant de Waterville was a regular Army officer and recently commissioned. He radiated courtesy and reasonableness even in the most frustrating circumstances with his 'squaddies'.

The 'passing out' photograph, which marked the end of our basic training, evokes a few memories. 'Lofty' Hatfield from Nottingham towered above us. He had a laconic view of life and became a successful civil engineer. He and his wife were welcome guests at my seventieth birthday. Sapper Stan Elsegood struggled to save the family name, always pronounced Elsie-good. To all corporals he was 'Ellsgood'. On one occasion, after a tirade of reprimand, the striped authority concluded, 'So f...ing watch it Ellsgood or whatever you call yerself – "Elsie-good".' 'That's better,' responded Stan, always ready to trade encouragement for abuse. It was not wise repartee.

We had one Etonian, Sapper Donner, even more other-worldly than me. His boots were the constant despair of authority. He did not get a commission. John Halton was the star intellectual of the troop. He was destined to become an outstanding mathematician and is now a professor at the University of North Carolina at Chapel Hill. He was to be a good friend at Cambridge and I became godfather to his first daughter. John quietly slid out of the Sappers and did his time as a sergeant in the Intelligence Corps. Troop Three of the No. Three Training Regiment, Royal Engineers, had little time to develop a group personality, but I do remember my fellow recruits with affection. There was a pervasive scepticism about National Service and its disciplines and its food. Doubtless these hardships were exaggerated but we learned to live together cheerfully enough.

For me this was most important; after the seclusion of Somerset rural life, I was beginning to cross the Rubicon of group living and friendship.

After the first six weeks of unmitigated hell the time came for those of us who had been pre-selected to sit for the examination which would decide who could be sent to Mons Barracks as trainee officers – a routine known as the War Office Selection Board (WOSB). This entailed going off to Lingfield for a couple of days and undergoing a series of tests designed to demonstrate aptitude, character and leadership qualities. We had to wear denims throughout, marked with huge identification numbers so that we were easily recognised. It was fairly physical, involving constructing edifices of logs and running through forests. Compared to the highly structured life at the training camp, it was a pleasantly informal interlude amongst congenial company. At one stage we were asked by a senior officer if we felt it was a fair method of testing. Not merely out of politeness we said we thought it was.

The WOSB results came soon afterwards. I was told merely that I had failed: no details. This was a terrible blow. Up until then I had never failed at anything of note to which I had put my mind.

In fact I came from school with a practically unbroken record of success. I had done very well at School Certificate, I had ended up as head of school and then got a Cambridge scholarship. My life until that moment had all been steady progress and I had had no real experience of defeat.

By chance some weeks later I saw my WOSB report. It did not lack candour. Under the character assessment they wrote that I was quiet and making a great effort to do well. However, I lacked the poise, inner self-confidence and general aura necessary to be a commissioned officer. It ended by saying that I was sitting the WOSB not because I wanted to be an officer but because it was what I thought was expected of me. This really stung me. Nothing in my pre-National Service days had prepared me for this moment. I regarded it as a necessary imposition which I had to go through between school and Cambridge, but I had not allowed for failure. I made the decision then and there that I would do everything to repudiate this judgement. Whatever I was going to do afterwards I was going to be a success. I didn't intend to go through life trying and failing.

It would be too strong to say that this was some Damascene moment that obliged a new direction to my life, but it was a moment of truth.

Of course the Army was absolutely right. It would have been very difficult for me if I had been commissioned. At that time I could not have stood up in front of rows of recruits and issued a stream of effective instructions. I had never been in the Army

Cadet Force at school. I had no experience of telling people what to do in such a way as they would do it. I could not easily have assumed the physical presence and mental assertiveness which was required to be a successful officer. It must have clearly struck the authorities that I was not the sort of material that would make a commissioned officer in a matter of weeks.

As an only child I was self-centred. The natural social unit for me was myself. Only very gradually in the Army was I learning to be with other people and form easy friendships. Living in such close proximity we were thrown together and formed a robustly negative attitude to military authority. In fact it was one of the best things that happened to me. I was forced to spend the full eighteen months' service in the rough and tumble of the other ranks. An excellent preparation for Cambridge and life thereafter.

16

TRAINING FOR A TRADE

At the end of our basic training at Cove the time came to move on. Having failed the WOSB, I had to be allocated to an Army trade. I was chosen to be a potential Royal Engineer clerk and was sent for training to Kitchener Barracks, Chatham. An engineer clerk was hardly a skilled trade, but it meant you needed a reasonably good standard of education. You became a lance corporal, a toe up the ladder.

It is difficult to describe how different was the atmosphere between basic training and training for a trade. Compared to Cove, Chatham was a picnic. Although we continued to wear Army uniform, the discipline was much less formal. There was very little parading and only occasional marching. I enjoyed working in a team of trainees but I didn't like being shouted at or accepting unquestioning instruction. This was why basic training had been such a difficult phase for me. Most of all, at No. 10 Training Regiment RE Chatham with small groups in the barrack room, we had time to form friendships. Meanwhile I had grown accustomed to the food. My only fear was that my learning was rusting away and I had no idea how I was going to pick up the intellectual sharpness I needed at university.

Most of those on the engineering clerks course had failed the WOSB. We weren't striving to go anywhere or trying to reach the officers' mess. There was a common bond as we marked time whilst the eighteen months of service was ticking away. We had more time on our hands and were not under as much pressure so we were able to socialise in a modest way. We were not loaded with riches.

The pay had been 28 shillings (£1.40) a week whilst doing basic training, rising thereafter to 35 shillings (£1.75). As a lance corporal I was paid 42 shillings (£2.10), but at least it was all spending money.

I could go out in the evenings and very occasionally go up to London during the weekend. I immediately made use of this greater freedom by joining the Chatham Young Conservatives! This was a source of astonishment to my fellow recruits. Not least because it was thought that the Young Conservative women were a lacklustre lot, 'all talk and no skirt'.

The only things I can remember of this passing political interest was a speech by Robert Mathew, then Tory candidate for Chatham and later MP for Honiton, and a talk by a local councillor who explained that town council spending shaped the national budget. It seemed a novel idea; but perhaps he was only before his time.

Here again sex ruled our lives. Even before I had been near a typewriter I was given a lecture by a wizened sergeant on sex and the Medway towns. The message was clear. The Rising Sun had to be avoided at all costs because 'it was a matelot's pub'. It was my early introduction to service rivalry. He also gave us the advice: 'Always use a durex even if it is like washing your feet with your socks on.'

At Chatham I first encountered two superb Army characteristics: 'skiving' and 'dumb insolence'. The former involved the calculated avoidance of any duty for as long as possible or the prolongation of any given task so as to avoid any subsequent work. This practice of idleness was inconceivable at Cove; but thereafter I discovered that Army life involved spurts of activity and prolonged periods of inaction. The trick was to use time on your terms rather than those of authority. The devices were limitless but the great art was to walk everywhere with a sense of purpose with papers in your hand; you should not amble aimlessly. You would rarely be stopped. 'Skiving' became a way of life. I well remember weeding the lawn in front of the officers' mess with a penknife. It was not intellectually stimulating but nor was it arduous; there was no need to hasten – who knew what other task lay ahead? With great method I took an inordinately long time, but the tedium may have confirmed me in a lifelong lack of enthusiasm for gardening.

'Dumb insolence' was conduct as close to the breach of formal discipline as was possible. It was a rather dangerous skill which on the whole I avoided. It usually involved a deliberate misinterpretation of orders, and this required a subtlety I possessed neither then nor since.

The engineering clerks' training involved lectures on typing, filing and general clerical duties. It was all rather rough and ready and we certainly couldn't have held down a job in a modern office. Typing took place at Gillingham at Brompton Barracks. We sat in a large classroom each with our Remington or Underwood typewriters hammering away. An attempt was made to teach us touch-typing, which the relaxed warrant officer soon abandoned. After a couple of lessons he gave up the struggle: 'All right, lads, you can look at your keyboards.'

Life was more casual and the hassle and swearing heavily reduced. In truth it was rather enjoyable. One memory stands out. This was marching from Chatham to Gillingham once a week behind the band of the Royal Engineers. We started the day forming up in close order and marched off to the Regimental tune. It was wonderful. I thoroughly enjoyed the music and really did feel a sense of collective identity and a personal loyalty to those around me rather than to the regiment. Many years later I did *Desert Island Discs* with Sue Lawley and included the Engineers' March in my choice. Happy memories – even in khaki.

Weekly inspection – a terror at Cove – was very different at Kitchener Barracks. You laid out all your Army possessions on your bed so that, at a glance, it could be seen that it was all there and in good order. At Cove the inspecting officer, accompanied by an NCO, would enter the barrack room. Then there was the piercing 'Squad Att----en----tion'. At Kitchener we remained motionless. The building, a Betjeman jewel, was an ageing Victorian barracks, but the floors were not up to the shock of thirty-two feet stamping to attention, so special dispensation had to be given for us to stand at ease instead. Predictably, had we known that the floor was in danger of imminent collapse, we would have brought our feet together with the greatest force.

Whilst the barracks at Chatham were functional and austere, those at Brompton were majestic. They were solidly built, faced with white plaster, and radiated a quiet and almost scholastic atmosphere. This was hardly surprising. It was the home of the School of Military Engineering (SME) where the most advanced military engineering skills were taught. The buildings seemed inhabited by officers and senior NCOs – either teaching or learning. We were lucky to do our training there. As would-be clerks we had no real connection with the SME; we were a sort of carbuncle attached to its side. The SME was headed up by a Brigadier Davey. He was a distant figure. I can't remember ever seeing him but I frequently saw his horse. It was rather an attractive bay which was looked after by a couple of grooms. A typically irreverent discussion took place about the brigadier and his f…ing horse. To many it was a provocative symbol of private authority. For once I did not share the popular view; I was sufficient a countryman to revere the horse independent of its military trappings.

At Chatham my views on living with colleagues in close quarters happily improved. I began to warm to their companionship and I look back on that period with affection. A small group of us did most things together. We were soulmates, non-officer material, middle-class and all looking forward to post-military professional careers. In such company I was even able to reveal my fanatical Toryism without provoking derision. There was Tinker Collen, Pat Brimilcombe, Bob Hatfield, commonly known as Lofty (a veteran from Cove), and Pat McCann. Tinker became an architect, Brim went to New Zealand and became an engineer, and Lofty was an executive with Wimpey. Pat McCann was posted to Ceylon and sadly committed suicide soon afterwards. Our main recreation was talking and drinking. We were tolerably fed for nothing in the camp so we hardly ever ate outside. Drinks were cheap in the NAAFI and I remember drinking vodka with Pat McCann one evening and ending up uncharacteristically, Russian-style, throwing my glass into the fireplace. It was an exaggerated and expensive gesture. When funds permitted we would go off and have a drink together in Chatham, always observing the warning to avoid the Rising Sun.

My final memory of Chatham was the weather. It was a lovely autumn. I can still remember the smell of the ripe apples lying rotting on the ground. There was a feeling of exhilaration as we came to the end of our training. I wanted to go abroad and, in my own quiet way, I wanted adventure, so I volunteered for an overseas posting.

17

TO THE CANAL ZONE

When the posting came I found I had been selected to go to the Suez Canal Zone. I was delighted but my father was horrified. He was very protective and desperate that I shouldn't be sent abroad. My parents had no wanderlust. Their honeymoon was spent at Bournemouth, and they never went abroad except for a short visit to Ireland after the war. My father enjoyed the food but thought the farming was 'very poor'.

Sadly, none of my Chatham friends were posted to Egypt. They were scattered around the world in Malaysia, Ceylon, British Army of the Rhine (BAOR) and Hong Kong. Malaysia and Hong Kong were considered to be attractive posts involving bush uniforms and hats for jungle warfare. The Canal Zone was judged to be humdrum – but it could have its moments.

We assembled at Chatham and were put on a train to London. We were weighed down with travelling kit but had to await our summer khaki drill until we reached Egypt. There was something festive about the departure but the Kitchener Barracks cookhouse did not rise to the occasion. We were provided with the most atrocious rubbery beef doorstep sandwiches. I got rid of mine as soon as possible by dropping them on the railway line. In London we changed trains for Harwich and then embarked for the Hook of Holland. The crossing was uneventful. We spent a night in a transit camp in very austere conditions. There were very few facilities, and the most ferocious wind whistled through our tin huts. Next morning we were put on a troop train which was to convey us practically non-stop across Europe. It was a fairly comfortable corridor train and we were accommodated six to a compartment. The challenge came when you had to sleep. There was only room for four, but what of the other two? The alternatives were sleeping on the seats or on the floor between the seats. There was the option of sleeping in the corridor, which was freezing cold, or, as a last resort, trying to sleep in the over-head luggage rack. We all took turns in sharing the discomfort, using our kit bags as a pillow and greatcoats as a blanket. It was all rather primitive and, after two nights sleeping fully clothed, the excitement of continental travel palled for some.

Most of my colleagues found the train journey rather boring. I didn't mind at all. I was delighted to be abroad for the first time and it was a thrill for me to be on a train going into the unknown. For much of the way the train broadly followed the route of the Tauntonvern Express which I was to take some eight years later when I visited the Communist Youth Camp at Peshtera in Bulgaria.

Everything was strange and exciting. I had a corner seat most of the time and sat with my nose against the window pane look-ing out at the passing countryside. The flatness of Holland was soon replaced by the Ruhr as we entered Germany. This was only a few years after the war so a great deal of the urban area consisted of ruins. It was night time when we went through Cologne and the sight of the jagged urban skyline lit up in the gloom of a handful of street lights made a huge impres-sion. Thereafter it was sleep – of sorts – as we jolted sedately across Germany.

It was exciting to wake up as dawn broke and find we were

in Bavaria and to have my first view of the snow-covered Alps stretching ahead. Going through Ulm my schoolboy history kept me company. Here in Bavaria I was seeing for myself the land over which the War of the Spanish Succession and the Battle of Blenheim had been fought.

The train made sporadic halts. In Austria, in the Tyrol, we got off at a little place called Traunstein to await another train to take us to Trieste. In early December it was freezing cold as we were in the Alps. We seemed to be hanging around for hours, bad tempered, numbed by cold and irritated. Finally we broke out into spontaneous and unmelodic song with the repetitious verses of 'Why Are We Waiting?'. It wafted down the valley. I guess this dirge of protest was a mild example of 'dumb insolence'. At least we did not sing 'Land of Hope and Glory'.

Eventually we arrived at Trieste and were allowed into the town for the evening. Trieste was indisputably Italian but it was still under Allied military government. It occupied a strategic position at the head of the Adriatic Sea and was a potential trouble spot because of Tito's ambitions for an extended Yugoslavia. The Allied military presence was low key but pervasive. I was fascinated by Trieste and the sheer novelty and excitement of being in my first continental town – at last I was walking on the streets of a European town redolent with history and the menace of current conflict.

Trieste had been untouched by the war and coming from the austerity of post-war Britain the market stalls seemed to be piled with treasures with their abundance of candles, nativity figures and Christmas goods. The fact that there was a powerful Allied military presence seemed no deterrent to the bustle and prosperity.

I append below my memories of Trieste which appeared in the school magazine – *The Morganian*.

A FLEETING VISIT

Trieste. I shall never hear that name without a host of jumbled recollections. The troop-train that had faithfully carried us across Europe groaned to a reluctant stop one Sunday morning. It was just dawn, and grey mist enveloped the train, obscuring from sight a dismal station. Soon a loquacious babble of Italian indicated that the new train orderlies were at work. Gradually the mist lifted, and it seemed, after spending the previous day in the Alps, that this was a new world.

We detrained and were marched to the quayside. It was then that I got my first impressions of Trieste. The buildings were tall, terribly official and stereotyped, like barrack blocks. The streets were wide, interlaced with busy tramways. Judging from the many and colourful posters that adorned every wall, the main industries of Trieste must be politics and opera. The city seemed terraced on the hills surrounding the bay. As the sun gathered height, and the sky became a pale whimsical blue, the large white buildings and slated roofs took on an almost Latin atmosphere. Waiting on the quayside is as pathetic as an unemployment queue: the grumblers complain until everyone becomes indifferent to fate and squats on kitbags. When finally we embarked it was soon known that two hours' shore leave would be granted. We settled in our new quarters, and in the evening were assembled on deck. The ship's RSM discoursed at some length on the fate of some predecessors who had overstayed leave. His audience was impatient. Eventually we surged down the gangway with just two hours of Trieste before us.

Although it was Sunday, nearly all the shops were open and gaily decorated with Christmas trimmings. Streetside cafés were everywhere. They sold very weak wine and had heavy fluorescent lighting. The wide main streets contrasted sharply with the narrow ill-lit alleys that led away from them. The shops were laden with luxury goods at fantastic prices. Madonnas and religious symbols were everywhere. The Italian Santa Claus wore a white cross on his crimson hat, differing from the iconoclastic English edition. One could hardly move for the chestnut vendors. All Trieste seemed to be in the streets that Sunday evening. For if the city sleeps by day, it is doubly vigorous at night. As time slipped by, all too soon we had to leave the children thronging around the commercial Santa Claus and the frantic police trying to control the crowds, and return to the ship.

Next morning we set sail. Trieste was still asleep on the hillside; the December sun valiantly trying to pierce the clouds. As we pulled out into the Adriatic, Trieste vanished on the skyline; leaving the memories – the neon lights, the chestnut stalls – and the crucifixes.

At Trieste we were expecting a troopship to take us from Italy to Egypt. I was prepared for the worst because of all the stories I had heard about vermin-infested sardine tins. In fact it turned out we were to travel in the comfort of a small civilian cruise ship and I had the luxury of a bunk cabin room to myself. I look back on the journey as an oasis of civilian comfort in the midst of my Army career. The ship took two to three days and I spent as much time as possible on deck. We sailed down the Adriatic and the Yugoslav coast looked dark and rugged. At night there were wonderful deep, black, cloudless skies and a full moon picking out all the islands. It was magic.

Eventually we pulled into Port Said. Almost at once I was hit by the heat, dust, noise and smell. Nothing could have been more different from Trieste than the chaos of this Egyptian port. Everything seemed to depend upon noise. Trade depended on noise as sellers shouted their wares; religion seemed to be by public address as muezzins called the faithful to prayer. The port

itself, in those days, before the advent of containers, reverberated
with shoutings and crashings as cargo was loaded and unloaded.
It was like a discordant symphony – but nonetheless fascinating
for a novice service traveller.

Port Said was very much an Egyptian town despite the British
military presence. The next few months were to remind me of
the delicate and uneasy relationship between our armed forces
and those of our Egyptian hosts. After the Second World War
the British had traded their overall political authority in Egypt
for a garrison of troops in the Canal Zone, which was a strip of
land on either side of the Suez Canal and included the towns
of Port Said, Ismaïlia and Suez. This gave Britain control over
the Suez Canal and the strategic link it provided between Europe
and the Far East.

The arrangement, whilst valuable to Britain's international
status, was hardly conducive to good Anglo-Egyptian relations.
It was not conceived as a partnership by the British soldiery.
The 'wogs' were at best tolerated or patronised, or more likely
despised. Scornfully we sang, 'King Farouk, King Farouk, hang
his bollocks on a hook; Queen Farida give us a bit buckshee.'
We might have been defending the Empire but we were hardly
ambassadors of partnership. I learned to appreciate this in the
months ahead.

18

FAYID

The journey from Port Said to Fayid was by train. Although the British had a very large military presence, they relied on a great deal of local support – hence our journey on Egyptian State Railways.

We chugged off and got as far as El Ballah, where the train broke down and we were delayed for hours. This was my first experience of the general lack of coordination and failure which characterised all the Egyptian support services. As squaddies we were stoical about our fate and dismissive of the Egyptians.

In the end we arrived at Fayid, a huge Army camp on the Great Bitter Lake. The camp consisted of a number of administrative buildings, whilst the living accommodation was mainly in tents. I had never been a Boy Scout and it was the first time in my life I had slept under canvas. The tents were quite good. They were reasonably spacious, with standing room and accommodation for four people. We were each allocated a camp bed and metal locker. Although the tents were cold in winter, they were very practical in view of the extremes of the climate.

For the first time my living companions were a problem. They provided a culture shock after my would-be officer colleagues at Cove and Chatham.

This was the first time I'd had to live in such a small unit so close to three others from very different backgrounds from myself. My worst fears were confirmed when one rather thuggish individual from Wolverhampton tried to steal my wallet. Apprehensive of life in Egypt I always slept with my wallet under my pillow. What I didn't realise was that as I slept I moved around and the wallet became exposed. I woke one night with a fright, aware that my neighbour was coming towards me. I judged it was for cash and not companionship. Immediately I jumped out of bed and stood facing him, at which he turned round and retreated.

One of the others came from Preston. He had a strong Lancastrian accent and had been a locomotive fireman shovelling coal. He was a good-natured person and talked about the railways incessantly. His great ambition was to return and gain promotion as a train driver. The only bone of contention was my face flannel. He picked on this and declared that 'only women use face flannels'. I had no succinct rejoinder.

The weather played a large part in our lives. In winter it was surprisingly cold and there was frost on the ground in the morning, but the temperature in the tent was perfectly reasonable.

I only experienced one *khamsin* or dust storm during my time. You could see it coming like a great brown cloud on the horizon behind the mountainous escarpment at the back of the camp called the Great Flea. It gave you plenty of notice. The moment it was spotted the word went round and we rushed back to our tents and pulled down all the ropes and tied the flaps and then waited for the storm. The wind preceded it with a great shrill whistle. The whole tent shook with the impact of the storm. Then came the sand behind it, a great whirling cloud of grit. There was nothing to do but to sit it out. It must have gone on for perhaps a couple of hours and was quite awe-inspiring. Despite all our efforts at closing the tent the sand got everywhere. It was in our clothes, in our bedding and up our noses. When we were quite sure it was over then came the business of clearing up. We swept and swept, trying to get the grit out of the folds of the tent and bring life back to normal.

I soon settled into the camp routine. In the winter we worked right through the day. Then as summer came we moved to a two-shift pattern. We started out early in the morning and then stopped at midday when it got very hot and returned to our tents. Then in the evening when it had cooled down, we would go back again to do another shift.

We had quite a lot of time on our hands and I now regret not making more use of the many facilities provided. Foolishly I chose not to learn to swim or play games and spent a great deal of my time in the cool of the tent, reading. I arranged for my parents to send me out the *Weekly Guardian* so I could keep abreast of international affairs. There was a good Army library which I used. The two books I mainly remember were H. A. L. Fisher's *History of Europe*, which kept me going for a long time, and *Christ Stopped at Eboli* by Carlo Levi.

Fayid Camp was the GHQ of British forces throughout the Middle East. It accommodated a whole series of different skills. Engineers mixed with artillery and intelligence. There was a good NAAFI where you could buy everything from clothes to cigarettes and also meet up with one's fellow men. Quite soon I came across kindred spirits.

I made a lot of short-term friends. We knew that when we left Egypt we might not see each other again, but there were two who became particular friends and I am still in contact with them. Hugh Easterling was billeted in a tent near me. We had much in common. Like me he was an only child, rather quiet and not particularly coordinated. I was attracted to his pleasant and kindly temperament and we discovered that we were both going on to Cambridge, he to Sidney Sussex, to read history like me. We formed an immediate bond and saw a lot of each other. The friendship has continued ever since. Neither of us swam or liked sitting in the sun. We were both interested in the life ahead and looking forward to going to Cambridge and studying. He subsequently had a career in banking and in retirement specialised in South Africa.

'Ginge' Hodson was a full corporal in the Intelligence Corps. Slightly built with a good head of flat ginger hair, he was an exhibitioner at Queens' College, Cambridge, in classics. His father had an outfitter's business in Liverpool. We were both of very similar temperament, bookish and not much interested in all the physical pursuits the Army had to offer. When time came for my leave it was natural I should take it with 'Ginge'.

As headquarters and nerve centre of the whole British Army east of Suez, Fayid had a very large Royal Engineer staff. The two officers with whom I came into most contact were Captain Jones and Captain J. J. Walker. The former came from Weston-super-Mare and was baldish, erect, remote and rather sharp in manner. I formed a negative view of him. Captain Walker was beaky with glasses and a slight scar by the side of his nose. He was kind and courteous and could have been a country solicitor. His pleasant voice carried with it the authority that comes when you treat people sympathetically. This was in sharp contrast to the barrack square kind of officer I had experienced in basic training.

Fayid had a relaxed atmosphere, rather like a large village. Despite the fact that there had never been good relations between the Egyptians and the British Army, I felt there was little threat of attack and no feeling that the political situation was deteriorating. Of course, I was wrong, but the great political rows came after I left. The real worry was theft. There was an enormous amount of pilfering and a great deal to steal. It centred around a huge Army store out in the desert on the tract of land leading to Tel el-Kabir, known as Tek. It was an enormous place filled with weaponry and supplies. It was essential that it should be protected, eventually by armed guards equipped with 'one bullet up the spout'.

Towards the end of my time the problem of theft was getting so bad that I was doing perimeter guard duty almost every other day. It was a twelve-hour guard with two hours on and four hours off. In multiples of three – two on and four off – we wandered round the perimeter endlessly. It was a lonely sleepless occupation. During our time off we lay on a bed beside the guard post. Your rifle was almost chained to you and you took such rest as you could, clad in full uniform and boots, ready to dash out if required. There was a blanket, but it was impossible to get comfortable weighed down with those great heavy boots. I could never catnap and still have miserable memories of it. Guard duty was one of the reasons that I was glad when my time was up.

Subsequently I had to face all-night sittings in the House of Commons. My experience of guard duty in Egypt stood me in good stead. There were two separate guard duties. Besides perimeter guard duty there was also guard duty of the tented accommodation. This was more informal. One evening I was doing this guard duty when over the skyline came Captain Wilkes, a cheerful regular soldier nearing the end of his time. He was as drunk as they come. 'Oh Corporal. You on guard eh? What about a fag?' A great gesture but I was a committed non-smoker.

I ended my Army career with two physical afflictions. One was a permanent sweat mark on my legs and the other was lace marks on my feet. For a long time afterwards I had raised weals where the bootlaces had cut into me.

When I arrived at Fayid I thought I was going to the Chief
Engineer's office. However, there was a vacancy in the MGA's
(Major General Administration) office so I spent the bulk of
my time there. I had no idea what I was in for, nor what MGA
meant. Fayid was headquarters for the British military presence
in the whole of North Africa and the Middle East up to and
including Aden. The MGA had a very senior role in supervising
this military empire. As filing clerk I found the military papers
fascinating.

The office itself was quite small. In overall charge was General
Brian Robertson, a remote and esteemed figure later to become
chairman of British Railways. On one of the very rare occasions
I came across him I managed to disgrace myself. I was taking
some papers from one hut to another when I saw him coming
and gave him the best salute that I ever could. 'Longest way up
shortest way down.' When I got to the hut the warrant officer
said 'Corporal! You have just saluted the C-in-C while not wearing your hat!' I had forgotten what a solecism it was to salute an
officer without a hat.

Major Ryle of the Royal Tank Regiment was the senior officer
after the C-in-C. He was a trim, slightly tetchy individual. Under
him was Lieutenant Whitehead, of whom I saw rather more. A
rather gaunt and angular man not temperamentally suited to
life in the Middle East, he had a very uneasy relationship with
the staff sergeant who sat with us in the outside office. It was an
upstairs–downstairs situation. The staff sergeant would come out
and tell us that the lieutenant had got it all wrong again, whilst
the lieutenant kept trying to pull rank.

One day the staff sergeant decided to get his own back. It was
the lieutenant's job to make a security check when we left the
office. Whitehead went round officiously slamming the safes
shut. There was one that was sticky. The staff knew that and

waited until the lieutenant had supposedly slammed it shut and stalked off. He then went up to the safe and gave it a great push at which it swung open. Immediately a telephone call was made to the guards to report a breach of security. All hell then broke loose and the lieutenant returned chastened by his negligence. It was a fantastic display of dumb insolence which we all hugely enjoyed.

The staff sergeant was a wonderful character who had been in the war. He was very competent, although with a rather rebellious attitude to authority which involved him being busted from staff sergeant from time to time. On one occasion he got drunk and started throwing stones on the NAAFI roof. As a result of this misdemeanour he was reduced to the rank of corporal but still continued with his job. He was exceptionally tolerant and allowed me to fix two slogans on the wall above my desk, 'Man was born free and is everywhere in chains' (Rousseau) and 'Workers of the world unite. You have nothing to lose but your chains' (Marx). I think I was pushing it.

Bob, the orderly, was a tall, slightly lugubrious gunner. His job was to collect the waste papers and make the tea. He had come to terms with the Army with difficulty. 'I don't know why I'm here. I'm from the Isle of Man. I don't think they have the right to call me up.' Philosophically he became resigned to his fate, possibly because of the relaxed and laid-back nature of the MGA office.

Bob's other claim to fame was that he was a great admirer of Ruby Duke. She was a dark-haired, vivacious Canadian working in our office and married to Colonel Duke. It made a huge difference to us all having a civilian in the office who was also a woman. Being Canadian, she wanted to be friends of everybody and was not used to the hierarchical nature of British military society.

With Mrs Duke doing the typing, most of my work consisted of filing. We were keeping records of the military and economic situation covering the entire Middle East. The scope of it all was absorbing. There would be reports from the military attaché in Ankara, also on conditions in Somalia and likewise from our people with Glubb Pasha's Transjordan Frontier Force. I remember one of Glubb's officers coming to the office wearing traditional Arab headgear and a khaki uniform. Office life was truly fascinating as I had the job of collating and filing all these reports. Faraway names had great prominence, and McKinnon Road took on a sort of romantic concept in my mind. It was in fact a railway station on the road from Mombasa to Nairobi. When I actually visited it thirty years later I was amazed at its insignificance. The Shifta featured prominently in reports. These bandits roamed and robbed their way round Africa. The British were concerned about the stability of the area and took a great interest in their activities.

For me it was great fun and fascinating to read about a British military presence over such a wide area based on the Canal Zone and Aden, and to a lesser extent in Libya, Cyprus, Jordan and Kenya. Sitting in the MGA's office I saw it all, not just a military view of things, but also the economic and political factors. It was gripping information and, when everyone went home, I often stayed late to read the files before packing them away. I could not have enjoyed a task more, and whilst the really hot stuff never came my way most of the papers were classified.

It wasn't particularly taxing work and I was not overstretched. It struck me that few National Servicemen were ever overstretched and that a great deal of time was spent waiting to do things. For me this meant that during the working day I had time to read through and study all these papers, which was a wonderful antidote to boredom.

At the MGA military discipline was at a minimum and on the whole the company was congenial. I was now getting closer to a reflective and academic world and away from the noise and shouting of the barrack square. It was a thoroughly untypical episode in normal National Service existence.

After three months or so I was transferred to my original posting, the Chief Engineer's office. The work was pedestrian, with little fascination, and was a great disappointment and let-down after the MGA's office. The office had a decidedly military structure. The Chief Engineer was Major General Broomhall, supported by a bevy of field officers. The engineer clerks were at the bottom of this pile. We occupied a large-ish office where we did our rather routine work. There were about a dozen fellow clerks and we made a cheerful team under the authority of Quartermaster Sergeant (Q) Wood. As you might imagine he was known as 'F... You'. Physically imposing with a large, bald, shiny head and a rather feline manner, he was always refer-ring to himself, 'So I said, Q, what happens now?' I found this very irritating. Capricious in his judgements, he did not exude leadership and he had favourites amongst his clerks of which I was certainly not one. Quinlan, a bright and cheery squaddie, was one of Q's favourites. When he came to depart on his last day in the office, he went around shaking hands. Q said, in a lachrymose and fruity voice, 'There was the best corporal I shall ever have.' Cynically we did not think it was just the typing.

Warrant Officer Harrison, who was senior to Q, came from Yorkshire. Quiet and precise, he led by example and was the sort of person I warmed to. His great claim to fame was having once played cricket with Jim Laker before he became a Surrey and England bowler. I can remember very little of what I did during my days in the office, apart from quite a lot of typing.

In my spare time I volunteered to do some freelance teaching of history and geography for the Education Corps, who were short staffed. This involved a small amount of extra pay and a welcome skive because it excused me from guard duty. I was then confronted with two WRACs wanting to learn geography for some Army test. The whole thing was a disaster. I had no idea how to handle these two women and they gave me a very hard time. They roughed me up and teased me as I struggled ineffectually against their dumb insolence. They were also skiving and doubtless could have given me a lesson or two.

The whole mistaken venture came to an end when the sergeant major discovered I was not doing this out of love but for money and to escape guard duty. The cash was withdrawn and I gave up my teaching career and resumed guard duty.

Quite a number of civilians and wives of officers like Ruby Duke worked alongside servicemen. One such was Mrs Bravant, married to Captain Bravant. I cannot remember how I originally met her, but she asked me if I would like to babysit Ian, aged four or five – old enough not to be too much of a challenge. He was an almost copybook child, very quiet and gentle but firmly disciplined by his loving parents. It was a cushy number as far as I was concerned. It provided the opportunity of spending an evening in an officer's house. Supper was delivered by some flunkey from the mess. It was an opportunity to eat rather better than the cookhouse and a valued chance to read. I struck up a very pleasant friendship with the Bravants, and kept up with them for a while after leaving the Army.

So I had a settled and tolerably pleasant routine. The weeks slid into months and letters home were cheerful.

19

CYPRUS

The Army encouraged troops to take their leave in special holi-day locations. Most of us took advantage of this, although we watched with envy as one of our number, Collins, whose father was a general, swanned off to ski in Lebanon. I was happy with the choice on offer. I could have gone to a camp at Alexandria, a hotel in Cairo or lodgings in Luxor, but decided on the leave facility in Cyprus.

My two weeks in Cyprus were wonderful. I was escaping from the Army, escaping from Egypt and above all from the sun-baked climate. I made the trip with Ginge Hodson, whom I have mentioned earlier.

The two weeks' leave fulfilled most of my expectations. The Army provided lodgings for us. They were congenial, totally British in décor and cuisine, and charged very cheap rates. We were mainly based at a small hotel in Platres, high up in the Troodos mountains. Because of the altitude it was cool in the evenings and the air was scented with the aroma of pine trees.

It was a good time to be in Cyprus. Although there was a certain amount of tension between the Greeks and the Turks, mutual abuse was still at the poster stage. You couldn't walk down the streets of Nicosia without seeing huge blue and white posters extolling 'ENOSIS' (union with Greece).

In 1950 Cyprus was still very much a backwater. There were not many cars and the military presence was unobtrusive. The few roads were mostly used by horses, carts and goats. It was another age. I remember looking at a big stretch of farmland. In one field a farmer was ploughing with camels and just next door his neighbour was using a large caterpillar tractor. There couldn't have been a more stark contrast between the old and the new. This mix was visible throughout Cyprus.

We wandered all over the island. We visited Kyrenia, Limassol and Paphos and travelled in Army buses or in the local squat black Cypriot ones. There was a very good local service and the buses were much smaller than the British ones. They were crowded with the peasantry, the priesthood in their stove hats and a mix of chickens, goats and every form of produce.

On a typical day we would decide on an area and visit monasteries on the way. In those days, before the influx of tourists spoiled it all, the monks were very hospitable and would invite us in and offer some refreshment.

I have photographs of many of the places we visited. Ginge was a keen photographer as well as having a great interest in ancient history. He went on to become a very distinguished archaeologist. We were both inherently academic and had a very bookish holiday. It was glorious to have a fortnight of wide-ranging conversation and companionship and to have a break from the tented world back at Fayid Camp. After the rigours of the Canal Zone it was so relaxing to be in civilian clothes in the summer sun, exploring the island. Compared to Egypt the abundance of flowers and greenery was paradise. May to June was a wonderful time to be there. Travel was cheap and the island was untouched by civil conflict or mass tourism.

After the hot and dusty days the cool evenings were a relief. We spent our time sitting in cafés in Nicosia amidst the noise and bustle of the crowded streets. It was my first opportunity to sample life in a foreign town at leisure and I loved it. My visits to Trieste and Port Said had been fleeting. The Canal Zone was solely a military complex and you could be anywhere as far as the outside world was concerned.

Ginge and I were very insular. When it came to food we were British to the core. In all our time there we tried to keep close to some Army establishment so that we could maintain our diet of beans, eggs, chips, sausages and beer. On a few occasions we tried our hand at a little Greek café and I sampled Commandaria wine, but not an olive or piece of feta cheese passed my lips. Once I bought a dried-up little cake from one of the many stalls but decided to stick to the safety of Army rations.

One of our few escapades was in Nicosia, when we went into a dingy café that turned out to be a brothel. We were sitting on bar stools having a drink – probably British beer – thinking about the egg and chips we were going to order when we noticed two or three rather nondescript women hanging around. One came forward and put her arms round Ginge and said in rough English something like, 'Want a good time, Corporal?' Ginge was quite unprepared for this. He reminded me of my father swatting a wasp as he ineffectually flapped his hands in the air saying 'Go away. Go away.' We realised we had made a ghastly mistake and tried to make a quick retreat. A dignified departure was impossible. There were two huge, menacing Alsatian dogs. We edged nervously away and missed a night of passion.

On another occasion we went to Famagusta to see the castle and its fortifications. Afterwards we started walking across a slightly marshy piece of land towards the suburb of Varosha. As we proceeded we saw something on the ground. It was a nest of snakes. To this day I have no idea whether or not they were harmful but we ran like men possessed.

With the small funds at our disposal we weren't great spenders. I bought some lace to give to my mother and a pair of nylon stockings from the NAAFI which were very difficult to obtain back home. For my father I bought a tankard on which was inscribed the Arabic for 'Coca Cola'. I do not think a drop of that beverage ever passed his lips.

All too soon our leave was over. We returned to Port Said in a corvette. The small flat-bottomed boat was not ideal in the Mediterranean swell. I remember finding a space on the open deck where I could lie full stretch. I awoke to find myself surrounded by a sea foaming with white horses and the corvette bobbing about like a corkscrew. I was as sick as could be, as were we all. We tottered off at Port Said into the Army hotel wondering how to celebrate, and decided on the cinema. The first thing on the screen was a boat at sea. I took one look at it and had to leave. It was too much.

I returned to Cyprus several times as an MP, including visits to the British Sovereign Base areas and Turkish North Cyprus. I had all the comforts of a parliamentary visitor but something was missing. The struggle for 'enosis', the Turkish invasion and mass tourism had each left their mark. The island had lost the magic of that first visit as a National Serviceman in 1950.

20

RELEASE

Soon after Ginge and I left Cyprus in the summer the prospect of release began to loom. In theory I should be out in September. We used to have great charts ticking off the weeks before we would be released. As we got increasingly 'demob happy' one of the squaddy slogans was 'Roll on Death: Demob is too slow'. I once wrote this on the outside of the envelope of the letter I sent to my parents as a joke. It really did upset them.

All seemed to be going well when suddenly, out of the sky, came the Korean War. There was no real means of knowing what was going on except from little snippets we gleaned from the *Egyptian Gazette*, the local English-language newspaper. We did not know whether we were going to be tipped into a major war. This did not seem merely a remote prospect as the United Nations troops were being pushed back along the Korean peninsula. We were all worried in case we were in the ante-room for World War Three. At the same time the United States beat England one–nil at football. This was a wholly unforeseen disaster which deeply disturbed the squaddies, for whom it marked the decline of Britain.

This background meant that what should have been a rather pleasant run to one's demob date became agonising, lest the conflict grow so serious that it affected our release. Of course we were right because quite soon the government announced the extension of National Service from eighteen months to two years.

Amidst the anxiety and gloom I was touched by good fortune. In early 1949 the armed forces had done a deal with the universities. All students starting their university careers in the autumn of 1950 would be called up in the spring of 1949. It was a neat arrangement: you would leave the forces one week and almost immediately start your studies. All university arrangements proceeded on this basis. What was a practicable idea suddenly became an immutable block to two years' National Service for student squaddies. The government decided to waive the six months' additional service for us and as a substitute required us to spend three years doing a fortnight's annual Territorial Camp.

It was a grand exchange: I subsequently did two weeks at Halton, near Lancaster. It rained non-stop. In 1952 we camped in glorious sunshine at Trawsfynydd near Barmouth. Memorably we all had to be enrolled in the British Legion Club in Llandudno to escape the Welsh licensing laws. Later we did a fortnight at Weymouth.

Meanwhile the result was that those of us going to university were treated not so much with envy but with outright resentment and anger. Why should a privileged few get out of service at eighteen months when the rest had to hang on for two years? Life was not exactly harmonious. We quickly learned not to flaunt our good fortune.

Eventually the day came when we embarked from Port Said on the *Dunera*, quite a large troopship. We were a mixed bag. As well as those taking early release, some were due to go home anyway. These included a lot of National Servicemen from Liverpool. The result was a nightmare journey.

All our worldly goods, including presents for the family, were in our kitbags. They could easily be slashed open and thieved. I felt I was surrounded by Scouse cut-throats. Apart from defending my wallet at Fayid Camp I had been cushioned throughout my Army service from the rougher elements. Now we were crowded into the troopship, with little privacy and no sense of security. I recall one overweight ginger-headed Liverpudlian whose sole contribution to social life was to rattle his mess tin and shout 'I want my f...ing connah'. Nothing was stolen but it was a very uneasy journey.

My companions were noisy. There was nothing much to do, but to help pass the time games were organised. My small success was winning the general knowledge quiz. En route we called at Tripoli but could not go ashore. When we got to the Bay of Biscay we hit a storm and I was violently seasick. It was hardly a triumphant return to Blighty.

Eventually we docked at Liverpool, sailing up St George's Channel. The weather became much more familiar and British, with grey skies and drizzly rain. We disembarked and got straight onto a troop train which took us down to the Aldershot area for the release procedures. There we hung around for a couple of weeks doing nothing – a sort of enforced skive. Release procedures ground slowly, under the paternal guidance of Warrant Officer Robert Offert, a local man known affectionately as 'Bob Offert of Andover'. He had a gentle Hampshire accent rather like the late Lord Denning.

Release was rather an anticlimax after all the pent-up antici-pation of the summer months. The time lingered, but eventually the magic day came. In my uniform, and with the huge kitbag that had survived the marauding Liverpudlians, I caught the train even though I knew I could not reach my parents by even-ing. I could not wait to have my first night away from the Army. I spent it at a lodging house in Bath.

As I stood fully kitted on the doorstep before a puzzled land-lord I explained, 'I'm not a deserter: just trying to get home.'

Next morning I got the train to Bridgwater where my parents were waiting for me. It was a wonderful homecoming. Hill Farm seemed almost exactly the same. My bedroom had been kept as a monument to my absence. Sadly I had only a brief time – barely a week – to prepare for Cambridge. Meanwhile I had to cast off the Army lifestyle. On the clothesline in the paddock, I hung up pairs and pairs of socks, a veritable footwear mountain, from my closing weeks of National Service. Now it was to be Cambridge and hopefully another world.

21

CAMBRIDGE: GOING UP

Cambridge was like a beacon on the horizon sustaining me during my National Service. In my mind there had always been a longish gap between leaving the Army and setting off for Cambridge. In the event there was a very short lapse of time between the two. It came upon me in a rush.

There was a tremendous bustle to sort out all my Army kit. Then there was an expedition to get some new clothes. I bought a tweed coat, a jumper and grey corduroy trousers. In an act of tremendous paternal generosity my father opened an account at Lloyds Bank, Bridgwater and presented me with a cheque book so that I could go through university life not too concerned about finance. His view was quite simple. He never wanted me to hold back when it was my turn to pay for a round of drinks. In fact, during my early Cambridge days, outings to the pub were largely at weekends. We also tended to pay for ourselves, but it was a wonderful gesture by my father.

Carter Paterson was booked to collect my trunk and, with great excitement and anticipation, I boarded the train to Cambridge. The first few days were hectic. Equipped with my cheque book, I made some initial purchases. Besides books, I bought the college scarf and tie. I also bought a gown. This essential piece of kit had to be worn on most occasions: in hall, at lectures and in the evening when out in the town. I still have it.

The choice of Jesus College had been that of my headmaster, Charles Key. It was not completely unknown since I had spent one night there when I went up for the scholarship examinations. To me the outline of the college buildings, at dusk, seemed rather austere and gaunt. Architecture aside I decided Jesus was a good choice since it was of modest size with around three hundred undergraduates.

I had little idea of what collegiate life would be like. I knew it would be a step up from the National Service barrack room. Looking back I realised it was surprisingly spartan, a hangover of post-war austerity. In September I received a note – touched with menace – saying, 'You are requested to come up on 6 October and you are advised to arrive in Cambridge before dusk...' The note concluded, 'Freshmen are reminded to bring RATION BOOKS.' I was told I was responsible for supplying the bedmaker with 'dusters, tea-cloths and swabs'; however, the college was intending to issue each bedmaker with four dusters and two swabs per staircase. This was no munificence. A charge would be made to the buttery bill as 'cleaning materials'.

Soon I received a formal printed Notice to Residents with the heading 'Gentlemen are requested to keep this paper for reference'. It was a list of instructions as detailed and minatory as that given by the Oswestry Borough to their council tenants. Musical instruments could be played between 1 p.m. and 10 p.m. 'and at no other time'. 'Gentlemen are not permitted to set up wireless aerials outside their college rooms.' There were nine regulations and those concerning gas fires and electric fires presumed we were latent pyromaniacs.

Other restraints prohibited the keeping of motor cars, and 'dogs may not be brought into College under any circumstances'.

Furthermore it was clearly established that 'the privilege of walking on the grass lawns in the Courts of the College is reserved to the Fellows'. Despite the litany of constraints, I never felt life at Cambridge was at all restricted. My modest social life and strong commitment to work ensured that I never wanted to stay out of college 'after hours' and then climb in illicitly. It was fairly easy and many did.

I have kept all my college bills. They are a fascinating commentary on life at Cambridge in the 1950s. My college open scholarship (worth £60 per annum) and my Somerset county scholarship (worth £75 per annum) paid for just over half my bill. My father paid the balance. I thought I was living royally on about £30 a month but I suspect continued wartime rationing played a part.

The college had two distinctive traditions. The first was quite a pronounced Anglican link through the Rustat Scholars. These were scholarships which had been provided historically for sons of the Anglican clergy. Although it wasn't overwhelming they did have some influence on the general ethos of the college. However, the much more significant tradition was that of rowing. For a college of its size it had a remarkable place on the river and a distinctive style of rowing introduced by an Australian coach, Steve Fairbairn, some fifty years earlier. The result was that members of the first boat tended to be the recognised elite in college society. The oarsmen generally sat together in hall at dinner and the college was understandably proud of its rowing record. Just gone down ahead of me had been the university cox Anthony Armstrong-Jones and I remember one of the college servants holding aloft a large plate of scrambled eggs and proclaiming 'As eaten by Mr Armstrong-Jones!' His reputation was still alive and was subsequently fortified by his skill as a photographer and not least his marriage to Princess Margaret.

Those of us who didn't row respected the college tradition and success. From the outset I had decided that I wasn't going to try and be a member of the rowing club. I wouldn't say that we were a nation apart but I think that non-rowers did feel that rowing dominated the college. However, it was a fairly tolerant situation. I opted to stay with cricket and hockey although my main interest was my work.

There was one incident, rather out of character. I saw in the paper an advertisement showing a lad exhausted over his oars and underneath was the caption 'Mother! Your son needs Horlicks.' I cut this out and sneaked up to the college notice board on which all the rowing club's fixtures and announcements were posted. I pinned it to the board and hastily retreated before I was spotted having made my own modest and irreverent gesture.

I suspect the rowing club was very Masonic. They all had nicknames such as Bungy Langton and Bimbo Mayhew-Saunders. The latter ended up as a great tycoon in the engineering world, chairman of John Brown. He came to see me when I was Trade Secretary about his firm's export promotion. I could say quite truthfully, 'I remember you well.' He looked thirty years older, as did I.

22

JESUS COLLEGE: LIFE

My rooms were situated in North House, a Victorian red-brick building detached from the main college buildings. It had originally been constructed as a residence for unmarried dons. Downstairs was Peter Hurcombe, an organ scholar who went on to great national recognition. However, the reason he sticks in my mind is that, despite college rules, he used to practise all hours of the day and night. My studies proceeded to the accompaniment of strains of Bach, Schumann and Debussy. Although he came from Minehead, quite near me in Somerset, I never got to know him.

Jesus was a very friendly college. Normally you would live in for your first year, and out thereafter. As a scholar I was given rooms of my own, which were mine for the full three years. Obviously I was at a great advantage. I couldn't say that my rooms were memorable. I had a bedroom and a sitting room and shared a lavatory with others on the same floor. For washing we had to make use of a communal bathhouse in the college. The sitting room had a fireplace for a coal fire but mercifully at the end of my first year this was replaced with a much more effective gas fire. The room looked over an open space beyond which were the college playing fields. It contained an imposing horse-chestnut tree with the most beautiful white flowers which always came out at the time of the examinations. The room itself was square and gaunt. There was a bookcase, a sofa and a great wicker armchair. Eventually, I brought a few prints including one of Dürer's hands. It did not relieve the gloom. I simply did not know how to make a room look homely. After National Service I was very well prepared for the bedroom with its unyielding iron bedstead and washstand.

These were still the days when the bedder would arrive every morning, bearing a ewer of hot water. She had the additional effect of encouraging one to get out of bed before her arrival. However, my neighbour Peter King found it very difficult to get up in the mornings. I would hear the plaintive cries of the bedder, 'Mr King, Mr King. You know what time it is', urging him to move so she could tidy up after him. I envied his lively courtship of his girlfriend Nancy. It was not without its dramas. As I sat at my books trying to master the intricacies of the medi-aeval papacy, Peter's rooms opposite mine had other activities. Occasionally there would be a trip-trip-trip down the staircase, followed by Peter shouting 'Nancy! Nancy!' In the monkish state of my first two years I was quite fascinated by someone manag-ing both to study and have a girlfriend.

My other neighbour was David Grenier. The son of a clergyman, major scholar and eventually City journalist and stockbroking executive, he was much more sedate. Although I remember one party when we both got drunk and David ended up with a rendition of 'Frigging in the Rigging' to the anguish of Mr Austen, the senior porter.

The focal point of college life was the hall where we ate our meals. It had a fine high ceiling and the walls were lined with the rogues' gallery of former distinguished college members. Cranmer was certainly its most famous son. Then there was Malthus, the notable nineteenth-century population expert, and more recently the portrait of Steve Fairbairn, the Australian coach who had inspired Jesus rowing. At the end there was the high table on a raised platform where the master, dons and their guests ate. It was common to eat nearly all one's meals in college. For dinner one had to wear a gown. This formality was offset by the casual seating arrangements. Huge refectory tables flanked by benches ran the whole length of the hall, set against the walls. To reach the far bench you had to step onto the table and over to the other side. It was a tricky manoeuvre considering that the table was laid for a three-course meal. The same procedure took place when one had finished and climbed back over the laggards ploughing through their stewed fruit and custard. Despite being still in the days of rationing, the authorities did their best. Certain things such as vegetables were abundant and the enormous quantity of both chips and celery on offer sticks clearly in my mind. Inevitably soup was followed by meat or fish and braised celery and chips. I used to think that the fen farmland must have been denuded of its celery beds and potato fields to feed us. In fact, after my time in the Army, I quite enjoyed the food. It was certainly no worse than I was used to and was served in infinitely more attractive circumstances.

In hall one tended to sit with one's friends. A main feature of dinner was the lengthy grace that had to be said at the beginning of the meal. Scholars and exhibitioners took it in turns and there was an unwritten understanding that one should either try and say the grace very slowly or very quickly. Saying it very slowly got a particular accolade of approval from one's colleagues. This would have been deemed 'dumb insolence' in the Army.

Eventually I received a handwritten note from the senior tutor, R. Y. Jennings, a distinguished international lawyer, ominously requesting me to go to his rooms as 'we had better try it over together first'. I understood why when I saw the text.

Oculi omnium in te aspiciunt et in te sperant, Deus. Tu das illis escam
tempore opportuno. Aperis tu manus, et imples omne animal benedictione tua.
Benedic nobis, Domine, et omnibus tuis donis, quae ex larga liberalitate
tua sumpturi sumus, per Jesum Christum Dominum nostrum.
    Deus est caritas. Qui manet in caritate manet in Deo et Deus in illo.
    Sit Deus in nobis, et nos maneamus in illo.

I got through it somehow.

The chapel has a distinguished history, having been the ancient church of the Nunnery of St Radegund. Its construction lasted from around 1140 to the first half of the thirteenth century. The nunnery fell upon poor times, allegedly becoming a brothel, and was suppressed by Bishop Alcock of Ely, who founded Jesus College in its place.

The trouble with Cambridge chapels is that King's is so overwhelmingly impressive that other colleges do not get a look in. Jesus had a good choral tradition, with its own choir and regular services. At this stage of my life I was not a great church attender. The habit had weakened during my spell in the Army and at that time I was going through a phase of not being particularly enchanted by the Church of England. In fact very occasionally I attended the Methodist church. The second obstacle to church was that there were so many other things going on. The biggest challenge to my hitherto very regular church attendance was membership of the Cambridge Film Society, the largest club in the university, with special showings on Sunday mornings. My friend Harry Hodgson and I were regular attenders. I can remember the films a good deal more than I can recall my lectures. I now realise what a superb programme we had: *Ivan the Terrible, Citizen Kane, Ninotchka* and *All Quiet on the Western Front*, to name just a few. The last mentioned was a powerful anti-war film. I really think it made me not a pacifist, but one who would seek any solution or appeasement to avoid war. It was a view that I held throughout my lifetime in politics.

In my last year there was a great furore involving Mark Boxer. I regret I took no part in the protest, not even as a spectator. I kept studiously to my books. Boxer was editor of a literary magazine, *Granta*, an edition of which contained a poem considered blasphemous. The editor was rusticated (temporarily expelled) and *Granta* was suppressed for six months. There was a massive and impressive student march with elements of hilarity, as a coffin purporting to contain Boxer was carried along King's Parade. Neal Ascherson, who became a renowned *Observer* journalist, published a cyclostyled broadsheet, *Granta and the Proctors*. He argued convincingly for press freedom, and it is inconceivable that such censorship would be applied today. Boxer suffered no harm and earned martyrdom. As an outstanding cartoonist he became one of Cambridge's best-known alumni. Years later – in the mid-1970s – he made a sketch of me, a supposed rising Tory.‡

---

‡ Reproduced on the back of the book jacket.

23

HISTORY

Although my Cambridge years were immensely happy, I am still daunted by recollections of the scope of the Historical Tripos. Part One, which took two years, had five subjects: Ancient History, Mediaeval European History, Political Thought, English Constitutional History 1485–1660, and English Constitutional History from 1660 to the Present Day. Part Two contained Modern European History, Theories of the Modern State and a special subject, Approach of World War One 1912–14. It was a fearful laundry list which encompassed lectures, reading and tutorials. I felt a strong commitment to my subject but I probably stood too close to the trees. I became more reflective after leaving Cambridge and more particularly after entering the Commons.

Having achieved an open scholarship in history, it was my natural instinct to continue with it, although quite a few people changed subject. My tutor was Vivian Fisher, whom I held in considerable awe. In his thirties, he appeared somewhat austere. Tall and dark, with a shock of hair, he did not have a very easy manner. I think he had been wounded in the war because he walked with a slight limp. We were not linked by a common interest since he was an Anglo-Saxon expert, which was not a period of history of which I had much understanding. He had researched the subject but had written only a modest amount compared with other Cambridge dons.

The form of our weekly meetings would be an essay which I had to read to him. He then made comments and invited counter-comments. I now realise that he was a kindly and probably very shy man. Every so often I would be invited to have tea: 'Well, Biffen, perhaps you could come and have tea on such and such a date. You'll like my wife. She's pretty.'

My first tutorial with Fisher was an uncomfortable affair. I stumbled through the essay relating to some generalised topic such as the virtues or drawbacks of moderation. I then underwent a harrowing period of cross-examination. Leaving his room I met a fellow undergraduate from Nottingham High School who, earlier that morning, had also had his first session with Fisher. He asked me how things had gone. I said they had been pretty rough and he riposted that after the tutorial he felt as if he had been chewed up and spat out. This was my first meeting with Harry Hodgson, who became a very close friend. I was best man at his wedding and godfather to his eldest son.

Gradually I overcame my anxiety and apprehension at my weekly meetings with Vivian Fisher, particularly when I was able to deal with more specific topics. I was then passed on to another college historian, Charles Wilson. With his easy charm he was a very different character. Rather portly and of medium height, he was very much a man of the world. An authority on Anglo-Dutch relations in the seventeenth century, he had made a study of Unilever, eventually becoming Professor of Modern History. Very much an economic historian, he represented Jesus College in the academic world of history at Cambridge. Although politics didn't intrude much in his teaching, he was generally on the liberal wing of the Conservatives. Eventually we went on to having tutorials in pairs. Harry and I attended together and, as we were by then close friends, this was a very congenial arrangement.

Fisher remained my director of studies but if I had to pick out one don at Jesus who was responsible for my guidance and tuition it was Charles Wilson. He was very easy to talk to and used non-academic language. Peter Mathias was one of his special pupils, an outstanding historian who had taken his degree just ahead of me. He was still at college and eventually became, like Wilson, an acknowledged economic historian.

Two other Jesus dons featured during my time. Dr Raby had been a career civil servant and had come to the college in retirement. A very quiet and rather withdrawn person, he didn't make much of an impact. I benefited more from the cutting edge of Fisher and Wilson than from his guidance. The fourth person was the formidable Maurice Cowling. He turned up just before the end of my third year so I only had a few sessions with him. He subsequently went on to Peterhouse, where he made a reputation as one of the most redoubtable and unyielding Conservative academics. I always think his illiberal views prevented him from getting a wider recognition within the academic community. He made a strong impression. Coming from Battersea Grammar School he was very aggressive in his tutorial techniques. I found some difficulty in handling his assertive line of reasoning but it certainly was helpful in disciplining my mind.

I had assumed my study at Cambridge would be centred on lectures. It is a pity I had not received some worldly advice on this matter. It was one of the disadvantages of having been at a school with no Oxbridge tradition. There was no one to warn me that lectures would take up a vast amount of time, that even the most distinguished academics were often poor communicators and that you had little opportunity to question the lecturer. The consequence was that I found my first year rather unsatisfactory.

My 'preliminary' exams at the end of my first year were a disappointment. I was placed in the second division of the second class – a 2.2. As a scholar I should have been at least in the first division, namely a 2.1. I improved my marks by studying more on my own account and spending no time at lectures in my second year. Also in my first year I was recovering learning skills that had rusted during National Service.

Most of the lectures were given in a suite of rooms at Mill Lane. We sat on rising tiers of benches with the lecturer before us on a podium. Lectures generally lasted an hour in sessions from 9 a.m. to 1 p.m.

Looking back at the *Cambridge University Reporter*, which lists all the 'Lectures proposed by the Board of the Faculty of History, 1951–52', there were upwards of fifty lectures. Most of these had some relevance to the subjects included in the Part One Tripos which I was studying.

I attended about ten lectures a week. I honestly cannot claim that any of the lecturers left much impression. An exception was Kenneth Pickthorn. He had been Conservative MP for Cambridge University until 1950, when such seats were abolished. Thenceforth he was MP for Carlton in Nottinghamshire. He taught Tudor constitutional history and was as starchy a lecturer as he was a politician. I can still hear the cracked voice elaborating upon the implications of 'praemunire' but even more I recall his final lecture before the end of the Michaelmas Term. There was a tradition that had developed to applaud. Otherwise lectures were held in total silence with no questions at the end. At the appropriate moment we gave our round of applause to Pickthorn. 'Stop. Stop. Stop!' he cried. 'I disagree with this entirely. It was a bad habit brought here by people from the London School of Economics. Once undergraduates start voicing approval they will think they can also show disapproval.'

Getting to know him years later in the House of Commons, I found him delightful company. He was a strong traditionalist and unmoved by fashion.

I very occasionally attended lectures outside my subject or those given by visitors outside Cambridge. Noel Annan from King's College was a superb lecturer on cultural topics and commanded a wide audience. He was a master of speech, and irreverent quips intertwined with mild socialism. He entertained, if not converted, his undergraduate audience. I was lucky enough to hear him in the Lords in the late 1990s. He had lost none of his verve but his audience was more stolid. Karl Popper was the most dynamic visiting lecturer. His rather modest presence did not prepare you for the onslaught as he laid about collectivism. I did not appreciate his arguments as I should. My history was devoted to the details of political events, such as the impact of the Industrial Revolution and its relationship to House of Commons electoral reform. I did not realise there was emerging a school of history, largely based upon London, with Popper, Oakeshott and von Hayek, who would successfully challenge the liberal collectivism that was dominant at Oxford and Cambridge and whose icon was Herbert Butterfield. Yet it was their teaching that so much influenced me and my politics from the 1960s onwards.

In my third year I made a special study of 'Europe 1912–1914, the origins of the First World War'. About two dozen of us did this. I decided I had to resume lectures as I couldn't have grasped the topic merely from books despite an extensive reading list, including Poincaré's memoirs in French. I struggled. The class was taken by a young don, Michael Vyvyan from Trinity.

Doubtless he was highly learned but he was not a fluent lecturer. Physically clumsy he always seemed to want to shift the table. We watched with fascination whilst he lifted it up, then brought it back and then moved it a bit somewhere else. His fidgeting dominated the small room.

All things considered I very much enjoyed my special subject. It probably had an effect on my subsequent political life. I didn't view the 1914 war as a culmination of historical events and inevitable consequences. I saw it as a very complicated motor accident. A whole series of incidents which reacted upon each other, and in happier circumstances war would have been avoided. It still affects my outlook on war and appeasement. I am a crypto-pacifist to this day. I felt that the 1914 tragedy should have been manageable and that the consequences of war were infinitely more dire than anyone could have foreseen.

24

COLLEGE ROUTINE AND MAY BALL

In my second year I made a breathtakingly radical decision and resolved to attend no lectures at all. My study would be entirely reading and handing in my weekly essay.

Obviously I had been disappointed only to get a 2.2. Holders of open scholarships were certainly expected to do better. It had taken me quite a while to settle down after National Service and I wasn't playing to my potential. This was certainly the view of my tutor, Vivian Fisher. He thought that I suffered from nervousness, saying, 'It is all there but you have difficulty in getting it out.' My decision not to go to lectures did not mean that I avoided work but that I worked much more on my terms. I found this less stressful. I was also quite pleased with how I was doing in the non-academic side of my Cambridge life, which was mainly politics. The irony of it is that at the end of my second year the papers at which I did best were those on ancient history. They were mainly responsible for my getting a First.

The pattern of my university life was pretty constant. My day would start with breakfast in the hall. I would then stay in my room reading the papers. I took two, *The Times* and the *Daily Worker*. *The Times* was more because of the very advantageous student subscription rate they offered. I had been reading it at home for some time. I had persuaded my parents to change from the *Daily Mail* to *The Times* just after D-Day. I read the *Daily Worker*, not out of sympathy, but because Communism fascinated me. It was an enjoyable quick read, and since it was permanently short of money it was a very flimsy paper. Years later when I met David Aaronovitch of *The Independent* I was able to ask him if he was related to the Aaronovitch who used to write for the *Daily Worker*. 'Yes, that was my father,' he said. It says something about my self-contained and introverted life that it came naturally for me to sit in my room, having finished with the papers and then proceeding with my reading and making notes. My solitude was broken by close college friends like Harry Hodgson, Roy Marlow and David Grenier dropping in for coffee.

I did not study non-stop and played games, mostly hockey, in the afternoon. In my last year I played squash almost every day. Pursuing my forlorn desire to be a wicket keeper, I also played cricket for a junior Jesus team. However, I was terrified of the fast bowling of Nick Mitchell. I found myself standing even further back than the slips, so to avoid further humiliation, I abandoned cricket. I played no other field sports apart from hockey. In my second and third years I played hockey for the Jesus 2nd XI as goalkeeper. It was a fairly exposed position and in those days before fancy face grilles you just had to hope the ball didn't come screaming past and hit you in the jaw. Although I had relatively little skill, I had a rather surprising disregard for personal safety and I was not intimidated as I had been at cricket. I would get out in front of the goal and kicking in all directions see off my attackers. The net result was more successful than might be imagined.

The Hockey Club annual dinner was held after an afternoon match. I was truly delighted with my fellow players' inscriptions on my dinner card of December 1952: 'They shall not pass'; 'May you repeat today's success many times'; 'You'd better wear a box next time, jolly well goaled.' The card is proof of my unexpected games skill, but few are convinced, particularly my family. I wisely left hockey when I went to Birmingham.

I ate both lunch and dinner in hall, and sometimes I would do a little reading after dinner, but there was competing social life. Club meetings were held in college, there were films and, of course, I would go to the Union at least once a week.

Immediately after the war, many Cambridge students were ex-servicemen. By 1950 the war generation had come and gone. Now we were only ex-National Servicemen and I think of Cambridge as a peacetime experience. The university had recaptured much of what I thought of as pre-war Cambridge. There was still rationing but there was not much austerity. May balls flourished and, for me, student life seemed tremendously relaxed.

Gowns had to be worn for lectures, meals and going out in the evenings. I suppose this was in order to increase one's visibility and promote good behaviour. In the evenings the proctors would roam the streets of Cambridge, searching out misbehaving undergraduates. If they couldn't get you for anything else there was always the tattered state of one's gown, resulting in a fine of 6/8d. Certain pubs such as the Pickerel were put out of bounds from time to time so as to avoid confrontation between undergraduates and American servicemen with their women of easy virtue.

Harry Hodgson, Dick Brown, Roy Marlow and I used to go on a modest pub crawl most weekends. Starting off at the Volunteer, drinking halves of Benskins bitter, we would go on to the Baron of Beef and, if in bounds, finish up at the Pickerel. It was a bachelor outing, not a woman in sight. The evening would normally end in one or other of our rooms drinking coffee and putting the world to rights.

The debating club, the Orators, was formed some time after I arrived at college and reflected the fact that there were a number

of people at Jesus interested in politics. The club membership
was about twenty. Prominent members were Peter Gadsden,
subsequently knighted and Lord Mayor of London, Patrick
Jenkin, who became Secretary of State for the Environment,
John Byrnell, Terence Mallinson, an accomplished thespian who
went on to run the family timber business, and Emmanuel Addo,
a charming and diminutive coal-black Ghanaian always attired
in a bow tie. Other members included Harry Hodgson, Dick
Brown and Roy Marlow, all of whom came from Nottingham
High School. Marlow worked for Unilever, then, as Foreign
Office late entrant, became ambassador to the Dominican
Republic and sadly died young. Although it was a fairly low-key
club we published a programme and met regularly after dinner
to debate a topic. Club membership was 1/6d a term – surely a
bargain to rub shoulders with a future Lord Mayor of London.
In no way did it rival the Cambridge Union as a debating forum
but it was a very good training ground. It enabled me to mix
with a wide range of people who shared my interest in politics.

Orator debating was very relaxed. Indeed it seems remarkable
the club was ever founded amidst the college rowing culture.
Chanticlere, the college magazine, reported, in Lent Term 1951,
that E. A. Addo had proposed that 'International Law and Order
is beyond the pale of human achievement'. Out of character I
opposed this sensible motion. E. A. A. was affectionately known
as 'Ee Aye Addio', the war chant of Merseyside footballers.

Cambridge had a host of clubs, many based upon colleges, but
even more open to university membership. They fell into broad
groups, based upon sporting, social, academic and public affairs.
I detail elsewhere my main club activities, namely the Union
and the Conservatives. Like most newcomers I signed up for a
number of clubs but my interest soon died away. There were
three whose membership I still recall. I joined the Cambridge

Scandinavian Society in the Michaelmas Term of 1952. This was entirely the result of a delightful time spent at a Danish folk high school at Roding in Slesvig. It had been a wild success socially. The Scandinavian Society was rather austere, more Kierkegaard than Greta Garbo. For the specialist there was 'Faeroese Music', a talk illustrated with gramophone records. The History Club I felt I had to join. Its president was the distinguished Dominican professor M. D. Knowles, but spending so much of my day doing history I was reluctant to give up my evenings to the same topic.

Cambridge was a great place for social-cum-dining clubs. The most renowned was the Pitt Club, which attracted the social elite. Long after my time it fell upon plebeian days and became a supermarket. Happily it is now a restaurant. A number of us, aping our betters, formed a dining club, the Viginti, for politically minded members. The dinners were held in the Music Room, Downing College. Rule Two stated 'that the membership is limited to twenty male persons who must be members of the Union or Conservative Association or Liberal Club'. You would have thought I had had enough of politics, but I did enjoy the dinners greatly.

I was quite reconciled to a monkish existence at Cambridge as I had had a very thin social life before going up. Drinking and going to films were part of a male-orientated life. Then came the great challenge of what I should do about the May ball. As it was one of the highlights of university life I thought I should go. I was incredibly shy and had no girlfriend. Apart from putting an advertisement in *The Times* for a partner, I didn't know what to do. Eventually my very good old school friend, Peter Thorak, now at Bristol University, kindly agreed that I could invite one of his many girlfriends. Jacqueline Tanner was extremely handsome and a superb partner. She had been at Roedean and was an enthusiastic student of English literature. I repeated the invitation a year later. For this second May ball she accepted and then cancelled at the last moment. In extremis I was rescued by Harry Hodgson. He was taking Pat Heywood, a friend from Nottingham who appeared in the original production of *Salad Days* and subsequently went on to play the nurse in Zeffirelli's *Romeo and Juliet*. Pat introduced me to a friend of hers, Diana Edwards-Jones, as my partner. She too was from the Bristol Old Vic Drama School, and became a producer on ITN. Later when I was appearing regularly on ITN, we would reflect together on the random nature of our first meeting and drink to it.

I remember the ball as most enjoyable but lacking in gallantry. Harry and I were on an exceedingly tight budget and decided we could only afford the basics. We took the poor men's way out as far as flowers for our partners were concerned. We bought none. Whilst in my rooms drinking Yugoslav Sylvaner Riesling (a flat economical wine, quite without sparkle) a knock came on the door. It was the photographer. The girls started adjusting themselves for action. We waved him away. For all our meanness we looked studiously decadent at 7 a.m. having danced the night away. Harry and I decided to atone for our lack of gallantry by punting the girls up the river to Grantchester for breakfast. It was fun but I don't think I have felt as shattered since, not even after a Commons all-night sitting.

25

CAMBRIDGE UNIVERSITY CONSERVATIVE ASSOCIATION

The Cambridge University Conservative Association was my first port of call for getting into university politics; I also became a regular attender at the Cambridge Union. In my very first week at college I received a visit from Patrick Jenkin, the CUCA college representative. He is one of those people who have the good fortune of hardly changing. He was looking much the same thirty years later when we were both members of the Thatcher Cabinet. The year 1950 was a memorable one for CUCA because my contemporaries included Geoffrey Howe and Douglas Hurd. Both became Foreign Secretary and both stood in vain for leadership of the Conservative Party. Another fellow member was Tony Buck, who became a Navy minister in the Heath government and with whom I shared a flat in Kennington Palace Court for some years.

CUCA was an impressive organisation. Its membership ran into four figures. With an ambitious programme of meeting every Sunday and frequently a second meeting during the week, it was able to attract major political speakers from the Conservative front bench and also well-known backbenchers. Socially the other benefits were two balls a year and a summer garden party. The balls were great occasions. The chairman and secretary wore white ties and association sashes. I hired an outfit and tried to look the part. One year we had the 1930s star Evelyn Laye do the cabaret. Our politics were pinkish but otherwise we revelled in nostalgia. Geoffrey Field of Trinity Hall, who became a teacher at Glenalmond and defected to the Liberals, was CUCA chairman when I was secretary. My note of the top table bill lists dinner £1.57, sherry 35p and champagne 50p, the latter being a share of a bottle costing £1.80. What memories! The invitation card for the ball in February 1951 must be a collector's piece. The cabaret was provided by Humphrey Lyttelton (and three other bands) and the invitation was in the names of Geoffrey Howe, Douglas Hurd and Patrick Jenkin. The price to dance with the men of tomorrow was £1.50 for a double ticket.

As secretary my own organising of the Conservative ball was flawed. I had forgotten to clear the plans with the proctor. University 'law and order' required such festivities to be reported and cleared. Anyway the law descended and I was reprimanded and fined £1 by the university for 'breach of University Regulations'. Perhaps it had a deterrent effect. I have a clean licence after fifty years of driving.

Without doubt CUCA was the premier social club for would-be politicians, although as a Labour spokesman said, 'It's all balls.' Actually we were rather a serious group of people with quite clear political ambitions. I hardly ever missed a meeting and in my last year became chairman. I enjoyed all the scheming and plotting that this involved.

Getting speakers was quite a responsibility. I had to field six speakers for Friday evenings and six for Sunday afternoons. Some I approached directly but most were provided with assistance from Conservative Central Office. There were no serious mishaps but I gave Sir Waldron Smithers a Saturday railway timetable for a Friday meeting. He spotted it and lived up to his reactionary reputation by vainly trying to enrol me in the Society for Individual Freedom. David Renton, then MP for Huntingdon, accepting the invitation, asked if he could bring his wife, explaining he would pay for her. Another MP, no names, asked Central Office to book a hotel room and emphasised he wanted his wife in another room. Central Office provided a Cabinet minister, Gwilym Lloyd George, then Minister of Food. He was the most prestigious name on the card but really quite dull. The speaker I most sought was Michael Oakeshott, an acknowledged Tory intellectual who had recently left Cambridge to lecture at the London School of Economics. Alas, he was unable to come because of his academic work.

My programme was not very exciting but the meetings were well attended with no disasters. My predecessor as chairman, Geoffrey Field, arranged a meeting for Robert Carr and a Conservative trade unionist, A. B. Matthews. It was held in the Masonic Hall and the caretaker and a friend, supplied with Guinness, sat at the back of the room and were horrified to hear Tories talking such modish rubbish as trade union rights and shop floor participation. They heckled and burped, and eventually Field had to expel them. The incident was more memorable than Carr's earnest progressive views.

One year was an *annus mirabilis* for the Jesus membership of CUCA. We persuaded Paul Mack, a member of the boat club, to stand for the committee and bring along his friends from the club, a lot of heavies who dominated the election. Solemnly, this was agreed to be bad form. John Byrnell, a man of great charm and the son of the vicar of Slaidburn, was responsible for this nifty bit of Tammany Hall electioneering.

A memorable CUCA officer was Hugh Thomas. He was the most innumerate treasurer you could imagine. Of course, his skills lay elsewhere, and his book on the Spanish Civil War remains a classic. His later politics led him first to Labour, then to being a foreign affairs adviser to Margaret Thatcher, and finally to the Liberal Democrats, but sitting on the cross benches.

As my time as chairman came to an end I tried to secure my succession. I picked as my protégé a charming, quiet Old Etonian called Tam Dalyell, who at that stage was still a Conservative. I did my utmost to promote his fortunes but with limited success, although he became an officer of the Union. After leaving Cambridge he went on to be a school teacher and fairly soon thereafter became a Labour MP. He was a champion of many causes and eventually was Father of the House of Commons.

Besides our regular weekly meetings we also practised open-air public speaking on the luckless Cambridge populace at Parker's Piece. We were very serious about our speaking and used to attend classes taken by Mrs Cuswell. She was very good. It is the only occasion I have ever taken formal speaking lessons and I am still very grateful for what she taught me. We worked in pairs for tuition. One person would be chairman and other the speaker. I was told that I was rather good at speaking but was the most dreadful chairman. The moment I introduced the speaker I would look at the floor as if I was condemned to a terrible ten minutes whilst my companion droned on. This criticism struck home. Thereafter I was always conscious that I should look approvingly at the speaker and be succinct but generous in my thank-you comments.

During the long vacation in September/October some members of CUCA would go on a Conservative speaking tour. In 1951 I went to Carlisle and in 1952 to Watford. The tour lasted for a short week and the local Association put us up in private homes. In 1951 I stayed with Mr and Mrs North, who were enthusiastic Conservatives. Mr North was an insurance agent and when the election was called he went out and insured his windows.

Under the eagle eye of the Carlisle agent we would be sent to speak outside factory gates and schools and also to do some straightforward canvassing. The speaking team for Carlisle was memorable. It consisted of Douglas Hurd, Hugh Thomas, Piers Dixon and me. Piers Dixon was the son of Sir Pierson Dixon, the diplomat. Piers had a moment of political involvement when he became Conservative Member of Parliament for Truro. We were quite an imposing little quartet.

During the speaking tour Clement Attlee called the 1951 general election. Suddenly it was real politics. I remember Douglas fulminating against public spending and how much it cost to finance the prison service and saying with great indignation that it cost more to keep someone at Wormwood Scrubs than at Eton. Douglas was a good speaker whilst Hugh was wonderfully fey with very much an intellectual's approach to any topic.

This visit was handsomely covered by the *Cumberland Evening News*, probably because it coincided with the calling of a general election. Under the heading 'Young Tories answer the hecklers', our open-air meeting was described as 'lively with questions'. Douglas Hurd was the star turn, and had a vintage heckler interrupt with shouts of 'We cannot support a capitalist policy' and 'The Tories want a war'. There was something incongruous about the rather smooth university Conservatives being matched against the young and noisy working class of Carlisle. No conversions were made but no heads were cracked.

The Conservative candidate was a road haulier called Noel O'Reilly who had an individual style of canvassing. The form was to find somewhere to park the campaign lorry and show a short film from the back of it to encourage people to gather round. This time the film was of Jackie Milburn scoring the crucial goal in a cup final. As Noel O'Reilly began his speech by saying 'there's our Jackie', I had a feeling of being miles away from Cambridge and Somerset and part of a great Tory tradition of North Country pride.

At the finish of the speaking tour I hitchhiked all the way home to Somerset. Despite my father's generosity, funds were limited and I didn't want to fritter it on buses. I stopped off in the Lake District. It was the first time I had been to the area and I was captivated by the scenery. Then came the great challenge of getting through Birmingham. However, in those pre-motorway days it was quite easy to get a lift.

After Somerset I returned to Cambridge and was confronted with the general election campaign itself. We believed that the participation of CUCA was vital to secure a Conservative victory and we all reported for duty. Douglas Hurd was then chairman and masterminded the plans. On 20 October I received a manuscript note: 'As regards your Cambridgeshire meeting on Monday, Captain Sanglier wants us to run a meeting at the village of Papworth St Agnes (near Huntingdon) which Mr Howard [the Tory candidate] will not be visiting. Will you take this on with Geoffrey Field? If you call in, I will give you details of times and transport.' It worked quite well, unlike the many election shambles I encountered later on. My job was to be sent out to evening meetings in the countryside. At that time it was still usual to have three or four political meetings a night and a warm-up speaker was needed to fill in time until the arrival of the candidate. I was sent out all over the place. Once in mid-Bedfordshire the candidate, Alan Lennox-Boyd, was struck down with laryngitis and, as he was sinking, they rushed him in front of a microphone and recorded his speech. I found myself warming up to a gramophone record. However, it was all very friendly and no one felt the need to ask me to answer questions concerning the recording.

The letter of thanks I received from Alan Lennox-Boyd has a special value. Twenty-five years later his son, Mark, came to help me when I was 'shadow Energy'. He was an invaluable companion and eventually became an MP and a minister at the Foreign Office. I am a godfather to his daughter.

One other aspect of CUCA was the rather solemn business of study groups covering many topical subjects which were advertised on our speakers card. I was chairman of a study group entitled 'Communism in Britain', and the meetings were held in my college rooms with a membership of four or five. It was at this stage that I added to my standard reading of *The Times* by subscribing to the *Daily Worker*. Some ultra-right-wing members purported not to be able to tell the difference. It wasn't a terribly intense group but I enjoyed it, and did a fair amount of reading to try to understand the nature of the Communist Party. I have the typescript of the report which was eventually submitted to the Association.

CUCA was affiliated to the Federation of University Conservative and Unionist Associations (FUCUA). This met twice a year at Hoddesdon, a rambling country house in Hertfordshire. There gathered members from all the university Conservative Associations and for a weekend they solemnly debated and passed resolutions and tried to be reasonably progressive. I think the Central African Federation and comprehensive schools tended to be touchstone issues. It was at Hoddesdon that I met people who became friends for life: Julian Critchley and John Bellak from Oxford and Ian Davison from the London School of Economics. They all subsequently stood for Parliament and Julian was Member for Chatham and subsequently Aldershot and a delightfully irreverent addition to Westminster.

In March 1953 at an FUCUA conference, Ian Davison
(London) and Stratton Mills (Belfast) proposed a welcome for
the 'political federation' of the six Common Market countries.
Stratton became an MP in 1959 but was a victim of 'the troubles'
and left the Ulster Unionist Party. Another progressive student
was Mark Carlisle (Manchester) arguing against corporal punishment. He entered Parliament and became Margaret Thatcher's
first Minister of Education, something of a dove amidst the kites.
He did not last long, but became an active member of the House
of Lords.

Being a member of CUCA was quite a serious political
commitment if one so desired. It included a prestigious list of
speakers, speaking lessons, speaking tours and study groups. It
was clearly more than a pretext for socialising. It considerably
developed my political experience and, combined with membership of the Union, confirmed that it was quite practical for me
to think of a political career with a view to becoming a Member
of Parliament.

26

CAMBRIDGE UNION

Whilst still at school I had more of an idea about the Union than I had about Cambridge. The university debating societies had a certain notoriety, not least because of the famous motion passed by the Oxford Union in the 1930s saying they would not defend King and Country. When I went up for my scholarship exams I had a furtive glance round the door of the Union and was struck by its resemblance to the House of Commons with a Speaker's Chair and banks of benches round the sides.

The Union had been founded in 1815 and was essentially a male club with a library, a dining room and squash courts. It was its debating chamber that attracted, indeed captivated me. Life subscription was £7.87½ p. I signed immediately.

Once at Cambridge I turned up on the first occasion possible for a freshers' meeting and attended my first debate. The Union met regularly on Thursdays, although other debates were included as events dictated. Although it was most widely known as a political nursery a great many of the debates were not political but general. Some of the most excruciating were the 'humorous' ones. Ironically I eventually developed a style of speaking in the House of Commons which was rather self-effacing and mildly humorous, whereas when I was debating at the Cambridge Union I was still an earnest and intense Young Conservative in a gown.

The Union hierarchy consisted of a president, a vice-president and a secretary. Mainly to give as many people as possible a turn, these were re-elected each term by the members of the Union. So in my time I knew nine presidents. A number of them were particularly effective. Julian Williams was president during my first term. Coming from a conservative family in Cornwall, he was not an outstanding speaker but more than made up for this with his ebullient personality. He became a friend and stood for Parliament in Birmingham All Saints in 1955 when I was working there. Sadly he was not elected, despite my strenuous efforts to help him. It was he who was instrumental in persuading me to apply for inclusion on the candidates list.

Greville Janner I remember as a dedicated politician. His father, Barnett, was a Labour Member of Parliament. Greville was thought by a few of the more waspish Conservatives not to conduct himself with the dignity expected of the chair. The result was that he was attacked by Archie Norman, a rather angular Tory and publisher of 'Saturn', an ephemeral political tract. There was only one edition. It sought to kill two birds with one stone, lampooning the established magazine, *Varsity*, and also Janner, the president of the Union.

One of the 'Saturn' features was a portrait of the president of the Union. This was a satirical piece about Greville, criticising his dreariness of speech and bemoaning the lack of sparkle you would expect from the president of the Union. One section was particularly effective and wounding. 'I rose to speak. "Mr President," I said, "last night you and I…" Here at last was an innuendo the president could understand. The president with a squeak cried, "Order! Order! Explain yourself."' I doubt if Janner was much fussed, and certainly Norman could never imagine that Janner would eventually be sponsoring an Archbishop of Canterbury (George Carey) as a member of the House of Lords.

Douglas Hurd and Geoffrey Howe were conventional pillars of the Union and both became president. They were competent rather than sparkling. The most amusing speaker I recollect who was president was Anthony Sampson, a member of the Labour Party and a man of great charm. Alas he did not become a politician.

On one occasion I thought there was a slightly dubious manoeuvre. Jack Ashley was president, and subsequently a Labour Member of Parliament and a great campaigner for the disabled. As president he retired early so that someone else could be squeezed in to be president for a fortnight. It was done for the benefit of Mr Gunter Mathur from India. It was assumed that Ashley and the progressives thought it would be a good gesture for Mr Mathur to finish his time having been president of the Union. There was also the ungenerous thought that no one back home would realise he had only been president for a fortnight. I do not believe this manoeuvre would have been connived for a British student.

The Union flattered itself as the 'establishment in waiting'. Such a view was confirmed by a visit from the Duke of Edinburgh. A privileged few, myself included, were invited 'to attend a small reception' after the main meeting. There was a strict dinner jacket rule, and the Duke used the privacy of the occasion to voice some robust remarks about journalists. We felt immensely grown up.

Election to the Union Committee took place each term involving the entire membership. The ballot paper was an enormous sheet with candidates listed alphabetically from which you had to choose up to nine names. The usual progression for an aspiring member of the Union was to start speaking in debates. If you made your mark with the president you would then be invited to be a teller counting votes at the end of the debate. This meant that your name would be printed at the foot of the debating sheet. After you had become a teller the next step would be an invitation to 'speak to the paper'. You were then listed with the visiting guest speakers at the head of the printed order paper. The furthest I got was to be elected to the Committee for a full year. I have a manuscript note sent to me by Graham Tayar of Jesus College, telling me I had won fifth place on the Union Standing Committee. I never managed to become secretary. I just missed it, coming second to Nicholas Tomalin, a member of the Labour Party whose distinguished journalistic career was sadly terminated by early death.

The Union debates were seriously reported every week in *Varsity*. Union Committee membership was competitive. I was on the Library Sub-committee and had great fun choosing the books. We were mostly aspirant politicians and thespians and delighted in meeting and plotting. When we had finished sorting out the Cold War we would turn to matters closer to home. There were always great debates about rules. The long-standing favourite was whether or not women should be allowed membership. I was for the preservation of the status quo. I consistently voted against the great change which, although inevitable, did not come until after I had left Cambridge.

I so much enjoyed the Union debates that I cannot pretend to be a fair critic. I would join in the 'morning after' inquests that took place in the Blue Boar or the KP as we dissected the speeches over an endless brew of coffee. There was much to gossip over such as Compton Mackenzie getting very ill-tempered whilst debating 'This House is bored with the Scots'. No one thought it was a serious subject – certainly not the lead undergraduate speaker, Edward Greenfield, who cut short his speech to play a gramophone record. He developed his skill, becoming music correspondent for *The Guardian* and having his own record programme on the BBC World Service until he was seventy. I first heard 'Hon. Wedgwood Benn' (as he was then described) in a debate in February 1952 when he was matched against Robert Boothby. They both knew how to play an undergraduate audience. It was a great evening.

Very occasionally the Union turned to religion. I attended the debate on 20 January 1953 when R. G. Moore (Trinity College) asserted that 'A strong Roman Catholic Church is a grave danger to democratic government'. The redoubtable Bishop Beck of Brentwood defended the Papacy, and the mood was good natured despite the title. There was an irony only to be revealed by time. Richard Moore's son Charles, of *Telegraph* fame, became a Roman Catholic convert.

I took an active part in debating and eventually had the real prize of being asked to speak to the paper in the annual 'no confidence' debate. It was usual for the new session of Parliament to open in October and coincide neatly with a 'no confidence' motion being debated early in the Michaelmas Term. A Conservative government had been in office for a year. The motion of 'no confidence in Her Majesty's Government' was proposed by Michael Hydleman, a Liberal from Downing College, and his supporting speaker was Herbert Morrison, a former Home Secretary and latterly Foreign Secretary. I spoke for the government and was partnered by Iain Macleod, then Minister of Health, who made by far the best speech.

The debate took place on 14 October 1952. It was a crowded house. The motion was lost by 256 votes to 527. An impressive figure considering many members would have chosen to leave the chamber immediately after the debate was concluded and not wait to vote. I think Hydleman and I were evenly matched. The

Cambridge Daily News reported that I had talked about the virtues of party unity – something that I rather neglected in the 1980s. I still remember evenings of high drama, largely on account of the crowded Union chamber. Unbeknownst to me was a young Labour student – one of the Labour minority – attending his first debate. Years later we met in Westminster and reminisced. It was Cecil Parkinson, who had become a Conservative MP, and subsequently became chairman of the party and a member of the Thatcher Cabinet. Alas, his conversion did not derive from my speech.

I remember how incredibly nervous I was. Tradition dictated that you wore a dinner jacket if you were speaking to the paper and I added to this a very dashing maroon bow tie.

Even in the Union 'make-believe' of politics we were naturally anxious about the press. The debates were faithfully reported by *Varsity* and the *Cambridge Review*. I did quite well. Richard Moore, a pillar of student Liberalism, approved of my remarks in a debate on pacifism. He reported in the *Cambridge Review* that I had 'made a thoroughly good speech in a sympathetic manner worthy of his sentiments which were so sound that a name is wanted for his sort of political position – Tory Whig perhaps'. The same debate was reported in *Varsity* by Tam Dalyell. He observed that I had 'made a first-rate debating speech … suffering from flu'. Either way I must have sounded an uncertain bet for conventional Conservatives.

In my last year, when I felt very much at home in Cambridge and in the Union, I acquired, at last, a girlfriend: Vuokko Liisa Lappalainen from the Davies Language School. I used to put her up in the Union gallery to watch all the drama and excitement and we would meet afterwards. My modest female social life did have a link with the Union.

It was wonderful work experience for an aspiring politician.

As a member of the Union you thought yourself omniscient, passing judgement on the rest of the world. It was an excellent club. The debating facilities were a foretaste of the House of Commons and it had quite a good library and squash courts where I played a great deal. A great feature was that the Union had permanent staff. Mr Elwood, who ran the place, had been in the Air Force during the war. His presence was the one element of stability, sanity and good sense amongst all these excitable young lads thinking they were just a touch away from the Cabinet.

Meanwhile I had never really prepared myself for the outside world. I so enjoyed Cambridge that I didn't much want to think further ahead. The 1950s was an age when you didn't really have a problem getting a job. Although an academic career was quite attractive, there were not that many places for post-graduate work. I was about ten years too soon. I had got a First, but when I did not get a double First I realised that a university career was not much of an option. I still hankered after a year or so of further academic study, thus postponing the day when I had to buckle down to a proper career. I thought that it would be nice to take a Master's degree at an American university, and I applied to several, including Cornell, where I was accepted. The difficulty then arose of finance. Again it was ten years before the public expansion of post-graduate education. The one fairly certain opportunity was to get a Rotary Scholarship. However, the Rotary Clubs took it in turns and it wasn't Bridgwater's year so all I got was a regretful letter of refusal.

In my trawl of overseas universities, I received a wide range of documents. I was offered an extension of my Jesus scholarship to study for a year in Bruges at a recently established institution called the Council of Europe College. Although I was fascinated by the idea of going to America and studying international relations, somehow I looked upon going to Bruges as merely a postponement of the real world so I turned it down. In retrospect I regret this decision. Spoken languages have never been my strong point and had I gone to Bruges there is the chance that I would have ended up learning tolerably good French.

The final exams hovered ever nearer. Although I had spent a good deal of time at the Union in my third year, I did not neglect my studies. I resumed lectures, at least for 'The Origins of the First World War', and did plenty of reading and attended my tutorials. I did not feel confident about getting a double First, and my uncertainty was justified. I got an Upper Second, which no more than matched my status as an open scholar. Matters were not improved by having a nose bleed during the examinations. I was disappointed not to end with a double First but I was not dejected or downcast. My studies, political activities and, latterly, even my social life had exceeded any expectations I had when I 'went up' in the autumn of 1950.

27

BIRMINGHAM

I decided not to pursue an academic career. Having sat my Finals, I tardily attended the University Appointments Board. Tentatively I asked them to put me on the job market. I also made enquiries on my own. This was not a success. I visited the West of England Engineering Employers, was instructed in the duties of managing the office stationery and was told the virtues of starting at the bottom. I was then turned down. The Reed Paper Group sounded better and my interviewer, the cricketer Mark Pawson, seemed a good deal more worldly than the Engineers of the West of England: again I was turned down.

Suitably chastened, I was invited to visit Birmingham to do a two-day group interview with Tube Investments. The invitation said the post would be in London. Actually it was in Birmingham. I am sure this was an honest mistake but the industrial austerity of Birmingham rather than the worldly life of London seemed like switch selling.

Eight of us were interviewed and two chosen, Michael Coleman Smith and me. Michael became a very good friend and later I introduced him to his wife. He was an excellent sportsman and had featured in *Wisden*. We were both employed by a marketing company, TI (Export) Ltd, but initially had to spend up to two years with companies that manufactured steel tubes.

My company was Tubes Ltd, whose factory was at Aston Cross, in the heart of Birmingham, sited adjacent to Ansells Brewery, the HP Sauce factory and a small manufacturer of glue. It was a far cry and smell from Cambridge or Somerset.

For a year I worked on the shop floor. At first I was a labourer; then I was in a team that forged the steel bar into a rough (or hollow) tube, and subsequently was in charge, although closely supervised, of a draw mill that produced the steel tube. It was an unknown world, acrid and exceptionally noisy. I worked in overalls but had one concession. I could use a junior canteen for lunch. I soon realised that Tubes Ltd had a hierarchy of canteens from the directors by degrees down to the shop floor operatives, with a special one for inspectors from the Royal Navy – invariably known as the 'Admir-ality'. I got used to the new world, but wondered where it would all lead.

Amidst the noise and seemingly endless days I would often think back upon Cambridge, the days of learning and student politics. I managed to conform to my new pattern of life but I did object to using a lavatory without a door handle. There was, of course, a loo hierarchy and I decided to risk using one with a handle. I had barely settled before the door was hammered by an angry employee, acting as a shop floor concierge, who bellowed, 'You're no bloody foreman.' My time as a trainee, little short of a year, also included a week on 'nights'. It was a different world, quieter, and with a workforce who positively preferred such strange hours.

The factory floor was a society as well as a workplace. I was fascinated by the extent of gambling. A foreman nominally regrinding the dies used for shaping the tubes was the shop floor's bookie. He had an assistant who trundled around the factory with a wheelbarrow carrying dies, but whose real task was to be a runner collecting bets. The bookie, whom I never patronised, was known as 'pudding', and his valuable activities were undermined when off-course betting was legalised.

Tubes Ltd was a non-union factory so I was deprived of the chance of becoming a bogus Tory trade unionist. My lasting memories of the shop floor and particularly the draw mill were ones of unrelenting noise.

Thursday was a break from my shop floor routine. I would spend the day at the technical college in Suffolk Street where I received some instruction in product control, economics and quality engineering. The course was dominated by Australians who were receiving apprenticeships from the General Electric Company. I learned very little but it made a welcome break not to be wearing overalls.

After a year on the shop floor I began work in the sales office of TI (Export) Ltd. The company handled the bulk of the export business of the twelve companies that comprised the Steel Tube Division. The offices were in John Bright Street, near New Street railway station and shortly to be demolished in the rebuilding of Birmingham city centre. The effective sales manager was Mr R. A. Grover, whose personal office was equipped with an amplifying machine into which he talked to the rest of us. It had a resonant boom, further complicated by the fact that Mr Grover talked to it without removing his pipe. I did not find much romance in being a trainee export salesman. There was no exotic travel; my only journeys were the daily suburban train trips from Wylde Green, Sutton Coldfield to Birmingham New Street. The route went through the industrial heartland, with the Erdington Coffin Manufacturers Company prominent on the skyline. It persists in my memory.

It was not difficult to master the art of quoting export prices. We all had barrel calculating machines which were hand manipulated. It was the age before the electronic calculator. TI (Export) was a friendly open-plan office and the sales staff, of whom there were about thirty, were divided into 'Europe' and 'The Rest of the World'. So I settled down to commercial life. It was monotonous and not well paid, but a good deal more congenial than the choking smoke and noise of the Aston tubemill. In 1957 the main board of TI, on the inspiration of the scientist Sir Ben Lockspeiser, a non-executive member, purchased an IBM 650 computer. It was to be used to assist in corporate planning. This was a pioneering development and reputed to be only the second such computer in the West Midlands, the other being with the General Electric Company.

Initially the machine was to be used to analyse the sales of the twelve companies in the steel tube division and to rationalise the manufacture and distribution of their various qualities of tubing. A small unit, rather grandly entitled the Economics and Statistics Office, was established under Kenneth Henderson. He had an economics degree which he constantly emphasised. I mainly recall his aversion to walking whenever he could summon a company car. It was the cause of ungenerous ribaldry. A 'Henderson' was the number of yards he would walk before summoning Tubes Ltd transport.

I was given the lordly task of collecting the punch cards from the twelve companies and handing them over to the engineers in charge of the computer. Unlike my sedentary life at TI Export this involved travel to Aberdare, Jarrow, Chesterfield and Sheffield. In addition I learned the back roads of the Black Country as I visited Oldbury, Halesowen, Wednesfield, Walsall and Wolverhampton. Each month I would hand over to Henderson the monthly analysis, which he then plotted against 'outside indicators', i.e. national statistics of bicycle, steel and general engineering output. There was little correlation. The work made only a negligible intellectual demand, but I spent

the lunch hour reading the *Financial Times*. This gave me a rudi-
mentary grasp of economics and some understanding of the
jargon used by the commentators. I also made friends with
the computer staff, including the programmers. They were
pioneers in a rapidly emerging profession.

My days with the Economics and Statistics Office were tolerably enjoyable but not really challenging. I knew I would have to
move on, but I decided to stay until I had fought Coventry East
in the general election. This was in October 1959. In March 1960
I was able to persuade the Economist Intelligence Unit that my
lunch time reading of the *Financial Times* might be put to better
use. I had been in Birmingham for six and a half years. It was a
long apprenticeship with little to show in executive progress, but
my political experiences and time spent in a provincial industrial
society were valuable. I had a slow start along the political path
but I suspect Birmingham and TI were better for me than the
London hothouse world of media and advertising.

I cannot pretend I had a wildly exciting social time in
Birmingham, but I had a very happy communal life in the
Midlands. I started with lodgings in Wylde Green, a suburb
of Sutton Coldfield, conveniently near the suburban railway
station. I had hardly been there for a few months before my close
Cambridge friend, Harry Hodgson, came to Birmingham, also
to work with Tube Investments. Together with Michael Coleman
Smith and Martin Morris, another TI graduate apprentice, we
rented a decaying Victorian house, 554 Chester Road. There
we lived, confined to the ground floor since the stairs were a
no-go area because of crumbling masonry. In the winter it was
so cold I used to line my blankets with newspaper. Actually I
enjoyed this communal living very much. The domestic learning
curve was steep. We acquired a pressure cooker. In my innocence
I tried to stew rhubarb and by the time I had discovered the

recommended cooking time, it had become atomised. The four
of us were bonded by our work and a feeling that we were intellectual immigrants in a materialist land.

Quite soon we moved to a spacious flat, coming to the end
of its lease, in the Hagley Road. We made new friends including Brian Haslett, who also worked for Tube Investments and
whom Harry, Michael and I had just missed at Cambridge.
When the Hagley Road lease ended we moved to the top floor
of 38 Clarendon Road, just in Edgbaston. The ground floor was
occupied by Maurice Culley, an accountant, and his wife Phyllis,
a paediatrician whose father farmed near Whitchurch, just
outside the Oswestry constituency. We had an active social life,
frequently entertaining, and we even had the services of a part-
time cook who otherwise worked for ICI.

As time proceeded I had an increasing number of political
commitments which I pursued single-mindedly. Also I began to
take an interest in classical music. A passing member of the flat,
David Younger, had an excellent collection of records, and the
Mozart Clarinet Quintet still haunts me. Years later I chose it
when asked to list my Desert Island Discs.

Whilst in Birmingham I became a fairly regular church-goer.
This was much due to Harry Hodgson, who was a High Anglican.
We attended St Jude's, soon to be destroyed in the rebuilding
of the city centre. In addition, Mark Thompson-McCausland,
also a passing member of 38 Clarendon Road, was a devout
Christian. He was eventually ordained, and used to take us to
Edgbaston Old Church for Wednesday morning communion,
which preceded breakfast at the vicarage. I once went on a weekend retreat at Mirfield. The silences, the prayers and the solitude
were impressive, and the visit did help me in wrestling with my
views on the British invasion of Suez.

This was a difficult period for me. I was opposed to the

invasion of Suez, but such a view was not held amongst the West Midland Tory activists. At a special meeting of the area council I was one of the two dissidents who voted against a congratulatory telegram to Sir Anthony Eden. The chairman sarcastically noted he could not send the missive 'unanimously' but only 'by acclamation'. The area council comprised those who would influence constituency selection committees. I was hardly promoting my career in being so openly critical of Suez. Happily it all died down, and when I was adopted by Coventry East my Suez behaviour was viewed with curiosity rather than hostility.

Harry Hodgson and I both played cricket for Tubes Ltd in the Birmingham Business League. Harry was a highly competent all-rounder: I was a rabbit, but much enjoyed spending Saturday afternoons playing rather keen cricket where winning was the objective. Two West Indians, recent immigrants now working at Tubes Ltd, joined the team. They were welcome additions to the side but I remember some unease in the team: 'It's all right now but there would be trouble if they became foremen.' At that stage – 1955 – it was inconceivable how immigration would change the character of Birmingham.

At this time I was strapped for money. My salary was modest but I was determined to live within it so there was not much cash for holidays. In 1956 I decided to try a cheap vacation. I wrote to the *Daily Worker*, as the paper was then called, and asked if I could visit a youth camp to 'learn about a people's democracy'. That was a good ploy. I was given free admission to a rally organised by the World Federation of Democratic Youth at Peshtera in Bulgaria. I then sold the story of my intended trip to the *Birmingham Evening Mail*, which paid for my rail fare. The newspaper heading CITY TORY PIERCES IRON CURTAIN resulted in a visit from an unassuming man, suitably dressed in a mackintosh, who enquired if I would report back on my visit noting any badges or designations worn by the Bulgarian or Soviet military. I agreed and decided I had scrounged enough and did not suggest a fee.

The camp was fascinating. It was badly organised and the food and drink ran out. I must have been an obvious misfit: I was approached by several vocal Bulgarian dissidents who told me that the camp was a great hoodwink. One had a powerful phrase: 'You want eyes like the searchlights on a British destroyer.' The return journey, on the route of the Tauern Express, was a disaster. The train broke down at Niš. Eventually we reached Belgrade, having missed connections. I planned to sleep in the station with the impoverished locals. However, I was moved on and had to sleep in the park. I reached Birmingham a day late with a watermelon which I donated to the Edgbaston vicarage. My TI boss, Mr Richard Young, reproached me for having over-stayed my holiday; I don't think he would have been mollified by the melon.

My visit to Bulgaria preceded by a few months the Soviet invasion of Hungary. I was incensed by this and did an open-air meeting with Denis Howell, then Labour MP for All Saints, when we called for the release of the Hungarian patriots Imre Nagy and Pál Maléter.

My Birmingham years added to my political apprenticeship. I started with the Sutton Coldfield Young Conservatives and I soon became treasurer. It was not a great test, and the incident I most remember concerned the local MP, Sir John Mellor. He had been critical of the Conservative leadership and an Association meeting was summoned to 'clear the air'. Sir John defended his views with little sign of contrition. He was undercut by the simplicity of an ageing blue rinse. 'Sir John, we love you,' she quavered, 'but we love Sir Winston even more.' Sir John did not stand at the subsequent general election.

In the early 1950s a number of graduates, foremost of which was Alan Bennett, a lecturer, formed the Birmingham Bow Group. I was an early member. We were modest in numbers but hardworking. With true Midlands insularity we insisted upon being the Birmingham Bow Group and not the Birmingham branch of the Bow Group. Our prestigious London colleagues patiently and reluctantly accepted our self-proclaimed status. Our numbers included Anthea Collins, who became a recognised university authority on geriatric care. We produced a pamphlet on graduates in industry.

The Birmingham Bow Group was a far cry from the Joseph Chamberlain caucus that had converted the city from Liberalism to Unionism in the 1880s. I encountered the successor party organisation, located in Empire House, in the 1955 general election. For the newly created All Saints division the Tories had adopted Julian Williams, whom I had known as president of the Cambridge Union. Williams arrived in Birmingham from the family estate in Cornwall and was pleased to add me to his campaign team. He was a man of great charm and enthused his band of Brummagem activists. All Saints was a predominantly working-class constituency and the Labour candidate was Denis Howell, later to be 'Minister for Rain' in the drought year of 1976. Howell was a good local candidate and to the right in Labour politics. He won by 1,307 votes and I was sorry that Julian left the national political arena. He became a respected public figure in Cornwall, living in Caerhays Castle and its beautiful gardens.

I enjoyed Birmingham politics but it was not for the faint hearted. Once Julian was confronted with a dubious political tactic. Taken aback, he demurred: 'Heavens, man, you can always apologise afterwards' was the reply. The All Saints division included the old Birmingham West constituency, which had been represented by Joseph Chamberlain 1876–1914. It still had a somewhat run-down working men's Conservative Club, which contained a magnificent throne-like chair. In a whispered voice I was told, 'That's where Mr Joseph sat.' The dramas of home rule and tariff reform still seemed to haunt the place.

When the election was over Julian Williams urged me to get on the candidates' list. It seemed a long shot but the treasurership of the Sutton Coldfield Conservatives had lost its appeal some time ago. I made my application to Central Office for inclusion on the candidates' list. My referees were Gerald Wills, the MP for Bridgwater, Sir Dirom Crawford, a senior Tory from Somerset, and Father Bubb, the priest of my Anglican church in Wylde Green. I do not know why I decided to include the Church, and I had no idea of Father Bubb's politics; perhaps instinctively I was assuring Central Office, forty years ahead of time, that there would be no sleaze.

I was interviewed by Donald Kaberry MP, a vice-chairman of the party and every inch a Yorkshireman. 'I see, Mr Biffen, you don't expect a winnable seat. I like a realist.' The hurdle of inclusion in the selection list being overcome, I was delighted to find myself selected shortly afterwards. I benefited from working in Birmingham. The Midlands had plenty of Labour seats suitable for a Tory trial run for Parliament. I would have had more difficulty had I been working in London where I would have been competing with metropolitan barristers, advertising executives and City accountants. The Coventry East Conservatives chose me from a shortlist of three, the others being a local councillor and an Ulster Presbyterian minister. It says much for the 1950s that I was selected without any enquiry: 'How might your wife help you?' Her existence, like a clean driving licence, was assumed. At my first meeting I was greeted with a huge bouquet of flowers, which given her non-existence had to be passed on to the Association chairman's wife.

I enjoyed Coventry. The seat was a Labour stronghold, represented by Richard Crossman. He was much disliked by Tory
Party workers. His Winchester and Oxford credentials did not
appeal: they felt he was a traitor to his class. I was fearful of his
formidable reputation. However, he spent the entire election in
London, where he was involved in Labour's national campaign.
I travelled around the constituency with a loudspeaker, proclaiming, 'Richard Crossman is an intellectual, but you can vote for
John Biffen.' It pleased my supporters but was a meaningless
slogan. I nursed Coventry assiduously. Most evenings I would
finish work in Aston and drive straight across to Coventry and
attend party meetings or go canvassing. My Association chairman, John Henderson, was an executive with an engineering
company. He was an excellent colleague and we talked the same
language. Throughout 1958 I built up a good relationship with
the local Association. Politics was quite sharp in Coventry, particularly at local level where the Labour Party was left inclined. I
think the Tories reacted by becoming further right. In such a
polarised situation there was some bewilderment when it was
discovered that the Industrial Chaplain Simon Phipps, a friend
of Princess Margaret, was a socialist.

I learned a good deal from my Coventry experience. I did the
usual tasks: factory gate meetings, talks to special interest groups
and pensioners and a good deal of door-to-door canvassing. It took
up a vast amount of time, which I did not begrudge. The election
result, always a foregone conclusion, was a mild disappointment.
Substantial council house-building resulted in an increase in
Richard Crossman's majority. The West Midlands Conservatives'
Central Office agent, Jack Galloway, had noted the enthusiasm
and – I suppose – the maturity with which I had campaigned. He
passed on the message to the Oswestry Conservatives when they
had to choose a by-election candidate in July 1961.

The 1959 general election concluded, I now set about finding a new job. I made an abortive attempt to join GKN and a Devon ball clay manufacturer, but by April 1960 I was in London and working for the Economist Intelligence Unit. Brian Walden, writing in *Now!* magazine in 1980, observed that 'he went to Birmingham. It was the wisest thing he ever did… In no time at all Biffen was sharing a flat with three other young men and the females were coming round in droves to their frequent parties. It did him a world of good.' I don't recall the regiment of women, but it was a wise decision.

Birmingham had been a long apprenticeship. I certainly benefited from the shop floor experience, had enjoyed bachelor communal living and had ended with a good political reputation in Coventry.

28

OSWESTRY: GETTING THERE AND ADOPTION

Adoption for Parliament is a random and capricious business. I was extraordinarily lucky. I left Coventry with the reputation of being a conscientious campaigner who worked well with the party enthusiasts. No one much cared that my opponent, Richard Crossman, had increased the Labour majority.

Meanwhile, in April 1960, I left Tube Investments and Birmingham and joined the Economist Intelligence Unit (EIU) and started working under the shadow of St James's Palace. The contrast was startling. My work, mostly overseas investment analysis, was highly political and light years from the industrial practices of Birmingham and the Black Country. My immediate boss was Tom McKitterick. He had twice stood for Parliament as a Labour candidate and was a strong Gaitskellite. He had maintained a keen interest in politics and in his spare time edited the *Political Quarterly*. I contributed an article, keeping to the anodyne topic of election statistics. The whole atmosphere at the EIU was informal and friendly. 'A home for failed academics,' acidly observed one of my friends. That was unfair; the managers, Geoffrey Brown and Bill Mills, made it a commercial success, although it paid poorly.

Once settled in the EIU I joined the Bow Group, a rather self-conscious organisation of Conservative graduates of liberal

leanings, particularly on colonial matters. I had been a founder
member of the Birmingham Bow Group, which had had a very
junior and acrimonious relationship with London. The parent
group had been established in the early 1950s. It made an impact
by the quality of its membership and its research. James Lemkin,
an early chairman of the Bow Group, produced the pamphlet
Coloured People in Britain, which was a pioneering work. Geoffrey
Howe in particular had distinguished himself as a politician/
lawyer and was already being tipped as a future law officer. I knew
many members from my university days and soon became librar-
ian in charge of publication of pamphlets written by members.
I managed to block every proposed pamphlet that came before
me as I felt the group, because of its growing reputation, was
in danger of diluting the high standards that had been set by
Geoffrey and the early pioneers. I was well positioned to become
chairman but I resigned from the committee when I became
an MP.

Meanwhile at the EIU I did not think seriously about
membership of the Commons. Of course my name was kept on
the Central Office list. But I did not realise the extent to which
I had earned the approval of the West Midlands chief agent,
Jack Galloway, who had been impressed by my showing at the
Coventry contest. I had received a couple of invitations from
constituencies to put forward my name for Labour-held seats
including Northampton; however, I decided it was too early in
the parliament to be tied to a marginal: something better might
turn up.

In June 1961 I was surprised and astonished to receive an invitation to meet the Oswestry constituency selection committee for
the pending by-election caused by the MP, David Ormsby-Gore,
becoming ambassador to Washington. His close family relationship with President Kennedy made it a classic appointment. I

duly took a day off work and travelled to the market town of Whitchurch, where I met the constituency executive committee in an upstairs room in the Victoria Hotel. I cannot recall any points made during the interview but I felt numb and fumbled my answers. Shortly thereafter I received the usual polite letter of rejection. Mentally I shrugged my shoulders and turned to my work on electronic component investments in Catalonia.

A few days later a telephone call transformed the situation. The most favoured candidate chosen by the committee had withdrawn. A new shortlist was compiled including the two runners-up at the Whitchurch interview. It seems that my performance was not as bad as I feared but I still felt the odds against me were overwhelming. Also the final selection clashed with the annual Bow Group ball. The matter was resolved over the telephone and my pathetic reason for declining the interview was overruled by the constituency agent. He was a dour Scot who was appalled that a serious prospective politician should walk away from such a challenge because of two Bow Group ball tickets. He was right. I told my partner, a Virginian banker's daughter, Robin Ould, that I was standing her up and that she should use the tickets. In my place she invited Anthony Wood, a young diplomat. He married Sarah Drew, whom I subsequently met and married after their divorce. It was an extraordinary coincidence.

On the fateful evening of the Bow Group ball I took a train from Paddington to Market Drayton and met the final selection committee, now a hundred strong, in an upstairs room at the Corbet Arms. There were four candidates. Major Mowat was the constituency chairman and came from Ellesmere. He was a kindly traditional squire. Colonel Grubb came from near Whitchurch and was with the Country Landowners Association. These two had been on the original shortlist. This had been expanded to include the 'runners-up' at the Whitchurch meeting,

Major Friend and myself. Jummy Friend came from the Market Drayton area and had been active in politics. Decidedly right wing, he was rumoured to be sympathetic to the League of Empire Loyalists. Although I was pitted against three local candidates the constituency was by no means at one. Later I was to discover that Oswestry regarded Market Drayton as outer Siberia and that there was no bond between Ellesmere and Whitchurch. The selection was by single transferable vote and the supporters of the three local candidates overwhelmingly gave me their second preferences. The committee members voted first for their pledged local grandee and secondly for my speech. I pipped Major Jummy Friend by two votes. Years later I met Jummy, who had retired to Jersey and was a friend and neighbour of my father-in-law. He was splendidly robust on the issues of Europe, had fought bravely in the war and was a great raconteur. He would have been a good companion in the smoking room but a nightmare for the whips.

At the meeting I think my natural diffidence was overcome by anger at missing the ball. I radiated self-confidence and gave a forthright and assertive speech about the Common Market. Ironically in the light of my later views, in the summer of 1961, influenced by my work at the EIU, I was much in favour of membership. The committee had no settled views on the topic but were obviously pleased to have a potential candidate who did.

My commitment to the Common Market was better known in London and the Bow Group. One letter I still treasure was from Kenneth Baker, later to be a Thatcher Cabinet minister and chairman of the party. 'For a European to get an agricultural constituency at the moment is almost miraculous,' he enthused. 'I can only assume that your experience as an interviewer for the Bow Group membership committee revealed to you the inexplicable workings of the minds of the adoption committee.'

In my moment of unexpected victory I telephoned my parents. Frustratingly they were out and I had to leave a message with Wiggy, our farm worker, at Putnell Farm. I also telephoned Robin at the Hurlingham Club; she was over the moon.

My selection caused a mild ripple in the political world. There were some wry comments that a Tory heartland seat should choose a National Service lance corporal when there were field officers available. That I was young, then aged thirty, and a Bow Group liberal was also noted. The selection committee were typical of Conservative activists. They were middle class, leaders in their community and traditional in their social attitudes. Only a minority had clear views on political issues. Julian Critchley described the event in an article titled 'Government by Greengrocer'. My main weakness in the eyes of the selection committee was the doubt as to whether I really came from the countryside and had rural instincts. That was of much more concern than the Common Market or Selwyn Lloyd's 'pay pause' (a six-month wages freeze).

The ecstasy of triumph was quickly replaced by apprehension. My description as a farmer's son (presumably with a working knowledge of the hill cow subsidy) was challenged. 'A London journalist' was the pejorative description. Supporters of Major Friend were mainly responsible for this and with such a narrow defeat I can hardly blame them. The chairman of the constituency Conservative Women took up the cudgels on my behalf. Maisie King Hay was originally from Donegal but left the country after 1922. She had endless enthusiasm and added me to the cause of Ulster. All this I witnessed from London, bewildered and apprehensive.

Once again Jack Galloway, the area agent, was the shrewd support. 'Are your folks still around? You'd better get them.' My parents were summoned for a constituency meeting which was technically to confirm the selection, but in reality was 'a chance for second thoughts'. My father played a magnificent role. Heavily built with a strong Somerset accent, he looked and sounded the part. His hallmark was a broad-brimmed felt hat sporting a pheasant's feather. He never altered his style and years later the hat particularly fascinated my young stepson, who claimed it on his death. My 'confirmation' was carried with a score of dissentients.

Next morning my father went round the Oswestry fat stock market displaying his omniscience on the pig, sheep and dairy trades and standing his round at the Golden Tankard. The Smithfield view was that the 'governor's a better bet than the lad'. Thereafter I kept my father far away in Somerset as a strategic reserve.

From late July until early November I had the tedious task of nursing the constituency. The decision to delay holding the by-election confirmed my belief that Conservative Central Office (Jack Galloway apart) lived in a distant planet. The three months after my selection saw increasing government unpopularity.

One decision, again by Jack Galloway, struck me as generous and enlightened. He called me to his office and said, 'Those Oswestry folk are rather grand, they will expect you to travel first class and stay in the Wynnstay' (a Trust House hotel and clearly the best in Oswestry). 'Do that and let me have the account.' It was a sensible judgement. The press made much of my grammar school background, which was almost unique for a seat which traditionally had provided a Commons berth for knights of the shire. It was best I should play my new role properly and not be confused with that of an impecunious journalist.

I still recall the summer of 1961. Every Friday I would leave the EIU and grandly travel first class to Gobowen, a village station near Oswestry. There I would painstakingly thread my way around villages and market towns with such magical names as Woore, Cockshut, Edstaston and Llanyblodwel. I yearned for the by-election and success, but wondered if Selwyn Lloyd and his wretched 'pay pause' would frustrate my goal.

29

OSWESTRY ELECTION

In the mid-1950s I had been asked to apply as a candidate for Stoke-on-Trent Central. The name had no romance – 'sounds like a signal box', said a member of the Birmingham bachelor flat I shared. Coventry East was better, but even that was an urban abstraction. Oswestry, by contrast, was magic. I had dropped back into my rural childhood.

Shropshire had a historic manufacturing area which had cradled the Industrial Revolution and looked towards Wolverhampton and the Black Country. The rest of the county was predominantly rural and stock-rearing. The 1832 Reform Bill had given the boroughs of Shrewsbury and Wenlock each two seats and the remainder of the county was divided into two seats, northern and southern, each with two members. In 1884 Gladstone gave the vote to rural workers and increased the number of country constituencies.

Oswestry became a single seat and its initial electorate was just over ten thousand, of whom 84.5 per cent voted in 1885. There was a further redistribution in 1918 and this added the townships of Whitchurch, Market Drayton and Wem to that of Oswestry. This was the constituency I inherited. It continued to be called Oswestry until 1983, when it was converted into North Shropshire, a triumph of geographic correctness.

The constituency had a strong Welsh presence along the county border and Oswestry, particularly on market day, was bilingual. I was given sensible advice by one of my Central Office minders who warned me not to refer to 'English' but always to say 'British'.

Rural Shropshire had a rather passive record of political commitment. The Conservative Party dominated the area and the big families dominated the Conservative Party. The Liberals snatched Oswestry in a by-election in 1904 but barely a year later it returned to the Conservative candidate, Mr Willie Bridgeman, notwithstanding the Liberal general election landslide. As late as the 1935 general election the Conservatives were returned unopposed. In normal political times the seat would be regarded as natural Tory territory. July to November 1961 were not normal months, as well I knew.

After a decade of power the Tory team, and especially Macmillan, were beginning to look tired. Oswestry was not a natural target for Peter Cook's satire but it made some impact. The 'pay pause' was not much understood but clearly economic management had faltered after the Macmillan dominance at the 1959 general election. Above all at by-elections voting Liberal was considered a natural way of giving a complacent government a necessary prod. There had been signs of this at the Ludlow by-election a year earlier. I did not approach the Oswestry by-election with unshakeable confidence, but I did not consider defeat likely.

The Labour Party had never been well established although Oswestry, the centre of the Cambrian Railways, had provided a railway workers vote. In 1961 we still used local rather than national political colours. Labour was green, confirming the influence of the farm workers' union, Liberals were red, and locally, as well as nationally, the Conservatives were blue.

Transport House, doubtless with Hugh Gaitskell's connivance, parachuted a brilliant candidate, Brian Walden, into the constituency. He was a first-class speaker and combined this skill with an easy manner and the shrewd use of populism.

In my view the problems of rural poverty and resentment against the landed wealthy could give Labour a good vote if they had organisation and a charismatic candidate. Even so I feared the Liberal more than I did Walden. They had a growing organisation and, after standing aside for three general elections, had re-entered the fray in 1959. Their candidate, John Buchanan, was a *Sunday Express* journalist. He had none of the panache of Brian Walden, but he was personable and likely to pick up Tory protesters.

There were plenty of protest topics ranging from NHS contracts for chemists to rural services. Some villages still did not have electricity and the Oswestry rural district had a declining population.

Finally John Dayton, a building contractor, arrived with a decorated double-decker bus proclaiming the ills of the Common Market. As the Patriotic Front candidate he livened up affairs and I gloomily concluded it could be at my expense. It was extraordinary that no newspaper commissioned a poll of the by-election. It would have shown a drop in Tory support and encouraged latent protesters to support the Liberals. Mercifully the election in November 1961 was a few months ahead of the dramatic Liberal victory at Orpington. That created a new political climate and I doubt if I could have held Oswestry in those circumstances.

Throughout the campaign I had the good fortune to stay with Ken and Florence Walmsley in Trefonen at their lovely seventeenth-century house, The Pentre. Florence was very other-worldly. She dismissed the media with an off-hand 'John Biffen can't see you, he's far too busy'.

My Central Office minders, four constituency agents seconded for the campaign, were helpful and our organisation was well ahead of our rivals. The campaign was based on village evening meetings, usually three per night, each lasting thirty to forty-five minutes including time for questions. This resulted in near on fifty such meetings. I was reasonably competent in my speeches, which were mainly devoted to rural topics, and enjoyed dealing with questions. We had a number of morning press conferences but the by-election was largely neglected by the national press. The local press and particularly the *Border Counties Advertiser*, Oswestry based and Liberal leaning, provided generous and factual coverage. The almost statutory meeting with the NFU was a relatively tame affair. I suspect Dayton made the biggest hit. On entering the NFU office, apparently he tossed his checked flat cap aside and, ignoring deficiency payments and lime subsidies, and referring to me and my two rivals, said, 'What do you want with three kids who know damn all about life?'

My minders had arranged public meetings to be addressed by national figures including Reginald Maudling, then Secretary of State for the Colonies, who gently harangued the electors of Wem. I asked if I could have a meeting for Enoch Powell. 'Oh not really,' said the minder, 'no one would understand him.' The campaign was lengthy but well mannered. Only the speech of Nicholas Ridley left a mild imprint. He made a risqué joke about a girl, her father and a bull. The blue rinses were unsettled but most of us were vastly amused. The master plan of my minders was to flood the constituency overnight with large posters. These were backed by reinforced cardboard and nailed to posts. They showed a nervous but smiling Biffen. They immediately disappeared from the hedgerows and reappeared as home-made livestock pens.

The by-election was the only occasion on which I was asked to dress down. I thought my working London suit was drab enough but I was instructed to wear a 'rat catcher' jacket.

It was a gloomy autumn made even more sombre by the Russians building the Berlin Wall. This serious development probably helped check the flow of protest votes. *The Times* reported the by-election on 3 November under the heading 'TV helps bring crisis home to Oswestry. Questioners are sometimes better briefed than candidate'. The subsequent text refers to how 'Mr Biffen is beginning to show signs of strain as he nears the end of his programme of fifty meetings'. How true.

The campaign closed on a lively note. My supporting speaker on the eve of the poll meeting was Ted Leather, the MP for North Somerset and a good knockabout performer. There was an audience of about 500 and the *Border Counties Advertiser* reported that 'parts of Mr Ted Leather's speech were virtually drowned by hecklers'. After growing tiredness I seem to have had a final spell of vigour, mainly directed at the Patriotic Front supporters, whom I described as 'a gay cavalier band of backward looking, emotional people'.

I was content with the campaign view of Duart Farquharson of the *Winnipeg Free Press*, who accompanied me on a day's canvassing. 'Like Canadian voters, the good folk of Oswestry contrive to give the impression of political apathy,' he wrote but conceded that the wider world, the Common Market and the Berlin Wall were making an impact. Farquharson flattered Brian Walden and me by observing, 'It is the quality of the contestants in this by-election which most strike the Canadian observer.' He had decided after a day's canvassing with me, that I was 'no airy intellectual or any sort of self-regarding superior'. I imagine an episode in Whitchurch confirmed his opinion: 'Canvassing in a working class district he roars with laughter on learning that the pretty young woman whose vote he has been courting is only sixteen. (Mr Biffen, unlike Mr Walden, is a bachelor.)'

The campaign, apart from the tearing down of posters and eve of poll excitement, was quiet and good natured. Old hands remembered nostalgically the elections a generation or two ago.

In measured style and political courtesy Walden and I were look-alikes at the count. Whilst our supporters kept to themselves in the Territorial Hall at Oswestry, we pursued a developing friendship over cribbage. The local paper decided this must be chess given our presumed intellect. The result reflected growing Tory unease, an accelerating Liberal revival and Walden's ability to hold together the Labour vote. A civic dignitary intoned from the steps of the Territorial Hall:

Biffen 12,428
Buchanan 8,647
Walden 8,519
Majority 3,781

It was not a good result but I put on a reasonable face for the *Border Counties Advertiser*. I told them my majority was higher than my own forecast in the office sweep and I had ten shillings on that, so you see I'm perfectly sincere about this. Well, almost.

My parents came up from Somerset for the count. In the moment of drama I valued their support. They embraced me and packed me off to the Commons as though I was attending a new school.

30

PROFUMO AND MY MAIDEN SPEECH

The drama of the by-election was speedily followed by my introduction to the Commons as Member for Oswestry. Sir Gerald Wills, who had been MP for my home constituency of Bridgwater since 1950, kindly hosted a lunch for my parents in the Commons on the day of my introduction. They then took their seats in the gallery for the modest theatre of my introduction. I was flanked by the Chief Whip, Martin Redmayne, and Gerald Wills. Together we marched from the bar of the House to the Speaker, breaking step for a reverential bow of the head en route. I had waited patiently with my sponsors until the Speaker had finished Parliamentary Questions and a private notice question on the East Goodwin lightship. The time seemed interminable, but, after the Speaker's welcoming handshake, I disappeared into the labyrinth of corridors and rooms behind his chair.

My early days in the Commons were a fearful challenge. As a by-election victor I was very much on my own. There was no 'group baptism' as there would have been for new Members after a general election. The Whips' Office seemed strangely remote, but I soon got the message, literally, as to when and where to vote. For the first couple of weeks I sat at the very back of the Commons chamber from where one could spectate but not

actually take part in the proceedings. It was as if I had a recru-
descence of schoolboy nerves. Soon I began to settle down. I
reached the Commons just before the reforms to improve MPs'
facilities that came after the 1964 general election. My secretary,
Mary Rose, called by twice a week. I had no desk or telephone
but I did have a numbered locker similar to the one in which I
kept my rugby kit at Dr Morgan's School. I also was assigned the
traditional peg and loop on which former members had hung
their swords. I used it to hang my coat. Mary Rose, who also
worked for Hugh Fraser, MP for Stafford and a political neighbour, was a splendid guide. She had a comprehensive knowledge
of Parliament and was engagingly cynical about politics.

I made friends with Julian Critchley, then MP for Aldershot.
We had met at gatherings of university Conservatives. He was
even then witty and irreverent. He was a valuable contact who
was able to answer questions such as what kind of expenses one
could claim. He was a lodger for a while in Netherton Grove
where I lived in a four-bachelor household as he disengaged
from his first marriage. I much enjoyed his friendship over three
decades despite the chasm between our political beliefs which
widened as Europe began to dominate domestic politics.

I had lived at Netherton Grove since I moved to London, joining Brian Haslett, who had also worked for Tube Investments.
We had the inevitable turnover of young business executives. It
was not a very political household but some were members of
the Bow Group. Nigel Vinson was an entrepreneur from Surrey
and had an occasional bed – three legs and a biscuit tin. He
made his fortune in plastic coatings and became a life peer and
strong supporter of Keith Joseph.

My early acquaintances tended to be MPs who had been
in the Bow Group and were in their early thirties: Tony Buck,
Richard Hornby and David Walder. The media occasionally

would select us as a kind of 'liberal avant garde', especially on issues like Rhodesia. It was flattering to have even modest press notice.

My first experience of parliamentary drudgery was to be selected for the standing committee of the Transport Bill. This provided the legal framework for the Beeching railway plan and a ragbag of other transport measures. Ernest Marples was the minister in charge but the leg work was done patiently by his junior minister, John Hay, in impressive style. The Bill was complex and lengthy but did not qualify for a guillotine. Three Labour ex-railwaymen MPs, Charles Mapp, Archie Manuel and Thomas Steele, talked ad nauseam. The hours sped by and the daily sittings got longer. I sat at the back working on a paper on the Congo for the Economist Intelligence Unit, hoping this moonlighting would not be spotted by the chairman. I never opened my mouth.

There was hardly any light relief but I recall that the inland waterways section of the Bill was not as ponderous as the railways. The champion of inland waterways was Wing Commander Grant Ferris, the MP for Nantwich and my immediate neighbour. He endeared himself to me, on arrival, by putting his arm around my shoulders and saying, 'Biff, old boy, don't visit the constituency too often.' I nodded and neglected his advice. He was always impeccably dressed, immensely courteous and self-important. As he rose to promote the waterways interest, the Labour benches would shout 'Come on, Admiral' or 'Here's Nelson'. It was an early occasion when my heart warmed to my opponents.

If the Transport Bill was the tedium of Westminster life the 'Profumo Affair', which followed shortly thereafter, was high drama.

I was effectively a cheerful prisoner of the Commons. I had no family life. My bachelor existence in Fulham was spartan and hence I spent my days and most evenings at Westminster. In these circumstances I find it extraordinary that I did not hear the whispers that linked the name of John Profumo, then Secretary of State for War, with Stephen Ward, Christine Keeler, Mandy Rice-Davies and Ivanov, the Russian embassy official. One evening the story was blown in a late-night Commons debate by such shrewd and forceful parliamentarians as Richard Crossman and Barbara Castle.

My innocence was shattered by Anthony Howard, then lobby correspondent for the *New Statesman*, who seemed to know all about it. Howard had a ready wit and a partisanship which frequently dipped his pen in acid where Tory ministers were concerned. He became one of the most gifted political commentators and his biography of R. A. Butler was an outstanding portrait of the Tory statesman. On this occasion the vitriol was laid aside. I reflected on the dire warnings of Tony Howard. I simply could not believe them. Unbeknown to me the Crossman–Castle accusation in debate had provoked a hurried midnight meeting of Profumo, Bill Deedes (Cabinet minister in charge of government public relations) and Iain Macleod, Leader of the House. They agreed on a statement to be given to the Commons next morning denying the accusations concerning Profumo's relationship with Christine Keeler. The annunciators read 'Secretary of State for War: A personal statement'. I was in my place in a House unusually well attended for a Friday morning. Profumo made a brief statement conclusively denying all.

I was delighted and wholly convinced. Immediately I went to the members' lobby where I met Anthony Howard. 'There,' I said with a touch of triumph. 'How about that.' Howard just shook his head and of course the last word was with him.

The Commons then went into recess and I did some company visiting for Grieveson Grant, the stockbrokers for whom I worked part time. In a Yorkshire hotel I heard the unwelcome bombshell that Profumo had misled the House. Although I was barely a parliamentary apprentice I realised the incident could detonate the government. I told Grieveson Grant to mark the reaction of Enoch Powell, as I thought he could be the austere moralist who might leave the government if he concluded there had been a cover up, and certainly he was no friend of Macmillan. Meanwhile, the story having broken, the media was now able to make the most of a drama involving sex, espionage and high politics.

I returned from the recess for a debate upon the 'Profumo Affair', which remains, over my thirty-six years in the Commons, the most memorable. In the late morning there had been an acrimonious meeting of the 1922 Committee of Conservative backbenchers. They wanted to put bluntly and privately what they would not say publicly. There had been a culpable cock-up. It was clear that a minority were not so much in a mood for closing ranks as for weakening the position of Macmillan. After the meeting I took my seat and did not leave the chamber during the six-hour debate. The Prime Minister was tired but dignified. I felt sympathy for him but his demeanour encouraged those who wanted a younger leader – chosen from the One Nation brigade which included Heath, Macleod and Maudling, and of course their mentor Butler. Harold Wilson was masterly. He was quietly analytical, wisely not moralising, but laying bare the mechanism of a government that – after more than a decade of power – was running out of steam. His peroration was a well-judged call for a new start and by implication an election. As the debate proceeded I moved my seat to the far end of the chamber opposite the Speaker; I wanted to watch the debate from the front row of the stalls. It was from here I saw the Nigel Birch speech. Technically it was superb. He and Powell had resigned from the Treasury in January 1958, Macmillan referring to their departure as a 'little local difficulty'. The estrangement, to put it mildly, was both political and personal.

Birch had a laconic speaking style. His poor sight meant that he spoke without notes and with effective brevity. I am told he kept a pad by his bedside on which he wrote down striking phrases for use in speeches. They were to come into their own on this occasion. With a mordant sarcastic wit he dealt with Lord Hailsham, Harold Wilson and *The Observer* and then concentrated on the requirement for Macmillan to retire. He concluded with the need for a younger man and a quote from Wordsworth: 'never glad confident morning again'. It was truly a hatchet job and the very force of it left the House stunned. He sat down amidst token applause.

Macmillan survived the Profumo debate, but the months afterwards were not happy for the Conservative Party. I attended debates, spoke at party meetings and was zealous in my visits to Oswestry. The fact that I had not made my maiden speech did concern me as – in my mind – it had become a lion in the path. Julian Critchley would advise me that it was a great opportunity, 'being called early – just like a Privy Counsellor'. I would have settled for an empty House. 'Crossbencher' in the *Sunday Express* then derided me as holding back until I deemed there was a sufficiently major occasion worthy of my oratory.

I had been in the House for eight months when I did speak. The Conservatives were struggling to regain popularity and Macmillan resolved to have a Cabinet reshuffle. It was not a modest shifting of the furniture; the removers had been called in. The centrepiece of the change was the replacement of Selwyn Lloyd as Chancellor of the Exchequer by Reginald Maudling. The political world was numbed by the scale of the changes, not least those who thought the Prime Minister needed changing as much as his team. The opposition forced a debate on the reshuffle and I felt I had to speak since my continued silence was becoming an embarrassment.

The occasion is still vivid in my mind. I sat tense on my perch on the rear bench clasping a small sheaf of handwritten notes. I did not realise that the rear bench was about the worst place from which to speak because of the acoustics. My speech was just about audible and was reconstructed – doubtless to my advantage – by the editors of Hansard. It was not a serious factor but I learned from it and never again sat on the rear bench in subsequent parliaments.

I was called after Emanuel Shinwell and before Jo Grimond. In the light of my subsequent politics my maiden speech was decidedly misleading. I championed a policy of income restraint – which I was vigorously denouncing by the next parliament. I spoke of the sacked Chancellor with affection and this pleased Nigel Birch. I also welcomed Christopher Chataway, who had just been made junior minister at Education, and was a Bow Grouper. Thus I nodded to the right and left. I made a brief and kindly comment on Europe. I also made the customary references to my predecessor, by then knighted as Sir David Ormsby-Gore, and to the Oswestry constituency. The speech lasted eighteen minutes. It was not innovative or radical but I think it was a success. The Commons is always exceptionally flattering on these occasions, but I think some of the bouquets I received were genuine. If the media took any note it was to remark that I was a Bow Grouper mildly left of centre and a pro-Common Market Tory who would fit into the post-Macmillan era. I fear I may have deceived them, but the thrust of my remarks reflected views I had acquired at the Economist Intelligence Unit. They did not bear the imprint of my admiration for Enoch Powell and the growing scepticism I had for government and Europe. I was still a Tory planner – just.

More immediately after I had made the speech I reclined on

the bench, mainly relieved that I had not swallowed words or phrases in a nervous spasm. Geoffrey Johnson-Smith slid alongside me: 'Well done. I bet you could do with a drink.' I had never heard a better speech.

Fairly soon after I passed two further milestones. I was invited by the Whips' Office to become a parliamentary private secretary (PPS). The post enabled you to work closely for a minister; the work was fairly modest and sometimes derided as 'bag-carrying'. You were expected always to support the government and certainly it was a rung in the climb to office. It was suggested I should be PPS to the Home Secretary, Henry Brooke. I now realise it was an offer of substance but I had no hesitation in turning it down as I needed a second income and did not want to be deflected from my work at Grieveson Grant where I had started as a member of their Research Desk. To the world at Westminster my priorities seemed curious but it demonstrated I was more committed to being an MP than an aspiring minister. Shortly afterwards I was asked personally by Robert Carr, Minister for Overseas Development, to be his PPS, but my answer was the same.

The second milestone was parliamentary rebellion. The issue was arcane, namely the extradition of Chief Enahoro to his Nigerian homeland under the provision of the Empire Fugitive Offenders Act. It was an unhappy situation for the Home Secretary, who felt, whatever his views, that he was clearly obliged by law to honour the request of the Nigerian government. As a backbencher I was free to make my own judgement on the quality of justice in Lagos, which I assumed was suspect. I decided to abstain when Labour challenged Brooke's decision. I was encouraged by the company of Ian Gilmour. We repaired to the smoking room, toasted our independence and watched the result on the ticker-tape. The reprimand was mild, almost sorrowful, and events proved it had no deterrence on my future behaviour.

31

MEDICAL PROBLEMS AND SUBTERFUGE

My early days in the Commons were not clouded by any medical problems. But soon I had recurring bouts of ill health which persisted for over fifteen years and had some impact upon my career.

The health of politicians is a natural topic of public interest and certainly Lord Moran's comments on Churchill's occasional 'black dog' depressions have helped the understanding of that man. Happily in Britain this concern has never been intrusive. Francis Pym retired from the front bench unwell with strain but returned to be Leader of the House and then Foreign Secretary. This was no consolation to me, but in retrospect I think I was more pre-occupied with my health than was merited.

I had no forewarning of the illness that struck in the autumn of 1963. I had been a nervous child – 'highly strung' was the meaningless phrase – and had to be coaxed through examinations. But my days in the Army and at university had been uneventful. In the autumn of 1963, after a holiday in Finland, I was struck down with sharp depression and tiredness. It was a shock when I was on the threshold of a career I had longed for. My London NHS doctor, Patrick Lovett, was sympathetic and very much a pioneer in the treatment of stress. The illness was not persistent but periodic, usually involving up to four days when I was quite unable to make speeches or master briefs. These bouts were followed by longer periods when I was fully active. I arranged my affairs and continued quietly as an MP, but it was no basis on which to fashion a political career.

Lovett eventually decided that I was suffering from 'manic depression' and treated me with Librium and Nardil tablets, which were supposed to offset the swings in my mood. This treatment had some initial effect and I was politically active in 1963–64, although having to conceal occasional bouts of gloom. Patrick Lovett eventually decided that Librium and Nardil were not resolving the recurring depression and that I should undergo therapy. I was referred to Dr A. Erskine, a soft-spoken Scot who had rooms in north London. I then spent the next ten years, until 1976, taking treatment with him twice a week. It was a painful business. I went early in the morning so that I could go on to work in the City. My eyes would flood with tears which cleared up as instantly as they commenced. Whatever the impact of the therapy, it did not cure the depression or make it more predictable or manageable. I much regret the lack of a friend or medical adviser who would have persuaded me to give up the treatment. Ten years was far too long to stay with something that at best was holding a position rather than curing it.

Meanwhile I arranged a political life that effectively concealed the situation. I was able to do the constituency work, occasionally pleading a stomach upset or cold when I felt exhausted at the thought of some fundraising function. As long as I voted no one missed my occasional inactivity in the Commons, although I once withdrew from the committee stage of a Prices and Incomes Bill, which caused comments as it was a subject on which I specialised. To this day I do not know whether the Whips' Office knew of my problem and that I was seeing a therapist. I think not.

The most significant factor of my disability was that I could not accept ministerial office. Frontbench work was generally exhausting but, above all, very structured. It simply was not possible to take a few days off at short notice. Up to 1970 I had the chance to do frontbench work but declined. A job was offered by the Chief Whip in the late 1960s. The offer was renewed after the February 1974 general election. Edward Heath saw me personally. I said I would accept shadow office if he would not lead the party at the forthcoming election. I regarded the interview as strictly private but my churlishness was reported in the *Financial Times*. There were also political reasons why I refused promotion, sometimes generously represented as a principled stance on Europe. But my anxiety over my health was also an undoubted factor.

This wholly unsatisfactory situation came to an end in January 1976 when Margaret Thatcher invited me to join her shadow Cabinet as Energy spokesman. The excuses for diffidence were exhausted: Edward Heath was gone and the European issue had been kicked into the long grass by the referendum. The shadow post was not a token one, but of Cabinet status. I bade farewell to Dr Erskine and never saw him again.

Shadow Energy, to which I refer elsewhere, was a success. I did not feel the stress onerously and to my surprise actually enjoyed this technical subject. In due course I was moved to Industry where the pressure was greater. I used to mark my diary every ten days as a kind of survival target. I mentioned this to Liz Forgan, an *Evening Standard* journalist. It was an asinine move. The resultant publicity, friendly but not helpful, was entirely my own fault. Soon after, but not, in my opinion, related to the *Evening Standard* article, I felt dreadfully stressed. At once I saw Humphrey Atkins, the Chief Whip, who was tactful and kindly. I then saw Margaret Thatcher, who was immensely considerate. She also told me that my ailment was 'a chemical imbalance' and told me to get it sorted out and return to her team. I could not have had better advice and her brisk approach certainly contrasted with the ten years' lugubrious and painstaking work of Dr Erskine.

My return to the back benches was a sad business, but I was immensely encouraged by the comradeship and optimism of Ian Gow, MP for Eastbourne, who had been a personal friend. At this time I had a long talk with my Shropshire doctor, John Symondson. I should have sought his advice earlier, but until 1970 I had effectively lived in London except at weekends. He told me of the alleged virtues of lithium carbonate in countering depression but warned that he had little direct experience in its use. This became evident from my reaction to his prescription, which was encouraging but not reliable. John Symondson then referred me to Peter Dally, a distinguished Harley Street consultant and lithium specialist. It was a masterly stroke. Dally was positive rather than passive when he analysed my problems. He changed the lithium dosage, varying the strength, quantity and incidence. My reactions were monitored by regular blood tests. It was only a matter of months before I was able to tell Margaret Thatcher that I was on the mend. In March 1978 John Symondson wrote a very supportive letter to her stating, 'I came to the conclusion that he never had any need of psychoanalysis whatsoever; he did not have a mixed-up personality in any way but was simply subject to the swings of mood from depression to elation which we all experience to a greater or lesser degree.'

In November 1978 I returned to the shadow Cabinet as spokesman on Small Businesses, about the most undemanding post that could be devised.

After the 1979 general election I joined the Cabinet as Chief Secretary to the Treasury. Meanwhile, I continued to see Dr Dally very occasionally, every other month or so. He would enquire about the lithium dosage, which was progressively reduced, and we would casually chat about my work. I said I found Cabinet life manageable but certainly stressful. 'I should jolly well hope so,' he said. The lithium treatment not only affected my political work. Marriage no longer seemed such a daunting challenge. Just ahead of my fiftieth birthday I married Sarah Wood, who was working for Nigel Lawson. We married on the eve of my birthday so that I could say I had taken the plunge at forty-nine. A late starter, I compensated by acquiring two young stepchildren, Nicholas and Lucy.

I have not been self-indulgent in describing the circumstances of my manic depression. There is no doubt that it had a sharp impact upon my political life in the mid-1960s and compelled me to leave the front bench in February 1977. In more general terms I think it made me more restrained and tentative in my political judgement and style and therefore a somewhat 'emollient monetarist', if that is not a contradiction in terms.

From the earliest time, I had sought membership of the Commons because the institution and its history fascinated me. I did not regard it as the ladder to ministerial office. Manic depression enhanced that diffidence, although eventually the experience of office proved exhilarating.

I can now discuss this health problem with candour. For years I felt I was walking on eggshells and could not share my anxieties privately or publicly. Dr Peter Dally encouraged me to make known the success of his treatment. It was argued that my story would help the countless numbers who cope with this condition. I hesitated as long as I was in the Commons, preferring the health book to remain closed. Now I am happy to open it.

32

SHADOW TECHNOLOGY AND THE WILSON GOVERNMENT

The 1964 general election was a long time coming. I had expected it in the spring but Alec Home held off until the autumn, almost the last possible date. After the 1961 'pay pause', the 'Profumo Affair', the departure of Macmillan and the controversial choice of his successor, Home, I began to look forward to the sweets of opposition. I rather favoured the prospect.

The Oswestry campaign was quiet. My Labour opponent, George Costley, came from Wolverhampton. He had none of the charisma of Brian Walden but he organised the Labour vote very well and pushed the Liberal, a young lawyer called Tom Crowther, into third place. The result was reasonably gratifying, namely:

Biffen 18,154
Costley 11,407
Crowther 8,745
Majority 6,747

Oswestry was returning to a pattern that had been sharply shaken by the by-election. One voter despairingly had written on his ballot 'Christine Keeler'.

Although Wilson had a small majority and was to call another election eighteen months later, my life was transformed. I now sat on the opposite side of the House and I chose the third bench below the gangway. The half nearest to the Speaker was occupied by the Liberals and I was the Tory marker for the remaining half. Relations with the Liberals were formal rather than friendly but I did like Alasdair Mackenzie, a Gaelic-speaking farmer who represented Ross and Cromarty. We talked of sheep and the seasons.

On the first day we crowded into the chamber trying to establish our places in the new parliament. I was struck by a handsome but rather elderly member. He seemed so mature compared with the other newcomers – as indeed he was, being Mr Speaker Hylton-Foster awaiting re-election. I had been under his daily authority for three years, but without his wig he was a changed man.

I soon settled down to an active life in opposition. I arranged my affairs so that I spent the mornings at Grieveson Grant and went on to Westminster after lunch for Question Time. Above all I regularly attended the Conservative backbench committees, which met in the afternoons. I balanced my relative silence in the chamber by being a regular contributor to discussions in the Finance Committee. It was the home of such 'sound money' men as Nigel Birch and Harry d'Avigdor-Goldsmid. Quite soon I became joint secretary of the Finance Committee. It was a prestigious move, but the duties were negligible. Harry Goldsmith (his democratic appellation) would depart to the smoking room instructing me to keep an eye on the debate and alert him and others when there was likely to be a vote.

I also attended the Agriculture Committee. The 1959 and 1964 general elections, had seen the election of a number of successful working farmers as opposed to landowners, including

Percy Browne and his successor, Peter Mills, who had regained and retained Torrington from the Liberals. I remember Peter Mills making an impassioned speech on the dismal state of the dairy industry and throwing his milk cheques on the floor. Quite a gesture from someone who was also a Church of England lay preacher.

I was settling down quite comfortably when the ladder of promotion was unexpectedly thrust before me. Edward Heath summoned me and suggested I should join the front bench as junior shadow spokesman on Technology. The Ministry of Technology was one of the new departments created by Harold Wilson in 1964. It was an imposing title, presumably representing Wilson's commitment to 'the white heat of technology'. In fact it was a gathering together of a few public research bodies and the sponsorship of the machine tool industry. More intriguing was the fact that the Cabinet minister in charge was Frank Cousins. He was an old-style trade union boss in the tradition of Ernest Bevin, but – in contrast – well to the left and a nuclear disarmer.

The invitation gave me no time to think of reasons why I should refuse. My spell as junior shadow Technology turned out to be a success and I much enjoyed it. It was clear that Heath wanted me to be aware of his patronage, which was reasonable enough. I replied by saying that he might like to know of my admiration of Enoch Powell. It was a genuine comment and not impertinence. In 1965 the leadership of Home was likely to be short term and the generation of Heath, Maudling and Macleod had their coterie of followers.

My shadow minister was Ernest Marples. I never really got to know him. He combined being a managerial politician with a great knack of folksiness. He was an entrepreneur but also had high regard for the French philosopher de Jouvenel, whose works he diligently underlined. Marples had no time for work on the opposition front bench and I was left to my own devices. I was in a totally new world as I tried to understand the scope and finances of the National Research and Development Corporation and Research Councils. There was really no politics in these worthy organisations; the challenge was Frank Cousins himself. I liked him but suspect he was a prickly colleague. The Commons does not much respect those who join it with a great reputation. There is a common starting line no matter what prominence has been gained in the trade union or industrial world. Cousins may have been a man of trade union action but he was no man of words. He stumbled as he ponderously read his brief and he hated Question Time when he had to think on his feet. We discovered this fear and then contrived to hold back our questions and table them for answer at the last moment. Of course it was gamesmanship, but in its way it helped unsettle him and, when he had policy differences with Wilson, he resigned from the Cabinet and then from Parliament. For him departure was a relief.

I had the baptism of my first frontbench speech. The debate was technically on the departmental budget and I had to wind up for the opposition. I carefully prepared a text which could be expanded to cover points made in the debate. The debate had to end on the dot at 10 p.m. The cardinal crime was to exceed or fall short of the allotted time and thereby leave Dick Marsh, the junior minister, winding up with a span of time he had not expected. As I studiously prepared my argument and the timing, the phone went. It was Dick Marsh, cheerful, irreverent and a rising Labour star. He told me his speech was based upon the theme 'All Tories are bastards'. I admired his brevity but alas his eventual speech showed the lifeless hand of his private office. The debate was generally constructive but ended in bedlam as Sydney Silverman, the campaigner against hanging, was alleged to have called someone a 'stinking stoat'. We had strayed from technology to the countryside. Dick Marsh and I became good friends – bonded by Euroscepticism. My speech went down quite well, not least because I had properly prepared it and certainly could not have been accused of inciting Sydney Silverman. Of course I was nervous, but as I got to the despatch box I gained confidence. In the public gallery sat Anne Williams, a very good friend from Oswestry who taught Latin in London. She wrote to my mother and said, 'When John got up to make his speech he looked up at me and winked.' Alas there is no record in Hansard. I was told that Alec Home came in for the closing speeches and commented favourably. Altogether it was a good night.

During my short tenure of shadow office I was invited to visit the United States on a State Department 'leader programme'. This was an honour because of the pleasure of the visit and because those chosen were supposed to be climbing up the ladder. I was accompanied by three MPs, Christopher Chataway, who became a junior Education minister, and two Labour MPs, Alf Morris, who was a powerful campaigner for the disabled, and Gordon Bagier. We were a happy team. I had never flown outside Europe and the Pan Am flight across the Atlantic was a novel and exciting experience.

The US State Department had a policy of placing those on the 'leader programme' with individual hosts rather than hotels. They wanted us to be with real America rather than travelling formally. As a result, I visited friends in Minnesota, Virginia and New York. I also took the opportunity to study investment banking in Wall Street, farming in Minnesota and machine tools in Wisconsin. The latter took account of my technology role. It was a wonderful experience, the more so as it really was so novel. My abiding memory was being booked into a Virginian hotel in Roanoke on a Sunday morning so that we could drink

Jack Daniel's bourbon within state law. There was also the bonus of a State Department daily living allowance so generous that I bought myself a dinner jacket.

The short parliaments between the two elections of 1964 and 1966 were good for me. After a painfully slow and hesitant start at Westminster I had become secretary to the backbench Finance Committee and a junior shadow spokesman, and had been singled out for a US leader programme. The early years of apprenticeship, listening and learning were paying off.

33

PRICES AND INCOMES BATTLES 1966-68

There is great advantage for a new MP to specialise in a topic which becomes politically prominent and runs for a number of years. It was my good fortune to take an interest in prices and incomes policies when they were at the heart of Wilson's economic programme throughout the latter half of the 1960s and featured in three major Bills – the Prices and Incomes Acts of 1966, 1967 and 1968.

The argument for state regulation of prices and incomes as a means of countering inflation had a long appeal to those who believed in a centralised and planned economy. It had been tried by the post-war Attlee government. The difficulties argue themselves: comprehensive control was hard to enforce and the trade unions resented interference with wage bargaining.

The Conservatives pursued a tentative liberal economic policy in the 1950s and price and income control was out of fashion, but it returned to favour after the 1959 general election. 'Economic growth' became the political watchword and Labour, with such skilled economists as Anthony Crosland and Roy Jenkins, argued plausibly that planning – indicative and not compulsory – would revitalise industry and allocate resources more rationally than the hit-and-miss of the market place. The policy would lead to more economic growth, more taxable income and more public spending on social services. It was argued that an unmerited rise in incomes would undermine these desirable and linked objectives and hence came the need for a policy that would keep incomes within the overall plan. It was also assumed that Labour would secure a reasonable chance of trade union cooperation in the pursuit of an incomes policy.

Of course these few sentences are a bald description of the policy, but I believe a fair one. I had first encountered the concept when I was working for the Economist Intelligence Unit. Many of the company's 'Young Turks' were much attracted by 'planification' as was being practised in France. I had never heard a squeak about it whilst I was fighting the 1959 general election campaign in Coventry. My Bow Group colleagues did not seem that inspired by it, but the Macmillan government was impressed. However, it proceeded with caution rather than enthusiasm.

All seemed to change with my Oswestry by-election. At the EIU I would muse on the topic with Charles Cooper, a splendidly laid-back South African with a planner's omniscience. Now I was confronted with Selwyn Lloyd's July 1961 measures, which included a pay pause appealing for a six-month wages standstill as a precursor to a 'planned expansion of incomes'; I suppose the new policy got a thin cheer in the EIU canteen, but it was ridiculed on the Welsh border. I defended it bravely and continued to do so in my early days at Westminster.

The decision by Enoch Powell not to serve under Alec Douglas-Home in 1963 altered the debate, certainly for me. He argued that income/price controls were ineffective and illiberal and took the politician's eye from the central issues of controlling public spending and also financing it without substantial borrowing.

The incipient debate within the Tory Party was interrupted by the 1964 general election. The Conservative defeat enabled it to be resumed with great vigour. At this point I decided to make it 'my subject' having been purged of my EIU planning heresies.

The Labour commitment to incomes policy and the National Plan now had no convincing Conservative alternative. Through my friendship with T. E. (Peter) Utley, who was then a leader writer on the *Daily Telegraph*, I had the chance to contribute an article for the paper. I argued that the Tories in 1961–64 had taken up planning and incomes policy 'out of curiosity rather than conviction'. I think that was an accurate judgement, but the mood was changing. The 1964 general election brought to Parliament Bow Group liberal-minded Tories like Geoffrey Howe, Terence Higgins and Patrick Jenkin. They did not share the view of the powerful Tory planners like Reginald Maudling and Robert Carr.

Quite soon an alternative economic policy began to emerge. It required restrained public spending, modest government borrowing, tougher competition laws and trade union reform. It was two-thirds the way to the Thatcherism of the 1980s and was eventually enshrined at a pre-election leadership meeting at Selsdon Park just before the 1970 general election.

Incomes policy in the 1960s was the daily political battle that became the touchstone of the wider economic debate. The argument was between Labour's voluntary planners and a cautious Conservative commitment to the social market economy which had been such a success in Germany.

The conflict and the clash of ideas suited my rather bookish temperament. That attraction was reinforced by the formidable quality of the Labour proponents of the policy, chief amongst whom was George Brown.

Meanwhile the 'voluntary' incomes policy soon acquired a legal framework and had become 'statutory'. A Labour government blanched at the thought of permanent wage controls so the law was repeated annually, hence a fresh Act for the three years 1966–68. It was also decided that each ministerial decision pegging pay would have to come to the Commons for a late-night debate on which we always forced a vote. I loved the cut and thrust of these short debates and took part in nearly all of them.

My view now is that the government vastly overplayed the significance of incomes policy. Once it was clear that it only had a marginal impact the rhetoric should have been turned down. The reverse happened. The policy was given a prime role in securing growth, maintaining the exchange rate and promoting productivity.

A particular attraction of the incomes policy debate was that it seriously divided Labour. Of course the Tories had their own problems, but only a few backbench old-timers like Cyril Osborne and Kenneth Lewis hankered after pay control. Labour had dozens of rebels, and Frank Cousins, formerly head of the Transport and General Workers' Union, left the Cabinet on the issue.

The Liberals usually voted with the government and I commented sarcastically upon this, referring to them as lap dogs. I sat immediately next to the Liberals and heard Eric Lubbock snort 'cheeky sod'. At once I picked up the phrase and ensured that it was printed in Hansard. It read well in Oswestry.

There was a group of youngish trade unionists including Eric Heffer and Stan Orme who expressed forthright opposition. Eric Heffer was the most prominent and eventually served a very short spell as a minister under Tony Benn at the Department of Industry. He was better on the back benches than in office. I liked Eric and once invited him to lunch at Grieveson Grant, the stockbrokers I advised. They would occasionally have Harold Lever or some other Labour millionaire as a guest, feeling they had to keep in touch with socialism. I thought Eric would be good for them. He played his role well. Leaning back in his chair with a brandy and cigar he fielded the first post-prandial question – critical of the trade unions. 'Being in a trade union', he reflected, 'is like being in a good regiment.' I assumed the political levy was like paying mess bills.

The most memorable legislation was the 1966 Prices and Incomes Bill. I sat on the standing committee. George Brown had been made Secretary of State for Economic Affairs and was in charge of the Bill. This was a signal to the world that the Treasury would have its wings clipped. Brown was a man of great courage and had been a loyal friend of Gaitskell with whom I had overlapped a few months before he died. The latter was impressive. Unfairly, I thought he contrasted sharply with Macmillan. He was articulate and idealistic, but he divided the Labour Party with his forthright rejection of nuclear disarmament. On Gaitskell's death Brown was defeated by Harold Wilson for the Labour leadership. It was a wounding blow for George, who did not conceal his resentment.

Harold Lever, not yet a minister, was the chairman of the standing committee. It was a crucial post. He had all the charm of a Jewish Labour millionaire. He once observed, 'I inherited a million, married a million and made a million.' The Bill initially provided for guidelines for price increases but the seamen's strike precipitated a panic and the government introduced a law freezing wages for six months. Lever had the unenviable task of deciding if this could be tacked onto the proposed Bill or whether it would have to be a separate Bill. The stakes were high. It was already late July and it was doubtful if the government could manage two Bills before MPs departed for long-booked family holidays. Ministers smiled when Lever ruled for a tacked-on Bill. It says much for his charm that the Tories did not contest his ruling.

The 1966 Prices and Incomes Bill set the pattern for the subsequent Bills of 1967 and 1968. After that the policy died peacefully.
The 1966 Bill was debated by a committee of twenty-five members.
It sat from 26 July until 4 August. George Brown had two able
frontbench lieutenants, Shirley Williams and William (Bill) Rodgers,
destined to become members of the Gang of Four who founded
the Social Democratic Party. They had entered the Commons in
1964 and were already skilled parliamentarians. The Conservatives
were led by Keith Joseph, whose scholarly defence of the market
economy made him a good foil to the Labour planners.

The Tories also had their rising stars: Terence Higgins and
Peter Hordern. Also part of the team was Norman St John-
Stevas, who regaled us with Cambridge Union oratory, which
was at least a diversion.

Frank Cousins had been put on the committee, presumably at
Harold Wilson's request. He had resigned from the government
because of the Bill and would soon resign from the Commons.
We met in Committee Room 10 each Tuesday and Thursday
morning. Cousins looked decidedly out of sorts and out of
place. His soulmate was George Perry, a sympathetic Labour
MP who barely spoke a word. A researcher from the Transport
and General Workers' Union was at the end of the room. A far
better opposition would have been provided by Eric Heffer and
Stan Orme. Cousins must have found it the greatest humiliation.
Once a trade union boss and a Cabinet minister, now an echo
of yesterday exiled by the heartless whips. Halfway through the
committee during a late night sitting, overcome by the futility of
it all, he stormed out of the room and was never seen again. I
would love to have glimpsed the whips' record of the occasion.

During the committee stage of the Bill a wholly unexpected
incident occurred. Someone slipped into the public seats
and started taking notes. When the session ended, she came

up and said how much she had enjoyed hearing me speak. This was Elizabeth Farrelly, a teacher from County Durham, who was taking notes for her MP, Charles Grey, who had the task of reporting daily Commons proceedings, known as 'messages', to the Queen. Her career had been spent teaching English and home economics in the East End. She also studied at Birkbeck College. Her charitable work resulted in Aneurin Bevan giving her a position with the Royal London Hospital. Many years later she was justly appointed an OBE.

Elizabeth Farrelly became a very good friend and over the years offered advice and consolation in the darker times. She was deeply interested in politics and would often drop in on the Commons. I well remember her calling the Roman Catholic priest at Oswestry during the February 1974 general election to get a local view, as I was so fearful about the outcome. He was quite confident and almost – but not quite – restored my morale.

Meanwhile, political careers were being played out before the public gallery of the standing committee. George Brown did not have a happy time at the Department of Economic Affairs. Temperamentally he was not well suited for the post of planner in chief. This showed in parliamentary debate and his departure was a sad personal anticlimax. I was in the Commons that evening. It was not entirely clear why he was going. It involved 'that man' – i.e. Wilson – and was all rather emotional. In the Commons tea room he addressed whoever would listen. Those who knew him well said 'when he's like this only Ron (his brother and MP for Finsbury) can handle him'. Ron was sent for, but George was determined to go. The tea room audience had consisted almost entirely of Labour MPs and as one of the few Tories there I felt I had been present at private grief. It was a sad exit.

The 1966 Prices and Incomes Bill was the high water mark of the legislation but, although it was an albatross, Labour persisted with Acts in the two following years. The Office of Economic Affairs was wound up in October 1969. Michael Stewart succeeded George Brown for a short period from August 1966 to August 1967. I felt no warmth towards him. What for him was precision I thought was pedantry. I am still bemused that he became Foreign Secretary in the late 1960s. After Michael Stewart and in its dying days the ministerial cup, tainted if not poisoned, was passed to Peter Shore. It was the first time I had met him. He was able and articulate but it was Euroscepticism that made a bond between us.

The experience of debating the Acts and the orders defining specific wage controls was exhilarating. My work at Grieveson Grant brought me many industrial contacts and I was able to brief myself for debates. More generally I found I could do a coherent twenty-minute set debate speech with a lively peroration and was equally at home doing the shorter and conversational style of the committee stage. I made some political impact and the topic and my style marked me as a 'Powellite' and not a 'Heathite'.

By the 1970 general election, after a slow start, I had made some mark in the Commons and was certainly at home there. Above all I relished studying the Labour Party and the background and reasons for their divisions over incomes policy. I found studying Labour – sympathetically and not abusively – a great advantage. It made me increasingly a House of Commons politician and stood me in great stead when I became Leader of the House. Prices and incomes mired the Labour government but for me it was a great opportunity to emerge from the facelessness of the back benches.

34

ENOCH POWELL

I first heard Enoch Powell at a Cambridge University Conservative meeting on 22 April 1951. The immediate impression was one of bewilderment. *The Times Guide to the House of Commons* had published the wrong Powell. I expected a bald frog-like figure: in fact he had a shock of black hair and looked half his published age. The lasting memory was of the speech. The voice was intense and rather nasal, but it was the argument that was really compelling. Most Tory speakers gave CUCA a rerun of their standard political speech. Powell was different. We had a scholarly analysis of political authority and the nature of government. It might have been the lecture room. I was not then to know it, but he soon became my political inspiration, my most favoured member of the One Nation Group of Tory MPs.

From my days at Cambridge onwards I looked to him as my political mentor. This was because of his reputation as an austere Treasury minister, a champion of post-imperial British nationalism, a sceptic of the European Union and a Cassandra warning against the consequences of the numbers and concentration of immigration which developed from the 1950s.

A number of biographies have been written about him, the weightiest by Simon Heffer. I also recommend those by Rob Shepherd and Patrick Cosgrave. I do not propose to analyse at length the man and his politics. My contribution is mainly anecdotal.

There are a host of memories that crowd in the years that followed my leaving university. From 1953 until 1960 I worked in Birmingham and met Powell occasionally at Conservative meetings as he was Member of Parliament for Wolverhampton South West.

At that time I did not appreciate the significance of his resignation from the Treasury in 1958 along with his Chancellor, Peter Thorneycroft, and fellow minister Nigel Birch. Later I realised it was a defining moment in the debate and division between 'sound money' Tories like Powell and those who favoured central planning, greater public spending and economic growth.

I was more impressed by his backbench speech when in July 1959 the Commons debated the Hola massacre. This concerned the killing of imprisoned Mau-Mau supporters who had been fighting against the British colonial government. There had been faulty administration to have allowed such killing and the matter was debated in the Commons. After waiting an age to be called to speak, Powell delivered a passionate oration arguing for British standards of justice in Kenya. The decolonisation of Africa was then becoming a major Westminster issue and I was firmly on the liberal wing, as were most members of the Bow Group. I read of the debate and wrote to him from Birmingham, where I was working. I received a handwritten reply from Enoch, a precise and legible script which I came to know well.

I had become Tory candidate for Coventry East and saw rather more of Powell at this time. In 1958 he had resigned from the Treasury and was on the back benches until the general election a year later. Political life quickened with the prospect of an election and it was a season of weekend conferences. I attended one when he vigorously questioned having a British military presence east of Suez. This view was rebutted by his fellow speaker, Hugh Fraser, MP for Stafford. It was an indication that he had moved well beyond the imperialism he championed a decade previously.

When I arrived at the Commons in 1961 Powell was Minister of Health. He was engaged in defending the Selwyn Lloyd 'pay pause' by restricting the increase in nurses' pay – never a popular hand for a minister. The central lobby was crammed with demonstrating nurses and as he made his way through the throng the cry went up: 'Enoch'. It was not approbation. 'Fame at last,' he observed when he got to the dining table. He was unmoved in the dispute by those who argued that nursing was a vocation. 'How fortunate to get the rate for the job and the satisfaction of a calling,' he observed. It was the kind of icy logic that left the Tory backbenchers full of unease.

I was unaware of the role played by Powell in the leadership contest to succeed Macmillan in 1963. Later I learned from his wife Pam that the fateful meeting of the Cabinet ministers who wanted Rab Butler as Prime Minister had been held in the Powell living room, festively decorated for one of their daughter's birthday parties. This was the backcloth for the famous comment by Powell to Butler that if he pulled the trigger the premiership was his, but it would make a lot of noise and there would be blood.

In 1962 I had written to the Chief Whip saying that when Macmillan eventually departed the Conservatives needed a Gaullist-style leadership – '*Vérité et sévérité*' – and that this pointed to Powell, then only Minister of Health. My view was almost unique. The letter had been sent whilst Macmillan was still in office but I sent a further note after he had resigned and a successor was being canvassed through 'taking of voices'. This note regretted that Powell was not a runner. I went on to favour Butler as first choice, vetoed Hailsham and as backstop accepted Home. Home emerged as leader.

Powell and Macleod both declined to serve under his leadership. Macleod became editor of *The Spectator* and his motives for 'not serving' were suspect. It was thought he was positioning himself for a general election defeat. I do not think Powell attracted the same doubts; his behaviour was judged to be eccentric rather than self-serving. I never discussed the matter with him but I welcomed the backbench speeches he now made concerning the market economy. He was opening up a wider debate.

After the 1964 general election defeat, Home stood down. There was a leadership contest in 1965. This time the choice was not by 'voices' but by a recorded vote of Members of Parliament. John Hay, who had been a junior Transport minister, proposed Enoch. I was asked to second the nomination. I was flattered but daunted by the potential publicity. I signed the nomination and then went to ground to escape the enquiries of the press and the bemusement of my colleagues. It was not a glorious episode.

Powell described his contest as 'leaving my visiting card'. He gathered a mere fifteen votes out of two hundred and ninety eight – 5 per cent. The select band of supporters were mainly Tory economic liberals but included Edith Pitt, his junior minister at Health. Earlier she had been welfare officer at Tubes Ltd, the Aston factory where I had worked as a trainee. Edith had an industrial working-class background and symbolised the people who provided much of Powell's support in the 1970s.

As the 1960s proceeded I began to see much more of Enoch. In opposition, under Heath's leadership, he did not confine himself to his shadow post – Defence – but ranged over the entire political spectrum. This irritated Heath, who liked his shadow team to behave like a government, albeit in exile. It also irritated Powell's fellow 'shadows' who felt he should keep off their grass. Going through the voting lobby one evening I heard Margaret Thatcher – hot if not incandescent – with Enoch about a speech of his which had trampled, without notice, over her subject of education.

His speeches were mainly about the economy and Britain's role in the world. His theme was that Britain must give up nostalgic memories of Empire and the era of Victorian dominance when Britain was supposed to be 'the workshop' of the world. Such memories belonged to a past beyond recall. Powell wanted the rediscovery of the virtues of the nation state. This would come from a vigorous pursuit of free enterprise. The successful entrepreneur and not the planner would determine Britain's post-imperial role. 'Meaningful patriotism' was his phrase. It intrigued and attracted me. There was nothing blimpish about his nationhood and his market economy was more than just money-making. He made no attempt to recruit adherents. His admirers generally belonged to the 'up to a point' school. Iain Macleod had once said he left the Powell express one stop before it crashed into the buffers. Many felt like that. I do not think he felt lonely or isolated as he set about challenging the Conservatism of the Macmillan years.

During this period I had become very friendly with T. E. (Peter) Utley. Blind from childhood, he had a razor-sharp mind, having obtained a starred first at Cambridge. He was a wonderful man and I would spend evenings at the King & Keys in Fleet Street, where he held court analysing the woes of the Conservatives as he chain smoked and consumed pints of beer. It was like attending a boozy tutorial. I would pass the beer not bothering to place it exactly before him as he seemed so much in charge that I could not believe in his disability. As an added attraction Peter had a vivacious 'guide', Lauren Wade. She knew exactly where to place the beer and help him light his cigarettes. We made quite a threesome; she came from Kenilworth and her father had a steel stockholding business within a stone's throw of my Birmingham workplace of Tubes Ltd. Suddenly I had something like a social life. Peter was then working for the *Daily Telegraph*, whose editorial policy was tentatively hostile to Heath. Peter developed hostility into an art form. I discussed with him my proposed speeches and my relations with Powell. At this stage Enoch made his notorious Birmingham speech on immigration and the dangers he foresaw, concluding, 'All I know is that to see and not to speak would be the great betrayal.'

Of course that speech changed Powell's career. Hitherto he had a niche following of Tory economic liberals such as Nick Ridley, Michael Alison and Peter Hordern. The immigration speech was made on 20 April 1968. I was in the United States at the time, lecturing for the Foreign Office. When I learned of the speech and his dismissal by Heath from the Tory front bench I sent a telegram of support. My host, a lecturer at Rockford College, was amazed, not because of the speech but because he thought the gesture would put an end to my career.

When I returned to England I made my way to the Powell home, 33 South Eaton Place. It was barricaded and coping with a deluge of mail. Enoch was reasonably calm but irritated: he could not find the Latin reference to the 'River Tiber' quote he had used in the speech.

After the Birmingham speech, Powell's political life was transformed. Not only because of its content but because he was sacked for it. He ceased to be just an economic ideologue and had become a major public figure. As Brian Walden said, 'he was like a Texan dirt farmer who had struck oil'.

I cannot add much to what has been written exhaustively about the circumstances of the speech. I believe Powell was determined to make it and wilfully did not discuss it with Cabinet colleagues when it certainly would have been spiked. Time has broadly vindicated his projection of the size of the immigrant-descended population, but the subsequent social dislocation has not justified the doom-laden language he used.

The language itself was a matter of controversy. Much of the speech was in the forceful analytical manner of Powell but the use of terms like 'piccaninnies' was saloon bar language. It was not necessary for the argument and not characteristic of Enoch. In retrospect I am sure he should have left 'the River Tiber foaming with much blood' in the original Latin, if it had to be used at all. The point of impending conflict was evident in the speech and needed no underlining.

Peter Utley was commissioned to write a book in the aftermath of the speech. *Enoch Powell: the man and his thinking* appeared within weeks. I was consulted by Peter and I think he produced a remarkably good – albeit favourable – analysis in such a short time. Lauren, his Girl Friday, removed the 'Powellism Works' sticker from her Mini. She championed his economics but, despite her 'Brummie' links, could not take the immigration speech.

I sat in the Commons in the following months whenever the twin subjects of race and immigration were debated. Enoch was a constant presence and would speak occasionally with controlled intensity. He often endured abuse. Andrew Faulds, a Labour MP and one-time thespian who featured on television as Carver Doone, was spectacularly offensive – shouting abuse from a seated position. Willie Hamilton, the Labour MP and anti-monarchist, declared he would not vote in a lobby 'soiled by the presence of Powell'.

It is intriguing to speculate what would have happened if Powell had not made the 'immigration' speech. I think he would have left the shadow Cabinet at some time. Heath and he were so different in character. Heath wanted a structured opposition, Powell wanted to range freely. Only one could be boss.

A handful of free-enterprise Tories were anxious to keep

Powell reasonably on side. Inspired by Nicholas Ridley we formed the Economic Dining Club. It concentrated wholly on economic affairs and never discussed immigration. It was an extraordinarily well-kept secret, partly because we took it in turns to host a monthly dinner in our own homes and away from the Commons. The meetings were a great success. Enoch was the professor and we all tried our hands at being disputatious pupils. We discovered that 'where there's Enoch there's argument'. The club continued after the 1970 general election and the membership was predominantly in favour of the Common Market, but Enoch (and I) were against. There was more unanimity over our hostility to Heath when he restored price and income controls in 1972. The group continued for a while after the 1974 general election but Powell had then left the Conservative Party and the Commons. An amusing judgement was that we chose Margaret Thatcher as a member after the February 1974 election rather than Geoffrey Howe – we were just ahead of the times.

Powell campaigned, albeit on his own terms, for a Tory victory at the 1970 general election. The Common Market was an emerging issue and the Tory establishment was anxious lest Powell should widen his gap with the leadership to include that topic. He did not oblige and soon developed a lively campaign against membership of the Common Market. It dominated his life before and after the 1970 election and he told me that he regarded the issues as more important than immigration.

There was a dignity and style about his personal campaign. He took his message to the continent, where he delivered speeches in German, French and Italian. Nicholas Ridley, then a strong European, wryly noted he used the term '*laboriste*' when he should have said '*travailliste*'. Powell would have appreciated the textual alertness. Immediately after Parliament had voted for Common

Market membership Powell told me he was thinking of leaving the Commons, but happily there were second thoughts.

During the 1970 parliament Powell invited a small group of MPs to meet him regularly. He called this little group the 'Privy Council'. It met every Thursday evening and discussed the week ahead. It included, amongst others, Ronald Bell, Fred Corfield, Richard Body (a Quaker) and James Ramsden. In temperament and outlook they ranged wider than the Economic Dining Club. James was fascinating; a huntsman, Etonian scholar and countryman, he embraced traditional Toryism. He became chairman of the trustees to the London Clinic and subsequently appointed me to the board. I enjoyed meetings of the 'Privy Council', which were largely devoted to offering advice to Enoch on his proposed speeches, which he almost totally ignored.

In the summer of 1973 it became clear that Powell was considering leaving the Conservative Party. Ronald Bell in particular tried to dissuade him. It seemed unthinkable to us that he could not find a formula that would enable him to continue as an independent-minded member for Wolverhampton South West. I have carbon copies of letters I sent to him, vainly trying to suggest how he could campaign against the Common Market and still stand on a Tory platform. The decision was just still open when the election came earlier than expected in February 1974 because of the miners' strike. I was at my constituency home in Kinton campaigning when the fateful letter from Enoch arrived. I recognised the typeface on the envelope and I knew it contained an advance copy of the speech he would make on the Common Market. My election assistant, Jonathan Bradley, whom I had met whilst holidaying in Albania, was dying to open it. I did not want to read it. I feared its contents and wanted to continue telling everyone that I did not know what his speech would say. In fact it said 'Vote Labour', which at heart I knew it would. I continued the election campaign in gloom. Doubtless, the Powell speech helped bring about the narrow defeat of Edward Heath but Labour did not bring Common Market membership to an end.

For a short period Powell was out of Parliament before being returned as an Ulster Unionist for South Down. The 'Privy Council' discussed this option. I never sought to dissuade him but I felt it was a second-best decision. From this time onwards I saw a great deal less of him. We were no longer both members of Conservative Party parliamentary committees and once I became a shadow minister and then a member of the Thatcher Cabinet I had almost no opportunity of meeting him by chance at Westminster. He worked tirelessly for the Ulster Unionists but I did not support his policy of fully integrating Northern Ireland with Great Britain.

To the very end (he was defeated in 1987) his speeches dominated the Commons. Members would come into the chamber to hear him. In those days there was no restriction on the length of speeches. His opening remarks were 'Polyfilla', using time to enable members to reach the chamber. He would then develop his argument without notes, in his flat voice with its Midlands intonation. It was precise and classically constructed. He must have been a Hansard writers' dream. Michael Foot, by contrast, was a romantic. His words were like a stream in flood and the pitch of voice and the mannerism combined to impart indignation and ridicule, all with the passion of a Cornish Celt.

Powell and Foot made a great contrasting debating couple, as was demonstrated in their hostility to the Labour government Bill in 1968 to reform the House of Lords. They were aided by John Boyd-Carpenter and Bob Sheldon, then a Labour MP. Richard Crossman, who had been in charge of the legislation, eventually came to the Commons and admitted he had to withdraw the

Bill because of the skilful opposition of backbenchers. Briskly he gabbled his words of climbdown. 'Eat it slowly,' snapped Powell, a one-liner that superbly fitted the occasion.

I have written about Powell the politician but I have many happy memories of the man and his family. I met his wife, Pam, when I was working in Birmingham in the late 1950s. She was a charming and ebullient person, in sharp contrast to her analytical and supposedly austere husband. The Powell household rang with laughter. Occasionally I stayed at their Wolverhampton home in Merridale Road and was struck by a photograph one of their daughters had taken of Enoch gently parting the leaves to reveal a blackbird's nest. An incongruous moment in a house under police protection because of a gun threat.

I remember a Sunday evening journey back to South Eaton Place after a Wolverhampton weekend. Pam, who had an Advanced Driving Licence, volunteered to take the wheel. Enoch brushed her aside and occupied the outside lane like a man possessed. Pam's 'Ohs and Ahs' subsided and I lay on the back seat, silent, with eyes averted. On arrival at South Eaton Place Powell emerged triumphant, saying, 'Never *legally* overtaken.' Life with him was in the fast lane, a terrifying absence of doubt, but quite a journey.

Very occasionally, Enoch and Pam came and stayed the weekend with us in Shropshire. The visits were both exhilarating and exhausting. There seemed quite a lot of walking along the Welsh borders and visits into Shropshire. I remember the trip to Moreton Corbet Church. I would have given it five minutes on a sunny afternoon but Enoch lovingly speculated on every aspect of its architecture and the role it would have played in village life.

He was a good trencherman. One weekend, Sarah, a great meal planner, had arranged a series of peak repasts with the occasional filler such as bacon and scrambled eggs for lesser

gastronomic occasions. Early evening after an enormous lunch
with friends he came downstairs magnificent in three-piece suit
and regimental tie. 'Enoch! Why are you looking so smart?'
said Sarah. 'For the pheasants,' he replied. Sarah recovered the
situation and at nil notice the next day's Sunday lunch became
Saturday's formal dinner. The incident became part of Tanat
House Powell folklore, as did stepson Nicholas's breakfast
conversation with Enoch. Nicholas in his mid-teens arrived early
and was alone with Powell. 'What are you going to do when you
grow up, Nicholas?' 'Oh, I hope to be a journalist.' There came
a reflective pause. 'But are you nasty enough?' Eighteen years
later Nicholas is a highly competent journalist with the *New York
Times* and is unquestionably 'nice' but he has wisely not joined
the Westminster lobby.

Enoch Powell, as a consequence of his political views and
conduct, never received deserved accolades from the political
or academic 'establishment'. This did not seem to disturb him
much, but I thought it reflected badly on the university world,
who opted for convention rather than intellectual distinction and
courageous speaking. I do not know if he would have liked to
have been made a life peer and I never asked him. I doubt that
he would have found the House of Lords very congenial. I would
have advised him against a peerage: like Edmund Burke he was
destined to be a Commons man.

His eightieth birthday was celebrated in grand style. A black
tie dinner was presided over by the Marquess of Salisbury at
the Hyde Park Hotel. I was there but my attendance was frac-
tured by a Commons vote. The one hundred and ten guests
were a varied collection representing a small number of keen
admirers in the media and the handful of parliamentarians who
were devoted to the man, if not all his causes. At dinner Enoch
was flanked by Margaret Thatcher and Lady Salisbury. The

My mother, Edith Annie Bennett (second from right), with her twelve brothers and sisters.

The Bennett grandparents, with their thirteen children (Edith seated on the left).

With a favourite bear.

ABOVE Hill Farm, my childhood home in Somerset.

With my mother, on the farm.

Victor Biffen with a prize-winning bull.

LEFT Ready for National
Service, 1949.

BELOW With friends at Jesus
College, Cambridge (JB front
row, far right).

LEFT Enjoying student life in the early 1950s.

BELOW 'May Week was in June.'

At the count. Coventry East by-election, 1959.

The MPs' cricket team, Shropshire.

Wearing my father's top hat at Sue Powell's wedding, with David and Jill Hutchinson Smith and their daughter Celia.

TOP 1978 visit to the Forties Oil Field.

MIDDLE Margaret Thatcher's 1979 Cabinet (JB back row, third from left).

BOTTOM With Sarah at the Oswestry Show, 1979.

TOP With Sarah, opening Frank Jones's food processing plant.

MIDDLE Campaigning in the 1987 general election, helped by Sarah, Nicholas and Lucy.

BOTTOM With Owen Paterson (left), who succeeded me as MP to the North Shropshire constituency.

TOP Investiture, 1997, with Sarah, Nicholas, Lucy, and Sarah's father and stepmother, Cyril and Penny Drew.

MIDDLE At the age of seventy-six.

BOTTOM Undergoing dialysis.

occasion, of course, did not reflect the wider audience in the country who felt he spoke for them in a way the political establishment would not.

Enoch Powell died in February 1998, his final years clouded by a debilitating illness. I had the daunting task of giving the address at his funeral service in St Margaret's, Westminster on 18 February.

Even if political fortunes had been otherwise I do not think he would ever have been Prime Minister. He might have been the Joseph Chamberlain of his age, powerful in Cabinet and representing a distinctive and popular viewpoint in the nation. For me he represented views that I supported generally but not unconditionally. Above all he was devoted to the House of Commons. A compelling oratory, courage and integrity set him apart.

35

EDWARD HEATH

I had no contact with Edward Heath until I reached the Commons. I had been aware of his reputation as a highly skilled Chief Whip who helped the Conservatives recover from the debacle of Suez. As a One Nation Tory I assumed we had sympathetic views. Once he took charge of the Common Market negotiations he became a hero and within months after I arrived at the Commons I saw him in action.

The next few years were to see a parting of the ways that was sharp and personal. I hope, nonetheless, I have such a sense of his considerable achievements that I can fairly write about them.

His election as leader in 1965 broke the patrician mould. Macleod had derided the 'magic circle' which secured the leadership of Lord Home in 1963, but Heath's success ended the dominance beyond recall. He was also a vigorous exponent of liberal economics, bravely challenging the Tory Party with the abolition of resale price maintenance and finally – as he will be remembered – securing British membership of what was then known as the Common Market.

I had a special reason to remember his effectiveness in handling the abolition of sale price maintenance. It was a trading practice much beloved by small shopkeepers and their many supporters on the Tory back benches. When Heath presented the

abolition Bill there was open parliamentary revolt and the Whips'
Office created a small committee representing the conflicting
interests with the task of finding a compromise. I was selected
to represent young Bow Group Tories sympathetic to Heath.
The shopkeepers' champion was Roy Wise, MP for Rugby. He
was pleased to be chosen and had first entered the Commons in
1931. 'Wise by name and not by nature' was the lame humour
of the smoking room. Heath was represented by Tony Kershaw,
his able parliamentary private secretary. The whips had chosen
well. The meetings were a pushover for the resale price maintenance Bill. Wise struggled – a lone voice – as he was forced to
make successive concessions. I can still hear his plaintive refrain
'I don't know how our lads will take it.' The committee was a
near-total victory for Edward Heath, although once during the
committee stage, his majority slipped to one vote. Brusquely he
commented, 'One is enough.'

In the early months of 1962 I would sit on the back benches
always present when he returned from a Common Market negotiating session in Brussels. It was an impressive performance.
He had a rather clipped voice and mastered a brief that often
considered the minutiae of trade – kangaroo meat was a memorable item. Questions to him quickly escalated to matters of
principle rather than details of shopping.

Sir Robin Turton was a persistent advocate of home agriculture and Commonwealth trade. He feared these were
endangered by Europe. Years later I was privileged to give the
address at his memorial service but in 1962 we were opposites at
the barricades. The Turton–Heath exchanges were memorable.
Turton, a tall, stooped figure, spoke with measured courtesy
which concealed a strong scepticism. Heath, at the despatch
box, half turning to reply, responded briskly. It seemed to me
– given my then Euro views – a clash between the nostalgic

politics of a passing age and the exciting challenges of Britain and Europe.

Quite soon I joined a small group of supportive MPs who met Heath in his ministerial rooms whenever he had reported to the Commons on the Brussels negotiations. I was overawed by the occasions, and as a tentative apprentice, made comments on agricultural issues and specifically the Milk Marketing Board. If the European negotiations had continued I think it is possible that I would have become one of the 'Heath European group' and I would have learned to adjust to his rather abrupt and distant moods. Initially these did not disquiet me. I was looking for a new style of Tory leadership in contrast to the Macmillan grouse moors caricature. My relations with Heath were never tested as de Gaulle put an end to the Common Market negotiations.

I was still with a group of young MPs who used to see him but we now discussed wider political issues both before the 1964 general election and afterwards. He was not a comfortable companion. I remember a group met him at Tony Buck's flat, which I subsequently shared. Tony was MP for Colchester and said after the meeting, 'He was very severe with you – not a bit friendly.' It was a fair point. The exchange had concerned my scepticism about Labour's National Plan. I think Heath felt it was unwise to open up hostilities during the short period of Labour government from 1964–66. By contrast I was dying for an argument against planning and incomes policy.

When I was on the front bench as junior shadow Technology I remember Heath coming in at Questions and growling 'I feel like a row'. To me it seemed impetuous and not the kind of leadership I would have got from Home or Maudling. Above all it was playing the man and not the ball. It was, of course, the reputation he earned as a bruiser and as an excellent organiser that got him the leadership over Maudling in 1964. Maudling was surprisingly laid back but his seeming laziness concealed a sharp intellectual command of a Conservatism based upon Keynesian economics. There was never any risk that I would have voted for him.

After his election as leader, Heath led the Tories briskly and very much as one might have expected. He was well served by Jim Prior as a parliamentary private secretary, but it was difficult to persuade Heath to relax in the smoking room and engage in low-grade political gossip. It was extraordinary that a person with such musical talents and a fine yachtsman seemed so socially restricted. The Tory Party, never happy in opposition, was querulous. Many yearned for more radical politics that would deliver trade union reform and lower taxes. Heath could accept these policies with reservations but he recoiled from the wider free-enterprise policies of Powell, which he regarded as unrealistic and dangerously romantic. His view was shared by Maudling and Macleod.

The knights of the smoking room, then a home of discontented gossip, decided to have a private dinner party with Heath as guest. All were to speak frankly as friends. We were entertained by Charles Taylor, the affluent Member for Eastbourne, in his elegantly furnished London flat. The surroundings were impressive and the wine flowed, but it did not mellow the discussion.

At the dinner was Douglas Glover, MP for Ormskirk, who had a grievance. Recently he had performed a procedural coup. The minister had finished his speech and sat down a minute early. Glover sprang to his feet and started talking. Acutely he realised he could not be shut up since only the Speaker could accept the closure motion which would end the debate. Speaker King was absent. He eventually turned up, well dined and wig slightly askew, but by then the debate had been automatically terminated at 10 p.m. and the government business lost. It was

a triumph for Glover but both front benches were secretly horrified. Glover felt he had not received proper acclaim from his
leader. With great dignity, but much feeling, he complained to
Heath and concluded by vigorously stubbing out his cigar butt.
Unfortunately he missed the ashtray and ground it into the
superbly polished table.

A buttoned-up Heath endured his hosts, who were complaining whilst protesting utmost loyalty. I only spoke briefly about
the need to attack Labour's National Plan and also to question
Keynes's alleged views on public spending and debt. It was
nonetheless enough to ensure that I was placed beside Heath at
his next dinner with the 1922 Executive. It was a genuine attempt
to see if we could have some personal rapport despite our different economic views. I was apprehensive about the dinner; my
command of music did not stretch much beyond popular classics
and I particularly disliked sailing. The dinner was punctuated by
a series of conversational dead ends, but he concluded by saying I
must come and see him at his rooms in the Albany. I turned up as
arranged and was put to wait in his sitting room. The walls were
lined with photographs of Heath either solo or accompanied by
political personalities. It was eerie. Then a member of his staff
told me that Heath had been called away. I never received an
apology or a suggested date for a replacement meeting.

The estrangement was total, although through an intermediary
I received an invitation to join the front bench which I declined.
The frozen relations became even icier after the passage of the
1972 European Communities Act and eventually the Counter
Inflation Bill fixing prices and incomes.

After his defeat in February 1974 I was asked to go and see
him. The message came whilst I was working at Grieveson
Grant and I had a good idea that the whips had told him that
my membership of the shadow Cabinet might strengthen his

beleaguered position. He had lost two elections out of three. I have described elsewhere my churlish reply – namely that he should make public his agreement to my request that he would not lead the Conservatives at the next election. It was out of character of me to be so outspoken but it was the culmination of a long period when policy differences were not tempered by any reasonable personal relations. I was not alone. In 1972 Nicholas Ridley and I joined forces to oppose the government control of prices and incomes. Thereafter, Ted Heath cut us both. What is more, he extended his froideur to my wife. Standing next to him on the stairs of the Bank of England waiting for lunch after the marriage of the Prince and Princess of Wales he responded to Sarah's polite greeting … until he realised to whom she was married. Conversation ceased immediately and thereafter she was added to his list of pariahs. It was a very sad business. I could disagree with Michael Foot or Tony Benn but understood and enjoyed discussing differences.

Heath was a powerful exponent of managerial conservatism as well as having a One Nation social policy. He had talented followers including Peter Walker and Michael Heseltine with whom I had cheerful relations. He might have emerged as an outstanding leader had he survived the miners' strike election of February 1974, but it was not to be. My hunch is that if he had been blessed with family life and the daily round of domestic compromise he would have been far better at political man management. Meanwhile his ideals will be remembered with more affection than the man.

36

BATTLE OVER EUROPE

I was a zealot for British membership of the Common Market from 1960, when I was working at the Economist Intelligence Unit. The enthusiasm died away after the 1966 general election. My election addresses in 1961, 1964 and 1966 were restrained rather than effusive on the topic, namely:

> 1961: I am sure we must negotiate, for the more Europe is united, the greater the contribution to the strength of the Free World in its struggle to meet the Communist challenge. Only negotiations will reveal if the terms of entry are satisfactory.
>
> 1964: No mention
>
> 1966: Our developing interest lies with Europe. A Conservative government would seek close relations with the Common Market.

The change then took place. The 1970 election address stated:

> I want our own agricultural, taxation, transport and fuel policies decided here at Westminster by British MPs and not by a European government or Parliament in Brussels. I would vote against signing the Treaty of Rome.

And in a speech at Market Drayton on 10 June 1970 I stated:

It is on this issue I believe that the British people are aching to be
heard. This evening I have raised my voice. I am not prepared
to be marched Prussian style through the Westminster lobbies
by the Common Market drill sergeants. I value British national
independence too highly.

The increasingly close association with Enoch Powell was crucial
in my conversion but it was hardly Damascus. I became aware
of a general lack of enthusiasm in the constituency. Many, and
not just the farmers, were content for the issue to sleep or even be
buried when de Gaulle vetoed British membership.

At Westminster things were rather different. After 1966 I
thought Harold Wilson was always agnostic but prepared to
negotiate membership. In his day George Brown had been a
volatile enthusiast. More important, by 1968 Roy Jenkins had
become a key figure in the government and he was a powerful
and convincing advocate of joining Europe. I had a mischievous
pipe dream. I expected Labour to win the 1970 general election and then Wilson would seek Common Market membership.
There would be ructions in the Cabinet from such ministers as
Barbara Castle and Fred Peart. The Tories, I judged, would be
sorely tempted by this situation and would press vigorously for
safeguards and encourage Labour's anti-marketeers. This would
be difficult for Edward Heath, whose natural desire would be to
support the government.

My analysis, of course, depended upon Labour winning the
election. But in reality and not pipe dream Edward Heath was
the victor. Even so I felt the public mood, certainly in Oswestry,
was against European membership and during the 1970 general
election campaign stated my opinions. By the summer of 1970
my anti-Common Market views were well known. They did not
cause much concern in the constituency. No one then considered

that I would carry my opposition to the lengths I did when the issue was debated at Westminster. In truth neither did I. The ringing words at Market Drayton rather assumed I would be an opposition MP who would not vote for Europe. For Edward Heath the 1970 election provided the chance for his life's ambition. He was aided by two outstanding lieutenants. Geoffrey Rippon was an indefatigable negotiator at Brussels and above all Francis Pym was an excellent organiser as the Chief Whip.

In the early stages of the Westminster debates I arranged three public meetings in the constituency so that I could, again, make known my position and learn the views of others. I decided not to have officers of the Conservative Association in the chair in view of the split between the government and myself. Instead I invited local dignitaries including the chairman of the NFU. The meetings were quite well attended and conducted in a friendly and not unhelpful fashion.

The Westminster debate was dominated by divided parties. The Conservatives had a number of anti-marketeers, from soft to hard line, perhaps fifty or so. These were more than offset by Labour pro-marketeers. Their number ranged to include members from both the right and centre including Roy Jenkins. Even in my partisan eyes they were of high quality. Pym's tactic was to provide plenty of debating time and votes on such generalised principles that strict party discipline was not enforced or required. This suited both Labour and Tory party managers since it enabled their minorities to let off steam. We talked ourselves to a standstill, but the time would come when the government would present a Bill to give effect to the pro-market House of Commons majority, namely the European Communities Bill 1972. Then it became a war of political nerves and pressure on the minorities to accept the party whip irrespective of their European views.

Labour insisted on a party vote against the Bill and with a heavy heart Roy Jenkins voted accordingly. It was rumoured that Bill Rodgers, another gifted Labour pro-marketeer, was sick after his act of apostasy. The Conservative anti-marketeers held their line rather better than their Labour pro-marketeer counterparts. A dozen Tories and five Ulster Unionists voted against the Bill but the government majority of eight was sufficient to guarantee the Bill through all its parliamentary stages.

That second reading debate still lives in memory. It was a three-day debate, 15–17 February 1972. I attended most of it but did not speak. Occasionally I would wander onto the terrace; the spring weather was fine and MPs gathered there to comment on how the debate was going. Enoch Powell's passionate speech denouncing legislation which would give away the 'independence and sovereignty of this House ... the very stones of this place would cry out against us...' made a mark. But Francis Pym had worked patiently and well. My somewhat inglorious contribution had been an attempted intervention in Geoffrey Rippon's speech. Magisterially he waved me down and I sank back in my seat. The whips, who were conducting a charm offensive, gave me their sympathy.

When the division bell rang I felt an emptiness in my stomach. The talking was over. I was sitting close to Derek Walker-Smith, the doyen of Tory anti-marketeers; he heaved himself out of his place and said with little apparent enthusiasm, 'Well, I suppose this is it.' I followed him into the 'No' lobby. The Tory rebels were modest in numbers – a mere fourteen. Ironically they did not include the two who had resigned from the government: Teddy Taylor, a junior minister from the Scottish Office, and Jasper More, my neighbour from Ludlow who had been a whip. More was a great friend through the European debate and thereafter. He had welcomed me on my arrival in Shropshire and was superb at guiding me through the pitfalls of county council politics.

I needed friends in Shropshire. My Oswestry evening surgery took place the day following the vote. My agent told me there had been a definite reaction from activists who had accepted my 'anti' views but felt that I should have supported the government in getting their business. This reaction was quite strong and led to a difficult annual meeting on 18 February 1972. It was made no easier by a power cut that plunged us into darkness. The meeting was confused and uneasy and eventually passed a resolution upholding both the Prime Minister and his policy and also me. The general view was that they were essentially supporting the Prime Minister and there was innocent surprise when the *Daily Telegraph* decided their support of me was more newsworthy.

My Association president, Mrs Eila Kynaston, was a tower of strength. There was no likelihood of deselection, but I nursed the constituency with even greater vigour. One evening I was working in the constituency office and answered the telephone. Hugh Richards, a substantial farmer, thought he was talking to the agent and told him, colourfully and at length, what he thought of 'bloody Biffen'. The scars healed fairly soon. At the Oswestry Agricultural Show in August 1972 I began to hear complaints against the Common Market and the French. At the subsequent February 1974 general election I had the irony of meeting constituents who intended voting Liberal as Heath had taken us into Europe; so much was the reward for my stand against the Common Market.

Whilst I was holding the line in the constituency I maintained my interest in the Bill, which had just squeaked by the second reading. The Tory anti-marketeers formed a group. Enoch replaced Walker-Smith as informal chairman and I became whip. Neil Marten was also at the centre of our activities. He was a dedicated anti-marketeer, the very opposite of a chauvinist with a charming light touch. It says something for the tolerance of the Conservative Party that Neil and I kept our seats on the 1922 Executive throughout this period.

My task as whip was not onerous. I kept an exercise book with the names of the group and how they had voted as the committee stage proceeded. It was important to recruit and hold those who generally supported the government but would occasionally support us – such as Hugh Fraser. Sadly I have to say the only time we mildly dented the government's majority was when Duncan Sandys held a large party for his friends – Euro-enthusiasts almost to a man. The hospitality was so good that the laggards missed the vote. I had never thought we could win a vote, but the battle was hard fought as just one successful amendment would have provoked a committee stage with who knows what consequences.

Powell told me he would not stay in a Parliament that was neutered by the provisions of the Rome Treaty. I do not know if that was a serious and settled view. He did, however, continue in Parliament to debate the issues of immigration in the context of the Ugandan Asians.

Meanwhile, the committee stage of the Bill had damaged the Labour Party rather than the government. Labour pro-marketeers simply could not maintain the hostility to the Bill they had been compelled to support at second reading. I suspect the managements of both parties were heartily relieved to see the back of the Bill in the summer of 1972. Soon new issues would replace Europe. In 1972 who could have believed that in February 1974 Heath, with an overall Commons majority and with seventeen months still to go before a general election was necessary, would decide to go to the polls early – and lose?

Europe dominated my life from the 1970 June election until the summer of 1972 when the European Communities Bill received its third reading, although there were other diversions including the marathon Industrial Relations Bill. At Westminster and in the constituency I felt drained by Europe. I was independent minded but never yearned for such prolonged controversy on such a scale. I was relieved when the Bill became law. I was as committed against it as anyone, scoring a high number of hostile votes, but I never displayed the commemoration plate that was struck for the 'antis'. It is still in the attic.

Alas, I had little time to sink back into conformity. The Heath government had scored a great success with its European legislation, but elsewhere it was ill starred. The Industrial Relations Act proved unenforceable and levels of government borrowing and spending produced the familiar signs of inflation. Heath decided to counter this economic situation with an Industry Bill, which empowered government spending on industry, and a Counter Inflation Bill to regulate pay and prices. I was opposed to both, and was partnered by Nicholas Ridley. He was no longer a minister: he said he had resigned and Heath said he was sacked. I campaigned with Nick from the autumn of 1972 until the general election in February 1974.

The Counter Inflation Bill was a memorable contest. On the second reading we had damned the measure with the faintest of praise and then supported it in the lobby. This was cynical but I was surprised when the 'selection committee' put both of us on the committee stage of the Bill. The committee of selection, which was an independent body, was either subtle or innocent in supposing that Ridley and I, having voted for the Bill, would be loyal to it throughout the committee stage.

The meetings were held in Room 10, a modest-sized room for a medium-sized committee. Maurice Macmillan, the Secretary of State for Employment, led for the government. He was a charming man and treated the rebels with great consideration. I doubt if his heart was in the measure; he was basically a free market Tory. Opposite him was Brian Walden. It was one of the few occasions that he had a Labour frontbench role. After a brilliant start in 1964 he was showing a lack of appetite for office unlike his Birmingham partner, Roy Hattersley. Walden could argue any case and he readily recognised the potential mischief in the Counter Inflation Bill. The arithmetic was simple. If Ridley and I voted against the government they would lose unless rescued by the sole Liberal, John Pardoe. Pardoe and I both came from Bridgwater and I had a rather better relationship with him than I did the Conservative whip. It soon became clear that the committee was now in the hands of a grouping of Labour–Tory dissidents – and occasionally Pardoe. We conducted our opposition with good humour, but were determined to carry our amendments. Macmillan very sensibly did not threaten or bluster. He knew that when the Bill was sent to the entire House of Commons for report stage the government whips would have a comfortable majority to reverse defeats in committee. Meanwhile, the press decided that the Counter Inflation Bill Committee was good copy. In particular David McKie of *The Guardian* much enjoyed the proceedings. The arguments were genuinely held and put without bitterness and represented Parliament at its controversial best. Francis Pym, the Chief Whip, offered us a meeting with Edward Heath. Nicholas and I politely declined; somehow it would have spoiled the occasion.

37

THE 1922 COMMITTEE AND EMERGENCE OF MARGARET THATCHER

I had enjoyed the brief period in 1965 whilst junior to Ernest Marples as 'shadow Technology' but the post was not renewed after the 1966 general election. Edward Heath did not want a cumbersome government in exile and relied upon officers of the party committees to do the junior 'shadow' chores. I had no great desire for shadow office but I was delighted to be invited to join the One Nation Dining Club.

The club had been established in the 1950 parliament. The founders included Macleod, Heath, Carr, Maudling and Powell. Their initial pamphlet on social policy, called 'One Nation', invested it with a reputation of scholarship and political skill. The group was highly regarded in the 1960s. I enjoyed the weekly dinner on a Wednesday. It was an occasion when politics and even the European issue were debated in a calm manner. The group had initially argued for a positive Tory social policy and for a market economy. We regarded ourselves as something of an elite and rightly so.

At this time I was also elected to the executive of the 1922 Committee, which consisted of House of Commons Tory back-benchers. The 1922 was created at that date as a result of the rank and file Conservative members rejecting their own Tory

leadership, who they believed was under the dubious influence of Lloyd George. From its origins the 1922 Executive was
concerned to have a close liaison and influence with the party
leader. The agenda of the executive ranged from the trivial to
the high drama of politics. Much time was spent discussing the
dining room wine cellar, which it was believed had deteriorated
under the stewardship of Robert Maxwell. But it was a topic
more than matched by anxiety over the party leadership.

The executive met on Thursday afternoons at 5.30 p.m. in
Committee Room 14. It was the largest of the committee rooms
and steeped with political drama. The full membership of the
1922 met at 6 p.m. immediately after the executive. My time
on the executive was to give me an insight into the workings of
the parliamentary Conservative Party and a direct link with the
leader and his team. It was from this position that I was able to
view the leadership of Edward Heath, both in opposition and
office, and subsequently his misfortunes which led to his replacement by Margaret Thatcher in 1975. It was the high drama of
politics and featured the clash of personalities and policies which
fundamentally recast the Conservative Party.

I was elected to the 1922 Executive in 1966. I had hardly settled
in before I became embroiled in the storm that followed Enoch
Powell's Birmingham speech on immigration, which resulted in his
dismissal from the shadow Cabinet. The party was in some turmoil
and inevitably the matter was discussed by the 1922 Executive.
Those sympathetic to the Powell position realised that Heath's
authority over the composition of the shadow Cabinet could not
be successfully challenged, but they took up another tactic.

They waited to demonstrate a firm line on immigration and
race relations without involving the person of Powell. The
Conservatives had voted for an amendment to the second reading of the Race Relations Bill and the opportunity arose when

the legislation now came back to the House for its third reading. It was then possible to vote against the Bill. Although very much a junior member I collected names for the amendment drawn entirely from the executive. The result was that the Bill, which had been subject to a frontbench amendment on its second reading, had an identical amendment by members of the 1922 Executive on the third reading. It was a splendid example of dumb insolence. The shadow Cabinet did not vote on the third reading as they had on the second. The disarray was near total. The incident demonstrated that the names of the 1922 Executive could be used to show, not least to the media, how divided the Conservatives were over the immigration issue, quite apart from the personality of Powell. In the excitement there were misunderstandings and mistakes and I recall how angry Cranley Onslow (later Chairman of the 1922) was that his name was listed for the 1922 amendment when he had not given his authority. I do not think that there was ever a repeat of the majority of the 1922 Executive trying to embarrass their betters on the front bench by this technique.

I just missed serving under the redoubtable chairmanship of John Morrison. He typified the classical chairman: a landed grandee, loyal but able to speak candidly to the leader and endowed with shrewdness which outstripped intellect. In political terms he was a 'good man to go tiger-hunting with'. His successors were William Anstruther-Gray 1964–66, Arthur Vere Harvey 1966–70 and Harry Legge-Bourke after 1970. Anstruther-Gray was charm personified. He became an imposing Deputy Speaker. In earlier days he had been asked by a Scottish Border Conservative Association if he would live in the constituency. 'No,' he replied. 'But I will certainly hunt in the constituency.' Vere Harvey had had a distinguished Air Force career and there was a period of relative quiet during his chairmanship.

Harry Legge-Bourke was landed gentry and ex-Army, but he had an independent streak and tolerated waywardness in others. Obliquely he had hinted to his constituents in March 1963 that Macmillan should retire. A military career spent partly in the Middle East had left him sympathetic to the Palestinian cause. He was a Eurosceptic before the pejorative term had been discovered and he was devoted to agriculture. When the Pig Industry Development Association addressed the Tory Agricultural Committee I remember Harry earnestly and with no trace of humour asking, 'Is PIDA prejudiced against the coloured pig?'

Memorably, he extended a protective arm when a handful of free market Conservatives, myself included, kept the Commons late on a Friday evening. We were opposing Conservative legislation that gave the state financial powers to support failing industries. We described it as a policy to save lame ducks. We talked with passion and at length and broke the fifty-year Friday sittings record. The Palace of Westminster car park was packed. Ministerial cars with their drivers, Members' wives waiting to leave for their constituency and the Friday round of surgeries and wine and cheese parties. Tempers rose. Even Tory monetarists sympathetic to our cause discovered the magic of wine and cheese but Legge-Bourke would brook no persecution from our fellow Tories. 'They are speaking from principle,' he said. All these splendid qualities made him a difficult companion for Edward Heath, who was impatient with parliamentary delay and was a committed reformer with a managerial style. The 1922 Executive meetings with him, under Legge-Bourke, were conducted with an icy courtesy; no bonhomie but no overt hostility.

Matters changed when Edward du Cann succeeded Harry. He had been a junior Trade minister under Heath in the early 1960s. They had disagreed on policy and Heath had emphasised his departmental authority without much tact. It is probable that du Cann got the chairmanship on the basis that he would 'stand up' to Heath, which he certainly did, albeit in oleaginous style, adding to the mutual antipathy. Heath should not have been distressed by this situation. His crucial role as Prime Minister made his position secure and the Whips' Office was in a better position to advise him about politics than the 1922 Executive, who tended to be consistently right of centre.

The miners' strike in 1972 changed this situation. Then the Tory mood was sombre. During the two years following the general election, economic policy had been gradually abandoned or U-turned. Now the policy was price and income control, a hallmark of Wilson's Labour policy. Most politicians, and certainly Tories, can bear with apostasy or U-turns if they work. The 1974 miners' strike tested to destruction the Tory wage controls and Heath decided that the issue should be resolved by a general election.

The Conservative defeat, albeit by a hair's breadth, under-mined Heath's position as leader. The general wisdom was that Harold Wilson, having sneaked into No. 10, would call another election in the autumn and would win. The 1922 Executive was now almost entirely anti-Heath and needed no encouraging from their chairman. Politics is so arbitrary: had Heath won by even a narrow majority, the executive would sullenly have accepted the reality of Prime Ministerial power.

During the summer of 1974 between the February and October elections, the executive reflected or plotted on the situation. Meanwhile Denis Healey introduced an electioneering and tax-cutting Budget. It was populist and economic nonsense but the shadow Cabinet decided we should sit on our hands. Peter Tapsell, a respected stockbroker, and I decided to rebel and vote against the Healey Budget. We took upwards of twenty colleagues into the lobby and earned a flattering leader in *The Times*. Sometimes martyrdom comes cheap.

The 1922 Executive decided they could not fomally challenge Heath's leadership should he lose the election. On the other hand they felt they could interpret the party constitution as suggesting that Edward Heath should offer himself for re-election. The unspoken thought was that he could not continue as leader if he had lost three general elections: 1966 and twice in 1974.

In July we agreed that the election would be in October and that we should meet as quickly as possible thereafter. There could be no security for a meeting in the Commons and du Cann therefore suggested that we meet at his City banking office, Keyser Ullmann in Milk Street. The election went as expected and Labour had a majority of forty-two over the Tories and three overall.

The clandestine meeting took place as arranged. I had no problems since I had a part-time job with the stockbrokers Grieveson Grant in nearby Gresham Street. Under the benign chairmanship of du Cann we held our inquest. Edward Heath was the scapegoat. The judgement was universal, including even Nigel Fisher, a Tory progressive. We agreed that the next move would be to discuss the propriety of a leadership election. The 1963 election of Alec Douglas-Home had been the last occasion when the leadership was decided by consultation. Thereafter the election was to be a ballot of Members of Parliament. The authors of the constitution requiring a leadership vote had not foreseen the circumstances of 1974, but we agreed a defeated leader should seek a new mandate from the parliamentary party.

Having made our discreet judgement we set about leaving. A bevy of journalists were waiting for us on the Milk Street pavement. Our story was blown and the secretive nature of our meeting told against us. Pilloried as the 'Milk Street Mafia', I have no doubt we created some sympathy for Edward Heath, struck down in his electoral defeat.

Edward du Cann and the 1922 Executive eventually triumphed; Heath did offer himself for re-election and to general surprise was defeated by Margaret Thatcher. She was something of a hard-line right-winger who had the courage to stand. Other members of Heath's Cabinet, notably Willie Whitelaw, did not put themselves forward in the first ballot out of loyalty.

I had no role in the leadership campaign in 1975. On the first ballot Heath offered himself for re-election and was supported by all his Cabinet colleagues, save Thatcher and Keith Joseph. These two had set themselves apart. Soon after the February 1974 defeat they had founded the Centre for Policy Studies. This was clearly a move to promote classical liberal economic policy – now bearing the fashionable designation of 'monetarism'. It was an attempt to revive free enterprise and promote trade union reform, which had been promised by the Conservative leader- ship at the Selsdon conference before the 1970 general election. This policy had subsequently been abandoned or thwarted. Keith Joseph did not harbour any leadership ambition, decid- ing quite rightly that he lacked the temperament. There was a possibility that Edward du Cann might stand, but he had served his purpose by helping to bring about the election.

It was assumed I would be in the Thatcher camp as I had been an opponent of income control and substantial government borrowing. Actually I supported William Whitelaw. I felt that radical economic policies had a better chance of being executed under his leadership. He was a shrewd 'fixer' and could reconcile the defeated Heathites to the difficulties of balancing the budget and to passing effective trade union law.

My immediate task was to vote tactically on the first ballot; the candidates were Ted Heath, Margaret Thatcher and Hugh

Fraser, a flamboyant and independent right-winger who was jokingly a self-proclaimed 'male chauvinist'. He got my vote but there was never the slightest doubt that he would lose. Margaret Thatcher polled well; Edward Heath stood down and, as I had hoped, Willie Whitelaw stood in the second ballot. He got my vote. I told no one including my constituents how I had voted. The assumption was that I voted for Thatcher on both first and second ballot; my actual behaviour, had it been known, would have been judged unexpected and probably somewhat bizarre.

‡

From 1968 until 1990 John kept a diary. He would write it up each day. From this point onward, I have included selected extracts from these diaries to complement the original text. I have also added explanatory details where possible.
  Sarah Biffen

‡

Thursday 7 February 1974

The election date was announced. Spencer Le Marchant told me as I was lunching Ian Gow. Gow told me that Prior had said Carrington had been impressed by me and would have liked to have me in the Ministry of Defence. I unburdened fairly fiercely and said I thought a Labour victory would more coincide with national interest. The news that Enoch was not standing caught everyone aghast. Peter Tapsell said it was a dreadful decision; Kenneth Lewis complained he would 'not be around when he was needed'. It has been a remarkable day. I know in my heart Enoch Powell is right – and I think the next eighteen months will and shall determine if I stay in politics.

Friday 22 February 1974

The campaign proceeds... At any rate we are now in the final stretch and I hope I can last out. Enoch Powell sent a copy of tomorrow's speech which I decided not to read until after delivery.

Saturday 23 February 1974

The campaign is beginning to take a toll. I felt very tired during the day, and was relieved to discover the same went for Jonathan Bradley.‡ The poor lad has had to do a vast amount of driving. In the morning I caught up with my mail completely, and then drove to Whitchurch. George Harris [Conservative supporter] drove me around the town and we did loudspeaker appeals wherever we went. Jonathan did canvassing on a rough housing estate and found evidence of switching from Labour to Liberal. I had the Powell speech in a sealed envelope which I gave to Jonathan – he thought I had exercised extraordinary self-restraint in not reading it.

Monday 25 February 1974

A fearful gloom has now possessed me. I truly believe the seat will be lost; or at best it will be touch and go. I do not know quite why the black dog has settled so firmly on my shoulder but canvassing in Maesbury did not help where I found tangible evidence of a swing towards the Liberals.

Tuesday 2 July 1974

I received the draft of the speech that Enoch plans to make at the end of the week on the EEC, and it is dreadful – going counter to all that was urged at last Wednesday's meeting. I wrote him a short and direct note saying that I thought this was a clear indication that he was going to ask people to vote Labour and I didn't

---

‡ John's 'candidate's friend' in the election campaign.

see much point in the rest of us trying to build bridges. I had quite an amusing meeting with the Europe Group when I did a 'Europe des Patries' paper. Michael Fidler is clearly anxious to protect himself against the consequences of Heath's EEC policy. [...] At dinner Jack d'Avigdor-Goldsmid told me he was fearful for the Midland marginals, and Winterton and Spence were both breathing anti-Heath noises. There is not much ebullience in the party and there is much coalition talk. I have agreed to go on Michael Heseltine's Industry Group.

Wednesday 3 July 1974

What a day. The lunch with Heath was disastrous: I said nothing until the end, but I then suggested that Labour had wider social backing than the Tories and this made it more likely that they would pursue orthodox economic policies designed to curtail inflation and that the Conservative Party needed a more emollient approach and to recapture the spirit of Baldwin. He got very bad tempered and so did I. The others present were slapped down for their various beliefs. Tugendhat advocated indexing and Lawson was anxious to curb trade union power. John Peyton told me that I was more than half responsible for the rift. Later in the evening Neil Marten assured me I was well to be 'in the clear' from any invitation to join a Heath government. Enoch Powell telephoned and we had a further discussion about his speech; I told him that it was impossible for me to collude with someone who was going to vote Labour. At least he recognised some force in the argument, and said, 'We are all waiting for the thunderstorm.' Certainly everything will be clearer in four months.

Saturday 12 October 1974

I had a long day which was faintly anticlimactic. I am gradually returning to the post-election world. I talked to Nick Ridley, and he says there is a plan to foist Whitelaw on the party as leader with Heath as shadow Foreign Affairs. Nick proposes to see Keith Joseph very quickly in order to ascertain what he would like. Meanwhile I have planned to see Nick tomorrow. I did a radio interview with Philip Goodhart on the leadership and was quite pleased when I heard the edited result. We both agreed we would be fighting the election under a new leader and whereas Philip thought the change would have come by this Christmas I said it would be Christmas twelvemonth. […] It is my instinct that the EEC renegotiated proposals will be endorsed by the government and put to the test in a referendum. It is also my hunch that it will not be long before Tory malaise sets in – once the three-year haul is appreciated.

Sunday 13 October 1974

In the morning Ian Gow telephoned and referred most kindly to my radio talk yesterday. He then told me that he was anxious for Joseph to be the leader but that Howe had told him that Joseph did not want the job. Later I went across to Nick Ridley's flat where the Selsdon Group had gathered (they were quite impressive young men and Patricia Hodgson was also there). Nick said Nora Beloff [journalist] had said that Joseph was bitterly regretting he had spoken at Preston and would be unwilling to stand as leader. I said that I thought the establishment would try and run a Whitelaw–Heath–Joseph ticket and this could only be frustrated if Joseph put his own hat in the ring. After the Selsdon Group departed Nick had a call from Jack Weatherill in which he said there was a Joseph–Thatcher determination to fight and that Whitelaw had received many blackballs. It was also apparent that du Cann was being smeared good and proper by his detractors. In the evening John O'Sullivan [journalist] telephoned me and he is most anxious to

propagate the cause of Joseph and I suspect there is some bewilderment that I am not a partisan.

Friday 18 October 1974

I have continued in the grips of a profound depression. I suppose
it was inevitable but I had hoped the problem had been simply
a matter of food poisoning. I fear the prospect of frontbench
responsibility – partly because I wonder how I could manage it,
partly because I want more leisure time, partly because I do not
want to risk my GG income. Why can't I be left alone and be an
influential rural backbencher with speaking opportunities? The
mood has laid upon me heavily.

Monday 18 November 1974

I was today offered a 'shadow appointment'. Edward Heath had
a word with me on the telephone and said he wanted a frank talk
with a view to broadening his team. I telephoned Edward du
Cann and told him that I would make my acceptance conditional
on the acknowledgment that I had indicated a preference for a
fresh leader by the next election and my commitment to the 1922
Executive view that the nature and timing of leadership and election should rest with the party. He did not feel able to make an
offer which would be accepted in these circumstances and there
the matter ended.

Monday 25 November 1974

The undercurrent of gossip at the House concerns the decision
of Margaret Thatcher to stand against Heath. I think she will do
well. Heath 140, Thatcher 90, Du Cann 40, and thus a second
ballot even though not persisted with. The main feature of the
day was a rather febrile meeting of the Conservative Home Affairs

Committee. Ostensibly we were going to talk about the Counter-Terrorist Bill, but in fact it was nothing but babble over the death penalty for terrorists. Jill Knight is putting down an amendment to bring in the death sentence, but there is no likelihood of this receiving frontbench support. Ian Gilmour spoke out against such a penalty in respect of Northern Ireland and the debate was incoherent. It appears a deal was done whereby the opposition praised the legislation in return for debates on Northern Ireland and the death penalty – the latter after Christmas.

Tuesday 4 February 1975
I cast my vote for Hugh Fraser in the leadership election and was shattered when I heard the result. The voting had been Thatcher 130, Heath 119, Fraser 16, Abstentions 11. I had discussions with several people in the lobby. They thought Thatcher would be hard to stop but quite soon it was apparent that Whitelaw would stand and personally I think Prior and Howe will also enter their names. I am saddened by the result. I would have liked to have seen a modest Heath victory with the chance of reconciliation with Powell at some future time. I imagine the next best thing would be a Whitelaw victory, and my instinct is that this is not likely. Gow will do all he can to ensure a good vote for Howe. Ridley thinks Margaret now has the leadership and 'she'll take some shifting'. The demise of Heath ends an era. After ten years I feel we can all breathe rather more easily, but I do not know what now happens. At least the EEC Referendum vote will be conducted in a rather more relaxed atmosphere.

Friday 14 February 1975
This has not been a happy day. As events proceeded I began to feel more and more certain that I could not take a post with the

shadow front bench. My nerves are now shot to pieces, and above all I would like to get away for a month or more. The death wish is now very powerful indeed.

Thursday 5 June 1975

I missed the *Farming Today* news but I gather that my recent remarks had been reported. At least a modest success on Britain's Black Day. Black because we are having a referendum and Black because the answer will be YES. How extraordinary that I should feel like this when I consider the mood of careless rapture and enthusiasm that I had for the EEC in 1961/63.

Tuesday 22 July 1975

It sticks in my gullet to write this but Heath made a remarkable speech in the House of Commons. It was fluent, sombre, a flash of self-deprecating humour – but without question one of the most impressive speeches I have ever heard delivered. Enoch, by contrast, seemed tired, rather arid and not at all in the mood of the House. The Labour people were delighted with Heath's speech, and it is bound to raise much speculation about his future. He has no need for further speeches for quite a while. It remains my judgement, however, that Labour are not going to fall asunder. This makes the Heath coalition strategy difficult to execute, but much could happen if Foot resigns on the intro-duction of a reserve Bill.

38

OPPOSITION FRONT BENCH

Following the Labour victory of 1945 Churchill did not have a shadow Cabinet. He conducted opposition much more informally. After Harold Wilson's victory in 1964 Ted Heath, by contrast, had a government in exile. It was an understandable technique; opposition shadows could concentrate on government ministers and also cultivate the media on their allotted subjects. Although I had briefly been shadow junior Technology in 1965–66 I had little idea just how onerous the work would be, but I had been given hints that Margaret Thatcher wanted me in her economic team.

I replaced Patrick Jenkin as shadow Energy. He was not pleased by the news. I had first met him at Jesus College when he had recruited me into the Cambridge University Conservatives. He was a lawyer and had worked with the industrial section of Distillers Company Ltd and took a keen technical and political interest in energy. He was now transferred to the role of shadow Social Security and I sensed his disappointment at being parted from the files of information he had accumulated. Generously he offered them to me.

More significantly I was given a small room on the top floor of the Commons main building. It could just about accommodate me and the Jenkin files. It was a mark of prestige to have a room to myself but I was sorry to leave the Cloisters. I had been there since the late 1960s. The Cloisters had been converted into cramped offices. One side was for Labour and one side for Tories. The Labour members constructed partitions around their desks, which seemed strange for the people's party. By contrast the Tories cheerfully accepted an open-plan office. I had good friends there: Michael McNair Wilson, Kenneth Lewis and Dick Body. We gossiped endlessly, bewailing our front bench and the whips. We also had Norman St John-Stevas, who was eased out because of his typing – the noise not the quality.

My prize inheritance was having Tony Benn as Secretary of State for Energy. It is a sad fact that there was more interest in Tony Benn at Westminster and beyond than in the Department of Energy. Benn had used the period of Conservative government from 1970–74 to rethink his position and had moved well to the left. He was a gifted public speaker, charismatic but not a good team player. He had plenty of establishment Labour enemies. He had been transferred to Energy from Industry where he had tried to promote worker participation and industrial planning agreements, thoroughly irritating both his Prime Minister and senior civil servants. An admirable adversary, he observed quite rightly that I would find it difficult to keep up with the many subjects within the Energy Department and offered to let me have a copy of his department's daily press notes. They were invaluable. Thereafter the Jenkin files collected dust. Benn wryly observed that as a minister John Davies had never offered him the Industry departmental notes when he had been the opposition spokesman.

Tony Benn thrived on publicity and chafed at the lack of interest shown by Westminster and the media in energy affairs. We once ran through forty-five minutes of oral questions and the one that got the most attention was from Rochdale's ample MP, Cyril Smith, on hypothermia. Benn and I hardly ever debated during the ten months I was shadow: the most constructive occasion was an exchange over European Community documents on nuclear policy. It passed totally unnoticed. It was extraordinary that subjects such as coal, gas, electricity, nuclear power and North Sea oil should be so neglected.

Labour had established the British National Oil Company (a publicly owned body) before I had arrived. The storm of opposition protest had died down. I much enjoyed meeting the management of the industries concerned. I was getting the feel of what it was like to be in the shadow Cabinet. The downside was I had to go to endless lunches. The oil companies were my most challenging hosts. They would put on the most impressive displays concerning the technical problems of oil and gas extraction and the financial problems associated with oil depletion. I had a good rapport with the American companies Conoco and Amoco. There was a general feeling of gloom that sometime in the first half of the twenty-first century we would run out of oil. I could understand why they used the argument but am now amused at how wrong they were.

I have so many happy memories of shadowing. The drilling platforms in the North Sea and the platform construction at Kishorn were masterpieces of technology. I also visited Shetland and fell in love with the islands. I was delighted to be asked to address an oil conference in Stavanger. The Norwegians were great hosts and there was a common bond between the two North Sea oil producers.

My day was made when I met Sheikh Yamani, the Arab oil tycoon, but it was little more than a handshake.

I missed the great controversy over the choice of UK nuclear power. There had been a furious debate between proposals of AGR (Advanced Gas-cooled Reactor, British) and PWR (Pressurised Water Reactor, American) designs. The nuclear debate was intellectually challenging and to my surprise I was obtaining a modest grasp of the technology. I also learned something about the potential of wind-, tidal- and barrage-generated electricity. I wrote an article for *The Spectator* on the Flowers Report, which underlined some of the environmental problems of nuclear power. I was flattered to receive a letter from Lord Rothschild (Victor). 'Thank you very much for sending me a copy of your piece on the nuclear power problem. I read it with great interest and if I may say so I thought that, unlike most people, you understand very clearly the problem.'

I was assisted in my role as shadow by a small group of MPs and a couple of peers. We were a happy team. Hamish Gray, MP for Ross and Cromarty, was particularly helpful and skilled in judging the Scottish aspects of North Sea oil. We were concerned with the advance of the Scottish National Party and for a year or more I attended the weekly meetings of the Scottish Parliamentary Conservative Party. I think it taught me how divided the Scottish Tories were over devolution.

Whilst I was shadow there was one significant Bill we had to handle. The Energy Bill was essentially technical legislation relating to the oil industry. I thought the briefing from Shell and BP was balanced and it was certainly helpful. I discovered I enjoyed leading a team, something I had never done at Tube Investments or the Economist Intelligence Unit. I think I was a tolerable success since I was more than content to listen to my fellow MPs.

The Conservative Research Department was a great help providing advice and research. Michael Portillo was the desk officer for energy. He had just come down from Cambridge where he had studied history under the parchment-dry supervision of Maurice Cowling, as I had done some twenty years earlier. I liked him and was not surprised that he became such a prominent Tory; but neither was I surprised that he did not make the leadership. We would often discuss the wider political issues; we were both Eurosceptics. At that time I hoped the enlargement of Europe to include Spain would alter its character. It was a mistaken judgement. Portillo and his fiancée Carolyn Eadie came to spend the weekend at my home in Kinton. It was a pleasant visit and memorable because I opened a fête with a few words in Welsh. Despite careful rehearsal I was deprived of my audience by a sudden torrential downpour. We were a good team at Energy and I came to have an understanding of the topic both technically and politically.

I was moved on after ten months. The post of shadow Industry was promotion but the pressures were greater. I had one major debate when I opened for the opposition. This was a debate on the Queen's Speech. I did my homework and in my view made a careful speech. It was moderate in content but crisply delivered. I was becoming increasingly familiar with the House notwithstanding my nervousness. I remember stumbling over some formality early in my speech and hearing the hostile hyena-like laughter of Jeremy Thorpe. I had never much liked him and even less at that moment.

Congratulatory notes are the small change of politics but I was pleased to hear from Nigel Lawson. He wrote, 'Very many congratulations on a brilliant speech. Just what we have been waiting for for so long.'

Stress shortened my stay as shadow Industry. I have written about my health in another chapter. I returned to the shadow Cabinet as spokesman on small business after a gap of twenty-one months. I had barely warmed the seat before the general election was called.

Life in the shadow Cabinet was fascinating. Margaret Thatcher was firmly in charge but we did have the informality of using our

Christian names. Once in government we addressed ourselves by our departmental titles. The leader of the opposition had a reasonably sized room behind the Speaker's chair, but it really could not easily accommodate twenty or so shadows around the oval table. I have an irreverent recollection of Patrick Jenkin being stuck between table and wall as he tried to slide out early from a meeting. He was too polite and possibly too self-conscious to call attention to his predicament.

I have two very clear memories of this period. First was the determination to research our economic and taxation policies very thoroughly. We had ample professional backing in the City and particularly benefited from the skills of Arthur Cockfield, who had earned a great reputation with Boots. He was later a colleague as a Treasury minister and also succeeded me as Trade Secretary. Margaret Thatcher wanted economic policy proposals in trustworthy hands. Geoffrey Howe as shadow Chancellor was diligent and happy to propose market economy solutions. He had the support of David Howell, John Nott and myself. Jim Prior, who concentrated on trade union reform, was a concession to the old regime of Edward Heath. I admit to prejudice but I believe the Tory opposition to Denis Healey from 1974–79 was not short-term opportunism but also provided the groundwork for effective tax reforms once we were elected.

Secondly, Margaret Thatcher was especially keen that we should plan to curb public spending. This proved a good deal more difficult. Howe proposed a round of shadow Treasury cuts and St John-Stevas, defending Education, did not fight fiercely; he just refused to take part in the exercise.

A major problem during my spell in the shadow Cabinet was the issue of Scottish devolution. Alick Buchanan-Smith argued with great firmness for the recognition of some form of devolution; Margaret Thatcher was strongly against, as I think were most Scottish Tory MPs. I was a witness to this struggle, fascinated but mercifully not involved. I do not think any of us supposed that by 1997 there would not be a single Scottish Conservative MP.

An eternal problem was the use of opposition debating time. If the government was unpopular the sound tactical judgement was to let the unpopularity fester: a debate provided by the opposition would often give ministers a chance to argue their case. The result was that we scraped around to find subjects that would not blow up in our faces. Thus no one was anxious to press for debates on their shadow topics. An exception was Sally Oppenheim, shadowing Consumer Affairs. She was indefatigable in seeking a debate on prices. It was a classic case where public discontent needed no fanning from Westminster. A debate led by Sally would inevitably bring Roy Hattersley into the arena – and that was hardly an equal debating contest. But she persisted in her requests.

My time in the shadow Cabinet left a strong impression on me. It was a happy period effectively presided over by Margaret Thatcher. She tightly controlled her economic ministers and that gave cohesion to the entire team. We were preparing detailed policies that were judged to improve the economy and above all would be enforceable. These were being developed in depth behind the scenes with expert financial and industrial advice. This strength was not so apparent in the general economic debates in the Commons. I had a deep regard for both James Callaghan and Denis Healey. Callaghan exuded gravitas and calm confidence and usually outperformed Margaret Thatcher at Prime Minister's Questions. Healey was an intellectual heavyweight and a bruiser. Geoffrey Howe batted manfully against him, but he was not equal in aggression. Happily, Labour's parliamentary strength was dissipated by the divisions over Scottish devolution and by the strikes in the public services in the Winter of Discontent. They could not have provided a better election backcloth for the Conservative Party and Thatcher and Howe did not miss the opportunity.

Thursday 30 October 1975

I had a most intriguing session with Mrs Thatcher. I had been called to her room to discuss some speech-writing, but it became clear there were other matters afoot. She said that in due course she would have to shuffle the shadow Cabinet and that she very much hoped I would think seriously before I decided and hoped we could make some arrangement. It now seems clear that something will happen within the next three months and 1976 should see me on the front bench. It is quite a thought.

Thursday 15 January 1976

I was summoned at 2.30 p.m. and asked to take over shadow Energy. This I accepted and I wonder to high heavens what will happen next. I explained to Margaret Thatcher that my original plan had been to be a 'respected backbencher' rather like Kenneth Pickthorn, and that the 1970–74 disputes had made life somewhat rancorous. I also said that ideally I would have liked a general and wide ranging economic brief – and she said that had been considered but that she had too many of these already. I then got clearance to speak in the devolution debate, and had a wrangle with the Speaker over the matter. I stuck to my point and literally sat it out until I was called quite late in the day. I then made a speech which I quite enjoyed – Enoch said, 'Your last speech in freedom; now you must go to prison.' He wrote me a most charming note – and later I dreamed something confused about the whole business.

Friday 16 January 1976

I continued life in a stunned and bewildered fashion. When I went to the Commons I had endless telephone calls. Mercifully I had rearranged that this weekend should be in London. I had two television interviews, and the most important was with Robin Day. This lasted for ten minutes, and he treated me very kindly. I declined the opportunity to 'hammer Benn' and in the short discussion we had afterwards Robin Day said, 'But you'll need TB as a bogey man.' I had quite an extended radio interview with *The World at One* and also a short ITV programme. In the early afternoon I had a long talk with Hamish Gray and he told me that there was no politics in the rate of depreciation and we also discussed the problems of a floor price for EEC Energy and the general personnel problems of the Energy Group.

Wednesday 21 January 1976

I will get on record my first impression of the shadow Cabinet. Margaret was charming but firm. We had a long argument about whether or not the party should vote at the conclusion of the economic debate on Thursday, which will be largely devoted to unemployment. The general view was that we should not vote, but Ian Gilmour thought we should. There were spirited anti-vote speeches by Geoffrey Howe and Angus Maude. Keith Joseph endorsed what was said, and Whitelaw was very sound. At the Business Committee there was general confusion and the mood was 60/40 that we should vote, although there were some sound voices in the minority including Christopher Tugendhat. Alas these voices did not prove decisive. When the shadow Cabinet reassembled in the evening there was a decision not to vote – almost everyone had turned around. Those who advocated no vote were Raison, Peyton, Joseph and myself. This small band were of little avail. Margaret Thatcher had already anticipated how matters would move, and Willie backed her, but with some reluctance. Maudling was wholly cynical in attitude.

Tuesday 16 March 1976

I was absolutely bowled over to hear that Harold Wilson had resigned. I quickly concluded that Jim Callaghan would get the leadership and that he will not be disposed to have an election until as late as possible – although the temptation to go in the autumn is there if it looks as if Labour could win. I had to handle the Energy debate on EEC documents in the evening. I was put out of joint because Tony Benn did not take part. Even so that particular rapid has now been negotiated, and I shall be curious to see what happens next. Every Labour MP I have spoken to thinks that Callaghan will get the job...

‡

Tuesday 22 February 1977

Today I went to see Mrs T. and told her that I wanted to pull out. She was immensely understanding, not least because she had taken her husband through a similar problem. I was also told how wonderfully well I had performed during the year and that a job would await me should the Tories win the next election. I could not have a happier resolution of a most miserable experience. I just wonder how Heath would have handled it. All day I had walked around in a daze and a state of bewilderment: I had slept atrociously and knew that I could not continue.

Wednesday 23 February 1977

I saw Humphrey Atkins and had a talk. I said I would be happy to serve in an MT Cabinet or in some fashion in the future. I also talked a while about my nervous problems. Altogether it was a tolerable interview and I told him I had hoped I had demonstrated that I was a loyal and cooperative colleague who looked most for means of reconciling views. I am in a fairly numb state, but I keep going. I do not want to enter the chamber until next week. I attended my last shadow Cabinet meeting. There was a sense of light-heartedness about it. Everyone was pleased that the Devolution Bill had foundered and Francis Pym was hero of the hour. I did a chat on the Jimmy Young show. My parents telephoned early in the morning. I had a lunch with IBM. John Hargreaves tells me he is leaving. The discussion confirmed my weariness of politics.

39

CHIEF SECRETARY TO THE TREASURY

I expected a good majority in the 1979 general election. The campaign was uneventful and the constituency had not then been enlarged to include Newport. At the start of the election I had the help of Sarah Wood and Colin Baillieu. I had known Colin from Bow Group days and he was an excellent 'candidate's friend' in 1979. Sarah and he decided that I lived in bachelor gloom, particularly when they discovered that I had never lit my drawing room fire. For eleven years it had been untouched except by crows and magpies. Perhaps the unlit fire was symbolic of my straitened social life. In my absence they attempted to remedy this defect with disastrous consequences; the whole place was smoked out. Mission accomplished, Sarah, who was working for Nigel Lawson, departed for Leicestershire to help him in his campaign.

Saturday 10 February 1979

Another very bad night's rest. I simply cannot understand why I should be taken thus. Undoubtedly the prospect of the debate has put me into a funk but I do wonder if the change of pills has had any effect.

Monday 12 February 1979

What a nightmare. No sleep again. I simply cannot understand why. I take 1 ½ Mogadon, but I cannot drop off – my stomach tingles with nerves and I twitch.

Tuesday 13 February 1979

The debate was a success. I spoke for twenty-five minutes and MT squeezed my arm and whispered 'Good luck'. I was heard in silence and I began to realise that this was because people were listening. The Tory benches were absolutely crowded and I sat down to a gratifying ovation. During the speech I heard Keith Joseph say, 'Doesn't he do this well.' I also managed to get some spontaneous humour – but what a relief to have it all behind me.

Thursday 8 March 1979

Julian Critchley told me that Windlesham had lunched Heath. The latter still thinks he will be recalled to be leader. Interim there is only one post he will take in a Thatcher government and that is Chancellor of the Exchequer. Specifically he refused Foreign Affairs although this was suggested by Windlesham. That really was a fascinating step.

Wednesday 14 March 1979

I went to the chamber to hear Callaghan make his Paris summit statement. It was absolutely fascinating. He dominated the entire proceedings. MT made a very pro-market speech and got severely mauled. Very few Tories were on their feet thereafter. When we got to shadow Cabinet she said, 'Where were all the marketers?' and Teddy Taylor piped up, 'There aren't any.' Jim Prior glowered.

General election campaign

Wednesday 18 April 1979

The weather was glorious and sunny, and we had a tiring but amiable day. In the evening Colin Baillieu and Sarah tried to light a fire in the living room and it smoked dreadfully. Furthermore Sarah managed to break the stylus on the record player – so it was an evening of dramatic incident. It says much for my temperament that I was not put out by all this. I had an uneventful day walking around the constituency. We covered the market and the villages of Selattyn, Weston Rhyn, Morda, Pant and Llanymynech. Poor Sarah was mortified by having my card torn up before her eyes. The general reception was quite good, but I think there could be 20 per cent undecided. Colin has the most direct approach. Sarah was quite fascinated by the Smithfield [Market], and we had a general chat with a number of farmers. David Smith told me that the Leicester police wanted to take my blood group – but I hadn't an idea. I am pleased my mood has stabilised. Sarah won at Scrabble.

Thursday 3 May 1979

We had a really busy day but it ended on a sour note. Tom Nicholas drove Candia [Younger]‡ and myself around the constituency, and we were on the go all the time. Even so we could not go back to Middle Farm as arranged and the evening meal at the Albright Hussey became an imposition which did not end until midnight. Colin got involved with a drunk and it was all rather unhappy. Meanwhile I had an excellent tour around the constituency despite the indifferent weather. Candia came into

---

‡ Daughter of John's Birmingham friend, David Younger.

every polling station and it really was a lesson in the constitution
for her. One polling clerk refused to tell me how many people had
voted – a proper thing to do. I had not realised it. There were
no outstanding incidents in our travels – but the camera did not
work whilst I swung in the playground at Cheswardine. We subsequently repaired the camera. We had lunch at Shawbury and did
a broad sweep across the constituency from Woore to Trefonen.
Tom was an excellent driver. I heard the radio and it was evident
that the Conservatives were going to win quite decisively.

The result in Oswestry was:

W. J. Biffen (C) 23,551
P. E. Sandlands Nielson (Lab) 10,150
D. J. Evans (Lib) 9,405

Immediately after the election I travelled to London. Most
members of the shadow Cabinet had been summoned for their
appointments but I had no idea what job I might be offered.
Shadow Small Business was really a non-post and I thought I
might be given something outside Cabinet rank. 'John,' said the
Prime Minister, 'I want you to be Chief Secretary. You really
need to keep a sharp eye on spending but don't be hard on the
parties celebrating the Queen's Birthday.' With these terms of
reference I went off to be sworn in as a member of the Privy
Council. Several other members of the Cabinet had not previously been Privy Counsellors and we were done together, rather
self-consciously kneeling and holding the Testament aloft.

As a newcomer to office I had the luxury of the official car,
a large Rover. I always sat in the back either reading or snatch-
ing a few moments' rest. My driver, Eric, was rather saturnine

and always complaining about the hours I worked. There was no remedy and Sarah said I should have someone more cheerful. When I left the Treasury I hope we found an arrangement so that he could drive someone with more suitable hours but I suspect he was morose by nature.

As I sat in my huge room I did not feel that comfortable with my team. I placed a copy of *Enoch Powell: principle in politics* by Roy Lewis prominently on my desk so I could be reminded of my mentor. No one ever commented upon it.

Saturday 5 May 1979

I was today made Chief Secretary to the Treasury and sworn a member of the PC [Privy Council]. The morning started with my walking to Downing Street. I had to wait quite a while and exchange general chat with Mark Carlisle and Angus Maude. MT then said she did not want me doing a non-job, but would I take Chief Secretary. Alastair Pirie, my private secretary, arrived and I am beginning to realise how much work there is. We then had rehearsals for the PC and finally were driven to the palace. It was a nerve-racking affair, particularly as I had to go first. I kissed hands and took the oath. I then returned and telephoned my parents. My mother was near to tears. I then tried to get an early night's rest.

Sunday 6 May 1979

The first day was pretty bloody – I had awful nerves and felt endlessly tired. I managed to read most of the papers I had been sent – but the words swam before my eyes and I cannot really understand what a Chief Secretary does. I kept wishing I could have become Chancellor of the Duchy of Lancaster – but I know this is better for me once I have learned to swim. Well here we

are – up to my neck in trouble but I am now a PC. My target is
at least a year – then I would like to escape to a more settled life
and marry. God help me with this job.

As Chief Secretary to the Treasury I had a vertical learning
curve. It was my role to supervise the spending of all government departments and the consequential paperwork was
enormous. Settling to read my first box I was much impressed by
the contents, which outlined the policies the Treasury's civil servants expected the Conservatives to pursue in the light of their
pre-election promises. Having never been in government or even
a parliamentary private secretary I was quite unfamiliar with the
red box. Every evening I took two or three home and frequently
could not start reading them until after 10 p.m. or finish until the
early hours. This was the fate of all ministers but I think it bore
most heavily on the Chief Secretary.

The red boxes followed me everywhere. They involved grinding hard work at unreasonable hours. Only once did they offer
a diversion. I finished constituency duties by having lunch
with John Gittins, local potato farmer. 'What about some spuds,
John?' At last the red box had a beneficial use. I repacked the
government papers and made a box available. I was confident
the box would be sent to my private office, but fate decreed it
was opened in the Treasury Central Registry. I am not sure if
the civil service thought it was frivolity or enterprise on my part.

My work involved looking at all departments' budgets, which
was helpful in giving me an overview of government. On the
other hand being in the Cabinet was my first experience of office
so I had little prior knowledge of how government worked. It
was a question of learning on the job and I didn't find it easy.

The Treasury had two Cabinet ministers: the Chancellor of

the Exchequer, who was arguably senior to the Foreign Secretary and the Home Secretary, and secondly the Chief Secretary to the Treasury. This post had been created to help the control of public spending and just about scraped into the Cabinet. My position meant that I had a senior civil servant who was effectively my permanent secretary. This was Sir Anthony Rawlinson. He was a commanding figure, intellectually and physically. He seemed to relish curbing public spending, in the course of which he showed little political partiality. I suspect he was broadly sympathetic to the public expenditure aspects of Geoffrey Howe's 'monetarist policy'. Sir Anthony was a great walker and died tragically in a mountaineering accident shortly after I had moved on to Trade.

The Treasury had an official in every government department and they formed a good idea of the prospective budgets. I have the strongest recollection of the package of public spending economies produced by the Treasury civil servants in the Health Department. They included 'accommodation charges' for hospital patients. I realised the official had to think the unthinkable but I decided we were not on the same planet.

Each year we had the public expenditure round when ministers and their advisers would visit the Treasury and argue their case. Sir Anthony had seen it all, but suddenly the routine was shattered. 'Chief Secretary,' he said, 'Mr Heseltine wants you to go and see him. That would not be appropriate.' The Heseltine ploy had failed but it was a sign of the liveliness that would attend his Cabinet career.

Quite soon Margaret Thatcher, doubtless supported by William Whitelaw and Geoffrey Howe, decided that a small group of ministers rather than the Chief Secretary alone should discuss departmental budgets. This was known ominously as the 'Star Chamber'. It was certainly a better way of handling public spending as the inquisitorial group was packed with ministers such as John Nott, then Secretary of State for Trade, who were tolerably sympathetic to the Treasury.

The Chief Secretary was a recent creation and at first my immediate Labour predecessor, Joel Barnett, had not been in the Cabinet. I felt the position was somewhat ambiguous. I was in the Cabinet but could only echo the views of the Chancellor. My Cabinet status was intended to reinforce his authority. This was no real problem because I had known Geoffrey Howe for many years as a friend and fellow Bow-Grouper. He was painstaking in his work as Chancellor. He consulted widely and often I chafed at the length of meetings when I had an office desk awaiting me loaded with papers. Our views were similar but not always identical. Geoffrey invited a range of opinions so I offered mine. I made clear that I was not enamoured by the Medium Term Financial Strategy. This was a monetary calculation and target based substantially on the Treasury forecast of public spending and revenues. I preferred to keep to the broad performance of actual public spending, revenue and borrowing as guides. The differences at this distance do not seem great, but at the time monetary measurement had become a talisman.

In late June 1981 I was interviewed by Robert Mackenzie, who was determined to pin me down as a monetarist ideologue. Exasperated, I responded, 'Can I tell you I've never met Milton Friedman. I've never read the works of Milton Friedman and I've never seen Milton Friedman on television. So my views are much more, if you like… simple is the wrong word but my views are much more home grown. I don't have to look to Chicago; I don't have to look to Hayek and to Central Europe for such inspiration. If I want to choose any philosopher kings I'd sooner look to Scotland for David Hume and Adam Smith.' Geoffrey accepted my heresy and we worked together happily enough. I do not think my views were ever leaked.

Wednesday 16 May 1979

We had a preliminary run over the 'savings' and they total around £3,000 million. She [MT] said she was appalled at how little had been achieved and at the politically sensitive areas. There followed a heated discussion and she dismissed the concept of cash limits, said cuts should be put in global and non-specific terms, and said she could not wear the VAT rate of 15 per cent but would take 12½ per cent. Over time she was worn down on these points and ended up by being a touch more reasonable. I thought she showed much of the old mood of petulance and I fear she may not back Geoffrey Howe.

Early in the job I unwittingly caused embarrassment when I spoke in Edinburgh. Spontaneously, in answer to a question, I said I thought the new policy concerning public spending and borrowing meant there would be 'three years of unparalleled austerity'. I felt it was legitimate to argue there would be short- and medium-term problems. The eventual pattern of investment and unemployment suggested that I was not far off the mark but the phraseology was not happy. I suspect the Treasury knights as well as the Chancellor thought I should learn the virtues of bromide language.

Thursday 24 May 1979

The high drama was when Geoffrey took me across to No. 10 and we had an animated discussion with the PM. It was in a delightful room with only her private secretary present. There was a Lowry painting over the fireplace. We argued long and hard in favour of a 15 per cent VAT and I really do think I was instrumental in getting her reluctant agreement. At first she thought the money could be secured by making the tax rebates non-payable. At heart she is worried that women are going to suffer from the Budget whilst the men will have the tax cuts.

Tuesday 12 June 1979

Budget day was an almighty scramble. We had a packed House but earlier we had a Budget Cabinet. There was a general feeling that Geoffrey Howe had been very brave and that the problem was whether the trade unions would cut up rough in the autumn. I had a job getting a seat fairly near Geoffrey Howe. He then delivered a very good speech and most clearly. It was heard with much anger from the left but I think the overall situation was 'Wait and See'. I then had to go off and do my rounds of visits to the media. I had a radio and TV and on the whole I was quite pleased with the performance on the various programmes. The journalists said I had been amazingly frank.

My sharpest memory of the Treasury was the first Budget presented by Geoffrey Howe. It contained cuts in direct taxation and a substantial increase in value added tax. Just before Budget day it was necessary to increase interest rates. I accompanied Howe to break the news to the Prime Minister. She took it very calmly. It was fascinating to have a ringside seat and watch relations between Margaret Thatcher and Geoffrey Howe. He was an immensely hard-working and loyal Chancellor; she reciprocated the loyalty but often with condescension and a lack of warmth. Furthermore she was inclined to pursue ideas she picked up from 'gurus' such as Alan Walters, a distinguished academic from Birmingham University. I found him an engaging and iconoclastic personality but I did not understand the principles let alone the nuances of his monetarism. His influence was resented by Nigel Lawson, who understood his views and found them wanting.

It was the task of the Chief Secretary to open for the government on the second day of the Budget debate. My opponent was Denis Healey. The Treasury officials held him in great awe. He outstripped them in intellectual authority but at the same time fought in the political gutter with relish and success. I rather enjoyed my frontbench tangle with Healey and got a good press, particularly from Andrew Alexander in the *Daily Mail*.

A further Budget responsibility of the Chief Secretary was to be in charge of the committee stage of the Finance Bill. It was a dreary task. My main objective was to get the business agreed without extensive debate and late night sittings. To that end I was disposed to make minor concessions. My second in command, Nigel Lawson, the Financial Secretary, was differently inclined. He was by far the most accomplished economist of the Treasury ministers but he was also supremely self-confident and could not avoid scoring points. I admired his skill but regretted the controversy it inflamed. I was well served by the range of Treasury civil servants who briefed me on public spending and upon the contents of the Budget.

Wednesday 20 June 1979

The Cabinet meeting was largely devoted to MPs'/ministers' pay. In the end we argued the Boyle recommendation but there was consternation when the PM and Lord Chancellor announced that they would not take their increases. MT said that such a gesture would give her moral authority – Jim Prior then turned deep red and said two members of the Cabinet should not take unilateral action without consulting colleagues. Eventually MT

got her way. I saw Prior in the lobby in the evening and said I
didn't think there was such a thing as moral authority in politics.
The weeks seem to pass by and I really do think I am something
in the swing of this job.

When I arrived at the Treasury I found I had been allocated
a 'special adviser', George Cardona, who had been with the
Conservative Research Department. I made it quite clear that
I didn't want a special adviser, primarily because I felt the role
would not fit easily with the traditional civil service. Geoffrey
Howe found a berth for Cardona and my decision caused no
awkwardness. I now realise I could have used someone to draft
the purely political speeches I had to make, but such work did
not constitute a full-time job. Since 1979 the use of special
advisers has become extensive as have the problems they can
create. Their potential for dispute with the civil service has been
evident recently, particularly where there has been a clash of
personalities.

Monday 29 October 1979

Work in the Treasury has been very hard and exciting. There
is great turmoil over the Pym affair [Francis Pym, Secretary of
State for Defence]. He appears to have triumphed totally and
now we have been asked to allocate the money for the Polaris
replacement from the Contingency Fund and not to discuss it
with ministers in the Cabinet. Wass and Rawlinson are very cagey
about the affair – and I suspect they will go along with the PM.

In November 1979 I married Sarah Wood, whom I had met when she was working for Nigel Lawson. We decided to have a quiet wedding. Not easy for a Cabinet minister. The ceremony was to be at Wandsworth Town Hall on Friday 2 November and I decided it was only reasonable I should tell the Treasury public relations officer, Mr Mower. I saw him on the Thursday evening and told him that the event was as secret as any Budget proposals. His face fell. He was endlessly explaining the impact of the Medium Term Financial Strategy, an arcane subject with only a distant silver lining. A marriage involving a mature if not crusty bachelor approaching fifty and all in the Treasury family, namely the Chief Secretary taking as a bride someone who had worked for the Financial Secretary. It almost gave monetarism a human face. Mr Mower loyally kept the secret and doubtless turned sadly to produce an erudite brief on double taxation relief with the Cayman Islands.

My wedding reception was held in Sarah's Battersea home. It was wholly non-political but was interrupted by a *Daily Express* journalist who had no idea what was happening. So I embarked with a household of a wife, two young stepchildren and a property in fashionable Battersea. I was to learn about the domestic budget as well as the national one.

Friday 2 November 1979

The weather was glorious and I got up and dressed in my new shirt and pants. David [Drew] borrowed a tie and Jonathan [Bradley] called to collect me. He had been detained by the traffic, and we reached Anhalt Road rather late. I was very pleased with the press I had received on account of the spending statement. We proceeded to Wandsworth Town Hall and Sarah and I were married by a most funereal man. Susie [Elwes, family friend] took quite a lot of pictures and we then returned to Anhalt Road and had a most pleasant party. Jonathan made a short speech and in the midst I had a call from the *Daily Express* who wanted to interview me on the 'cuts programme'. Eventually I told the 'D Ex' that we were married after being tackled by *The Sun*. We drove to Middle Wallop to the Fifehead Manor. It was a superb hotel and we had Dover sole for supper. We were both quite tired after the strains of the past two weeks.

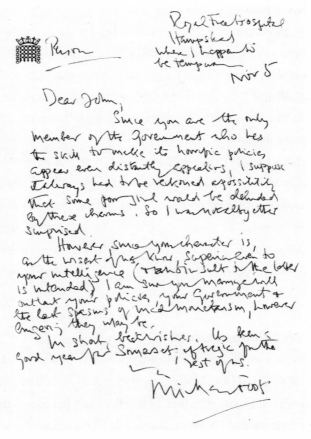

Letter received from Michael Foot on the occasion of John's marriage‡

Tuesday 1 January 1980

So I start 1980 – the year of my half-century. I cannot but reflect that 1979 was an annus mirabilis, and great thanks to Dr Dally. My ambitions for 1980 are somewhat prosaic. I will weigh [myself] when I return to London and thereafter lose 9lbs. I will attend church twice a month and I will try and drink rather less. With Sarah at my side I believe I can deal with the 'grey periods' more easily. She has been and remains an inspiration.

Tuesday 8 January 1980

Back at work. The main fascination was an early meeting to discuss the steel strike. Prior was quite immoderate in his behaviour. Joseph was not there to defend Industry, but Prior made it quite clear that he thought the BSC management was largely at fault. He also made dire noises about the bad way that the D of I had conducted negotiations and had failed to keep contact with the CBI. Generally speaking I had a useful and quite busy day.

Wednesday 9 January 1980

The first ministers' meeting of 1980! Nigel Lawson was in full spate of saying we had to do all kinds of horrors when it was realised that the tea lady was present. Geoffrey Howe does not seem to have got far with Jenkin in the indexation/social services argument.

Saturday 19 January 1980

I got up rather late and reluctantly and Sarah and I went to the Purcell Room where I had to give a Commonwealth Parliamentary Committee talk. I felt mopish but came through the test rather well. The speech was well received.

Sunday 20 January 1980

There is no doubt that the speech has caused something of a

furore. When I read the *Sunday Times* I decided I had better have
a word with Alastair Pirie but I was beaten to it by a call from the
BBC. I did a radio interview with them and triggered yet another
story by agreeing on the likelihood of taxes on drink and tobacco.
Altogether it has caused something of a storm, but I do not regret
placing on record 'three years of austerity'.

Monday 21 January 1980

I almost feel like public enemy No. 1. There has been considerable
press coverage of my Saturday speech and Sunday radio talk. I
was told that Patrick Jenkin felt very injured by what I had done;
but I decided not to apologise in the note that Alastair Pirie sent
him. Geoffrey Howe twitted me about the Budget revelations and
I sensed he was angry despite his good humour. We had a quick
huddle and he discussed the Budget date. It was decided to postpone it for a day to avoid the clash with the enthronement of the
Archbishop of Canterbury. I had a lunch meeting with the OR
Society. The place was full of reporters – doubtless awaiting a
further indiscretion! Actually it was a dull official speech. Gordon
Pepper [senior partner, Greenwell Stockbrokers] was there and
told me that he thought things were going quite well, but that
the government could not afford to let money growth get out of
hand therefore it must err in the opposite direction. Nigel Lawson
thinks we must get interest rates down ahead of the Budget.

Tuesday 22 January 1980

Well it certainly never rains… Today the newspapers are full of
a written answer I gave to Arthur Lewis on the Royal Household
and the economy drive. I really feel fed up with it all and only
pleased that my black mood does not get any worse. I know I
shall adjust to married life – and at this very moment Sarah is a
great help. I had breakfast at No. 10. We talked somewhat about

Defence: the PM is adamant that she will not take Pym's resignation. She is, however, quite fed up. The ministers' meeting was
not eventful. Max Berezowski [Polish journalist and friend] came
and saw me in my splendour as Chief Secretary – we did not
get around to Yugoslavia. I am apprehensive about PMQs on
Thursday – the fur might fly. I spoke to an Industrial Lunch – a
pleasant occasion and rather encouraging. I got back to Anhalt
Road fairly early after giving Jonathan and Anne Bradley a drink.
Jonathan is now a subsidiary director of Morgan, Grenfell &
Co. Sarah has been attending the closure of Kennington Palace
Court [John's flat].

Wednesday 23 January 1980

The bad luck dogs me and I am not yet through. After the morning
meeting Geoffrey Howe asked me to stay behind and told me that
the PM had expressed her displeasure over the Saturday speech.
I feel crestfallen and still numbed by what being married actually means. However, I know that things will balance out. At 'E'
[Committee] we had a rather patchy and inconclusive talk about
the taxation of social security benefits. I was taken aback when the
Prime Minister – yet again – returned to the hare of having an
index lower than the r.p.i. She is trapped as we all are by the sheer
size of borrowing and the spending cuts necessary to reduce it.

Thursday 24 January 1980

Geoffrey Howe called a rushed meeting ahead of the Cabinet.
The entire social service programme is now coming apart. The
PM now veers towards a cutback on retirement pensions.
The Cabinet itself lasted from 10 a.m. until 1.15 p.m. It was
scrappy. I survived questions. It was a B performance – and I
sensed that MT was displeased: 'I should think not,' she said
when I parried with 'I shall not reveal my ambitions.'

Friday 25 January 1980

The morning was fairly quiet. There was not much talk at the minutes meeting but Geoffrey Howe did ask for reactions on the evidence to be sent to the Treasury Committee. I sent a minute emphasising the wisdom of being cautious about the medium-term financial plan. After lunch I went across to No. 10 for a major session on public spending cuts. We had over two hours. MT was in a difficult mood and rejected any action on retirement pensions. Geoffrey Howe had originally withheld from her information about the 3 per cent cash limit squeeze. Eventually we moved towards this and both Douglas Wass and Anthony Rawlinson suggested we could axe the limits and I fear it will become the easy option. It is interesting that Rawlinson is prepared to prostitute cash limits in this fashion. It was also tacitly agreed that Geoffrey Howe could cheat over the uprating inflation formula for retirement pensions. In the evening we drove to Somerset.

Tuesday 29 January 1980

I had breakfast at No. 10, so at least I have not been frozen out of that – yet. The conversation was fascinating. There is now unfolding a plot which will force upon Jim Prior the acceptance of a major trade union reform in the wake of the steel strike. The PM is set upon it and enthusiastically supported by Howe and Joseph. I think the incident could risk the resignation of Prior. [Leon] Brittan is much involved. The day seemed largely devoted to meetings; but in the evening we saw the draft paper on public spending that will be presented to Cabinet. I think we have gone as far as we can. In the evening I spoke to the annual dinner of the domestic electrical appliance people. I was sat next to Lord Plowden. He told me that he had pressed upon the Prime Minister the need for reductions in excise duties and that she had been most unenthusiastic.

Thursday 31 January 1980

We had the great Cabinet meeting to resolve the public spending cuts. It was a bad day for me as I lost my temper with Norman St John-Stevas over his allegation that the package was biased against the poor and needed some cuts affecting the rich. I suggested the arts programme and there was an outburst – Nicholas Edwards also shouting and bellowing. Altogether things are not going my way these days and I only hope the phase will pass. Altogether we secured quite good results from the exercise – even a modest increase in the prescription charge. I still think that Geoffrey Howe will have a horrendous task to ensure his PSBR [Public Sector Borrowing Requirement] remains below £10 billion. I had an excellent lunch with Bonnie Angelo [*Time* magazine] and a couple of her journalists while we discussed welfare in the West. I had a quiet evening back at Anhalt Road. Suddenly life seems terribly quiet. Sarah is fussed that I am taking Anafranil.

Monday 4 February 1980

Geoffrey Howe told me that he had consulted with the PM, Joseph and Whitelaw. It is now clear that moves will be taken to strengthen the Trade Union Bill. At lunch I visited Scott Goff [stockbrokers] etc. It was pleasant to meet David Grenier again. I was in quite a chirpy mood and enjoyed handling the questions. I fancy that the City is expecting a tighter Budget than is likely. Meanwhile Geoffrey Howe is not pleased with the CBI reaction which has suggested there is no need for increases in indirect taxation. We had an absurdly long meeting of 'H' [Committee]. It was mainly memorable for a great diatribe by Hailsham over a private Bill by Lord Scarman on interpretation. He threatened to resign. I am irked by plans to graft Nigel Lawson on to my lunch with the bankers on Thursday. In the evening I returned to Sarah after a good session with Tim Renton. He says gas prices have caused alarm and that [Tony] Marlow has made an impression as a new MP.

Tuesday 5 February 1980

I had breakfast at No. 10 and the conversation turned to the proposed trade union changes. I reported that Jim Prior had made his resignation comment. There are thought to be three hard line opponents: Prior, Walker, and St John-Stevas. The last mentioned had apparently thought of resigning the Arts but keeping his other two posts. It was decided no approach should be made to Walker as he was resolute and would immediately spread the word to the back benches. The PM hinted she would resign if she could not get her way.

Wednesday 6 February 1980

We had a meeting of 'E' [committee] at the PM's room in the afternoon. It was devoted to union law. Prior had moved quite a way on the issue of secondary action. Percival tried to explain things but often could not be heard or understood. We then touched upon the question of sanctions. Hailsham proved a valuable and uncertain ally of Prior but otherwise the voices were as expected. There is a question mark over Heseltine. Prior threatened to resign – but broadly speaking things were calm. Battle will continue next week. Keith Renshaw [journalist] gave me lunch and told me Mikardo was making Silkin favourite for the Labour leadership. He also advised me to stick to my Purcell Room speech. I also saw Fred Emery [journalist] and suggested we might dine one evening.

Monday 18 February 1980

I had a tiring day. The critical occasion was the discussion of the Medium Term Financial Plan. I stoutly maintained my opposition to the publication of the figures. I could sense the hostility of Sir

Douglas Wass and Sir A. Rawlinson. Rysie [Sir William Ryrie, senior Treasury civil servant] was mildly an ally, but otherwise it was an unpleasant business. Geoffrey Howe will have to report the matter to the PM – and I think it should go to the Cabinet. Later we discussed outlines for the Budget. Lawson and Burns [Terry Burns, special adviser] talked quite a lot. Geoffrey Howe was being advised generally for a £9 billion PSBR. I opted for one as near £8 billion as possible. Once again I sensed being an outsider in the discussion. I attended a dinner given by Geoffrey Howe to financial journalists. I rather enjoyed myself and became very relaxed and made mildly dismissive noises about MTFP, tax initiatives and cash limits. Ian Gow tells me the PM is in the dumps.

Tuesday 19 February 1980

Breakfast at No. 10 was fairly unhappy. The PM was jumpy and wanted action to be taken against the banks. She was also very concerned that there should be an honourable end to the steel strike. It was a morose occasion. She also said that she had given up fighting the trade union issue. I think she is going through a bad patch.

Monday 3 March 1980

We had an enormous morning session on monetary affairs. The Governor of the Bank was summoned and I thought the whole business was embarrassing. He had not been given a Budget outline and had to read it first time in the presence of officials. I sensed quite a breakdown in relations. When the Governor started his dissertation on the financial strategy Geoffrey Howe took out a handful of coins and started counting them in a detached manner. At any rate the Governor delivered a most powerful broadside against the strategy and said he could not endorse it in evidence to the select committee. Furthermore he argued that such a plan would make EMS membership unlikely.

Tuesday 4 March 1980

The breakfast meeting was entirely devoted to the EEC budget contribution and the next moves. Everyone is aware of the problems that will be created with the Heathite wing of the party if we engage on a policy of withholding. However, the general mood is for robust action: Nott spoke vigorously but I wonder how long the vigour will last. Denis Thatcher was strongly critical of the EEC. I had a chance thereafter to send a letter to the Chancellor, copy to the PM, stating my opposition to money strategy.

Tuesday 11 March 1980

The day started with breakfast at No. 10. Subsequently Geoffrey Howe told me that he had entered a caveat about these breakfasts and that he thought that they should be on a rotating basis. In the afternoon 'E' discussed the denationalisation of BNOC [British National Oil Corporation]. It was a bad meeting and D. Howell was not given the authority to give a fairly specific indication of how he could sell off the operation next year. The FO are worried stiff about the Commission.

Wednesday 12 March 1980

We had dinner with Elsie [Donald, friend and author]. Peter Calvocoressi [publisher] was there – said he didn't ever agree with Ronald Butt but was at one with him in opposing Thatcher interference with the Olympic Games. Adam and Caroline Raphael were there. I had a great battle with Norman St John-Stevas before the PM to ensure that £350,000 grant to Covent Garden Appeal came from next year's Budget. Won. Sir Robert Armstrong [Cabinet Secretary] in the end didn't mind using Arts budget provided Covent Garden got the cash.

Wednesday 26 March 1980

The Budget was a marathon. It lasted for two hours. I was sat next to Margaret Thatcher and she was worried that the Tory benches were not cheering enough. There was the same worry in the pre-Budget Cabinet. There was a muted response, and Jenkin was anxious to enlist support for his agony-situation over child benefit.

Thursday 27 March 1980

The day ended with the TV show involving Joel Barnett, Alan Fisher, Sarah Hogg and myself. It was quite an ordeal – not least because it lasted an hour under the arc-lights. The difficult point in the programme was the question of Princess Anne and her overspending. Sarah enjoyed the whole thing enormously. Earlier I had taken part in the Budget debate. It was not bad – my speech was undoubtedly too long but it has some good knockabout. On the whole I managed to score off of Healey much to the pleasure of the Tory backbenchers who want to see someone match him. In the morning we had a rather desultory Cabinet meeting. We were warned that the Easter–Whitsun period was likely to be intensely busy. However, that will not be too bad provided I get decent sleep.

Tuesday 1 April 1980

In the afternoon I had to speak to the Finance Committee. I talked about the public spending paper and had a fairly critical reaction. Fortunately I defused much of the likely attack by arguing that it was a very modest document. Instead I had a lot of sniping and I vigorously exchanged blows with Elaine Kellett-Bowman over the damage done to rural areas. Both [Toby] Jessel and [Michael] Latham referred to me as 'Mr Biffen' and Nick Budgen said you cannot have power and popularity.

Thursday 3 April 1980

I had a busier morning than expected. I did not feel particularly well disposed as I had something of a hangover from the previous night. There were two meetings: the first on Energy passed without much talk. The PM accepts a larger round and some element of cash bidding. Then we got on to the AGR programme. I probably ended my career for all time by suggesting that the PWR was not the last word. The PM is adamant in believing that the AGR is a dubious design and that the CEGB [Central Electricity Generating Board] are incompetent beyond belief. She wants Heysham [power station] delayed (cancelled?) in order to facilitate the nuclear PWR programme.

Tuesday 20 May 1980

A rotten night; and poor Sarah had an even worse one. I really think she feels for me. Breakfast at Downing Street was pretty grim. At last we had the diversion of the Iranian sanctions to divert attention. However, she is quite unwilling to face up to the impending clash between cash limits and comparability/research. All she can do is to rail on about MPs' pay. We had a businesslike discussion of the Finance Bill and ended the morning with a session on PMQs. I had a sandwich lunch. In the early afternoon we started the standing committee of the Finance Bill. My paranoiac fears were realised and there was a row over notes on clauses which I handled badly and then had to retreat. Needless to say Lawson took a hawkish and unhelpful line. I sat in on the debates for quite a while and answered one amendment. I was sweating with nerves – but in the event answered the debate tolerably well. I got back at 1 a.m. A bad start – but at least something began.

Wednesday 21 May 1980

A better night; but I still feel wretched. Why the fear? I think it is the standing committee that I fear and that my ignorance will be rumbled. The main event in the morning was addressing the women's conference as part of the Treasury liaison. Actually I did myself a good turn. The conference was quite large and the Treasury team had a series of dull questions. I then seized the chance to make an impassioned plea for discipline. It went down well and slightly stole Geoffrey Howe's thunder. I had lunch with the Institute of Directors. Mather [Graham, Institute of Directors] was bumbling but pleasant and he knew about Blue Cheshire Cheese. Goldsmith [Walter, IoD] confirmed my view that he is not a friend. In the afternoon I attended a meeting planned for the local authority trade union reps. Heseltine handled it superbly.

Thursday 22 May 1980

I had a terrifying night and was sick with nerves. Such a thing has not happened for ages. The result was that I started the day with precious little sleep. Happily it all turned out well. The 'E' meeting passed off fairly quietly and I supported Heseltine in holding back from a system of cash limits for individual local authorities. The Cabinet meeting was fairly quiet except that it was clear that MT is unwilling to make the adjustments considered necessary by the FO. Treasury Questions turned out to be fairly quiet. Two questioners dropped out; and I managed to hold up my end despite nerves and a croaking voice. The triumph, however, was in the standing committee of the Finance Bill. The row over notes on clauses was resolved; and we then had amiable debates which lasted until 11.30 p.m. I found form with a lightness of touch, and Adam Raphael dropped by and congratulated me on the performance. A day which released me from the prison house of fear.

Saturday 31 May 1980

A dead quiet day and in some ways extremely sad. I felt very lonely – now I realise how Sarah and Lucy give life to this place.

In the evening I read back over the diaries for 1967 and 1968. The pain and nostalgia came back – and I can *still* feel the anguish of depression. I simply would not have believed that I could pull out of the trough. I worked from 7.15 onwards grinding at the notes on clauses and the boxes. I had to cut open the canvas bag to fetch one box: poor Alistair Pirie [Private Secretary] could think of no other way in view of the error over the key. I was telephoned by Keith Renshaw and Hugo Young over the EEC deal. I am not enamoured of it, and I think the savings on the budget will be used to dress up the RPI to offset the 5 per cent increase in CAP. I called Sarah, and it seems that she is now coping with her father.

Monday 2 June 1980

A good day. The Cabinet discussed the Brussels package. It was commended in low-key. One or two spending ministers were anxious to know what were the gains to the Treasury, and there was the usual sickening chorus from the sheep lobby – Whitelaw, Prior, Edwards and Younger. John Nott was not particularly successful in his attack on the deal – he got caught into details. I then made a contribution arguing we had only got such progress by brisk negotiating; the price (CAP) was demonstrably high; and the whole debate would be with us come the next election.

Wednesday 4 June 1980

In the morning I did the draft of the press release for the King's Lynn speech. In the evening I went to show it to Ian Gow and ended up by having a talk with MT. She told me how she wanted to stroke the RPI; and I said it couldn't be done at a stroke. She complained bitterly about the electricity industry and wanted Weinstock [Arnold, Chairman of GEC] to sort it out. However, she admitted she had never asked him. I was pleased to learn that she would favour any funds for direct tax to be used for raising thresholds.

Tuesday 10 June 1980

The day was dominated by the extremely unpleasant experience of the standing committee. I had imagined that we would make swift progress, but everything became slow and laborious. In the late evening Lawson was nutty enough to refer to the late Dr Broughton in disparaging terms. It caused a row and we soldiered on until 4.15 a.m. I had the last clause dealing with mortgage relief, and it was handled moderately. At that time I felt really tired. Morale on the committee has been quite good, but we cannot risk many rants like these. Sarah and I had a picnic lunch at the Treasury after walking around the park and watching the ducks. The day was quiet – I did some modest homework on the Finance Bill and read leisurely. There is now a plan afoot that Sarah and I should go to Ascot on Friday week. The general political mood is quiet. At the No. 10 breakfast it was significant that MT did not even mention Roy Jenkins.

Tuesday 17 June 1980

After the bad night's rest it was something of a nightmare day. I had to go to Downing Street for breakfast. She was in her usual non-stop talking mood. She is put out by the CPRS [Central Policy Review Staff] paper on pay, and thinks we are not being tough enough. The theme was taken up again at 'E' when there was a long dissertation from Geoffrey and a sharp but quite effective reply from Soames. It is quite clear that he does not think he can contain the civil service pay settlement within a 10 per cent cash limit. I had a sandwich lunch and then went to the meeting of the Finance Committee officers at No. 11. They were in quite good heart but Bill Clark said there would have to be a movement in MLR [minimum lending rate] to keep people happy. Rather surprisingly Jock Bruce-Gardyne argued for some tax on banks. We had the fifth meeting of the Finance Bill Standing

Committee. It lasted until 2 a.m. and Peter Rees handled it brilliantly. I had very little to do on my clauses and managed to edge by – numbed and somewhat depressed.

Wednesday 18 June 1980

Apparently the PSBR is running at least £2,000 million above target. This is shock news and there were even hints that it might produce a July fiscal package. I doubt this: at least there can be no question of indirect tax increases. The general mood was that we could afford to let MLR ease off – by one point. I expect that will happen soon.

Thursday 19 June 1980

I continue to feel in a grey patch and am desperately tired. Even so I got by. At a 9 a.m. meeting Mr Kitcat [civil servant] told me that Heseltine planned to send individual letters to local authorities indicating current expenditure ceilings. Alas we have to tread this path – we have no ultimate legal authority. The Cabinet was largely devoted to 'top pay'. I argued that ministerial example would be practically meaningless. The PM obviously did not think so. I am glad it was decided that staging was sacrosanct and there will be some abatement of the uprating. That was confirmed to me in so many words by Edward du Cann. The standing committee of the Finance Bill ploughed on until 10 p.m. It was a quiet occasion for me; but Peter Rees was masterly. MT came and watched the closing passages of the debate. We then had drinks in the Tory committee room and she was very relaxed and talked about the EEC – showing much Gaullist sentiment. She thinks Carter will win the Presidency.

Tuesday 1 July 1980

The major event was the debate on the Liberal Supply Day. Sarah came to watch and brought Lucy, who stayed in my room. I had to speak after David Steel and had a good time. I really did enjoy myself engaging in both solid argument and knockabout. I was congratulated afterwards by a number of MPs – and I think genuinely so. The day started with breakfast at No. 10. We had the most tremendous rows about the Top Salary Review Board and the pay of MPs etc. I spoke with almost unparalleled feeling as I resented the PM dismissing Geoffrey Howe's view as lacking in courage. We returned to the subject at Cabinet and I let fly and was told I was arguing 'Biffenisms' – 'None the worse for that,' I retorted. The debate was really quite fierce, and I do find the emotions of MT on the problem quite terrifying. She does lean towards government by public abuse where incomes are concerned.

Wednesday 17 September 1980

We had a meeting of 'E' called at 9 a.m. There is one common characteristic to all 'E' meetings. Geoffrey Howe constantly scribbles notes that he passes to near neighbours. Some are cryptic and some rather flat. The recipients scribble a riposte and they are then returned. Howe then tears them up. Today we had a session on the finances of steel, shipbuilding, transport and finally my own paper seeking £413 million savings on NI investment plans. The steel discussion was quite a trial, and Heseltine demanded that we thought of the UK steel industry and not just the BSC. This opened up a new line of debate and revealed Heseltine as a formidable member of the committee not bound by his officials. I had the bruising experience of lunch with the EEF [Engineering Employers' Federation] and defending and expounding government policy. There is growing demand that MLR should fall; and I suspect that the major manufacturers are now feeling a pinch.

Tuesday 23 September 1980

I continue to feel dispirited about the political/economic situation.

It is so difficult to reconcile the expansion of Money Supply M3 and the sharp recession. I had a short spell with Geoffrey Howe after a meeting to do with the organisation of expenditure divisions. I told him he must dwell upon this paradox at the party conference and this touched upon the credibility of the entire policy. He told me he would be doing this, but I confess I have doubts as to the extent he will. He believes the policy is being bizarrely affected by the impact of oil from the North Sea, and likens it to the impact of precious metals from South America and Spain in the sixteenth century.

Wednesday 24 September 1980

The grey mood persists. I do fret about the harshness of the recession and the apparent laxity of the M3. I had a discussion with Nigel Lawson about this. He was absolutely tired out after a visit to Brussels which involved an all-night marathon. He accepted my view that Geoffrey Howe was shell shocked. I suspect the intemperate behaviour of the Prime Minister explains part of this.

Tuesday 7 October 1980

In the afternoon Sir A. Rawlinson arrived with the news that the forecast was difficult – but really in line with expectations. The only thing that really seems to have caught people napping was the deterioration in NI finances. He seemed reasonably happy about matters – not having ever been much of an optimist. He warmed to my comment in *The Guardian* that there are no ultimate solutions in politics. It now seems that the sought formula will be a 3 per cent rather than a 2 per cent reduction in LA [local authority] budgets and a general 2 per cent cash limit squeeze. He thought this would cover the bad state of NI finances. I had lunch with Ian Gow in my office; he was annoyed at the pro-EEC tone of Thorneycroft's speech.

Wednesday 8 October 1980

Sarah and I went to Brighton. The weather was good but the conference was hideous. I was on the platform only for the Prior speech. There is no debate in the Tory Party over industrial relations, and the Prior speech was really an appeal to those who wanted an alternative economic policy – one couched in such terms as 'fairness'. I hardly applauded – anyone – and this was noted by the press, who were curious as to whether it had political significance. Sarah was quite agitated over this. After the speech I went behind the platform where Geoffrey Howe was much agitated because Angus Maude had said the better money supply figures could presage a fall in interest rates. Sarah and I were royally entertained to dinner at Wheelers by Hugo Young and Michael Jones.

Monday 13 October 1980

In the afternoon I attended the meeting called to discuss monetary targets etc. under the chairmanship of the PM. The Governor opened with a lengthy exposition which lasted for nearly forty minutes. It was a lugubrious affair, and the upshot was that he was worried about the reliability of M3 and about the depressed state of industry. In the subsequent conversation he showed himself to be sceptical about novel methods of funding debt. Lawson was foremost in advocating innovations and the PM reprimanded the Governor for the general conservatism of the Bank. I said nothing until I had to leave when I spoke up sharply saying the fault was the large borrowing requirement and no technical changes could bridge that gap. I felt that the Bank team appreciated my foolhardy remarks. I must confess I was partly inspired to this view by lunch at Hill Samuel, where I discovered there was no great love for a reverence of M3.

Friday 24 October 1980

The press is full of my letter seeking £400 million from the MoD, which the latter have leaked. I decided the best thing was to lie low. T. Mathews [press officer] told me that he had declined media interviews. I feel that the episode is bound to strengthen the hands of Defence, and as I was driven north I heard on the car radio that a number of Tories were exploding in wrath.

Monday 27 October 1980

Today saw the start of the 'Star Chamber Interviews', designed to decide the 1981/82 spending. The nastiest and most ill-tempered meeting was conducted with Jim Prior. We were all crowded in Geoffrey Howe's room in the Commons with occasional unstoppable telephone interruptions. Prior argued with fluency and bitterness against the policy. In effect he was arguing for a much larger PSBR because he believed it could be financed because of savings and indeed at a lower MLR. He was abrasive and rather curt with the Tory official who tried to defend the proposals. I disliked his macroeconomics and his manner, but I do concede that the Treasury are being mean minded about allowing the programmes to expand so little – and pedantic in claiming there is an advantage to him of having the spending transferred from the Reserve Allowance. We also saw Carlisle and Jenkin; and the Commons reassembled.

Tuesday 28 October 1980

A second day devoted to the 'Star Chamber'. Once again it was a long, drawn-out exercise but not as exhausting as I had feared. The exchanges with Pym were much the most significant. It was difficult to judge how he plans to play this. He argued fiercely that 3 per cent was merely the threshold above which one had to move to secure adequate defences, and for an instance it seemed that this was neither related to the national economy or the NATO target. Soames pressed him to accept the 2 per cent squeeze, and there was at least an inkling that he might do this.

Tuesday 4 November 1980

The Cabinet meeting started at 10 a.m. and lasted until after 12.30 p.m. At the end MT waited until Norman St John-Stevas had left the room, and with only Geoffrey Howe and myself there she said she would have to seek a reshuffle in December. She was clearly irked by the economic comments of Peter Carrington, who wanted a 'pick and choose' exercise on the 2 per cent cut on cash-limited programmes. Prior was belligerent over his Employment aids – and I did a 50/50 compromise with him. I thought the Treasury brief quite absurdly restrictive. The real row developed over Defence – Pym got quite manic over the Chiefs of Staff and the world defence role of Britain. He offered £150 million; but I think Soames and Whitelaw would wear £250 million and the PM offered to 'help' Pym with the Chiefs of Staff. In the evening Sarah and I attended the election party at the US Embassy. We were too tired to enjoy it.

Thursday 6 November 1980

The event was Question Time. I had not performed in the House since July and I was deadly nervous. I nibbled at a cheese sandwich beforehand and tried to brief myself for whatever might be. As it turned out I had a good run. Several of the questions for Geoffrey lapsed and I had the bulk of Question Time. Somehow I alighted upon self-deprecatory humour and this opened up situations where I could be outrageously dismissive. I had a great time turning comments to the disadvantage of Denis Healey, and I am glad that I do not find him an intimidating parliamentary performer. I hope I was not too curt with Michael Latham. Apparently Margaret Thatcher was listening to much of this and enjoying it all hugely. In the morning at Cabinet we had decided to announce an RSG pay figure of 6 per cent and the irony is that none of us, civil service or politicians, in the Treasury believes this figure. I wish it were 7 or 8 per cent.

Monday 10 November 1980

The great news of the day was that Michael Foot was elected
leader of the Labour Party. I can hardly believe it. I remember
the wagging finger and the flowing mane as he berated the Wilson
government on the 3R of the 1966 Prices and Incomes Act and I
was still waiting to be called. It was a tremendous recollection –
the radical passion. The news must be good for Steel and Jenkins,
and perhaps it will persuade some Heathites to bolt the party, but
I doubt it. I suppose Foot will have to be very robust with his left
wing – but it will be easy to parody him as radical and unreal, a
throw back to Lansbury.

Wednesday 19 November 1980

The final Cabinet to deal with the public spending was an anticlimax. The Defence agreement, announced at the outset at
£200 million, was accepted. Thereafter there were desultory talks
about the Social Security package and a 1 per cent abatement
was agreed quite without enthusiasm. The main point was that
much had been made of the 'leaks' from the previous meeting,
and as I was the last to leave I witnessed a fascinating conversation between the PM and Robert Armstrong. The latter clearly
thinks that St John-Stevas has been talking to the press, whereas
the PM thinks that Jim Prior has been doing so in addition. There
is no doubt that the Cabinet has moved into an unhappy phase.

Wednesday 26 November 1980

I was decidedly in a grey mood, but it seemed to be contained
by the end of the day. It was a dreadful day. In the morning the
[Treasury] ministers discussed the future over the NI earnings
limit non-disclosure. The discussion classified the problem and I
agreed to do radio and TV interviews. This I did, and at ITN saw
Sarah Cullen looking as splendid as ever. The general view was

that I had handled the affair in a desirable low key – but in the evening I learned that Geoffrey Howe was upset that the interviews were being quoted against him. In the early evening I spoke to the PPSs. My theme was public spending but I also gave my own rationale of economic policy. I really do think that it went well: I had kind words from John Selwyn Gummer and plenty of questions. The mood is anxious rather than hostile – and the waywardness of M3 is the problem in exposition. Greyness less at end of day – no Anafranil.

Thursday 27 November 1980

Why are we in such disarray and why do I feel so grey? The latter I cannot tell; but I think we have lost intellectual coherence and must make a change in tack and be seen to be doing so.

Tuesday 16 December 1980

After a long break we returned to the morning breakfast routine. I was given an oblique dressing down by MT for my Finance Committee speech. 'Do we have any more Biffenism to come?' However, much the most important point was the BL [British Leyland] plan and her deep hostility to Michael Edwardes. She said Denis (T) must look at the figures, and Joseph fought valiantly to have a good word said for Edwardes. Heaven knows the figures are difficult enough, but passion cannot will them away.

Monday 22 December 1980

A nasty day. I saw the *Now!* article and it said my honeymoon was over and that Thatcher believed I was lazy. It said Geoffrey Howe would have the chance to make good speeches if he did not have to spend so much time doing my job. It was a hatchet job – but I wonder who is doing it: Lawson or Adam Ridley [special adviser] or possibly George Cardona. Or it might be No. 11/10 press office. The other disagreeable experience was attending a meeting summoned by the PM to have an inquest on why Hawk aircraft has not been sold to UAE. She told the company what an informed person her son was and how outwitted had been the FO and MoD by the French. She stormed and was offensive to the last degree. Ian Gilmour was never allowed to complete a sentence, and senior civil servants were treated like recalcitrant children. All this will end in tears.

‡

In January 1981 I was having a Christmas break at Kinton when I was telephoned and asked to move to be Secretary of State for Trade. I suspect that the Prime Minister felt that I was not tough enough at curbing public spending but she wanted to keep me in the team because I was generally supportive of the 'monetarist' policy.

I have three general views about my first spell of Cabinet office. First and by far the most important was the exhilaration of being at the centre of Treasury policies, which were at the heart of the 'Thatcher revolution'. This covered not only the taxation changes and public spending and borrowing decisions contained in the Budget; it also involved scrapping exchange rate control. The policies had been carefully planned during our years in opposition and carried out in the face of some Treasury suspicion. Sir Douglas Wass was permanent secretary at the Treasury. He was a rather distant character, intellectually powerful and with clear views. As he was a Keynesian he did not sit comfortably with the economics and social policies of Friedman and Hayek. In my experience he behaved with great courtesy even if he was not 'one of us'. It says much for Geoffrey Howe that he coped well with this situation.

Secondly I found the control of public spending a difficult task, although I was assisted by the 'Star Chamber' technique.

Thirdly my Chief Secretary work gave me an insight into all government departments that was invaluable in the following six years. My time at the Treasury had not been particularly happy or successful but it was an excellent apprenticeship for my work as Leader of the House.

Sunday 4 January 1981

Around 9 p.m. I was called to the telephone. Clive Whitmore [PPS to the Prime Minister] was on the line and pressed me to explain how I would be getting back to London. Eventually MT came on the line and asked me if I would accept the Board of Trade. She was absolutely delighted when I said that I would. She told me that John Nott was being moved, but not to the Treasury. I suspect he is replacing Ian Gilmour at the FO. She said Norman Tebbit was moving to Industry and that Cecil Parkinson would remain at Trade and that Lord Lyell would be joining the department. MT suggested that the move would widen my experience – and I am very much inclined to agree. Sarah was very pleased with the news and we spent quite a while talking about it. It really does seem not a bad move. With luck I shall be able to play out this parliament as a Secretary of State and that really will have provided me with ballast for a future career.

40

TRADE

When I went to Trade I succeeded John Nott, who had become Secretary of State for Defence. He was as near a 'soul mate' as I had in the Cabinet. With sound money credentials he was as mildly agnostic about monetarism as he was about everything. He was a good man to follow.

My move to Trade was providential and I really enjoyed it. I was now a proper minister with a department of my own. Unlike the Treasury it was a manageable size and I soon got to know the key civil servants. I had an outstanding permanent secretary in Sir Kenneth Clucas. He was placidity personified, whilst having a razor-sharp mind. I once witnessed his end of a telephone call from the Prime Minister. She was on an Easter visit to the Gulf and had become agitated over trade deals with one of the sheikhdoms. It was a lengthy monologue with Clucas barely able to utter a word; telephone handbagging in spades. The one-sided conversation over, he put the phone down and observed, 'Prime Ministers should use the recess to go on holiday.' He spared me the nature of her call.

Thursday 8 January 1981

I hope I can revert to my avowed wish to write about only one or possibly two things each day. I went to Windsor Castle to receive the Seal of Office. It was a grey and sombre day – apt for the funeral of the Countess of Athlone. Eric took the car into the inner courtyard of the castle and I had a glimpse of the limousines as they drove after the cortège. Soames had attended the funeral and we joined him in a lovely room overlooking the castle grounds. There was almost farce when Norman Fowler practically cracked a cane chair. The ceremony itself was brief. Leon Brittan was sworn with the Orthodox Jewish book. The Queen complained about the harassment they had received at Sandringham from the press. And so I have achieved my ambition to receive a seal as Secretary of State. Also I attended my first Cabinet as Secretary of State for Trade – but it was largely devoted to ILEA [Inner London Education Authority].

Friday 9 January 1981

The day at Trade was quite active. I was instructed into some of the mysteries of the Companies Bill. I think we may lose the clauses on the registry of names in the Lords and then be unable to reinstate them in the Commons. In the morning and afternoon I did some walking of the bounds and in one room found the desk at which Mr Gladstone had worked – it had been brought in by a Principal whose father had bought it from the old Board.

Wednesday 14 January 1981

The memorable incident was a confusion in the corridor, as a consequence of which the Saudi ambassador was wheeled in under the mistaken impression that he was the Indian high commissioner. When the latter did arrive I had my first tedious discussion – his English being very faltering. I was told on all sides it would be even worse when I got to India. I had lunch with Adam Raphael – he confessed regret that Norman St John-Stevas had been sacked, but did say he had forecast this and had been frozen out for his pains. I had my first 'E' as Trade and strongly supported Geoffrey Howe, who wanted to maintain the 6 per cent pay factor and not lift it to 7½ in light of the LA (local authority) manuals settlement. Eventually it was decided to settle at 7 per cent for the pay factor. That is a fair compromise, but it is clear the cash limits cannot be used to influence rather than fix pay and still remain traditional cash limits.

‡
‡

John Nott had left me a pleasurable piece of unfinished business, a trip to India. It was a new experience for me. I stayed at the high commission and had a memorable visit to see the Taj Mahal by moonlight – almost the only person there. The high commissioner was very anxious to do a deal with the Indians but to use UK credits to finance it. I suppose such trade can extend British influence but it did not seem very commercially attractive to me. He was a shrewd operator. He had me under his roof and tackled me, bleary eyed, before breakfast. I demurred briefly but decided I was not sufficiently experienced to fight the issue.

Saturday 17 January 1981
We arrived in India after a long and tedious flight. There was a moment when I thought I did not have any lithium tablets. I will only record two instances in the day. First I am not at ease with the ambassador [High Commissioner]. I thought he should not have intervened when I was talking to a civil servant from the Indian Commerce Department in order to correct a general

comment I had made on civil servants and politicians. It was a small point – but I thought he tended to be didactic at lunch and afterwards. We shall see how he shapes up. Secondly on arrival at Agra we were taken to see the Taj Mahal in the moonlight. It was superb. It was ghostly and haunting. The mosque was magnificent with its ivory carvings and precious stones – and the echo was arresting. It lived up to its reputation, and I shall ever remember it. How Sarah would have loved it.

Monday 19 January 1981

My work got under way. I had the first meeting with Mr Mukharjee. He was a diminutive but friendly man. My main objective is to get the steel works confirmed for Davy, and to get progress on work for a power station, railways and coal mining plant. The ambassador is a helpful aide, but jumpy about possible misunderstandings. One has arisen. Gavin Dick, of the Department of Trade, is a cryptic and surly individual who has upset the Indians considerably. I may have to take him to one side – and the prospect does not daunt me. I still find it difficult to believe I am a Secretary of State, and still want to walk after people rather than ahead of them. In the early evening we visited the Red Fort – I shall long remember it: the parakeets swooping and squawking and the long slow trains hooting and snaking to the distant and endless plains. I had a vegetarian dinner – rather good.

Wednesday 21 January 1981

Quite a day. In the morning the high commissioner came to my room with the proposal to spend £200,000 per annum on trade promotion, and I turned it down. Stuart [Hampson, private secretary], who was observing the exchanges, said he was furious. I do have only a modest opinion of him. He had not consulted any Trade officials – although in fairness it was too early for him to have done so. My talk to the FT conference went well, or rather the ad-libbing at the conclusion. I managed to work in some humour and colourful reference to India. I called upon Mukharjee and delivered my initiative – a trade mission and follow-up studies. I think it will be accepted. The high commissioner was silent throughout. We had an excellent curry barbecue lunch and I talked with Aranachulam, the chairman of Tube Investments India, who knows Tom Barnsley [TI colleague]. In the afternoon I had the ordeal of an Indian press conference – it was quite a grilling. Now I feel that matters are downhill.

Thursday 22 January 1981

The climax was a truly hardworking day. I felt quite drained at the conclusion. In the morning I had a relaxed chat with the British journalists, including Peter Niesewand of *The Guardian*. It passed without event and much of the time was spent on the coal industry prospects. I do find the Indian habit of serving tea during such conferences a great irritant. I was then conveyed to the Ministry of Commerce where I signed the agreement with Mukharjee and we exchanged very short speeches and gifts. I understand I have a metal picture – not what will hang at Anhalt Road. Earlier I had attended the Indian Engineer employers and we had quite a useful talk. I find the standing wearisome and my endless doses of mango squash are dispiriting. In the evening a party was given at the high commission and Cyril Pitts made some spirited attacks upon Indian economic planning which I would have liked to have made.

During my time at Trade I had endless opportunities for travel but passed many of them to Cecil Parkinson, my Minister of State. He was an excellent businessman and a skilled accountant with much charm. In happier personal circumstances he would have become Foreign Secretary and in my view would have worked well with Margaret Thatcher, particularly on the European issue.

My concern, however, was to stay at Westminster and keep a close eye on domestic politics. I did less than half a dozen trips of which two were memorable. One was to Finland. I asked to see the home of Field Marshal Mannerheim, who had led the Finnish resistance to the Soviet invasion of 1939–40. I had barely concluded the visit when I was recalled to London for a hastily summoned Cabinet meeting. Sarah, who was with me, took over my duties in visits to the Arctic Circle and the Wärtsilä ship yard.

The other striking visit was to Iraq in order to coincide with the British exhibitors present at the Baghdad Trade Fair. On landing I was presented with a fine Swiss watch with the dial unfortunately obscured by the head of Saddam Hussein. The British ambassador whispered, 'Wear the thing as long as you are here.' The visit was eerie. I was not allowed to stay at the embassy but had to reside at a government guest house. It was luxurious with a great deal of gadgetry. I assumed that the place was bugged and all my discussions with my staff took place out of doors.

On another trip when I returned from a visit to Japan and Korea I was so grateful to be back in Britain with the prospect of home cooking that, at Heathrow, I sank to my knees and kissed the tarmac. It seems that the Pope subsequently picked up my habit.

Shortly after becoming Trade Secretary I was embroiled in the bid by Rupert Murdoch for the *Times* newspapers. When I returned from the Indian trip I was met at the airport by an official who told me that Murdoch had made a bid for *The Times* which would be accepted as they were loss-making and in financial difficulties. The Trade Department was involved as it was responsible for the competition and regulatory activities of the government. As the law stood newspaper mergers and takeovers would normally be referred to the Monopolies Commission for comment, but if it was a loss-making situation the Trade Secretary had the option of letting the bid go ahead without a reference.

Sunday 25 January 1981

I had a quiet day and ended with a study of the *Times* brief. It is a nasty problem. All the arguments for a quiet life suggest the Murdoch deal should be referred to the Monopolies and Mergers Commission [MMC]. On the other hand the Murdoch deal has the advantage that it is the bird in the hand, that the terms suggest that the essential character of *The Times* will be preserved, and that the print unions are content. I have had no hassle from telephone calls – only Fred Emery contacting me.

Monday 26 January 1981

I am certainly encountering the strains of office. I had a restless night and got to the Trade Office laden with anxieties. I had the officials discuss with me the issues. They made no formal recommendation, but Knighton and Clucas both favour non referral. We decided to press Thomson to extend the deadline to enable an eight-week reference to the MMC. Brunton argued he could not extend the deadlines as the union redundancies fell interim. Then we had Murdoch. He was prepared for an MMC investigation but would want a new contract on account of the delay. Then we had the journalists from *The Times* and the *Sunday Times*, and I thought they were mainly concerned with editorial freedom. 'E' informally advised we should not refer, and the PM was

strongly inclined to that view. I decided not to refer but to attach
conditions and this was left with the Trade officials. The debate is
tomorrow. What a day.

I had hardly left the plane when I was told I would be requested
to let the deal go ahead. I was also told that Murdoch was the
only serious bidder although Maxwell 'was making noises'. I was
then given a brief to read over the weekend to prepare me for
action on Monday morning. Sarah and I spent the weekend with
friends in Sussex, Colin and Renata Baillieu. He subsequently
became a valued member of the Monopolies Commission.

The whole episode came upon me with great speed. I had no
particular knowledge of the newspaper industry and no favourites although I had made a close friendship with Peter Utley
when he was at the *Daily Telegraph*. Unlike many people I had no
strong feelings about Rupert Murdoch but I welcomed the political changes he had made to *The Sun* newspaper. Also I actually
enjoyed reading it. I would have been delighted if the *Sunday
Times* had been profitable (*The Times* was too deeply in the red).
For then the proposed deal with Murdoch would automatically
have gone to the Monopolies Commission. As it was the buck
was clearly with me.

What followed my weekend's briefing proceeded at great
speed. Long afterwards I wrote two letters to investigative journalists seeking to set out the sequence of events. At that time I
kept a simple daily record of events – more a pocket book than
a diary. It proved invaluable as a record since it confirmed it had
all happened much faster than I had later recollected.

Sir Kenneth Clucas was at my elbow throughout. The meetings
were held in my ministerial room. They included representa-
tives of *The Times*, Mr Brunton and his team, then advisers to

Rupert Murdoch, with Murdoch himself present but silent. Finally there were the journalists from *The Times/Sunday Times*. The *Times* management told me their financial position was dire and they wanted a deal with Murdoch otherwise they would fold. Murdoch's advisers repeated the offer, the terms of which were well known, and the meetings were calm and businesslike. In sharp contrast was the meeting with the journalists. There were a lot of them. They all wanted to speak. They had the deepest suspicion and hostility towards Murdoch and generally behaved as if the newspapers were effectively their property and they should choose who might be nominal owners. The meeting was good theatre but I was not convinced. The trade unions did not seek a meeting with me but there was evidence they would accept the Murdoch bid, fearing unemployment if *The Times* collapsed.

Meanwhile senior people in the Trade Department, guided by Clucas, were devising a system of government-appointed directors who would have the responsibility of seeing that the *Times* standards would be maintained. I accepted the proposal without enthusiasm but I thought it would reassure middle class opinion.

John Smith, as shadow Trade Secretary, requested an emergency debate which was granted by the Speaker. Committee 'E' met in great haste to consider the situation. It was obvious the decision would have to be announced in that debate. The Prime Minister did not make known her views directly to me, but I judged she wanted the deal to go through as I did.

The debate was not comfortable. John Smith was in cracking form. Hostility to the Murdoch bid was growing and it was powerfully expressed by Jonathan Aitken from the Tory back bench. I stuck closely to my brief, aided by the fact that Murdoch had offered the editorship to Harold Evans, a one-time editor of the *Sunday Times* and now a leader of the vehemently protesting journalists. Evans accepted; should our paths have crossed I would have shared a bottle of champagne with him. The storm subsided but in time it was the unions and not the journalists who felt the innovative drive of Murdoch.

Subsequently when I had more time to reflect upon the episode I became critical of the legislation that enabled the deal. The decision turned upon profit figures but these were inevitably subject to subsequent revision. The *Times* deal relied upon both *The Times* and the *Sunday Times* being loss-making. There was no doubt about the former but it was a closer-run thing for the *Sunday Times*. Their figures were revised in the months following my decision but mercifully did not tip them into profit. It seemed to me this was an area of ambiguity.

Tuesday 27 January 1981

Today was possibly quite an important one in my political career. I had to handle the Murdoch bid debate. The morning was spent either awaiting the draft of the speech or else amending it. When the text arrived I felt it was too flat and needed to be given a new dimension, and I also felt that the reasons given for judging the *Sunday Times* were too peremptory. Stuart Hampson did an excellent job in extending the speech and giving it more life. It was indeed a difficult House. Once interruptions started they were difficult to stem. There was incredulity about the financial figures I quoted for *The Times*. John Smith exploited the general increase rather well; and Jonathan Aitken made a formidable attack. I was helped by some rather absurd allegations of favours towards Murdoch. MT heard my speech and the wind-up. She was absolutely delighted with how things had been handled, and referred to me in handsome terms.

Wednesday 4 February 1981

I had a truly exhausting day and at the end I felt quite exhausted. In the morning I attended my first meeting of the NEDC [National Economic Development Council]. It was quite worse than anything I had feared. I thought Murray put his case lugubriously but quite well. Moss Evans was not easy to follow, but had a pleasing manner. Terry Duffy was an embarrassment and Drain was nearly silent. Pennock was quite shrewd in his arguments, but Beckett was long winded and not terribly impressive. Prior was the best government performer, able to link the particular and specifically industrial problem to the general political proposition. Chandler has a great problem since his voice is earnest and rather squeaky. Geoffrey Howe was constructive and the PM presided over it all rather like an impatient schoolmistress. In the evening I had to talk to the Bow Group. It was a great burden after such a long day.

Thursday 5 February 1981

I had my economic debate wind-up. It went quite well and earned the approval of MT. Even so it was a fearful strain and I cannot easily convey how exhausting it all was. MT opened the debate and did so effectively and with authority – she got a good press. Michael Foot was rather long winded and the speech had plenty of style but not much economic argument. Stephen Dorrell made a competent Heathite speech. Peter Shore wound up well but was thrown by William Waldegrave, who spotted that it was important for Ulysses to have his sailors' ears stopped with wax because of the siren songs. My own speech was interrupted frequently but I kept to the theme which I had prepared. Also I managed to end on the hour to the immense relief of the whips. It was an experience to have to battle through a rough and rowdy wind-up – and succeed!! Lord be praised.

Sunday 22 February 1981

I had a powerful day. I suspect it will mark some turning point in my political life. The interview with Brian Walden was gruelling. It lasted thirty-five minutes and I found myself wishing that it would end. The discussion did not turn much upon the concepts discerned at the Cabinet meeting. I was primed heavily on trade union authority, and also the collapse of government's economic policy. Afterwards I went to the Commons and did some work on textiles and footwear for Thursday's debate. I had a telephone call from Lord Thorneycroft congratulating me and asking if I had cleared the line with MT. He was anxious to urge the line on her, and said he would ask her to discuss policy with me.

Monday 23 February 1981

I had a rather anxious day as I wanted to see the press and parliamentary reactions to *Weekend World*. On the whole things have gone quite well – I was told that No. 10 were briefing that I had done well in a difficult situation – and the press gave the entire incident handsome coverage. At an 'E' meeting on the miners the PM made a short and kindly reference – but that could have been a protective move. Francis Pym was evidently very pleased with what I had said, Geoffrey Howe observed I had become the enfant terrible of *Weekend World*. At the end of the day I felt I had established myself just a shade more in the political world. I saw Dr Dally in the morning and he seemed pleased but said I should take four lithium tablets each day. Sarah came back from Idaho and seemed in very good heart – she had made friends. It was great to see her home.

Shortly after the *Times* takeover Tiny Rowland, on behalf of Lonrho, made a bid for *The Observer*. The bid had to be considered by the Department of Trade. But unlike *The Times* in this case there was no question of it avoiding consideration by the Monopolies Commission. As with *The Times*, we proposed the new ownership should have a panel of independent directors. It was a modest move designed to placate those who were hostile to private media magnates such as Murdoch and Rowland. Although not in the same suspicion class as Murdoch, the latter was viewed warily; Ted Heath had talked of Lonrho as 'the unacceptable face of capitalism'. In return Rowland had great hostility to the Trade Department but it related to controversies that pre-dated my arrival. Edward du Cann, MP for Taunton and one-time chairman of the 1922 Committee of Tory backbenchers, was a business associate of Rowland who made arrangements for him to call and see me. 'John, old boy, can I bring round Tiny; he'd so like to see you.' In the meetings that followed I always had a couple of top officials present. They were bizarre. Rowland would deliver a monologue, starting in a whisper but ending in a rasping Germanic full-throated crescendo. The onslaught was on the general behaviour of the government rather than the shortcomings of the Trade Department. Du Cann sat like a silent acolyte and there was general relief when they left. Bill Beckett, the department's authority on monopolies and mergers, once observed at the departure of Tiny, 'Well, Secretary of State, we can now take our hands out of the piranha bowl.'

The *Times/Observer* bids, competition policy generally and British trade promotion were topical matters I discussed with ministers. They were a good team. Sally Oppenheim was Minister of State for Consumer Protection and possibly under-employed in that capacity. Consequently she was able to make regular visits to the hairdresser and was always immaculately coiffed. Cecil Parkinson had been a highly successful accountant and was adept at handling business delegations. Reginald Eyre was a political companion from the Birmingham Bow Group and handled company law. When I became Trade Secretary he was working on a Bill providing the framework for Lloyd's of London. It required a professional hand.

Thursday 5 March 1981

In the afternoon I had a visit from Tiny Rowland flanked by du Cann and Duncan Sandys. They explained that they wished to purchase *The Observer* and I explained my position under the law. Then came the bombshell. Rowland would purchase the paper himself if the Lonrho purchase was referred to the MMC. This would mean that *his* purchase could not be referred. The whole thing looks like making a Charlie of me, but Tim Renton argued later that Rowland could at least be inconvenienced if I tried to persuade Atlantic Richfield that he should not be sold the paper under such terms. Tim thought that Atlantic Richfield were sufficiently interested in North Sea oil that they might respond. Earlier the Cabinet had decided upon a public holiday for Charles and Diana – Prior, the PM and myself being against.

I followed the usual technique of having an early morning ministers' meeting. It worked rather well and kept us in touch with all aspects of the department and with politics generally. One morning Cecil turned up looking distraught. The previous evening he had foolishly left his red box in his own instead of the ministerial car and his vehicle was stolen. Cecil was in a great state and asked me if he should offer his resignation. I said that was dotty and that the car would be found and in it the red box. It was. But what a scrape. I was delighted that not a word appeared in the newspapers.

I have referred to the invaluable support I received from
my permanent secretary, Sir Kenneth Clucas. I also had great
help from my private office, which was initially run by Stuart
Hampson. He was outstanding and so much better than anyone
I had experienced at the Treasury. He left fairly soon after I
arrived to join the John Lewis Partnership, eventually becoming
chairman. He was duly knighted and also became chairman of
the Royal Society of Arts and an evangelist for wider social obli-
gations for business. His calm efficiency was tested one morning
when I was trapped in the lift between floors. I was an innocent
victim but quite unable to move. Bureaucrats to a man, my staff
continued to address me, waist downwards, as 'Secretary of
State' whilst I was past formality and could only shout 'Get me
out of this bloody thing.'

During my time at Trade there were two Cabinet meetings
which dealt with major situations where I took an independent
view. The first concerned the management of economic policy.
Geoffrey Howe had introduced a toughish Budget in the spring
of 1981 but, with strong support from the Prime Minister, decided
on additional public spending cuts in the autumn. A Cabinet
meeting was held to confirm this. The Prime Minister and
Chancellor were supported by Keith Joseph and Leon Brittan,
my successor as Chief Secretary. John Nott and I jumped ship
and joined the wets. We both felt that Treasury policy was being
pushed a bridge too far economically and certainly politically.
The Prime Minister was furious and sent her parliamentary
private secretary, Ian Gow, to chastise us. Ian was a long-standing
friend, much more than a political acquaintance. I listened to
his admonition. 'Margaret was very upset. I do hope you realise
that.' I really did feel unmoved. Of course it had not been easy
for me but I figured we were in the Cabinet for our judgement as
well as our support. I was glad John Nott thought likewise.

Tuesday 10 March 1981

In the morning I attended the Cabinet to discuss the Budget. Geoffrey Howe presented his proposals in a very low key. Jim Prior at once opened up an attack. He attacked the decision to go for a PSBR of £10,500 million and got quite excited in his accusation that the Treasury were indifferent to the recession. He said that current policies would create three to three and a quarter million unemployed. Howe had given a bad impression about the date and the scale of unemployment turndown. David Howell annoyed Prior by talking about taking the bellows to the economy. Gilmour and Walker also attacked the Budget, and kept on talking about it as deflationary. Pym half condemned and half supported the Budget – but Jenkin, Nott, Joseph, Edwards, Younger, Howell and Fowler supported. Hailsham said we must keep our nerve, Whitelaw said we must not spend too much too soon, Jopling said the party was fragile and disagreements must not become public. I strongly supported Geoffrey Howe and said the recession was on its way out.

Friday 20 March 1981

The day started with the arranged meeting with Rowland. I was extremely nervous and murmured rather than spoke. I told him I wished to refer the Lonrho bid to the MMC. It was clear that he hankered after a personal purchase, and we had a slightly edgy discussion about the issues that might arise in that event. Later I heard – via the radio – that he was making a personal purchase. I have found the whole business wearing and not exhilarating, and there are only tears in it for me. Sarah drove up to Middle Farm. Spring has arrived, but everything is damnably wet. We had the AGM. It was a low-key affair. Morale is bad, but there was no open bitchiness. The questions were pointed but fair. [Kenneth]

Pettigree complained about the reference of the Lonrho bid for House of Fraser to the MMC. Mike Woodcock [agent] came back for a drink and showed an alarming lack of political touch about the Social Democrats.

Sunday 22 March 1981

Not a happy day – far too much hassle. I stayed abed until 10 a.m. and got up to a wet and windy day. The skies were grey and the clouds raced by in the wind. I had a telephone call from Mike Garrod asking me if I would do a radio interview on the Rowland–*Observer* bid. I declined, but I felt bad and cowardly about it. I went to church with Michael Spicer: Cropthorne Church is truly delightful. I played Sarah at table tennis – the first game for ages, David Gow played tennis in a howling gale. We had a good lunch party, and I warmed to Michael and Ann Spicer. In the afternoon Sarah and I took the Gow dog for a walk up Bredon Hill. We drove to London and called upon Sally Oppenheim. She seemed to think that Rowland would be vulnerable under s.57 of the Fair Trading Act, but she also took a balanced view about the PNQ.

Monday 23 March 1981

Not a happy day. I am going through a period of strain but so far I have no need of anti-depressants and I sleep fairly well. I fear that Lib/Soc Dem will sweep me from Oswestry and that I will then be unable to get a job and married responsibilities will be overwhelming. I am also distressed over the *Observer*/Lonrho affair. The matter gets more complex. I heard from London that there is now a chance that Rowland may have infringed company law. I suppose the sooner we can pass the parcel to the DPP the better it will be. I left London in pouring rain to get to Portugal. I had a couple of meetings including one with their Minister for

Community Affairs. It was quite clear that there was a price for EEC membership which he thought it would be difficult to justify. We had an excellent dinner – ewe's milk cheese ended the meal. I talked too long – but only just!

Tuesday 7 April 1981

Thirty-two years ago I joined the Army – the memory is still strong. I had quite an eventful day. In the afternoon I visited Col. Johnson and with Bob Boscawen and Stuart Hampson I discussed the royal T-shirts. It was an interesting exchange: Johnson said it was the Queen and not the Lord Chamberlain who had been determined to issue the guidelines banning such textiles. I argued quietly but firmly that it would be impossible to describe the imported garments I had as being in bad taste.

Tuesday 14 April 1981

I continue to hobble around. Three things to note. The Cabinet was very protracted and we spent the entire time on the issue of civil service pay. The PM was very much in a 'Joan of Arc' mood and demanding a tough line, but regretting the weakness of her colleagues. I think Soames showed great forbearance. GH was profoundly unhappy over the granting of any arbitration. In the end I think we gave Soames just about the minimum negotiating hand he could use. Secondly I had a rather disagreeable lunch with the Clark brothers of Plessey Ltd. Their finance director was particularly wearisome, asserting all kinds of shortcomings within government that I know are untrue. It was a good example of the gulf between industry and politics. In the evening Sarah brought across Jeremy Cooper and we had a picnic supper. We were joined by Cecil Parkinson, who was in robust form and who emphasised his lack of enthusiasm for Humphrey Atkins.

Monday 22 June 1981

I had a terribly rushed day. It ended with the Mackenzie interview. He had a terribly bad throat which put him at a considerable disadvantage. The interview seemed to go well enough, and I managed to take the initiative two or three times. Earlier I had a talk with the secretary about the MMC report on *The Observer*. It was useful. I have decided to accept the MMC report – not happily but because it seems the most defensible course. In the afternoon I had to greet Mr Hassan Ali, the Iraqi Trade Minister. It was a pleasant occasion although Ali is reputed to be a thug. I received oriental gifts – dates, a rug and a book. Later I had a session at No. 10 when we discussed the problems of Merseyside. The CPRS report was quickly put aside and we had a debate as to whether we needed a commissioner or a minister to galvanise local government into action in the area.

Wednesday 24 June 1981

It was an endless and hard-working day. I had Harold Wilson come to see me about the film industry. He was easy-going and it was not difficult to flatter him. He loved reminiscing [about] the 1945 parliament and told me the bonfire of controls was created because he announced it on 5 November. He had the habit of making one-up comments showing him to have been the hero.

Thursday 25 June 1981

[At] lunch at the US embassy… I was sat next to Michael Jopling. Bush made a short speech and Healey asked truculent and rambling questions. Callaghan buttonholed me and asked me to postpone coming to a quick decision on *The Observer*. In the evening I watched the Mackenzie TV programme. I was reasonably pleased by it.

Monday 29 June 1981

Quite a day; and one I am glad to have over. Freddie Laker
arrived in the afternoon with his lawyer and I broke the news that
I was not withdrawing the BA privilege in Hong Kong, so there
would be no Laker Hong Kong route. He was voluble but not
histrionic until Trefgarne told him he was 'oversimplifying'. At
that he flew into a good natured rage and walked out. Curiously
I was not displeased with Trefgarne as I did not know how we
would get the meeting over.

Tuesday 30 June 1981

In the morning Mr Rowland, Lord Shawcross and others came to
see me. They were very relaxed about the *Observer* purchase and
conditions. It was a difficult interview because it was so bland.
Their main concern was the freedom to sell. In the afternoon
Gloria [Hooper] brought her posse of MEPs. Sally Oppenheim
strikes a forthright note in wanting to avoid consumerism, and I
note that several of the MEPs now use Eurospeak.

Wednesday 1 July 1981

I had a crowded and somewhat distraught day. *The Observer*
obtruded nastily. Donald Trelford and John Cole came to see me
and I was subject to a somewhat hysterical tirade on the Lonrho
bid. It was an avid and unhappy mutiny, and I now fear there
will be a stormy time in the Commons. John Smith has recommended the Minority Report, but I would be doubtful if the
matter extended to a debate.

Thursday 2 July 1981

The morning was a marathon of committees, including Cabinet.
I shall treasure two memories. There was a general bitch about
Fitzgerald ending with a scathing reference that his Foreign

Minister was a university hydrologist. 'What's that, a wet?' shouted an unidentified member of the Cabinet. Later we were discussing a wedding present for Charles and Diana, and the coffee tables were rejected and silver candlesticks chosen instead – at £35 a head. John Nott (rightly) complained that this was more than he would give for any present to his family. I had lunch with Mr Lewis, the US ambassador. A whole trade retinue accompanied me – which I dislike. Mr Knighton told me that progress was being made with *The Observer*; Trelford was apparently a good deal more reasonable.

Monday 7 September 1981

Back at work – and thus do I feel it. Already my mood is much dominated by thoughts of the SDP. The Labour Party news is getting worse, and it really does look as if Benn will storm the ramparts. I had lunch with Hamish McRae and Frances Cairncross. They told me *The Guardian* was losing out to *The Times*, and also that they now felt Labour was moving towards serious weakening. Poor Michael Foot: he could have been remembered as a great parliamentarian and now he will be remembered as a weak leader.

Trade visit to Iraq

Friday 2 October 1981

I had a rather nightmare journey, it coming so quickly after the Atlantic flight. The day started at the office. Somehow things seem in hand and I agreed the letter for the PM on Bank legislation. The department are obviously more nervous of Treasury intentions than I am. The Iraqi ambassador was at the airport to bid me farewell. The flight was long and tedious, but I had

an amiable chat with John Rose [private secretary]. At Baghdad
I was greeted by Hassan Ali and [Stephen] Egerton in stygian
alarm. The black-out was partial but not ineffective. We had
desultory greetings and then I was taken to a palatial guest house
where I had a substantial suite. I had a briefing talk with Roy
Williams and two others. I then retired to bed, exhausted and
disorientated. Graham Pope is dead. The seat will go SDP.

Saturday 3 October 1981

I was rushed to the Palace in order to be with other Trade ministers in line to be met by Hussain. He was a charismatic man
and with presence. It was all quite well staged. After lunch at the
ambassador's residence I had a rest and then went around
the fair – endless generators. In the evening I rested, had supper
with the Trade team and thankfully went to bed.

‡

Tuesday 20 October 1981

The first Cabinet and a wearing one. Doubtless I have incurred
the wrath of the PM but I placed on record my belief that the
Treasury would have to sanction more public spending and that
it would have to be financed by taxation. I was called second – the
PM doubtless hoping I would sustain the Treasury. The debate
lasted a long time but there was no real acrimony except when
Carrington told the PM quite sharply that he was not going to
be interrupted. Heseltine made a speech demanding more public
spending capital, financed by no improvement in welfare benefits
or public sector pay. Whitelaw made a contribution which clearly
identified him with the 'appeasers'. Walker was not very precise
or very convincing when he said we would only get greater output
with more investment.

Friday 23 October 1981

I heard the news of an SDP/Lib victory over the Tories by 10 per cent, and it froze my heart. I had supposed they would win by 5 per cent but it does seem there was a late switch of Labour votes. On this basis Crosby should certainly go SDP and there will be great ructions within the Tory Party. I am pleased I spoke up as I did in Cabinet.

Monday 26 October 1981

I had quite a long session with MT. The talk involved John Nott, Ian Gow and myself. I provided her with a draft outline of a speech for the censure debate. John Nott and I did this, but her heart was not in the theme, which argued that there had been a modest but justifiable increase in public spending. She berated me for having said £2 billion would do and then opposing the Treasury for having conceded no more than £3.5 billion. She railed against all ministers for not having cut public spending by administrative methods in their departments. She believes that if she had twenty MTs in the Cabinet they would get the spending cuts without loss to programmes. John Nott argued courageously against this, and tried to bring some realism into the talk. He also said we would have to abandon Trident before long and MT seemed to agree to that. Signed a Brazilian trade deal.

Wednesday 25 November 1981

A sad and depressing day. The plans to rescue Laker are coming to nought. The Attorney General says it would be illegal to continue the interest rate subsidy on planes that Laker would lease back. We had a hasty consideration of s.8 aid, but that does not seem a runner. Earlier I had a talk with Peter Jenkins on government economic policy. I said that I thought the Chancellor of the Exchequer would recommend joining the EMS and that it would be argued that fixed exchange rates would supply a needed discipline. I had an exhausting morning at 'E' when we considered a replacement for the referendum (no alternative was selected). Once again I used my voice to obscure the difficulties of Leon Brittan. He speaks at length and loses his audience but his mastery of intricacy is enviable. I did a lunch time meeting [in] North Ealing. Harry Greenway was quite optimistic.

Monday 25 January 1982

It has been a day of relentless hard work. I returned to No. 10 in the afternoon. MT put on a highly charged performance when discerning the fortunes of British Leyland. There is nothing she will hear in mitigation of [Michael] Edwardes. Geoffrey Howe and the rest of us then had a good moan after she had left the room since none of us want to see it closed this side of a general election.

Trade visit to Japan

Tuesday 2 February 1982

I continued to feel absolutely worn out and tired. This apart I had a pleasant day. I have a lovely suite of rooms, a ready supply of drink and TV in Japanese and also the BBC World Service. Cortazzi [ambassador to Japan] is brusque, talks endlessly through and over everything, but is informative and helpful. He so obviously enjoys talking in Japanese. My morning meeting was with the Japanese CBI and it lasted around two hours. It was calm and I thought it was all right – but everything is inscrutable. I had lunch with some bankers. They disapproved of monetarism and floating exchange rates; and above all were totally self-centred. In the afternoon I went around the SBAC exhibition. The men who conducted the tour had appalling breath. The exhibition was grim – but it was the centrepiece of my visit. We had dinner

with Abe – possibly a future PM. It was good value, and the food
was pleasant. The day went better than feared.

Wednesday 3 February 1982

Once again to my surprise things went quite well. The day started
with a visit to Mr Abe – with whom I had dined the previous evening. I received a truly worthwhile present – a bedside clock/radio.
There are enough dials to fly an aeroplane. Later in the day I saw
the Minister of Transport, and also caucus leaders of LDP. My
message was always the same – the need to secure the purchase
of capital goods and particularly the BAe 146. The replies were
oblique, but the main purpose was to register a message. I had a
genuine success at the British Chamber of Commerce where I did
a domestic political tour d'horizon. I received a number of thanks,
and it was good for morale. There was a substantial all-male dinner
party. I joked about not having a TV set and the boss of Hitachi
immediately wished to send me one. It took a while to dissuade him.

‡

Wednesday 24 February 1982

The great drama was the Lonrho meeting. There was a great
performance by Tiny Rowland. He was passionate and spoke
at length with populist style references to shareholders. Earlier
Duncan Sandys had spoken briefly and du Cann not long – but
he strongly attacked the MMC. I reacted quite sharply and
defended the MMC, and also made a spirited riposte to Rowland
saying there was no prejudice against Lonrho in the Department
of Trade. I also stated I would initially refer the new bid to the
OFT. I do not know how this will proceed. I am anxious to keep
the ball out of my court and he is anxious that I should play it.
On the whole I thought the meeting went off quite well.

Thursday 25 February 1982

I was apprehensive on how the day would go. It passed off quite well. The Cabinet was quiet and passed without effort into a meeting of 'E'. We had a short discussion on the Thames Barrage and it appears that the TUC are lending a hand. Actually the discussion tailed off into an attempt to analyse how it was that Ken Livingstone got so much publicity. My own paper on Trade went quite well. There was general agreement that more should be spent on ATP and I was relieved that the CPRS proposal to select export winners was turned down. We also had a broadly helpful discussion on non-tariff barriers within the EEC. Later I saw the PM on my own to discuss the Anglo-Japanese trade problems. She was determined that something should be done about it all and favoured macro-economic action bearing on the exchange rate. She was very severe against the EMS and was scathing that Belgium had not been permitted the devaluation she sought.

Thursday 25 March 1982

As the day proceeded I felt increasingly groggy. I seem to be overworked and have aches and pains. My day ended doing the TV marathon on the Hillhead by-election. This was with Roy Hattersley and Shirley Williams. They snapped and snarled a good deal and enabled me to be 'the nice guy'. Even so I found the result dreadfully depressing as it will give the SDP an immense publicity boost and a major effective leader in the Commons. On the other hand it could have been a worse result – and both Labour and Conservative had reasons for satisfaction. Earlier I had taken the Queen's Export Award winners to their drinks at Buckingham Palace. It was a scramble but I had a pleasant time talking to Arthur Knight [chairman, Queen's Award Committee] about the role of NIs, and I also met someone called Griffiths from Staveley who came originally from Knockin Heath. Ian Gow tipped me off to oppose the Prior paper on Northern Ireland.

‡

The second occasion when I took an independent view was the last Cabinet meeting I attended before being made Leader of the House. The purpose of the meeting was to decide whether or not we should send a task force to recapture the Falkland Islands. I had discussed the matter with my private office. I had misgivings about the proposed venture. I thought the distance made it near impossible and certainly highly risky. I decided it would be better to try negotiations, however unpalatable. My private office agreed. At the Cabinet meeting the Prime Minister took all the voices individually and I was the only opponent to the despatch of the task force. It was remarkable that there was no leak of that meeting.

Friday 2 April 1982

Much drama. I arrived at the Trade Department to be told that there was a Cabinet at 9.30. We were told that the Argentines were expected to attack the Falklands at 10 a.m. and that we had no more than ninety marines defending the place. It was arranged that Parliament would be informed. I went to the House and thought Atkins did quite a good job explaining the situation – but everyone knew the islands had fallen and would want to know what next. We then had a Cabinet in the evening. We had a joint security assessment (*not* endorsed by the MoD) which effectively said that the islands could not be recaptured. This assessment was not accepted and there then followed a most tense discussion about whether or not the fleet should put to sea. Alone, I argued there it should not, and Hailsham was particularly bellicose. I believe the whole climate will change over the days that we sail towards Falklands.

Saturday 3 April 1982

Early in the morning we had a meeting with Geoffrey Howe. Jenkin and Havers were there, but no one from the FCO. It was absurd, particularly as the nature of the economic action depended, amongst other factors, how much at war we were. It was a dispiriting meeting, but we cobbled together some innocuous economic phrases for the debate. The debate itself was a near disaster. MT spoke tolerably well, but could not resist the temptation of partisan nit-picking. Michael Foot was extremely good – hit just the right note between bipartisan unity and a scathing attack on the competence of the government. Powell was ugly and evil in his remarks about the marines. Finally John Nott wound up with a lame speech which foolishly attacked the opposition and simply fell below the level of the occasion. The TV subsequently talked of demands for resignation.

Sunday 4 April 1982

I had a desultory day working through my papers. In the morning I went to church – Palm Sunday. It was quite a moving little service – we processed around the church. I then cycled to Hughie's [Elwes]. Sarah was most surprised that I was able to climb the hill. Chloe pulled Bella's tail dreadfully. She is not a disciplined child. Lunch was marked by excellent ice-cream. In the early afternoon I drove to Windsor Castle. When I arrived there was no equerry to meet me, but eventually I was given a nursery tea and read the *Sunday Express*. I joined John Nott and Francis Pym and we had a PC. It concerned the power to requisition the *Canberra*. John Nott seemed in cheerful voice, but gave me the impression that the matter would end in conflict.

I was just about to leave for a visit to Latin America. I was not enthusiastic about foreign travel but I was looking forward to my first ever visit to Brazil and Venezuela. I was to be accompanied by Sarah since it was judged that there would be a great deal of entertaining on the trip. Suddenly it was cancelled. I reflected on Harold Wilson's dictum 'a week is a long time in politics'.

I had thoroughly enjoyed my stint as Trade Secretary. It was exhilarating to have a department and one that was manageable in size and had a congenial executive team. The *Times* episode, although uncomfortable, had been a great test of political and parliamentary judgement. I would not say I had matured but I had gained valuable experience.

41

LEADER OF THE HOUSE

The Argentinian occupation of the Falklands in 1982 led to a major government change. Lord Carrington resigned as Foreign Secretary and took his two ministers with him. It was a selfless act and wholly in character. Francis Pym became Foreign Secretary and I was asked to fill his position as Leader of the House. I was quite unprepared for the offer and hesitated whilst I quickly considered items on my Trade desk. Even I realised it was quite a leg up. 'You'll be Lord President of the Council,' said Margaret Thatcher and the deal was clinched. Within fourteen months that appointment was removed from me and transferred to William Whitelaw on grounds of seniority. But I had the consolation of keeping the red box.

Monday 19 April 1982

The main feature of the day was lunch. MT entertained a group of us including Ian Gow and the Chief Whip. Others included Parkinson, Younger, Whitelaw, Walker and Hurd. The PM got increasingly restless about the 'softness' of the party and terms which involved some part of the Argentine claim. She then started on a theme that the Soviets had a major influence in the Galtieri move and it was all part of the Red design. I got

the suspicion that she had been talking to General Walker.
Whitelaw kept prodding me (physically) to argue against her –
and this I did, counselling that there was not – necessarily – fault
in FCO before the seizure of the islands. It was a disturbing
lunch. In the evening I saw Michael Cocks – a handy talk. He will
never forgive John Stradling Thomas for his behaviour as pairing
whip at the time of the Aircraft and Shipbuilding Bill. Also he
was quite contemptuous of the antics of Tony Benn, whose seat
he thinks could be lost.

I was Leader of the House from April 1982 to June 1987. They were
my happiest years in Parliament and, I think, my most successful.
The job was a glorious hybrid – part Commons and part government. I had two offices, one in Whitehall and one in the Commons.
The former was an imposing and spacious room recently decorated
in salmon pink by Norman St John-Stevas when he was Leader of
the House. My enormous desk made the furniture at the Treasury
and Trade seem like wartime utility. I had only one objection. A
huge oil painting of James II hung on the wall behind me. I think it
was a piece of popery left behind by Norman St John-Stevas and,
admittedly without evidence, I thought that my ancestors would
have fought with Monmouth against James at Sedgemoor.

At lunch time the office, which numbered about six, would
transfer to the Leader's room in the Commons, close to the
chamber. It was quite compact and dominated by a large painting of a House of Commons point to point race and a smaller
one of William Wilberforce, who campaigned against slavery.
It also had a substantial drinks cupboard to facilitate business
after 6 p.m. The room had its history: it was here that Profumo
was interviewed by Macleod, then Leader, when the fateful statement concerning Christine Keeler was agreed.

My civil servant support, three executives and three secretaries, were on secondment from other departments. The Ministry of Defence was the main recruiting ground. David Heyhoe, an admirable and laid-back personality, was the senior official. Relations were more relaxed than at the Treasury. I knew almost as much about Commons procedures and personalities as did my civil servants. This was particularly true concerning the Labour Party. So we operated as a team. At meetings Heyhoe was a natural sceptic with a shrewd understanding of MPs' motives. Life tended to be a series of daily crises; storms at or after *Question Time*, meetings with the chairmen of select committees and Cabinet committees. I always looked forward to the inquest with David that followed these events and particularly after the meeting with the press lobby on Thursday afternoons. An unofficial member of my team was Derek Howe. He had found himself a corner somewhere in the office and had close links with the press. He was very supportive but in no sense a personal assistant. He was a mystery man.

My work involved close links with the Prime Minister. In addition to Cabinet meetings I attended a great many committee meetings, usually with a watching brief prepared by No. 10. Occasionally I was asked to prepare a speech for the Prime Minister – a task farmed out to many. I was very pleased to draft a speech for her to make on the death of Macmillan. I do not think either of us were uncritical admirers of him but I am vain enough to think I would have worded the contrived praise more happily. However, my text was mangled up before being used; a usual fate for all contributors.

I was also a member of the 'Kitchen Cabinet', which met on Monday morning. It included the Chief Whip, initially Michael Jopling, then John Wakeham, Norman Tebbit, the party chairman and of course, Willie Whitelaw. It was one of the most outspoken of committees and frequently featured the Prime Minister in handbag mood with Conservative Central Office. Norman patiently parried the charges whilst I wondered why he had been so keen to get the post.

My relative closeness to the Prime Minister was recognised when I deputised for her in answering Prime Minister's Questions. It was a prestigious task although I could not conceivably be considered as Deputy Prime Minister unlike the Chancellor of the Exchequer or Foreign Secretary. Prime Minister's Questions was a most taxing job. I would get a red box on Wednesday night with a brief outline of the questions and suggested answers. I would spend up to ninety minutes on Thursday morning rehearsing all the government successes I hoped to include in my answers. The questions and answers were general and could range over everything. Finally I would always have a lunch of smoked salmon sandwiches and read the early edition of the *Evening Standard*.

Tuesday 20 April 1982

I had my launch in speech-making – having to present the time-table motion on the Employment Bill. Sarah was in the gallery together with Alan and Patrea [More Nisbet]. It was a successful debut. The content was a helpful blend of text and my own work; I enjoyed and provoked the repartee. Altogether it was a plus, and my office clearly enjoyed the performance. Ian Gow saw me and said he had been worried by yesterday's lunch. He feels the dilemma will be that the terms of a Falkland settlement will be disagreeable, but that fighting will not make them much better. The PM is playing the islanders' card – and that is certainly the one most likely to win the Labour Party.

My first performance was lacklustre whilst I struggled with the enormous briefing folder. But eventually I got into the swing of things and enjoyed the contest. I managed with shorter notes rather than a large brief. I had my own style, 'the soft answer that turneth away wrath', and also oblique self-criticism. I had no concealed handbag. I respected, indeed liked, Michael Foot and Neil Kinnock, who were the leaders of the opposition who confronted me. I would go into the chamber at least a quarter of an hour before I was due to be called. I needed to absorb the atmosphere, which was constantly changing. Usually I was fairly sure footed but I once made a chance remark that could be construed as anti-homosexual. At once Neil Kinnock was down my throat and I learned to watch my words even more carefully in the electric atmosphere of Prime Minister's questions.

My announcement of Next Week's Business came after Prime Minister's Questions and this was followed by up to half an hour devoted to me being cross-examined. It was an occasion when members often made points which they had been unable to make in speeches. I was tolerably quick witted and I think the House and I enjoyed these verbal duels. I listened to an assault from Dennis Skinner sarcastically sympathising with me, to which I responded, 'Us grammar school boys must stick together.' The riposte went down well. Skinner, well to the left, had been to Tupton Hall Grammar School and I had long been waiting to use the phrase. The exchange was mentioned in the *Alan Clark Diaries*.

Today reports of Next Week's Business read rather flat in Hansard, but on the day in a crowded House they conveyed a lively and often humorous atmosphere. They were played out in front of a full press lobby, which was to my benefit when I met the press downstairs immediately afterwards. It was a friendly occasion but fraught with possible misunderstanding. The journalists themselves were divided between those who wanted the proceedings 'on the record' and those who preferred 'off the record'. I did not mind either but I was opposed to switching from 'on' to 'off' during a briefing. Most journalists wanted 'off the record'.

Leaders of the House seem to have an occupational hazard of indiscretion. Bernard Ingham, the Prime Minister's press officer, had to cope with Norman St John-Stevas, Francis Pym and me. I do not think any of us fitted his bill. I enjoyed my weekly tangle with the press. I treated it as a battle of wits and I tried to avoid being cross-examined on departmental matters so I tended to confine myself to broad policy and even philosophic issues. A consequence of my briefing role was endless lunches with journalists. They were good company and I ate superbly. I had been asked to include 'government–press relations' in my role as Leader but sought to be excused. I felt it put me too close to the government and also it was a non-job. It was given to Angus Maude.

Tuesday 4 May 1982

At 8.15 p.m. I was called to attend a meeting and we had the sickening news that we had lost a destroyer and a Harrier. The PM was clearly and deeply upset by the event. John Nott handled it quietly and also said that the Argentine aircraft carrier had been located. We all agreed it should be disabled – sunk, but Pym also made a speech outlining the dangers to a diplomatic solution. I argued that we had to secure a task force success in order to have any chance of a diplomatic initiative.

Tuesday 11 May 1982

The Cabinet meeting was quite long and somewhat unsatisfactory.

John Nott seemed anxious to cover himself against further disasters and we were unhappy to learn that an Argentinian submarine was sailing towards the *Canberra*. It was also clear that the idea of UN Trusteeship was at a disadvantage as it would enable massive Argentinian immigration into the islands. Somehow the meeting was subdued. I sensed that there would be a preference for a landing in the islands as a means of breaking the issue. In the evening there was great excitement when Labour officially asked for a Falklands debate. We were all resolved to concede one, although Michael Jopling would have preferred a delay. We all – Whitelaw and Pym especially – believe that Labour is much divided over Falklands and hope we can give them diversions by denying debating time.

Thursday 20 May 1982

The Cabinet was tense. It was obvious that diplomacy had been set aside. The naval option was in everyone's mind, and the PM read out the defence assessment including the questions of air cover. She asked if anyone disagreed with the decision to proceed with the naval option if necessary. No voice was raised against. We all left the room feeling rather drained and weary. The debate in the afternoon was a success for the government. MT did well and Michael Foot made a lacklustre but supportive speech. I missed the main debate but I was told that Callaghan had done well. Healey sat down leaving Pym with thirty-five minutes within which to wind up. What a bad trick. My lobby went rather better. I had a quite pleasant evening. Sarah and I were taken to *Eugene Onegin* at the Royal Opera House in Covent Garden by Bryan Rigby and his wife. I suspect a major day in the political calendar.

‡

As Leader I was part of the 'usual channels' – i.e. the whips' offices of the two major parties and the Leader of the House and his shadow. I worked very closely and generally in harmony with Michael Jopling and John Wakeham, who were government Chief Whips in my term of office. Jopling was not a very good guide during my early weeks. We were in the midst of the Falklands War and immense distress was caused when HMS *Sheffield* was sunk. There was great clamour from the Labour benches for a statement. The 1939–45 war occasioned a great deal of restraint in parliamentary debating of the conflict, but I knew this was a novel situation. I was new to the job and needed guidance. Jopling said 'don't give way' and so I rode out the storm but not before business was lost in the row. I should have met the opposition request and allowed a statement. That apart Jopling and I worked together rather well. He was fairly traditional and neither of us wanted much reform of Parliament.

When Jopling was made Minister of Agriculture he was succeeded by John Wakeham, a brilliant and highly political businessman. We were some way apart, particularly on the European issue. He lost his wife in the IRA bombing of the Grand Hotel at the Brighton conference and I much admired how he rallied from that tragedy. My opposite shadow Leader was John Silkin. I bore him a grudge since he had closured a debate in the 1974 parliament when I was still trying to speak. I was in such a temper I stormed out of the chamber without waiting to vote against the closure. Now all was changed. He was charming, considerate and a powerful Eurosceptic. The opposition Chief Whip was Michael Cocks. He and Tony Benn were locked in Labour controversy in Bristol where they both had their seats. I found little to commend Cocks. He decided upon bully tactics as far as I was concerned and I chose to contrive as much charm as I could muster. I could not have outbullied him. To my relief, after the 1983 general election Derek Foster became Labour Chief Whip. I liked him. He was a member of the Salvation Army and, unusually for the 'usual channels', was a teetotaller. There was a fraternity about the 'usual channels'. We were required to negotiate and agree on all the procedures that enabled Parliament to function and not get mired in unnecessary controversy.

The task of promoting this fell substantially on a civil servant who worked closely with the Chief Whip. In my day this was Murdo Maclean. He was an enigma with an encyclopaedic knowledge of procedure and a good judgement of politicians. He kept their company all hours of the day and night and despite coming from Stornoway was an accomplished drinking companion. Instinctively I tried to keep a little aloof, fearing he would get to know as much about me as he seemed to know about everyone else.

Monday 4 October 1982

The day seemed to centre around the *Panorama* TV show. In the morning I was summoned to No. 10 and the PM – who asked kindly after Sarah – was most anxious to emphasise how dangerous was Fred Emery and the *Panorama* programme. She is clearly worried by the impact of the Think Tank episode. I was then visited by Leon Brittan and he told me how his speech did not merit the radical interpretation it had received. He also said that Geoffrey Howe had asked him to come and see me. Thus battered with advice I went to the TV centre. The producer was not happy with the first run: reluctantly I agreed to another, but it was stilted and had to be abandoned. The third one stood. I thought Emery was gentle, and I was tolerably happy. In the evening Sarah and I watched the programme including the Heath contribution. Altogether it was not a bad day – I think I am reconciled to my work.

Wednesday 6 October 1982

Inevitably I think of today as the occasion when I spoke to the Conservative conference. It was the last debate and the hall was very empty. It would have been quite impossible to get a standing ovation – but I confess to being very satisfied with the speech. The press were heavily represented even though it was too late in the day to provide copy, and the weekend press were also there. In the evening I was constantly congratulated on the performance – and after a generous discount for flattery I still felt pleased. Geoffrey Smith of *The Times* gave supper to Sarah and me; and it was hilarious when Ted Heath came into the restaurant surrounded by a posse of journalists. The bile felt by Geoffrey Smith and myself rapidly surfaced. We had quite a round of media parties. It has been an exhausting day; and one I am glad to have over.

Monday 15 November 1982

The Lord Mayor's banquet was something of a strain. The original great panic was when the front collar stud proved quite useless. Perhaps it was a back stud. At any rate we had to make a quick dash to Dora Dibben [Sarah's aunt] and borrow one. It transpired that Kenneth [Dibben] was a Mason. The banquet was glittering and Sarah was lucky to be sat next to Justice Lane. He was excellent company and inclined to weary of the use of the Falklands. Lord Scarman was opposite. A sheriff and his wife were on my left. The speeches lasted too long and only that of the PM was distinctive. It hit the right note. Earlier I had a pleasant lunch with Lord McAlpine and assembled company. Geoffrey Lloyd was there – he will not write a biography. I think he was pleased that I remembered he had fought Southwark. Lord

McAlpine told me quite clearly that he thought the PM suffered from her chemistry degree and that it encouraged her to believe she had scientific judgements which she did not.

Monday 28 February 1983

The meeting with the PM was interesting. It was clear that she had been rattled by the Bermondsey result. I tried to develop the thesis that we should fight not only a Labour Party, but also the threat of a hung parliament. Parkinson was blaming Labour for calling an early by-election in Darlington. However, he is anxious to deflect the blame. At any rate we both agreed that it was impossible to have a calm and measured discussion with her – a view shared by Jopling. My PMQs went rather well, and Nicholas quite enjoyed watching it. I had a delightful evening with Sarah at the IBA dinner. We met Lady Falkender, and I can understand why she is such an attractive femme fatale. We talked a good deal about Harvey Rhodes. I sat next to Lady Thomson. She was most charming, and Sarah made her number with Lord T. making her repertoire of Scots children's ditties.

Monday 14 March 1983

Just before lunch the MORI was published showing the Alliance at 30, ahead of Labour (27). I was with Whitelaw and Parkinson at the time. I did not think the figures any worse than I feared, but subsequently learned they were about the same as the post-Bermondsey poll. That is hard. There was general gloom, and the PM was ill at ease. However, she authorised that Labour be given an opposition day ahead of Darlington. Jopling had been keen to get her permission as he feared a row – possibly a rancorous post-Darlington inquest. I had lunch with Extel, and there met the boss of London Transport. He is marrying Margot Norman. Lord Marsh [industrialist] was also there. He was particularly scornful of the SDP, the Darlington candidate having advocated Shillingdon as a workers' co-op. In the afternoon we had the first Estimates debates. Higgins thought they had gone well and only objected to the ministerial answer. I got back to Sarah after attending a TIPS launch (Anthony Steen idea). George Young said the SDP would win Darlington and Angela Hooper told me how fed up she was with Cecil Parkinson.

Tuesday 15 March 1983

The Budget was generally judged to be a success. All was revealed to the Cabinet. It got a good hearing. The PM chided Geoffrey Howe for not sounding enthusiastic enough about the pension calculation changes. Jenkin sounded suitably pleased, and even Prior conceded that – unlike past times – he supported the Budget. In the House it was a dreary performance. The content was well accepted, but the style was leaden footed and the overall length desperate. Sarah (in the gallery) thought so. I doubt if it will do much for Darlington (SDP 50, Lab 35, C 15) but it could help in the longer term. The EDC [Economic Dining Club] met at the home of Nick Ridley. Actually the Budget was not all that much discussed. I remember the occasion for the grief shown by Jock Bruce-Gardyne over his non-selection at Tatton. The successful candidate [Neil Hamilton] was derided as a fascist second-hand car salesman. However, what was noteworthy was that the Alliance was taken very seriously indeed, and it is now respectable to talk in terms of an election April 1984.

Wednesday 16 March 1983

I feel somewhat gloomy because of the Alliance breakthrough. I suppose I shall live with this for some time to come. The meeting at Smith Square was an insipid affair. I got the impression that Sir Anthony Garner did not know what was going on or else thought it was impolite to tell. During the morning I did a draft press release attacking Roy Jenkins, and which received the broad approval of Ian Gow. I also had lunch with a trio of journalists who confirmed my gloom by saying that the SDP would get plenty of coverage and offset the Falklands phase. I do feel there is much in this. I also went to the Palace and witnessed the pricking of the High Sheriffs. It was a fascinating PC. In the afternoon I took the Services Committee rapidly through the agenda and my objective was gained – the confirmation of Phase One of the Bridge Street site. Ian Lloyd was half opposed because it was not ambitious enough.

Thursday 17 March 1983

The Cabinet meeting was quite calm, hardly any bickering. It seems we are in a post-Budget calm, although things will liven up again after Easter. However, earlier I had a rather rough meeting with Jim Prior over the Disqualification Act. This problem never involved Northern Ireland initially; it arose because of statements made by the Secretary of State for Northern Ireland in the context of the Act. We are asked to bail him out. I fear that he and I clashed quite sharply, and the Heyhoe [David Heyhoe, John's private secretary] compromise of publishing the official's analysis – but not recommendations – is really quite a victory for Prior. I wish I had decided to take the matter higher. I had a good time during Business Questions – I am now much more in the swim. I saw the dissident pig farmers and we had a sensible talk. I then did three parties, including the one where Sarah was ball president. It went well enough, but the Orman supper was full of garlic.

Thursday 24 March 1983

The Darlington result was quite dramatic. Sarah and I were collected by the taxi and taken to Wells Street. On the way I heard

that an exit poll had established that Labour had won and that
the SDP was not a good third. At the studio things were generally
predictable – Mrs Williams was late. When the programme got
under way it was a long grind. Williams and Hattersley spat at
each other – but alas this did not continue all that long. I think I
was reasonably articulate. The result is good. It puts the Alliance
more firmly into third place, and with luck they can be kept under
control. The Labour Party will keep Foot. Derek Howe confirmed
that this pleased the PM. I had quite a good recess motion debate.
It was a challenge, as I had to cool down the aggro that had arisen
between Bob Cryer and myself over the question of privilege,
after he had attacked Laker for accusing him of pocketing money.

Thursday 7 April 1983

Thirty-four years ago I joined the Army. I thought about it a good
deal during the day – how then (1949) I was plunged into gloom,
misery and fear; indeed a future did not seem to exist. And now?
Politics has flourished in a way I never thought possible. If I am
never more than Leader of the House it will be success indeed.
In 1949 I would never have dreamed of being more than an MP
– and indeed the appetite for more tangible power has come late
in life and only after Dr Dally and John Symondson.

Monday 11 April 1983

I have a strong feeling that my political fortunes are in decline.
The meeting with the PM was not happy. I feel very much the
small boy at these meetings, and I find she is all too anxious to hit
down any ideas. I have in mind my suggestion that Jock Bruce-
Gardyne wanted to get back into journalism to be a runner for the
editorship of the *Daily Telegraph*. I also note with moody resignation that Jopling has now moved against blocking a Tebbit trade
union Bill. It is a question of nodding at the largest hat. Jopling

also told me that William Hickey is the great driver – 60,000 per annum. I cannot believe it.

Tuesday 19 April 1983

It really has been a dreadful day of drama. It started calmly and I thought I was going to have a dead morning. However, it transpired that the PM had seen the proposed amendment to the Wigley motion, and she was horrified that it specified a date. I convinced Ian Gow that the specified date was the most likely way of 'cooling it'. I had a babel of advice from CCO and the PM tried to railroad me (via Gow) into adjourning or voting down the Wigley motion. Sarah was in the room when Ian Gow was applying the pressure by telephone. I slammed down the receiver and threw my chair against the wall – leaving a noticeable dent. She applauded such a display of temper. Eventually we got the relevant permission of the PM to stand by the original plan – and M. Jopling and I felt at least something was salvaged. I handled the Wigley motion with brevity and some gentle humour. Bill Cash called for a picnic supper; he was intense, much grieved by his selection misfortunes.

Wednesday 20 April 1983

The drama continues. Ian Gow called by to ascertain whether the 10 May writ could give rise to an election date at Cardiff on 26 May. Possibly it could – but it strains credulity. Meanwhile Jopling said that 'she was venomous' and her venom was directed at him and me. Heyhoe is deeply upset by it all and fears that his promotion prospects are seriously prejudiced. So are mine!! But it is a serious matter for him.

Sunday 1 May 1983

What a May Day. The weather was foul. We looked around

Hereford very briskly – it was cold and forbidding. Then we drove to Naunton in pouring rain. The Ridleys were like an oasis. The house is so comfortable: the hot baths, drinks, excellent food and good political conversation. Nick said Jock Bruce-Gardyne had taken non-selection very badly indeed. After dinner he said he was much disappointed with life under Thatcher and he contemplated returning to the back benches and making a nuisance of himself.

Thursday 5 May 1983

I had two fairly exhausting sessions on MPs' pay. My main recollection was of the insensate distaste which the PM has for MPs and her determination to hold back their pay as much as she can. The distaste did not extend to severance payments and only partially to the pension proposals. Tebbit was the strong supporter and also showed contempt for MPs. However, the news that £12,000 paid in principle for 1980 would not be £18,000/£19,000 slightly dampened the PM's ardour. In the end roughly the right decision was taken, namely that the report should be published and that the salary levels should be criticised in general terms – but the decisions should be taken in the next parliament. I had quite a good exchange with Michael Foot, and managed to get past the lobby without too much difficulty.

Friday 6 May 1983

I had a busy day. Jopling and Parkinson talked with me about the Chequers meeting. They are both determined to have an early election, but said it was important not to lean on her; otherwise she would make a statement that would pre-empt the meeting on Sunday.

Sunday 8 May 1983

I went to Chequers by car, arriving just after noon. There were a posse of photographers waiting to greet us. The house party consisted of PM, Whitelaw, Parkinson, Tebbit, Jopling, Howe and myself, plus Wolfson, Shrimsley, Gow and Mount. The pre-lunch session was devoted to an analysis of the current situation by opinion polls and local elections. On balance they were quite satisfactory – showing an overall Tory lead of fifty. I doubt if the charts properly refined tactical voting and thus underplayed the likely number of Alliance seats. After lunch we discussed Thursday dates in June. Whitelaw advised an early announcement and an early poll. I said there must be an early announcement. Everyone was agreed on the announcement factors but the majority appeared to favour 23 June. She then gave an ugly display of megalomania – contrasting her rock-like qualities with an India-rubber Cabinet. She actually pointed out the difference between herself and the rest of the Cabinet. Eventually she calmed – said nothing was ready and we started to gloss up the manifesto – what a day. I left early for the *Observer* party, much to her disgust and disapproval.

Sunday 15 May 1983

A terrible day and a horrid blight on the end of a pleasant weekend. When we returned Sarah went in first and said, 'We've been burgled.' And we had. The great tragedy was that my watch [John's father's gold fob watch] had been stolen as well as the cufflinks that Sarah had given me. Sarah had lost silver and also her gold watch. The burglars had taken gold and silver objects. It could have been much worse. However, we felt heartily sickened by it all. To make matters worse Ben [son of Anhalt Road neighbour] had used the house and not locked the door properly. The CID man was very good in going over the house. Sarah was emotional and distraught. We were befriended by the Mervis pair [John and Margaret, neighbours] who gave us scrambled egg and sympathy there. What an appalling start to the election. I feel numbed by the nastiness of it and also by the great sadness in losing the watch. It has meant so much to me.

Monday 16 May 1983

I continued the day in great misery. The burglary dominated all. I could think of little that ameliorated the blow; and above all I felt dreadfully tired on account of the poor sleep. At the end of the day Anthony [Wood, Sarah's ex-husband] arrived and we had a pasta supper. Meanwhile I had collected Nicholas from the train. He seemed remarkably cheerful in view of his impending day of tests at St Edward's. He was fascinated by the burglary. The general view of both Anthony and Sarah is that he should go to St Edward's unless it is too much of a struggle to be there. At the office I had a quiet day. I managed to do three press releases, and after that I had a day of nothing. I had farewell drinks with the office before departing. They seemed genuinely sorry that I was going. I shall miss them a great deal although I think there have been some failings more recently. A sad and farewell day.

The 'usual channels' remained something of a mystery, but I much enjoyed being part of the undercover system. I thought it worked very effectively and it rested upon a remarkable degree of consensus. The adversarial nature of Commons politics could only proceed by agreement of the usual channels. It fitted my own belief that those in power should have the humility to remember that one day they too would be in opposition and those in opposition should have the responsibility to remember that one day they would be in power.

The business arrangements were presented to the Cabinet as first item of business for Thursday morning. There was a convention that it should be accepted. Nigel Lawson, then Chancellor of the Exchequer, was disposed to dispute. The Prime Minister always backed the Chief Whip and me and Nigel, for all his cleverness, would argue knowing his cause was doomed.

The departmental select committees had been set up by my predecessor, Norman St John-Stevas. When I became Leader they had become well established and were, in my view, a constructive aspect of Parliament. I cannot recall any of their reports causing much distress to ministers. The Prime Minister, however, was deeply disturbed that information would be made available to a foreign affairs committee that included Ian Mikardo. I could see no reason for such a restriction and I resented that Mikardo's reliability should be questioned. In the end we found some compromise.

Friday 10 June 1983

In the mid-evening I had a telephone call from No. 10 asking me to continue as Leader of the House but that I should hand over Lord President of the Council so that Willie Whitelaw might have it. This means that I will become Lord Privy Seal or Chancellor of the Duchy of Lancaster.

Saturday 11 June 1983

In the afternoon I went to Buckingham Palace. It was a sad moment as I watched Willie Whitelaw sworn in as LPC [Lord President of the Council]. I was sworn as LPS [Lord Privy Seal] not moments afterwards. I was surprised and angered to learn that Nigel Lawson has become Chancellor of the Exchequer and also that the Department of Trade has been broken up. It seems that Pym has been given an ultimatum and was still at home mulling it over.

Thursday 16 June 1983

We had our first Cabinet, and John Wakeham thought it was quite a bedlam. It lasted far too long and was largely devoted to textual criticism of the Queen's Speech. The PM was in robust mood attacking everything in sight. We also heard plans on the withholding arrangements should the Community budget talks fail.

Monday 4 July 1983

A day largely spent on MPs' pay. I was so disgusted with a *Daily Telegraph* leader that I sent a letter to Bill Deedes – not my favourite character. I saw Alan Beith, who clearly favoured Plowden [report on MPs' pay] or most of it, and also was strongly concerned to see the allowances confirmed. John Silkin was adamant that there should be full Plowden, and said he thought the Skinner group on this issue would be negligible. Edward du Cann was fascinating. He bemoaned that Plowden was not being paid in full, but still hankered on a pay deal to run unamended through a parliament, wished to have a non-indexed pension fund and at the end accepted that a deal should be struck between 4 per cent and full Plowden. I then had a longish session with John Wakeham and concluded staging Plowden plus no other annual increment or else one third Plowden plus annual increments. I think this could be the basis of progress if we can clear it with the PM and small group of ministers.

Tuesday 5 July 1983

The meeting with the PM on pay was a miserable experience. Later Michael Heseltine discussed her emotional and vindictive attitude. I am convinced she will have to go before 1987 when matters mend. In the event there was acceptance of the formula of 10 per cent across the board. Later I saw Jack Dormand, who was adamant that overwhelmingly Labour would vote for full Plowden. I also saw Dykes, Haselhurst, Hicks and Knox. They all wanted full Plowden. Nigel Lawson is to present a £500 million public spending package – I can see gloom on Thursday and a procedural wrangle. The Treasury will not be a joyous haven. Ian Gow did well with his maiden speech as a minister.

Tuesday 4 October 1983

I had a brisk day. In the morning we had a good meeting of 'E'. I joined with the Lord Chancellor in attacking the idea of an independent prosecution system, and I think we might even have delayed it somewhat. There was a lively argument over the extension of voting to British overseas, and Ian Gow fought firmly to see that it was not confined to the EC. In the afternoon I attended a meeting presided over by Geoffrey Howe concerning the Strasbourg elections. Cecil Parkinson was clearly anxious over the fissiparous nature of the Liberals. We had an amiable meeting – Sir H. Plumb [MEP] seemed rather keen to keep on side.

Wednesday 5 October 1983

The evening news that jolted me was that No. 10 had asked me to do Prime Minister's Questions next month when she is away, and secondly that Cecil Parkinson was issuing a statement about his affair with his secretary. It was a dramatic business, and John Wakeham was jumping up and down. It is all so sad.

Thursday 6 October 1983

The thought in all our minds was Cecil Parkinson. I got to the office and sent him a note, saying 'All the best'. At Cabinet no reference was made to the affair, but Jenkin whispered support across the table. The Cabinet meeting was very brief and we then had a short session on the party conference. I had a slightly frantic session with Murdo Maclean over SDP broadcasting time. It seems he was trying to convince himself that he was protecting me – as usual I couldn't quite see it that way.

Monday 17 October 1983
In a sense it was the first full day back. Richard Page [John's parliamentary private secretary] was worried by how the media had handled my Blackpool performance, and feared I was being boxed as a semi-wet anti-Thatcherite. The PM's pre-lunch and lunch was an event. She was persuaded not to directly rebuff the David Owen appeal. It was a discussion where the outcome was genuinely the result of exchanged views – I am glad we have found touch.

Monday 24 October 1983
Richard Page told me I had one year in which to establish I was not a political loner. Really it does not matter to me since I believe this will be my last parliament. I spoke to the Westminster Young Conservatives, a holistic and radical lot – but I praised Enoch Powell.

Tuesday 25 October 1983
What a day. I went to a meeting to discuss Hong Kong and when I arrived the PM was poring over tape reports of the American invasion of Grenada. As far as I can see the PM was taken aback by it all. In view of the fairly bland statement yesterday I suggested that Geoffrey Howe would have to say that he had not been consulted, and that he regretted the fact. The latter point was disputed by Tebbit. In the event Geoffrey Howe got an absolute roasting. He should have been less compliant to the US action.

Wednesday 26 October 1983
In the morning we had a meeting which touched upon Grenada

and the Cruise issue. Once again I noticed that the PM was assertive and 'non-stop'. Geoffrey Howe seems to have had half a dozen points to discuss, but he only got past the first one! Heseltine secured his point of delay in having to make a Cruise statement – and typically tried to push beyond that. The SO 10 debate was not a happy occasion. Geoffrey Howe made a more coherent speech, and almost appeared critical of the Americans. Healey was bruising, but spoiled his case by the charge of deceit. The mood on the back benches was most unhappy. Later I saw Geoffrey Howe as I was speaking to his Tandridge Club. He was in a good mood and quite happy to have the FO debate next Thursday. Hugh Fraser reproached me for having a Cruise debate on Monday.

Thursday 27 October 1983

Crisis after crisis. Today it was announced by Harold Evans that I had misled the House over the *Times* affair. It was raised by Kinnock and also by Kilroy-Silk and Wrigglesworth. I feel I am an unlikely and unpromising target for the charge of deceit – but we shall see. I had my first exchange with Kinnock. It was amiable enough, and I was satisfied with my own performance. However, later I learned there had been trouble in the 1922 and Douglas Hogg had inflamed feelings over the decision to have the Cruise debate as speedily as we had decided. I also was told later after the vote that Tony Buck was miffed at not being consulted.

Sunday 30 October 1983

I felt much troubled by the Evans/*Times* business. I am not convinced that it will go away. As a consequence I felt low and gloomy. The *Sunday Telegraph* had a fierce and attacking piece by Ivan Fallon. In the morning I went to church with Colin [Baillieu] and the children. It was a pleasant service, and afterwards I did

some idle work and also read the Nicolson diary. Colin and I had
great guesses concerning the name of the MP for St Marylebone
up to 1945. Eventually I remembered it was Cunningham-Reid.
Colin advised against disclosing [my thoughts] to MT about leaving politics.

Monday 31 October 1983

The day, at least in my mind, was dominated by the Evans/ *Times*
affair. I had been uneasy as I reflected on the situation and my
fears were not dissolved when I met the accountant together with
Beckett and Cooke [civil servants]. They wanted to say as little
as possible, but I dug in my toes and got a much more specific
handling of the items left out of account when preparing the
balance sheet for the 1981 debate. Richard Page was particularly
helpful and very tough.

Tuesday 1 November 1983

Once again quite a lot of the day was devoted to the Evans/ *Times*
affair. Evans made a radio charge that it was the biggest cover-up
since Profumo. The tack now is that different rates were applied
to the *Observer* bid from the *Sunday Times* bid. I had lunch with
John Cole. He was not particularly sympathetic over the Evans
affair – he claimed to believe that I was opposed to any MMC
examination of a newspaper merger. In the early evening I had a
letter from Alf Morris which enclosed a somewhat hysterical and
offensive letter from Evans. I went to Dugald Barr [family friend];
he and Sarah had been to a Langton Gallery exhibition of *Private
Eye* drawings. We had a scratch supper and a mild gossip – but I
felt tired and careworn from the Evans business.

Wednesday 2 November 1983

The *Times*/Evans affair proceeds. I studied the papers on the

Observer deal, and it is clear that it was considered on the same basis as the *Sunday Times*. The Speaker told me that he thought the topic was ebbing, and would not come before him. It seemed likely – tho' not spoken – that he would not grant an adjournment debate. Richard Page suggested I should take legal action (Tim Renton was doubtful), and I must consider it in view of Gow's judgement that some damage has been done. Jonathan Aitken came to see me late at night and said Evans was running the line that I had handled the *Observer* differently. I was able to explain exactly what the position was. Aitken advised a low-key reaction and said Evans was deeply upset by the whole *Times* episode.

Saturday 12 November 1983

Essentially the day was Dorneywood. The Dorneywood dinner party included (with spouses) Lord Whitelaw, the Belgian ambassador, Lord Denham and Sir Neville Leigh. The food was atrocious. I did not find the table conversation very good. Over brandy, however, Willie Whitelaw told us categorically that the order to sink the *Belgrano* was given when she was steaming towards the UK fleet but then it took five hours for the decision to reach the submarine. At the end of the evening Willie Whitelaw started reflecting and mentioned the occasion when Quintin Hogg had observed Ramsay and a Mini and had expostulated 'A stupid car for a stupid man'. Whitelaw also said that Howe had gained votes for the Tories in 1964, and speculated how it all might have been different.

Monday 14 November 1983

There was high drama over the Cruise missiles. Michael Havers had told me on Thursday that they would be landing on Tuesday. The *Sunday Times* carried the story and Michael Havers then asked the US to bring them over a day early. He made the statement to a relatively low-key House of Commons, and it went off fairly well.

Thursday 17 November 1983

The day was fraught but generally successful. I had quite a lively exchange with Kinnock and enjoyed it. Otherwise Next Week's Business went calmly with only one question (from Sedgemore) on the *Times*/Evans. Nigel Lawson presented his statement in a low-key manner. The follow-up of questions was lethargic, but altogether it was a useful afternoon. I then attended the Hong Kong Committee meeting, and there was a surprising and welcome view that we had no cards and should not deceive ourselves. This issue was put by Heseltine and Tebbit amongst others. I also spoke in that vein.

Tuesday 22 November 1983

Well, I survived the Prime Minister's Questions spot – without glory and without disgrace. I had the horror of running out of questions in the folder. It was disgraceful organisation on the part of the No. 10 machinery. We had devised plenty of briefing and advanced questions, but I was unable to use the briefing and had to ad lib. I had played the Irish questions fairly well and refused to condemn the OUP for boycotting the Assembly. I rather fluffed the questions to which I had no answer. Richard Page was helpful.

Thursday 24 November 1983

A triumph. Prime Minister's Questions were a smooth and almost effortless success. I developed the technique of answering the question that had not been asked, and I played down Hattersley very effectively. His question had been too clever by half. Even so the fifteen minutes seemed to drag, and I was dying to make the bell before any slip. The day had started with a final homework on PMQs and I was much happier with the technique now employed. I had a few punchy facts on a number of topics and these covered no more than three pages. I had my usual bacon sandwich lunch and felt nervous – but the planning paid off.

Tuesday 29 November 1983

Prime Minister's Questions went off very well. Once again we had organised the briefing material a good deal better. However, the row and racket was nearly all about the NGA [National Graphical Association] dispute, and Kinnock was subdued, and in conjunction with Tom King I managed to berate the Labour Party without getting drawn into the merits of the dispute. There were kindly comments afterwards, but even so I was heartily glad to have got the drama over.

Wednesday 30 November 1983

I was immensely pleased with the newspaper reports of my handling of Prime Minister's Questions. There is no doubt that it has lifted my standing quite considerably. However, I had the anguish of the most awful stomach ache and a general unease. I had to call off my lunch with Stratton Mills and make do with but a short conversation. He does seem such an echo from another and more civilised age.

Wednesday 7 December 1983

The PM delivered her Athens statement. It was a litany of disappointment; but I shall remember it because of the inept Kinnock speech. It never ended – and as lame question followed lame question, the Tories shouted 'More, more'.

Thursday 8 December 1983

Cabinet was largely devoted to a monologue by the PM on the Athens summit. She had harsh words for everyone – the French because Mitterrand went back on the word of Delors, the Community generally for not saying no to increased spending and the Irish for the way they had lobbied. I cannot see how things will be much better next time round.

Tuesday 17 January 1984

Hugo Young gave me lunch, and he told me how fed up he was with the new editor of the *Sunday Times* [Andrew Neil], and also that Murdoch had [instructed] Neil to clip the wings of Young. Earlier we had a lengthy meeting about the 1984–85 session – quite useful I thought.

Thursday 1 March 1984

It was a long day and I felt absolutely poleaxed by the end of it. The Cabinet rumbled along with little or nothing happening. However, the legislative programme was held generally intact and the Treasury had to yield the TSB law. Although it was resolved that there should be gas privatisation Peter Walker did not say a single thing. There was then a short meeting on the Falklands. Geoffrey Howe had the most minuscule proposals of talks with the Argentinians which would allow them the ritual of asserting sovereignty. She blew up and treated us to a horrifying display of paranoia. Michael Havers is deeply concerned about it.

Tuesday 20 March 1984

Once again I had Prime Minister's Questions. It was an ordeal. I had the briefing session in the morning and it was thought nothing would be said about the summit but that the coal dispute would come up. We also feared that the *Panorama* broadcast might be resuscitated. When I went to my place at 3.08 I was all of a twitch. There was no Sarah in the gallery but she came in later.‡ I had a dreadful question from Kinnock on old age pensioners' spectacles – but that was really the only one that floored me. I still have problems handling my papers – but managed to get through. It seemed tough and noisy, but my wicket was intact.

Thursday 3 May 1984

I felt quite tired, but managed to get through the day. Cabinet drifted along with no real point except that Peter Walker gave a good report on the coal situation. He argued that Scargill might turn nasty in the next few days and that the coming six weeks were critical. I also got the feeling that stocks were holding well and that we could run for several months.

Thursday 10 May 1984

The Cabinet was a calm affair except that the PM was in a most excitable mood about the coal strike and demanding that the law be invoked against the strikers. Everyone was aghast as they thought we had been doing rather well. The Business Questions went well; I was tired but there was no really critical hassle – and I had as relaxed a time as ever with the lobby.

Thursday 14 June 1984

I felt very tired, but the day passed off quite well. I had a bad Cabinet in as much as I tried to emphasise that the NCB were still willing for talks – but this was countered by those who said we should emphasise the only way was for miners to defy the union and return to work. I managed Next Week's Business in an empty

---

‡ Sarah Biffen always sat in the gallery for John's Prime Minister's Questions and major debates.

House of Commons and had a quiet but good natured lobby. I voted in the Strasbourg election and spoiled my ballot paper with 'Stuff Brussels'.

Move from Middle Farm to Tanat House

Sunday 2 September 1984

We got up fairly early and cleaned up the cottage, and then went to Tanat House and deposited some excess baggage. Sarah drove me to the Strensham service area where Albert met me. He then drove at breakneck speed to Chequers. I used the journey to get through LPS papers and also my constituency post. There was little excitement in either. The Chequers lunch was a desperately dull affair; Tebbit, Ridley, Jenkin, the PM and Mark were there. She is hoist with her *FT* interview proposition that only a drift back can cure the strike. She seems to have no idea how this can be achieved, and she has a Götterdämmerung of the power stations closing and public anger compelling the miners to return to work.

Thursday 20 September 1984

Albert [government driver] warned me that the gypsies have taken possession at the top of Anhalt Road. He met me in an absolute downpour of rain. I had protracted Cabinet. It started at 10 a.m. and lasted until 12.45 p.m. The time was mainly devoted to the miners' strike and only incidentally to the party conference. Much of the strike discussion was devoted to the issue of magistrates' courts and exemplary sentencing. At the end I made a strong plea that we should give greater prominence to the numbers still working in the pits, their success in getting the movement of coal and the return to work – albeit modest.

Brighton bomb

Friday 12 October 1984

The longest day. At 2.54 there was a tremendous explosion in the Grand Hotel. I was awake at the time, and could hardly believe the thunderous noise that I heard. I jumped between the beds and then we both crossed the room and dressed. We went down the stairs – a sniff of cordite and some debris – and then on to the sea front. The hotel had been torn apart. The place was thronged with the dispossessed. The night was fullish moon and balmy. The Metropole hotel had a bomb scare. At the Beach hotel I was approached by someone from Williton who said they would tell my parents. I did some TV, turned up at the conference at 9.30 and tried to do business as usual. I had a talk with Alfred Sherman about the civil war; Sarah and I got our kit from our room. We attended the Leader's Speech. Then we drove to Colin Baillieu's and had something of an unwinding evening. I learned that John Wakeham had been badly hurt.

Monday 29 October 1984

There was much anxiety over the prospects of the Police Bill. Eldon Griffiths threatened to cut up rough. The PM was most sympathetic to the rebels, but eventually conceded. I wanted to blame the Lords for the concession, but the others were worried that rejecting the Scarman amendment would be seen as a racialist gesture. As the day progressed the situation was complicated by Kinnock insisting upon speaking first in the Tuesday debate. Lawson resisted furiously, but eventually a session with the PM resulted in victory for the 'managers' – which was unexpected. The Downing Street lunch was much dominated by the Libyan affair. I said that its importance was that it blocked off UK support for Scargill; and given the output from the working miners and imports we would be able to endure forever.

Tuesday 13 November 1984

I had to wind-up the Queen's Speech debate, and it went tolerably well. My speech opened with a reply to the points that had been argued by Pym. He had made a powerful speech concerning unemployment. I had described it as a menu without prices – and entered the lists with humour. I then had a turgid piece which dealt with procedure and opposition days. My section on Queen's Speech legislation did not go well; but I ad-libbed the final pieces on unemployment tolerably well, although I had to jettison a small but valuable section. Altogether it did not go badly; and I was glad to have it over.

Tuesday 19 March 1985

Budget day. The Cabinet met at 10.30 to hear the Lawson plan. We had a diversion as we tried to understand the proposed increase in the reserve and the reasons for it. I *think* it means a more realistic attitude to demand-led expenditure. I like the general tone of the Budget: few tax changes and no ease on the borrowing requirement. Later the Budget was well delivered and received. The Canavan Budget – delivered as a prologue – was good humoured and entertaining. Even so it was a diversion we did not need. Kinnock made a very spirited rejoinder to the Chancellor. I thought it was one of the best I have heard.

Sunday 23 June 1985

Today we had the Chequers talk on public spending. I got there at about 3.45 and was the first minister to arrive. Nick Edwards was reticent about the outcome of the Brecon by-election. Gowrie confessed he had gone to Athens after all. Rees made a slide presentation; it was downbeat. The Chancellor opened the discussion. Everyone took part except Lord Hailsham. I spoke third – breaking my diffidence – and argued that spending plans must enable a rehabilitation of our fortunes in Education and Environment; that we must extol the virtues of public spending in the context of wealth creation, and that great care was needed not to present tax cuts as an aid to entrepreneurs. The last point rattled the PM. The discussion was generally good natured, and I was pleased that my theme was taken up, and Fowler, Jenkin and Howe all spoke well of it privately. However, the Walker and Heseltine contributions rather misfired. By most counts the PM should have been happy.

Tuesday 25 June 1985

I showed the final draft of my speech to Michael Alison – I thought it was very loyalist. However, it appears that the PM disapproves. She thinks it wrong to talk of the next general election when we should give the impression of a dispassionate government; secondly that we should give no currency to the idea that anyone was accusing us of social indifference. Clearly there is now bad blood and Sunday evening marked a decisive point.

Monday 22 July 1985

I had a fearfully busy day. [The] 'Kitchen Cabinet' had met and discussed the TSRB [Top Salaries Review Board] award. The PM was anxious that a robust line should be undertaken; but I was horrified when she wanted to quote the PM/Hailsham practice of not taking full salaries. Wakeham was rather bland about the likely size of the rebellion. It was my opinion that it would be higher... MT annoyed with what she thinks I have been saying about public spending.

Tuesday 23 July 1985

What a day. It ended with the debate on the order increasing Hailsham's salary, and this I opened with a ten-minute speech that was heavily interrupted but not destroyed. There followed a debate which was noisy and entertaining but hardly closely argued. The Labour Party decided to sit it out and allow the Tories to tear themselves apart. I did a vigorous wind-up which got generous praise and pleased me no end. I had been so fearful that it would be a disaster.

‡

Wednesday 13 November 1985

I had a long hard day. It started with a meeting at No. 10 on EMS. Brian Griffiths [head of Prime Minister's Policy Unit] said, 'Great things are expected of you.' He was quiet throughout the meeting but was decisively against the move to join. Lawson, Howe and the Bank were strongly in favour. Tebbit was opaque but in favour, Brittan was in favour as was Whitelaw. I argued that the Heath/ Pym endorsement would underline a charge which would weaken the PM's authority and I argued against it on liberal grounds. I had to wind up the debate. It was a noisy and somewhat hostile House. I had a difficult first five minutes or so as I did my written text, but otherwise I felt happy and truculent. The timing was diffi-cult, but I ended with seven seconds to spare – which impressed the whips.

‡

Wednesday 20 November 1985

Today Parliament debated TV. I spoke eighth in the debate and read a tightly prepared text which lasted around twelve minutes. It ended with an analogy with the 1867 Reform Bill and called it 'a leap in the dark'. The phrase was widely quoted despite its lack of originality. The debate was good. Ashton, Powell, Foot and

Bryan all spoke splendidly, and Heath was as authoritarian as ever. Altogether it was a good introduction to a voting shambles and a surprise defeat of the motion by 275–263. The broadcasters were chagrined. Earlier I had done four interviews, three TV and one radio, on the topic. The exchanges with Robin Day were rather sharp, but I simply did not know how the PM would vote. In the end she voted against.

Thursday 12 December 1985

The meeting with Tom King on Northern Irish affairs made it clear to me that he is under great strain. I begin to wonder if the Agreement can last so very much longer – six months? Cabinet was memorable for a furious row between the PM and Heseltine over Westlands. I [think] that she actually shed a tear of rage.

The select committee procedure was used as a device to enquire into the Westland helicopter affair, which had resulted in the resignation of Michael Heseltine from the Cabinet. It was judged that use of the Tribunals of Inquiry (Evidence) 1921 Act would be too protracted. The consequential select committee enquiry was reasonably satisfactory from the government point of view. The Prime Minister, following precedent, did not give evidence but the Cabinet Secretary, Sir Robert Armstrong, batted manfully on her behalf. The Westland affair was not a happy episode for me. I had to take part in the crucial debate on 27 January 1986. I tried a rallying wind-up speech claiming it was 'not our Dunkirk but our Alamein', quite misjudging the mood of the House. I should have played it dead dull. I had not attended the Cabinet committee where Heseltine had argued his case. I would have been against him on the merits of the choice between an American link with Westland or a continental helicopter supplier. I liked Heseltine, notwithstanding his party conference populist speeches, and was glad to welcome him as a guest speaker in North Shropshire after he had left office.

Monday 27 January 1986

The day. It was not a disaster, but certainly not a triumph. Had I known it was going to be such a noisy and hostile House I would have been more nervous. In the morning I spent much of the time reviewing the draft speech for the PM. Whitelaw presided over a team which included the Chief Whip, Howe, Hurd, Sir Robert Armstrong and Wicks [Nigel, Private Secretary to the PM]. Howe and Hurd were impressive and sharp in their observations. I gather the PM reluctantly accepted the revised draft and Brittan was only squared late in the day. The debate was highly dramatic. Kinnock spoke badly, and Owen well. Heseltine made a dramatic intervention of support and Brittan a brief one accepting blame. Foot was good, as was John Smith. I had to speak against a torrent of noise. It was a sketchy speech although it made use of material on collective responsibility. I avoided answering the debate. Sarah and I had a lovely music evening at the Russian Embassy.

Tuesday 28 January 1986

Very much the day after. I felt quite exhausted by yesterday. The press comment has been very skimpy and not very generous. However, a member spoke kindly and Richard Page reported well. I saw Geoffrey Howe and discussed the situation with him. He spoke of the PM's bossy and intemperate manner that had led to the needless alienation of Heseltine over the Westland affair. He also spoke of the weak organisation within the Private Office and the overweening confidence of Bernard Ingham. We were much in agreement and I cannot now see how she is secure, and I think she should go before the next election and probably won't.

My work involved a close liaison with the Speaker. His decisions, particularly on whether or not to allow private notice questions, could be crucial to the day's business. I would never attempt to influence his opinion, which paradoxically was the best way of doing so. Speaker Thomas had an obvious sympathy for authority and for government. If he had to suspend a member for misconduct (often a quest for martyrdom) it was my task to propose suspension and name the member. This had to be done with precision and no fluffing of lines. I always carried a card in my wallet bearing the required words and had pencilled Ian Paisley as the expected culprit. How wrong I was. Ian Paisley was the master of both order and disorder with always an eye on his North Antrim constituency. He never troubled me. I had little chance to meet Northern Ireland MPs but quite often I would join the Unionist MPs at their table in the dining room. They were a rather beleaguered group and their cause was not really understood by most British MPs. I had two agreeable parliamentary private secretaries: Tim Renton and Richard Page. Tim was a friend with a successful career in the City. He voted against the government upon some financial matter and the Chief Whip insisted on his resignation. I contested such heavy-handedness in vain and he had to go. But Tim had the last laugh; he became Chief Whip and subsequently Minister for the Arts. He enjoyed the latter job more than the Whips' Office. Sarah and I spent two happy holidays with Alice and Tim at their croft on Tiree. They were sunshine days.

Richard Page was with me for the bulk of my time as Leader. He was a valuable foil, being – like Renton – a Euro-enthusiast.

Richard was a worldly businessman and could explain the graduation of horsepower rating for the MPs' motor mileage allowances. It was an art lost upon me. MPs' pay and allowances were a quagmire for the Leader. Margaret Thatcher decided increases in pay were vote losers but she was more relaxed on allowances for secretarial and research work, motoring and second home expenses. Over many years the MPs' total income became biased against direct pay and in favour of allowances. It was a manageable compromise until its impact was felt on pensions, which were related only to pay. There was little I could do against a Prime Ministerial brick wall.

Meanwhile allowances went up by even more than I had planned, Edward Leigh, the MP for Gainsborough, moved a resolution for a very substantial increase in secretarial allowances and I had prepared a reasoned contrary view for the wind-up of the debate. I was outmanoeuvred. Suddenly I realised Leigh had organised the debate to lapse in silence. Not a voice was raised; I had to answer well before the time when the whips had summoned the 'payroll' vote of government members and Leigh carried the day. It was a clever ambush but my amour-propre was pricked. Not all was lost. My wife was my secretary.

Occasionally I had to answer open-ended debates that could run very late. I had no deputy and had to man the government bench unaided. One such debate was the discussion on whether the House should adjourn for a recess. This could be high drama as it was such a debate that led to Neville Chamberlain's resignation in 1940. I had more pedestrian issues as members pleaded for by-passes, war widows and fertiliser grants. There was one trick I learned quite soon: my wind-up must refer, generously if not effusively, to every person who had taken part in the debate. On one painful occasion Tam Dalyell had the last of a series of debates and was not reached until breakfast time. I had known Tam at Cambridge where he was an aspiring Tory. Throughout his lively parliamentary career we remained friends. That night I looked back on university times and wondered if salad day memories could transfer an all-night sitting into the tinsel of a May ball. It could not. One compensation was that my private secretary would replace the carafe of water on the despatch box with vodka and tonic.

A chore of leading the House was the requirement that I should move the guillotine whenever Bills were being debated at great length and endangering the flow of government business. Guillotines had been introduced in 1887 to counter the disruptive behaviour of Irish Nationalist MPs. A century later it had become routine and the occasion of a lot of low-grade humbug about the death of parliamentary democracy. The one guillotine I took seriously was that on the Bill creating the European Single Market. This was no easy task after my opposition to membership of the Common Market. I reluctantly accepted the Bill. It was the only major blot of apostasy on my Eurosceptic record. I insisted on writing the guillotine speech without civil service assistance. It had a weasel-like merit and I had Bill Cash with me in the lobby. I also guillotined the Scottish Poll Tax Bill, but I was happier a year later denouncing the English counterpart, having recently returned to the back benches. Margaret Thatcher called the bill her flagship and I called it the *Titanic*.

It was the capacity for surprise that really enlivened life in the Commons. I was in my room in dinner jacket after some wearisome formal occasion when I was summoned by a whip to go the chamber. Alan Clark was speaking from the front bench and had inflamed the Labour Party. I decided we had a very good Speaker who could keep order. Had I turned up in a dinner jacket like a poor man's Jeeves, the House, already smouldering, would have ignited. Eventually the storm blew itself out but it was the last thing I expected after my duty dinner.

There was an immensely sad occasion when Michael Roberts, MP, a junior Welsh Minister, collapsed from a stroke whilst speaking from the despatch box in 1983. Michael Jopling and I were deemed to be in charge of this tragic event, which was not anticipated in Erskine May's guide to parliamentary procedure. Michael was highly successful in clearing the public gallery and, perhaps surprisingly, also the press gallery.

At the trivial end of the scale I was taken aback when George Cunningham MP stormed into my room, past the staff in the outer office. Slamming down his keys he remonstrated on the difficulty of parking his car. It was a problem that stumped me but I had a warm spot for George since it was his proposed voting formula, a majority being required of all those entitled to vote rather than actually voting, that scuppered Scottish devolution in 1979.

Monday 24 February 1986

The weather remains bitterly cold and I had a busy start to the week. When I saw John Wakeham he told me what a drubbing he had received from the PM because Peter Morrison and I had said the House could consider the British Leyland deal after the conclusion of negotiations. Willie Whitelaw had also borne the brunt of her fury and had said that it indicated she would 'take the Tory Party under'. In fact we had quite an amiable 'Kitchen Cabinet' and lunch although she did much of the talking.

Saturday 8 March 1986

I have the most awful cold and would much rather I was in bed for the weekend rather than travelling. However, I got a certain amount of sleep and David Morris collected us at 10.50 a.m. We had a quiet journey to Northolt and there met Jim Callaghan. He was an excellent travelling companion, and I was pleased when he volunteered that he would 'put me up' for the Other Club. We had a light lunch on the plane. At Lisbon airport we boarded a car and were driven to our hotel with police outriders flagging down everything and amidst great panic. We have a superb hotel. In the afternoon we drove to the riverside and also did a short walk in a park.

Inauguration ceremony of Portuguese President

Sunday 9 March 1986

I had a surprisingly good night's rest, although the cold made me feel very heavy and unsocial. Sarah and I had breakfast in our rooms. Eventually we were motored to the National Assembly. The organisation was fairly chaotic, but eventually I was sat in a balcony just behind Vice-President Bush. The building was quite imposing, but the thing I remember was the tremendous amount of smoking by the deputies. Soares spoke for a long time. The lunch was held in a lovely old royal palace. The Carringtons were there, and he spoke witheringly of the PM and the insular attitude of the British. I thought he seemed a rather unhappy man. At lunch I was next to the Danish Minister of Education, quite the dullest man. Then we did some shopping and caught the plane. It was a dull return. I felt rather dyspeptic, and was glad to reach Anhalt Road. I did about 1½ hours' work and then got to bed.

Monday 24 March 1986

The great event was the Denholmes statement by Douglas Hurd. The HO decided to make the statement and Michael Havers

was most anxious that he should not be asked to take part. I
said he must make sure that Hurd could answer on behalf of
the Attorney General. Hurd did a splendid blocking job, but
he did pass off an uncomfortable number of replies to the AG.
However, all in all it was quite a reasonable exercise in damage
limitation. We had a meeting of the BL Committee. Channon
told us that the General Motors talks had broken down. There
was indecision over what should happen next, but the management buyout is generally favoured. I suspect we could run into
quite a lot of storm over this; but at least the GM bid is avoided.
The PM was more than usually self-righteous at lunch today. She
can see no strength or generosity in her opponents and was bewildered that the Fulham poll was not better. Everyone else thought
it was an extraordinarily good poll. Somehow the week has
started badly.

Monday 14 April 1986

I had a fearful day. It started with Breakfast TV and I had quite
a pleasant interview with Selina Scott, although there was some
mild concern that I had chosen Samantha Fox as one of my five
newspaper cuttings. I then got to the office and seemed to be
always out of breath. There was then called a meeting of OD
[Cabinet Committee Overseas/Defence] and the PM told us that
the decision had been taken to accede to the US request to use
Oxford airbases for attacks on Libya. She had taken Howe and
Younger with her and Willie Whitelaw later. It was a tense meeting as Lawson, Tebbit, Hurd and myself all opposed the decision.
The Shops Bill was a shambles and we lost by fourteen votes.
Hurd exceeded his brief and said there would be no guillotine.
We had a terrible time trying to haul back the position. It was
probably just as well that we lost – we could not have put it on the
statute book without a much bigger majority.

Thursday 17 April 1986

A day full of stress and tension. At Cabinet we had a long discussion on Libya. Somehow or other the PM did not hit the right note, and at the conclusion there was a strong outburst by Whitelaw against Reagan. It was pyrotechnic. Finally I said I feared the US insensitivity towards the UK and that notwithstanding a deeply divided UK opinion and isolation from other European countries we would be requested a second round of bombing. I said that was not on. Ken Baker afterwards told me how much he agreed. I felt sick about it all. It is a real strain, and I do think I would resign if we sanctioned further use of the bases.

Tuesday 6 May 1986

I had the task of answering Prime Minister's Questions. It was – as ever – quite a trial. I had a fair amount of constituency post to handle. Tim Flesher [Private Secretary to the PM] arrived with the briefing and I decided nuclear fallout would be the major story. I was pleased that Kenneth Baker, at my suggestion, agreed to make a statement. This shielded me from the general wrath, but I had rowdy and forceful exchanges on Wapping. I managed to draw a line between Neil Kinnock and Tony Benn. On the whole I think it went quite well.

Thursday 8 May 1986

We had quite an exciting Cabinet. The PM was agitated because of the Privileges Committee report, and feared the government would be manoeuvred into being anti-press. I said I sought no whipping on the matter and was extremely happy to have the matter resolved as House of Commons business. Actually I am quite happy to see the report contested as I do not think Rossi was damaged very much by it all. I had the matter again at the lobby and at Next Week's Business. On the whole I was content with

the way I managed to spread the caution. In the evening we had
a splendid dinner party. It really was a great success. Michael and
Jill Foot, Tim and Margaret Flesher, Ian and Maureen Davison
and Willie and Gaia Mostyn-Owen. The food was good and
I much enjoyed talking to Jill Foot. They brought in their dog
'Dizzy', who is a Tibetan spaniel. He was quite delightful. Such
a civilised evening.

Friday 9 May 1986

I was mortified by the election results. I simply did not think they
would be so bad – Ryedale was unbelievable and West Derby was
only just saved. It was grim. The only practical consolation
was that we held Wandsworth. I saw Willie Whitelaw in the
morning. He said we would have the PM leading us at the next
election and it was pointless to argue otherwise. However, he did
agree with the general thesis that we did not appear to 'listen'. I
talked for a short while about the Privileges Committee, but it all
seems on another planet.

42

OUT OF FAVOUR

I never harboured ministerial ambitions and did not discuss my future with the Prime Minister. I would like to have been Leader just longer than Herbert Morrison, who had held the post for five years and nine months in the 1945 Labour government. However, my end came unplanned and touched by controversy. In May 1986 I was asked by Central Office to be available for a TV interview with Brian Walden. The subject would be the by-election results expected from the West Derbyshire and the Ryedale constituencies. I explained to the TV company that I had a very heavy weekend programme of constituency engagements and could not return to London. They arranged for the interview to take place in Birmingham. Brian was an old friend and a skilled interviewer. However, I was far too relaxed in my discussion with him and speculated on the Conservative need to have a broader base than rely on the undoubted dominance of the Prime Minister. The passage that was picked up by the press was as follows:

Nobody seriously supposes that the Prime Minister would be Prime Minister throughout the entire period of the next parliament. So therefore there is nothing extraordinary about the balanced ticket of the Prime Minister and some of the most powerful in the Conservative Party, one of whom probably would become Prime Minister in due course, being represented as a team.

It was foolish of me to have spoken these words but hardly a hanging offence. I can vouch that there was no intent of disloyalty. When I got to London I realised a storm was in prospect. I had no call from Margaret Thatcher but Willie Whitelaw saw me and quite properly pointed out the embarrassment my remarks had caused. I asked John Wakeham how best I could mend the bridge. 'Say something nice about her,' he said. This I did, but a curtain had come down.

Brian Walden at once wrote in the *Evening Standard*, 'I was disappointed to see the general reaction to Mr Biffen's disinterested comments. Of course he is not involved in any plot. He is the most loyal and straightforward of men.' The letter I most appreciated was handwritten by Sir Kenneth Clucas, who had been permanent secretary during my time at the Trade Department. 'I was appalled by the latest press report that Mrs Thatcher had been so angry that she had considered reshuffling you out. (She had always had great difficulty in recognising who her real friends were.) So I write as a fervent member of the John Biffen fan club to say how right I think you are.'

Bernard Ingham, meanwhile, had briefed the press on the whole episode. He described me as semi-detached and the press interpreted this as meaning I was on borrowed time. I did not think the view was just that of Ingham but they conveyed the sentiments of the Prime Minister. I was asked to comment on this and said I thought Ingham was the sewer not the sewage. The next thirteen months were pretty miserable. I was put out to dry, although I remained in office until the 1987 general election. I had the consolation of a handwritten note from Willie

Whitelaw dated 3 June 1987. 'I have been increasingly angry and upset at the way you are being treated. I hasten to add that I personally would be very sad if the silly rumours were true as I greatly enjoy our close association.'

Sunday 11 May 1986

Another awful day. The weather was bad, grey and damp. I went to the ATV studios and did the interview with Brian Walden. It was a marathon lasting nearly thirty minutes. I felt uncomfortable when I was pressed on the question of Mrs T. and I devised the response of the 'balanced ticket'. It was an ingenious retort, but I was aware that the ice was thin.

Monday 12 May 1986

The storm has broken. All the papers carry the most high profile interpretations of the *Weekend World* interview. It is lead story in the *Times* and *Guardian* and features generally. Later in the day I was summoned by Willie Whitelaw, who gave me a direct and somewhat magisterial telling-off for the reference to the 'balanced ticket'. He thought there was advantage in seeing her, but he would check with John Wakeham first. I then had a chat with Richard Page, who thought that party reaction had been favourable by 2–1. There is no doubt that there is now a considerable storm. I shall be glad to nudge through the week.

Tuesday 13 May 1986

The papers reflected the full blast of the *Weekend World* interview. There has been powerful No. 10 briefing describing me as 'maverick', 'eccentric' and 'semi-detached' etc. Richard Page thought there had been an overreaction by Ingham. I felt decidedly 'frozen out' and the whole business induced some stress, but all manageable. Prime Minister's Questions were a delicate period. Actually the PM did exchange a few words, so it was not frozen silence. The meeting on the privilege debate went quite well, and we established that the vote should be completely free. That suited me. I could see enmity where Tebbit was concerned.

Wednesday 14 May 1986

Today's hurdle was the Press Gallery lunch. The editor of the *Shropshire Star* was there. The audience was clearly hopeful of a continuation of the *Weekend World* interview. However, I did a jokey introduction followed by a rather low-key analysis of the Tory market economy. It was received glumly, and I hope it damped down the matter. The worst aspect of the press was that *The Times* had a Bevins article talking about a 'Biffen camp' and preparedness to resign. In the evening I went to the Caldecote party. Plowden was there and he was pleased with the *Weekend World*.

Thursday 15 May 1986

The drama rumbles on, but at least it is getting a little less deafening. The press reports of Wednesday's speech have been very muted. Cabinet was quiet, but the PM was brittle over her Perth speech and at one stage turned to Kenneth Clarke and said, 'I am asking you for cooperation and not argument.' I made a modest intervention in a committee under her chairmanship on conference security. Prime Minister's Questions passed without incident and Next Week's Business was very low key. However, the lobby pursued me over the balanced ticket, but it was manageable.

Tuesday 3 June 1986

I seem to have had an extremely busy day. It ended with a three-hour debate on the Channel Tunnel Bill SOs, and I got through a low-key piece lasting ten minutes and which had only one interruption. I then had a chance to listen to some vigorous Kent protests, and got home at 1.40. I sat by the PM for her questions: there was not a single word. I will not be the first to speak.

Monday 9 June 1986

Ken Baker told me that when he was given the Education task the PM spent some time talking to him about my disgraceful behaviour. He said he thought I should know, and that he thought it extraordinary that she should speak thus about a colleague behind his back. He thinks Tebbit has a plan to remove Edwards, Jopling and myself. He advocated going rough – and it so happens that Peter Jenkins had written an article saying she would be unwise to sack me in the autumn as I might stand against her.

Wednesday 18 June 1986

In the afternoon I saw Cecil Parkinson. We talked generally about South Africa and public spending issues. He then confirmed that the PM had been very upset over the remarks about her going in the next parliament and that she was still 'simmering'. He advised that I should go and see her, since it was important that she had confidence in colleagues and was so dismissive of everyone just now. Giles Radice [John's pair] advised that I should keep going as usual; that her position was not so strong that she would sack me and that I had appeared subdued since the episode. Colin Brown and Peter Hitchens told me how subdued I appeared at the lobby lunch – and I responded with some spirit saying I was vulnerable to everyone in the room.

Thursday 19 June 1986

I had a day of continuing sadness. I just would like to know the future, and I suppose wake up with a sustained income. The PM announced a General Election Committee and I was very sorry not to be included on it. Inclusion would have settled my future.

Thursday 26 June 1986

It was a great success. Now I really do not think I can be put on the streets in September. I felt pretty nervous beforehand. In the morning there had been the usual briefing. The great dilemma was whether or not to have references to South Africa or rather hide behind the Hague meeting. In the end I decided I had to meet the SA challenge. The PM spot was marked by robust arguing over the South Africa issue with Kinnock and emphasising that effective [progress] was in the context of partner cooperation, and then, with great mischief, saying Owen had been helpful on sanctions. He rose, full of anger, and got trapped in a bog of procedure. Ian Gow and Dennis Skinner both made great pleas of order. It went well. The back benches enjoyed it.

Tuesday 15 July 1986

A long day. I saw the PM in the morning and it was thirty or forty minutes and alone. She made no reference to the *Weekend World* broadcast or subsequent events. She observed I was not a member of the A-Group but said she would like to have talks with me from time to time about the coming election – she wanted her own point of reference. We talked quite a bit about the election and I repeated that I thought we should build on recent policies and repeated my Tyler conference speech. It means I am now back in the clear and likely to do this job for the remainder of the parliament.

Tuesday 29 July 1986

I had a fairly pleasant day; but there is no doubt that I do feel tired. In the morning I had a talk with Edward du Cann. He feels very concerned about the present low morale of the party; he also agreed that there should be some monitoring of MPs' expenses. Later I saw Lord Plowden and we covered the territory again. He felt that there should be some monitoring but was concerned about how practical it might be. We also had a lively meeting on education and discrimination in Northern Ireland. There is a lighter atmosphere in these meetings.

Tuesday 28 October 1986

I read over the final text of the Westland speech. It is dull beyond belief and scheduled to last twenty-seven minutes. I fear that it will go badly, but it will fill up time.

Wednesday 29 October 1986

The debate. I was reasonably happy that I would get through. In the morning I had a short chat with Robert Armstrong and also went over to the MoD and talked to George Younger about the general tactic. Officials were rather keen that there should not be too much common identity with the select committees. George Younger opened with a thirty-minute speech that was largely about helicopters and certainly boring. Denzil Davies was good, but it soon became clear that there was only modest steam in the debate. There was a dramatic suspending of Tam Dalyell whilst I was having some supper. Peter Shore spoke with eloquence and passion but left me with thirty-two minutes. I thought I would run out of speech but there were just enough interruptions. Porter said it was dreadfully boring – and it most certainly was.

Monday 17 November 1986

Not a happy day. The 'Kitchen Cabinet' meetings are not what they were. The meeting had been in progress before I arrived and the A-Team (a continuation I suspect) proceeds after I finish.

I sense hostility on the part of the PM. She thinks the Speaker is weak (i.e. he often disagrees with her), and she is determined not to report her US visit to the Commons. Tebbit is determined to 'stand up' to the Speaker and later in his Questions planted enough linked questions to dominate his period and make a nonsense of it all. It is a deliberate attempt to destroy authority. I hate it all.

Tuesday 18 November 1986

Things improved a touch. I saw Willie Whitelaw and he is concerned that the PM is going through an anti-Parliament phase, and secondly Tebbit is refusing to let the BBC issue go away. I felt at least someone was prepared to talk to me – and sympathetically.

Tuesday 25 November 1986

At the moment we have two major Bills likely to cause procedural problems. The first is the Education Bill, which we are determined to get by Christmas. The second is the Rates Bill – indemnifying past mistakes – which is becoming complex and cannot be secured in time. John Wakeham thinks that we must drop rate-capping in order to get Labour acceptance of the Bill. I think this is so, but it will cause a furore. There was a great storm after Questions over the Spy business. Kinnock made a long assertion that his honour had been impugned; and the Speaker said it had not. I saw the Speaker afterwards and told him that I feel Kinnock should have been ruled out of order. We had quite a long talk, and he told me he was prepared to pack it in. I hope he does and thus exposes the small-minded bullying of the PM.

Thursday 15 January 1987

I had my first Next Week's Business and it went rather well; I got

my ration of laughs and it contrasted with the general scratchi-
ness. I also had an interesting lobby in which the question of
Tebbit–Thatcher relations was raised. Oakley has an article in
The Times which is damaging to Tebbit, and Peter Morrison
telephoned me to secure sympathetic handling of it all in the
lobby. Richard Page tells me it would be difficult for the PM to
dump me and that I might be offered chairmanship of the party.
It's a thought.

Monday 16 March 1987

Once again the 'Kitchen Cabinet' demonstrated the lack of
rapport with the PM. She did at least talk about Truro and
wondered why things had not gone better. Her view was that we
might have missed out on the pensioner vote, but she decided
tax cuts were the best way to counter this. She also said she
would have voted for Lord Blake at Oxford. The great message,
however, was that of tax cuts.

Thursday 19 March 1987

By the end of the day I felt really tired – the exhaustion coming
from a lack of sleep rather than very hard work. At the Cabinet
we discussed the political outlook. There is now much anxiety
over the challenge that comes from the Alliance. Tebbit still
argued that Labour was the main enemy and the Alliance should
be attacked… I spoke with vigour on my theme of linking main-
stream Labour with Alliance and I was delighted that the theme
was developed so well. There is now a tide running towards June.
I had the usual run at Next Week's Business and quite a good
lobby. There is no doubt they are running things for June.

Saturday 21 March 1987

The day ended with the grim news that the Liberals have moved into second place in the Gallup poll provided for Central Office. Curiously I am getting indifferent to the election as I am weary of Westminster and actively dislike the constituency zealots. In the morning I had a rather light load of surgery work, but the journeys remain the same. After the Newport surgery I called upon Mr Wood and his small team and discussed the campaign to save the Adams School. I think it is a battle that could be won, but only with a Conservative Education Secretary.

Thursday 2 April 1987

The PM reported back on the Russian trip. It was an extraordinary occasion. She was full of enthusiasm, and was impressed that the Russians were no longer actively promoting world Communism. She also was impressed by the signs of more 'openness' – but otherwise it was obvious there had been no substantial movement on nuclear arms. She went on at great length: 'Am I going on too long?' – 'No, No.' I thought Kinnock just about survived the statement, but he is looking smaller and weaker. The [Keith] Best affair moves briskly. He is desperately pleased for any lifeline. Alison [Smith, private secretary] did a note suggesting he was unlikely to be protected. I did the recess adjournment motion. It ran the full three hours, and it was quite a good-natured affair. I was satisfied.

Saturday 25 April 1987

I feel dreadfully low and I cannot avoid waking very early. I feel the loss of Leader of House so very much, and cannot think positively about what comes next. I wish I had the temperament to be angry. I had my ration of surgeries and the weather was magnificent. I had modest clients at all places and they fully took up my time.

Thursday 30 April 1987

How near to the end. Cabinet was preceded with a stiff talk from the PM about ministerial speculation on election dates. I had the impression that all this was directed at me, but I think I was wrong to make that judgement. Cabinet was fairly brief but we had a dreadfully long session upon benefit changes to do with the abolition of rates. Tebbit drily observed he was glad this was not the first press conference on the subject. I had a straightforward Next Week's Business – but Skinner observed he had heard I was to be chopped, and I riposted by thanking him for his character reference. The lobby was good. The date of the election is clearly known. Jonathan Bradley came to see me and more or less offered me a non-executive directorship with Tyndall. I attended a reception at No. 10 and met Aled Griffiths [Shropshire farmer]. We had a good dinner with Robin Ibbs [banker].

Tuesday 5 May 1987

Three papers (*Star, Sun, Times*) carry the story that I will go. I am surprisingly calm about it all. Baker tells me it is a foolish move. I had a good lunch with journalists from the *Sunday Telegraph* and there is much talk about the proposed changes and the political attitude they reveal. The general view was that it would inaugurate a third term which would be marked by intolerance. The mood generally is that 11 June is now a racing certainty. I had to do a token contribution to the Chevening Bill. We also had a Committee discussion on family courts and put it to touch. I saw Enoch Powell in a Speaker's gathering. He seemed quite cheerful – philosophic about his wife's distaste for electioneering.

Wednesday 6 May 1987

I had an exceedingly quiet day. In the morning I was left in the office with little to do. All is happening elsewhere and I am being excluded. There is no question of me being at Chequers as in the last election. I had a good lunch with Bevins and Carvel and we discussed my future quite cheerfully. It was decided I would be gentlemanly but antagonistic in the back benches but Walker and Heseltine would be just antagonistic. There was a very lively session whilst she vigorously defended her stance over not having an MI5 enquiry. At the request of Richard Page I had tried to congratulate her, but the noise was too great. Richard and Madeleine Page gave us an excellent dinner to mark the end of an era – he would not have continued as PPS.

Friday 12 June 1987

I was somewhat taxed by the number of media people at the count. I reprimanded the editor of the *Whitchurch Herald* for his straw poll. He was an unimpressive man. There was gloom when the bar closed at 1 a.m. Eventually the declaration was made at 3.30 a.m. I was relieved with the majority (which was up) but there was no denying that the share of the poll was down. Sarah and I were driven by Owen [Paterson] back to Tanat House. Then we had limited sleep and returned to London by car. In the afternoon I heard that Enoch had been defeated. It was a dreadful blow. We both felt quite overcome with fatigue. We went across to the Walters' for a drink. The general mood is one of great delight at the extent of the victory – even Battersea has fallen. We had biscuits and cheese and that spoiled our supper. We had an early night. I fell asleep and Sarah watched TV.

With the onset of the election there was a farewell chorus from the Labour benches when I made my last appearance at the despatch box. I realised my time was up and used the election campaign to get in a few blows, asserting I would 'rather go on my feet than stay on my knees'.

The final departure was rather a farce. The Prime Minister vainly called me at Tanat House whilst I was in London awaiting execution. Eventually I saw her in No. 10. Enoch Powell had once told me: if you are going to be fired, get it in writing. When I saw Margaret Thatcher I asked if we could exchange letters and she agreed. My letter said in part: 'There has been a steady rise in social spending in health and education. This should increase in substantial terms. There must be a balance between a successful economic policy and a progressive social policy which provides resources for the National Health Service, in particular and also for state education.' It made clear what had been a growing personal view.

Thereafter I became adopted as an icon by the anti-Thatcher media but I neither sought nor deserved such a role. Meanwhile, I was obliged to Bernard Ingham for the title of this book, *Semi-Detached*.

Saturday 13 June 1987

Quite early I had a telephone call from the PM announcing she had 'bad news for me'. I am out. I agreed that I would see her that afternoon. We then went to the Scotts' to watch the Trooping of the Colour [Northern Ireland Office]. It was a good view, but I felt dreadfully tired. Nick Scott's wife let drop a remark which persuaded me that King did not run as happy a ship as Hurd or Prior had done. In the afternoon I went to see the PM. It was a very frosty interview. She was disturbed when I said my letter wanted to be in the context that she had asked for the resignation and not that I had offered it. I was interested that she thought the Labour Party was against devolution in Scotland. There it is. Wicks wanted the letter that day and I told him it would be Monday. I am out, but not down and not really sad.

Tuesday 16 June 1987

Not an entirely happy day. There were three incidents that provoked sadness. First my lunch with Kleinwort Benson was a lacklustre affair. I was examined at length and not very charitably – Beaumont managed to get the sense of my resignation letter wrong. However, even more sad was that no hint was made of a possible job. Secondly I saw Tony Buck, who commented 'You old fool'. He might have been more understanding. Thirdly I had an absurd letter from Gloria [Hooper] suggesting I had made the right decision. The main good thing is that I have Francis Pym's old office. It is quite large and fairly quiet and very central to the chamber. I shall like it there. There has been a bungle over the post and it appears to be at Tanat House or Anhalt Road but not the House of Commons. I did, however, have a few nice letters. I had a pleasant morning at the Crumbys' [close friends, Tom and Rose] – but just now I feel uprooted. Talked to mother, who was relieved to hear me.

Wednesday 17 June 1987

Things were decidedly gloomy today. I had to wait quite a long time at Anhalt Road when I wanted to be in the office. Also it rained steadily and the house was gloom and misery. Finally Sarah drove me there and I had a half morning working very hard. I feel so disoriented and have no files. I did a radio broadcast with Dennis Skinner. I was surprised that he still stressed unemployment as one of the big factors. I watched part of the election of the Speaker but I had to hurry away to catch the train. Westminster–Euston is twenty-five minutes. I shall learn to be an 'ordinary joe' in no time.

Monday 6 July 1987

I slept badly and in my dressing room, and I was fearful of the breakfast TV interview. Actually it went well and I managed to tone down the remarks in the Turner article and the accompanying *Sunday Telegraph* piece. However, the article etc. has been a great error. The use of the term 'Stalinist' has made me appear bitter and over the top. Several MPs warned me about it, including Richard Body. I had a hostile editorial in the *Sunday Telegraph*. I feel bad about it. I had a good lunch with Antony Graham [headhunter and friend] and he explained some of the techniques about getting a job. This is also a headache. I attended the meeting of the Environment Committee. I thought Ridley got quite a good reception, but there was a strong mood for transferring the education cost to central government. I had a good time as host to the Economic Dining Club. Cecil Parkinson was very critical of the PM and her sycophants in an embarrassing way, and Ian Gow assured me that Wakeham had plotted to get my job. I feel harassed and hassled.

Tuesday 7 July 1987

I had a bad day as I begin to realise just how unwise has been the Graham Turner interview and the 'Stalinist' jibe. I appear harsh and embittered, and spoiling for a fight. In fact I am relaxed about the life on the back benches but anxious about getting more money. I am cautious and Fabian by temperament – not a bruiser. The positive thing is considerable publicity and the appearance of being tough and thus commanding some respect. However, this is not me!!

Sunday 25 October 1987

I feel boxed in and on the edge of a great gloom. The logistics seem so bad. I find Westminster travel bad, the weight of hand luggage a burden, and the post currently more than I can cope with. I think the Sicilian pile-up was the start, and I have struggled since.

Thursday 31 December 1987

And so the year ends. What a dreadful one it has been. Sarah's knee operation, which has been painful and slow curing; the death of my father; the dispiriting closing days as Leader of the House; the dismissal from office; the disappointing development of non-political work/income; the great sense of political emptiness on the back benches and a lack of drive in seeking a role. It has been an utterly wretched and miserable year and I end it in gloom with no optimism for the future or active will to live. We saw the old year out/new year in at the Horseshoe. Not many people were there. In the afternoon Sarah and I went for a short walk, and in the morning I did some modest shopping in Oswestry. The weather remains mild to the end.

43

MARGARET THATCHER

I first heard Margaret Thatcher at a Cambridge University Conservative Association meeting in 1953. I was in my last year as a student and she had just come down from Oxford. She talked about economics and referred to esoteric matters like 'City opinion'. In shorthand terms I thought she was very right-wing.

I did not come across her again until eight years later when I became an MP two years after she had entered the Commons as Member for Finchley. Her qualities were soon recognised by the Whips' Office. She was then a junior minister, as Joint Parliamentary Secretary at the Ministry of Pensions and National Insurance. I had little interest in that topic, but in opposition 1964–70 came to know her better because of our shared views in opposition to Labour's policies of national planning and incomes control.

The 1964–66 Tory intake included a group of thrusting young Bow Group liberals, chief amongst whom were Geoffrey Howe, Patrick Jenkin, Jock Bruce-Gardyne, Terence Higgins and Peter Hordern. We soon settled down to opposing Labour's economic policies. Margaret Thatcher did not hunt with that pack but her views were broadly similar. In the Commons she did not sparkle. At that time she had a rather high-pitched voice and it says much for her professionalism that when she became leader she

corrected this. I was never at ease with her in conversation; she
seemed intense and a more dedicated combatant than me.
During the mid-sixties I went with a delegation of Conservative
MPs to Sweden. The group included Sir Brandon Rhys-
Williams, a somewhat didactic character who had strong views
on social security. Amongst the party was Margaret Thatcher,
then answering from the front bench on this topic. Brandon,
ever an evangelist, tried to convert her from her orthodoxy. It
was the indefatigable meeting the immovable. Exhausted and
irritated, Brandon came to me and said, 'It's impossible to talk to
that woman.' I am sure it was her determination and unwilling-
ness to accept error merely for compromise that secured her a
place in Ted Heath's Cabinet.

Whilst Margaret Thatcher was Minister of Education she
came to my constituency and opened a refurbished village school
at Welshampton. She spoke to a Conservative supper club in
the evening, which was a great success, but what I remember
most are her views on de Gaulle. He had just announced the
French would have a referendum on British membership of
the Common Market. It was a tactical move wholly within the
context of French domestic politics. She almost took it personally,
wondering why he had the effrontery to question the virtues of
the Common Market and above all by the technique of a referendum. Little did I realise she was an undercover Eurosceptic.

I came to know Margaret Thatcher very well after the February
1974 general election defeat and her emergence as a challenger
to Ted Heath. Over the years two qualities much impressed me.
She was an immensely kind person, especially to her domestic
employees, and was very courageous. The staff in her No. 10
flat were friends whose views she noted. She was a thoughtful
employer and would remember the children's birthdays. She
was also happy to pass on their views. 'All this crime; Ethel says

"string 'em up".' This vox populi was delivered to a breakfast table of economic Cabinet ministers, everyone wringing wet on capital punishment. Margaret Thatcher had firm principles but she also practised populist politics, supporting mortgage tax relief, designed to aid the middle classes.

She was extremely kind to me when I withdrew from the shadow Cabinet in 1977. I thought my frontbench days were finished but she persevered to keep the door half open and I ended up serving eight years in the Cabinet. I was often struck between the contrast of the understanding and sympathy she showed in private and the 'iron lady' she was happy to project in public.

She also had great courage. Her decision to challenge Heath is now seen through a backward glance as a decisiveness which gained her an outstanding victory. It did not seem like that at the time. Many thought it was a foolish and an impertinent gesture. During her election campaign I took her to Grieveson Grant for a stockbrokers' lunch. We had a guest from one of the pension funds who was ill mannered enough to enquire why she was opposing Edward Heath and rocking the boat. She dealt with this comment with an arctic cool. As we returned to Westminster together she snorted, 'John. Where on earth did you find him?' It was one of the many instances where she would find incredulity and prejudice in her quest to become leader.

She had a puritanical devotion to work and did not relax easily. This enabled Denis Healey to make the quip – not without merit – 'Ted Heath in drag'.

I had an amiable relationship with her in Cabinet (at least until my last year) and on most issues was very much on her side. However, my usefulness was hampered by two factors. Temperamentally I am as happy listening to a debate as speaking and secondly I had a rather soft voice. This was not helped by having a seat at the far end of the table. One day she took me aside. 'Chief Secretary. Please speak up and not just on Treasury matters.' Loyally I obeyed. At the next meeting I cleared my throat and intervened with a mildly dissenting view. After Cabinet I said, 'Well Prime Minister, I spoke up.' The reply settled the matter: 'I meant speak up for me.'

A serious difference of opinion arose over a Cabinet discussion of public spending in October 1981. Geoffrey Howe proposed a further cut in public spending. John Nott and I challenged these plans. She expected us as economic liberals to be dutiful lieutenants in Cabinet.

Her parliamentary private secretary, Ian Gow, made it clear how surprised and upset she was. I was unrepentant and thought then, as I do now, that it was a questionable economic decision.

At times Margaret Thatcher had almost tunnel vision in trying to achieve or reject policies. Such determination was often a strength but ultimately a weakness. She was skilled in finding the long grass to postpone crucial judgements. Her Chancellor and Foreign Secretary, then Nigel Lawson and Geoffrey Howe, wanted to move towards a fixed exchange rate for sterling. She opposed. Eventually we had a fairly large meeting of ministers and officials including the Governor of the Bank of England. The debate was predictable. She then took the voices. She had the support only of Keith Joseph and myself. All the big guns, including the Governor, were against her. Given the strength of the voices I assumed – at long last – there would there be a decision. Undeterred she said, 'Well, gentlemen, that's it: we do nothing.'

She was not a great parliamentarian but one speech was superb. She had been toppled from the premiership but made a last contribution from the front bench. It was devoted to a recent meeting of the European Council where she had said 'No, no, no' to proposed measures of economic and monetary integration. She asserted her Euroscepticism, now free from Cabinet collective responsibility. 'I'm enjoying this,' she said. It was a wonderful and passionate finale.

In 2000 I was asked by Hofstra University, a private institution on Long Island, to give a lecture on the Thatcher government of 1979–87. It was a great occasion. Cabinet memories were recalled by old-timers including John Nott and Cecil Parkinson. Margaret Thatcher had flown in, travel-worn but resolutely presiding before a doting American audience. I was delighted to give the lecture on her two parliaments as Premier. They were the years of her great success and formidable leadership and contrasted with what followed. It is important to recall her early years in office.

She had become Prime Minister in 1979 in circumstances of deep national unease. Government authority was at a discount. The trade unions were not merely hostile to change but they also had privileged legal powers. Overall the most powerful economic and political factor was the rapid rise in inflation. Lenin's dictum – that if you wished to destroy a nation, first debauch its currency – seemed terrifyingly prophetic.

In 1977 the Labour government had called in the International Monetary Fund for advice. Labour took some account of their proposals and introduced a measure of control over public spending with tighter monetary discipline – even some sales of public assets. It was, however, a modest reform programme compared with the Thatcher plans initiated after the 1979 election. Healey was an agnostic monetarist; she was a true believer.

Margaret Thatcher had a near-manic desire to check and reverse socialism. Her premiership was even more radical than that of Asquith and the Liberals before the First War and Attlee and Labour after 1945. She was not frustrated in any of her major objectives.

She placed her closest economic sympathisers in key Cabinet positions and outmanoeuvred many traditional Tories – effectively derided as 'wets'. The subsequent government programme could have been jointly written by the International Monetary Fund and Milton Friedman of Chicago University. Trade union law was fundamentally and effectively reformed. Foreign exchange and price and income controls were abolished. The Chancellor of the Exchequer, Geoffrey Howe, introduced monetary targets and used increases in value added tax to finance cuts in income tax.

The government pressed ahead with the sale of public sector housing and all the major utilities, even water.

The popularity of this fundamental programme is very much a matter of personal judgement. The public often wills the end but shrinks from the means. In my view effective trade union reform was immensely popular. The privatisation of utilities and public housing was also popular. On the other hand measures designed to liberalise the economy such as abolishing exchange, income and price controls had only a modest public impact.

Crucially I judge the broad thrust of her economic and fiscal policy to have been less than popular. Enthusiasm for cuts in income tax was fully offset by resentment against the substituted increase in value added tax. The modest controls over public spending combined with the high interest rates resulted in levels of unemployment and bankruptcy that brought censure from academic economists and more significantly led to considerable public disillusion. But the trough in electoral support was not fatally deep. Margaret Thatcher and the government held firm and fortunes were assisted by the successful war with Argentina over the Falkland Islands. She led the Conservatives to victory in the general election in 1983.

I do not disparage her will and determination but she was

powerfully assisted by the collapse of the opposition. Throughout this period the Labour Party was in turmoil and decline.

The left under the charismatic leadership of Tony Benn made a serious, albeit unsuccessful, challenge for power. This revealed deep divisions within Labour. These ranged from defence, Europe and public ownership to general economic policy and provoked a reaction from the Labour moderates.

On this occasion these Labour moderates were prepared to challenge their beleaguered party leadership with the creation of a Social Democratic Party under the leadership of Roy Jenkins. It was a brave gesture and nearly succeeded in breaking the political mould. The Conservative and Labour Parties are not strangers to sharp doctrinal conflicts but the Westminster electoral system does not encourage breakaway parties.

The Social Democrats, with the partnership of the Liberal Party, had a profound and immediate influence. The impact can be measured in the general election results. In 1979 the Conservatives secured 44 per cent of the vote, in 1983 it had been shaved to 42.4 per cent and in 1987 stood at 42.2 per cent. The pattern is clear: despite domination at Westminster, full implementation of its economic policy and the near collapse of Labour, the Conservatives could only maintain their popular vote. Over this period Labour's misery was total. A general election vote of 37 per cent in 1979 slid critically to 28 per cent in 1983 and edged upwards to a figure of 31 per cent in 1987. The Liberal–SDP vote tells a contrasting story, namely 14 per cent in 1979 rising with SDP to 26 per cent in 1983 and falling back slightly to 23 per cent in 1987.

Opposition disarray enhanced Margaret Thatcher's authority and she knew how to use it.

These figures can be interpreted endlessly, but my own view is that the Thatcherite dominance in the Cabinet room and Westminster never led to a major realignment of popular votes to the advantage of Conservatives. The inability of the Conservatives to convert their Westminster authority into popular support touches upon a residual attachment of the British to collective politics. Thatcherism for all its supremacy and style was unable to convert many entrenched attitudes.

The disintegration of Labour at Westminster from 1979 to 1987 concealed the fact that the British public still retained powerful residual preferences for high public spending and a collectivist economy. Tony Benn bemoaned that the Conservatives had instituted 'irreversible changes'. He was only partly correct. His socialism of public ownership and trade union power had a diminished support but John Smith and Tony Blair from the 1990s onwards were able to fashion a policy of regulation of the utilities, low increases in taxation and the rhetoric of an improving public sector. This was encapsulated in the style of New Labour. To me it is a poor substitute for what it sought to replace but it helped create the 1997 general election Labour landslide. Margaret Thatcher can take satisfaction that she not only gave life and success to the Tories but she also impelled Labour to change. It has been no mean triumph.

I observed the Tory fortunes after 1987 from the back benches in a philosophical but not bitter mood. What went wrong and why did her leadership end in such humiliation? I think she was driven by a self-confident belief that she, uniquely, could bring about necessary and fundamental changes. She wanted to alter the political landscape far faster than I thought prudent. I was a self-confessed 'consolidator', which she regarded as 'wetness' or appeasement. In another age I would have been for Baldwin, she for Churchill. I did not think the nation wanted a perpetual revolution of Tory radicalism. Instead of buttressing the successes of 1979–87 Margaret Thatcher ploughed ahead with further major reforms. She persisted with the community charge (poll tax) despite the unhappy experience of such a tax in Scotland and the worldly scepticism of Nigel Lawson and the Treasury.

Another factor in her decline was the distance that developed between her and the two key Cabinet ministers, the Chancellor and the Foreign Secretary. The general thrust of economic policy after 1987 reflected the fact that Nigel Lawson wanted to modify the principles on which Thatcherite policy had been pursued in the early 1980s. He wanted to move towards a fixed exchange rate with the consequential clash with Thatcher and her economic guru, Alan Walters. It resulted in the resignation of Lawson. It was a confrontation between two self-confident and determined personalities and it weakened the government.

Margaret Thatcher's clash with Geoffrey Howe, as Foreign Secretary, was even more damaging. His was the assassin's hand when she was slain. Geoffrey was an ambitious politician who, as Solicitor General, was the key author of the European Communities Act. It was obvious he would pursue an active pro-European policy. He found ready allies within the Foreign Office and over several years conducted a policy that Margaret Thatcher sought to thwart. From the back benches I supported her stance against Lawson and Howe, but I feared that her policy differences with them exacerbated by personal sharpness would prove fatal.

The cohesion of government would have been better served if in the mid-1980s John Moore had become Chancellor and Cecil Parkinson been Foreign Secretary. Alas this was not to be. Moore retired from politics, taking his considerable skills to the City, whilst Cecil Parkinson's personal problems blocked his planned promotion to the Foreign Office. A Thatcher–Parkinson European policy would have been unacceptable to many officials in the Foreign Office but I think it would have developed a British form of Gaullism that would have resisted the centralising ambitions of the European Commission under Jacques Delors and the Maastricht Treaty which paved the way for economic and monetary union.

Margaret Thatcher was unable to judge when it was appropriate to retire or to provide an orderly succession. Retiring is a skill that eludes many political leaders and in Thatcher's case her failure damaged Tories over a long term. I felt the need for a change of pace, if not direction, after the major policy initiatives of the early 1980s. In 1990 I voted for Douglas Hurd as her successor as I felt he was traditional and would hold the party together after its phase of radicalism. I had to swallow my Euroscepticism in making that choice, and – as usual – I backed the losing candidate.

I hardly saw Margaret Thatcher after she left the leadership, but I was delighted to meet her at a memorial party for Peter Utley. We talked about Europe. It was clear we were on the same side, but I was a Tory Fabian cautiously taking a long view and she was still crusading.

In May 2004 the Conservative Way Forward Group gave a dinner to celebrate the twenty-fifth anniversary of Margaret Thatcher's premiership. It was a pity they did not invite all fourteen surviving members of the 1979 Cabinet. Incredibly I was the only member present and found it a moving occasion. Disregarding the doctors' advice she made a speech. It was a vintage performance. The voice was weak but the spirit was as robust as ever.

A generation of historians will busily argue about her overall contribution and her personality and the policies will provide a rich study. It was a privilege to have served in her ministry and I feel personally indebted to her. Her qualities of courage and determination made her outstanding, but beyond a point they were self-defeating.

44

ELECTION OF BETTY BOOTHROYD AS SPEAKER

On 27 April 1992 I proposed Betty Boothroyd as Speaker. It was something of a parliamentary occasion in two ways. The Commons had never before chosen a woman, and a Labour Speaker was selected despite an overall majority of Conservatives. Also it was unusual to have so many candidates openly scrambling for the post.

As the 1987–92 parliament was coming to a close Speaker Weatherill announced he would be standing down. The new parliament would have to choose a fresh Speaker. Whilst Leader of the House I had had experience of working with the Speaker, mainly with Speaker Thomas. He was an old-style authoritarian and traditionalist and was more severe with dissidents than I would have been. He was also a Eurosceptic and a Methodist with a charming Welsh lilt. I got on well with him, but he had favourites and I would not have liked to cross him.

As a backbencher I had served under Speakers Hylton-Foster, King and Lloyd. Like most MPs I was neurotic about not being called to speak; but the persecution was in my febrile mind. The opportunities to speak were limited as there was no time limit in the 1960s and most backbenchers spoke for twenty minutes in debate. Secondly, it took a while for a newcomer to become known to the Speaker. I was diffident, being elected in 1961 and

asking my first oral question in 1965. I would never go to the
Speaker and ask when I would be called, but once Nigel Birch
asked the Speaker to move me up the list as he approved of my
'sound money' views. The Speaker obliged. I think I felt greatest
resentment when Speaker King turned down my request for a
ministerial statement when foot and mouth disease broke out in
Oswestry in 1967. I took it personally but I now realise neither he
nor his clerks would understand what a rural scourge the disease
could be.

In the 1970s I met a businessman at one of the never-ending
parties who said, 'I used to dine with Selwyn and he'd say, "I'm
going to put you in the gallery and then call John Biffen – he's
good value."' Without an Equity card I hope I entertained well.

The selection of Speaker is a matter for the House of Commons,
but the Prime Minister, the party leaders and the 'usual channels'
(i.e. the whips' offices) always took a keen interest. All the Speakers
I knew had been ministers or senior whips. The exception was
Speaker King, who was the first Labour MP to hold the post.
After the 1983 general election Margaret Thatcher was anxious
that Francis Pym, then Foreign Secretary, should succeed Selwyn
Lloyd, who had retired as Speaker. Francis was not taking the
proposed patronage gratefully. He wanted to remain in the active
world of Conservative politics where he had been Edward Heath's
outstanding Chief Whip and a soft-spoken but liberal member of
the Thatcher Cabinet. I was given the task by Margaret Thatcher
of visiting him at home and making a last plea that he should
accept nomination as Speaker. Francis and I both recognised it
was a futile call and parted good friends. Bernard Weatherill filled
the post with great distinction: a product of the Whips' Office,
he had, nonetheless, an instinctive sympathy with backbenchers. On the announcement of his retirement in 1991 the field
for his successor was open. I judged that the impending general

election would return a Labour government. At the time it seemed a reasonable view and I assumed a Labour House of Commons would select a Labour Speaker. I contacted Betty Boothroyd and said I would support her if she stood as Speaker. During my time as Leader of the House (1982–87), I had been impressed by how well she had handled committees. She was a no-nonsense chairman but happily not a pedant. Our politics were poles apart as she was a Euro-enthusiast.

My proffered support was genuine and strictly personal: no others were involved. The gesture hardly amounted to a plan let alone a plot. I assumed my support would enable her to demonstrate to any Labour rival that she had some Conservative support, the more so as I had been Leader of the House. The general election transformed the situation. John Major and the Conservatives won. Immediately I received a call from Betty Boothroyd: she enquired if 'bets were off' in view of the Tory victory. I said, 'No. I still hope that you will be Speaker.' There then followed another call and she asked if I would nominate her and I agreed. She chose Gwyneth Dunwoody as her seconder, a highly effective and independent-minded Labour MP. I then issued a statement: 'Betty Boothroyd has been an effective Deputy Speaker. On ability and merit she now deserves to be Speaker and I shall certainly support her.' In essence it was a backbencher's ticket.

The campaign that followed was unusual and somewhat public. Boothroyd had only one significant Labour rival, Harold Walker. A trade union stalwart and a former minister, he had been Deputy Speaker. Age was against him and he was decidedly less than charismatic. His bandwagon was stuck from the outset.

I still do not know why the Conservatives with the aid of their whips could not settle on a single candidate. Eventually Peter

Brooke emerged as the front runner. He had great presence, a respectable ministerial career and a deep regard for Parliament. He would have been a strong candidate had he been the sole Conservative standard bearer and had to make an early public bid. It was his misfortune that both Terence Higgins and Giles Shaw mounted serious campaigns for the Speakership and competed for the Conservative vote. Terence Higgins had been a Treasury minister but in more noteworthy fashion had made a career through office in the select committees, a relatively new force in Commons politics. Giles Shaw was a former minister and subsequently on the panel of a standing committee. Higgins was rather formal and Shaw diminutive and effervescent. They were unintentional spoilers. They were both friends of mine and Shaw had been a contemporary at Cambridge where he had sparkled as a Union debater. He was good company but he was disappointed by my action. I learned from a mutual friend that he expected better of me. Giles had never told me of his Speakership ambitions, but had he done so it would not have deflected me from my support for Betty Boothroyd. Selecting a Speaker is not an old pal's act.

The Commons normally voted for Speakers when only two candidates were standing. The Father of the House, Edward Heath, presided over the ballot. The provisions for a vote when there were more than two candidates were convoluted and wholly unsatisfactory. Heath explained the situation: 'I shall first call for a candidate to be proposed … after which a debate may follow … at this point an amendment may be proposed … to leave out the first name and insert another name…' Heath then called on Peter Brooke, who accepted nomination. I was called to move an amendment proposing Betty Boothroyd. If that had failed the other candidates would have been called in turn. It was an unenviable task for Heath. Boothroyd was a natural choice, being the sole Labour candidate, but Heath judged that Brooke was the strongest of the Conservative candidates and gave him the first round in the contest. It was a decision naturally regretted by Higgins and Shaw but I think Heath was right. My own view was that a single transferable vote should have been used to determine the Speakership, when there were more than two candidates. The subsequent shambles when Speaker Martin succeeded Betty Boothroyd in 2000 confirms me in that view.

The Commons was packed on the afternoon of 27 April. As ever I felt nervous as I awaited the summons from Edward Heath to move the amendment adopting Betty Boothroyd. I was in my usual place below the gangway two rows back. My speech was reasonably short – eight minutes – and I soon lost my nerves and made a restrained but spirited appeal on behalf of the backbench qualities of Betty Boothroyd. I was determined not to make reference to the fact that once she had been a Tiller Girl. It was a passing episode that had been excessively seized upon by the media. The speech seemed to go quite well but my confidence in the outcome was uncertain. Peter Brooke made a charming and humorous speech but the votes had been resolved before members had entered the chamber, let alone having heard the speeches.

Betty Boothroyd was duly elected and as the House stood to acclaim the result I heard John Major call across to me, 'Congratulations, John,' which was a kindly comment since I had spiked the establishment choice.

Tradition requires that the Speaker elect must always show great reluctance to ascend to the chair. Historically the post was fraught with danger, the holder acting as an intermediary between an imperious monarch and a truculent Commons. The proposer and seconder must take him or her by the arms and drag her to the chair. This piece of theatre was charmingly

described in a sketch by Matthew Parris in *The Times*, part of
which I repeat below.

Was it the changeability of an April day, or providence, which
sent a sudden beam of sunshine through the windows of the
Commons yesterday to bathe Sir Edward Heath in light as he
took the Chair for the selection of a Speaker?

Sir Edward's great day had arrived. His smile said it all: 'I
am still here. She's gone! Yippee!' Few of us in our lifetimes will
see again a look of more profound pleasure spread across an old
gentleman's face. Sir Edward looked as though he had been prac-
tising all morning: the bows were just so, not too deep, not too
perfunctory, each impeccably timed, each undertaken with slow
dignity and gruff expression. He resembled Edward Bear doing
his stoutness exercises in front of a mirror...

Betty Boothroyd's posse were a varied lot. The Tories' best
intellectual, John Biffen (proposing her), advanced of our one-time
Tiller girl, not one but two constitutional hypotheses: the doctrine
of 'constructive myopia' and the concept of 'fraternity in suffering'.
Tony Benn as the 'Uncle of the House' praised her candidature as
untainted by Labour and opposition whips. 'The usual channels',
he added, 'are the most polluted waterways on earth'...

Betty Boothroyd spoke well: graceful but confident. The vote
over, John Biffen and Gwyneth Dunwoody enacted the ritual
of dragging her, unwilling, to the Speaker's chair. Frankly, Miss
Boothroyd did not look unwilling. Mr Biffen, a rather slighter
figure than either of the ladies and holding Miss Boothroyd by
the hand, looked like a little boy being helped over the road
by two lollipop ladies.

Mr Major quoted a previous Speaker, 'I'm tired, I'm weary,
I'm sick of all this', and wished Betty Boothroyd better luck.

So do we.

The choice of Betty Boothroyd was a happy one. It vindicated my belief that she was clearly an excellent candidate – the best for the job – whoever won the general election and whatever the party conventions observed by the 'usual channels'. It was an episode where I could champion the abilities of backbenchers to buck the party caucuses. I was part of the action and not a fascinated spectator.

In 2001 Betty Boothroyd was appointed to the House of Lords. She asked me if I would be one of her two sponsors when she took the oath. It was one of my great sadnesses that I was unable to accept as I was then seriously ill with renal failure. It was a miserable epitaph to one of the most satisfying episodes in my Westminster life.

45

FINAL TIME IN THE COMMONS

Shortly after the 1992 general election I decided I would stand down at the end of that parliament. I had always thought I would leave at around sixty-five and I was experiencing some signs of ill health. This turned out to be a cancerous cyst on the kidney which was operated on in the autumn of 1997. Contributing to my decision was the fact that I had had a good general election and the result, North Shropshire including Newport, produced the highest ever Conservative vote and majority.

W. J. Biffen (C) 32,443
H. J. Stevens (Lib) 16,232
R. J. Hawkins (Lab) 15,550
Majority 16,211

I had relished my parliamentary career every bit as much as I had hoped. I enjoyed representing a rural constituency. I had a good working relationship with the local Conservatives and my time at Westminster, in government or on the back benches, had been lively. After leaving the Cabinet in 1987 my views had become more independent. I felt the government should place more emphasis on health and education spending and less on the reduction of income tax. In March 1988 I tabled an amendment to prevent the basic rate of income tax being reduced from 27 per cent to 25 per cent.

I thought John Major did quite well in the Herculean task of following Margaret Thatcher in 1990. There were tensions and uncertainties in the post-Thatcher era and – heretically but realistically – I thought a Tory defeat in 1992 would enable the party to recover a direction for domestic affairs and resolve a European policy whilst in opposition.

The 1992 parliament was a disaster. One great problem was that the recovery from an economic dip – hardly a recession – was slow. Towards the end of the parliament the economy improved but Tory fortunes remained static. I would vainly tell constituents, as the election drew near: 'The votes of protest will be replaced by the votes of choice.' It proved to be facile optimism.

One adverse factor was the number of Tory MPs whose marital misfortunes or petty greed had given rise to the charge of sleaze. It was an unfair accusation but it stuck and reinforced the view that after eighteen years of power the Tories were complacent, were not attending to detail and above all had become boring. All these charges were to a degree true. This was the background for the Maastricht Treaty, which provided for greater European centralisation and fatally split the Conservative Party.

It was quite clear in 1992 that Europe would feature in the new parliament and I judged that some new MPs were sceptical. Sarah and I gave a dinner party for Iain Duncan Smith, Bernard Jenkin, Barry Legg and Alan Duncan. We also had Hugo Young and Adam Raphael. These two liberal journalists were taken aback by the militancy of my guests. I thought they reflected the changing mood amongst Tory constituency workers. I reckoned there was a growing cleavage between the continental political elite and the British public. The former was most powerfully represented by Jacques Delors, whose market brand of socialism was much respected by Geoffrey Howe. Delors, as President of the Commission, emphasised the social policies of Europe and helped persuade the Labour Party that Brussels was a welcome alternative to Thatcherism. It was a master stroke and enabled Labour's leader, John Smith, to move the party towards his own strong Euro-integrationist view. Above all Delors was in a hurry; he envisaged up to 80 per cent of European political decisions being taken at Brussels level. The objective had to be secured speedily. He had the bicycle theory – if you did not keep pedalling you would fall off.

The Maastricht Treaty marked a major step forward for the Delors approach. John Major recognised the divisions within the Tory Party, which were then latent rather than overt. At Maastricht he secured an exemption for Britain from the Social Chapter, with its considerable business regulation, and kicked into the long grass Britain's obligation to join a European single currency. He believed these successes would persuade Conservative MPs that the overall package was acceptable. He should have been at our dinner table with Iain Duncan Smith and Hugo Young.

Many Tory MPs felt that Europe should evolve pragmatically. They would have preferred to amble on a leisurely walk rather than take a Delors cycle ride. A number of these Conservatives formed a group. I do not recall whether we ever had a name but we were recognised as the Maastricht Group. I was the most senior, by parliamentary service, by ministerial experience and by my record of Euroscepticism from the late 1960s onwards. I was therefore slightly miffed that I was not asked to take the chair. Michael Spicer took charge and I had the role of 'elder statesman', a position I shared with Peter Tapsell. Michael Spicer was a good chairman. He kept in touch with the Whips' Office and was reasonably sceptic in a group that contained many wayward figures. Like the biblical cave of Adullam we collected a whole range of discontents and our numbers became an embarrassment to John Major, and not merely on European policy. We would meet weekly in a downstairs committee room. It was all rather more public than conspiratorial. The Maastricht Treaty and its painful progress through the Commons was our exclusive business. Once Michael Spicer and I met the Chief Whip and separately the group had a meeting with John Major. I then argued that the European policy should be evolutionary and I suspect he had some sympathy with that view. Our numbers included Bill Cash, MP for Stafford. Like many he had started as a supporter of membership of the European Community but had become an obdurate opponent. He propounded his views with considerable knowledge and at great length. He is reputed to have worn down Michael Heseltine by his persistence. Chris Gill, MP for Ludlow, was also a dedicated sceptic and by chance a good partner in the battles I fought for the Shropshire education budget.

The Maastricht Treaty became an albatross for John Major. There were two reasons. John Smith led the Labour Party with great tactical skill. He put aside his own Euro-enthusiasm and fought the Bill at all stages. My pair, Giles Radice, was a great supporter of Maastricht and would anxiously ask me if the Tory sceptics were seriously committed to their opposition as he was being compelled by Smith to vote with them. Who would blink first?

The second factor that added to the agony was the Danish referendum. Denmark's vote of 'no' (soon to be reversed) raised sceptic morale and delayed the passage of the Maastricht Bill.

I was an active supporter of the sceptics but I made it clear that I was no longer prepared for all-night marathon sittings. I think this was partly because of my health, but at the time I did not realise it. I decided to make my position quite clear to the whips on 13 January 1993. I said I would not stay late, but would otherwise support all Conservative sceptic amendments except the referendum and reserved my position on procedural votes. My whip was David Lightbown, a bulky and intimidating person. He left me well alone but his generally aggressive methods of persuasion became part of Maastricht folklore. I had no idea what problems Maastricht was causing John Major within his Cabinet but it is now clear that several, including Portillo and Redwood, were closet sceptics.

The debate ended with the new drama of a vote that might be treated as a confidence motion – that is the government would resign if defeated. I decided I would vote with the government. That decision was not influenced by a short conversation I had with Douglas Hurd, who mildly regretted we had not talked together more often about the issue. I thought that a nonsensical and insincere comment. The disputed Maastricht provisions were not negotiable; they were genuine matters of principle, as painful for me as for my pair, Giles Radice. There is no doubt that Maastricht revealed a deep division in the Conservative Party that was exploited by John Smith. The division had long-term harmful consequences, as it persisted well beyond 2000 when the party might have reunited around a policy of European enlargement with institutions favouring the nation rather than a centralised continent.

Iain Duncan Smith produced a post-Maastricht pamphlet to which I wrote a foreword. The authors were Duncan Smith, Bernard Jenkin, Barry Legg and Walter Sweeney, all of whom had been active parliamentary opponents of the Maastricht legislation. John Major had called his negotiations, which excluded Britain from the Social Chapter and postponed a decision on a single currency, a victory: 'Game, Set and Match'. This claim was parodied effectively by the pamphlet. I concluded, 'It would be tragic if the thoughtfully argued debates of Iain Duncan Smith and his colleagues about the future of Europe should presage irreconcilable divisions in the Tory Party. It need not happen and it must not happen; but the precious quality of tolerance will be needed to ensure it does not.' Amen to that.

During the parliament John Smith died. I had known him quite well, as he was my shadow when I was Secretary of State for Trade. He was a shrewd and effective opponent. Neil Kinnock had done much to reform Labour but John Smith always looked more electable. If he had lived and become Prime Minister I believe he would have quickly sought membership of the euro.

I spent rather more time than usual on Shropshire politics. I had the most dependable support from Chris Gill. We were both champions of rural schools and believed they were disadvantaged by the spending formula of the Department of Education. I enjoyed working with the county council and the topic became one more issue where I voted against the government. I was also disenchanted by the idea of splitting the county in two, one half based upon the growing new town of Telford and the remainder the rump of rural Shropshire. I wrote to the minister, John Gummer, saying Shropshire had a proven history of being both the cradle of the Industrial Revolution at Ironbridge and the pastoral lands of the Marches. To me it seemed foolish to tear up a partnership that had survived two hundred years. My Tory and historical judgements were cast aside. I became a Shropshire nationalist, impatient with Westminster and Whitehall, let alone Brussels.

In August 1996 my mother died. She had moved from Williton to a house in Llanyblodwel and had made new friends. It was so pleasant to see her each weekend rather than every other month when I would have to go to Somerset. Her death was relatively sudden but not unexpected. I was telephoned at the Commons, informed that she was fading and asked to come at once to her nursing home at West Felton. I thought it courteous to tell the whip I was departing. 'Oh,' he responded, 'can you wait until after the next vote?'

I took an interest in whom the North Shropshire Conservatives would choose as my successor. They chose Owen Paterson. He had fought Wrexham in 1992 and helped me in the 1987 general election. He proved to be an excellent MP, dedicated to constituency work and a prominent Eurosceptic at Westminster. We had an excellent relationship, made secure by making a clean break from the constituency although Sarah and I continued to live at Llanyblodwel.

I remained an active member until the dissolution of parliament in 1997. It was quite obvious that a Tory recovery was most unlikely and my last year was devoted to damage limitation. I made my last speech in 1996 on the issue of BSE. This disease was having the most devastating impact upon cattle. I believe that its origins and implications divided veterinary opinion but I knew plenty of farmers who believed it had been caused by government changes in animal feed regulations. It was a judgement they decided naturally since it required financial compensation.

The intractable problems of BSE were added to all the other difficulties of the Major government. It produced a landslide defeat even greater than in 1906. But I was delighted that Owen Paterson retained North Shropshire.

On my last day in the Commons I was interviewed by the BBC and made some fairly obvious remarks about the possible scale of the Conservative defeat and possible changes in the leadership. I was then telephoned by one of the whips, Andrew MacKay. He must have some merit since he married the prettiest girl in the press lobby (Julie Kirkbride). However, he did not endear himself to me by his threatening manner. I had not spent thirty-six years in the Commons to be pushed around by a junior Mafioso. I was both sorry and glad to move on.

46

LORDS

In 1997 I became a life peer. It was customary for Conservative ex-Cabinet ministers to be sent to the Lords. It was a comfortable sunset home. I had no desire to treat it as a club, merely using the dining and library facilities; but I had no idea how I would continue my political interests. When I received the letter asking me if I would wish to go to the Lords I telephoned Sarah, who was with her family in South Africa. I had been asked to keep it confidential, so somewhat mischievously I asked if she would mind changing her name. She got the message.

However, changing one's name was not a simple matter. We discussed the matter with Garter King of Arms, Mr Peter Gwynn-Jones, whom Sarah had known since her youth. 'Your title?' he queried. 'Lord Biffen of Tanat,' we said in unison, thinking of the river that ran past the Horseshoe in Llanyblodwel. 'You can't have a river.' I was stumped and thought it would be impertinent to remind him that Anthony Eden was able to have Avon as his title. In the end I was allowed 'Tanat'. I was delighted. The valley straddled England and Wales; it was truly border country and the Welsh villages still had many Welsh speakers.

Our next triumph was getting to the head of the queue of those waiting to be sworn in. I was shortly going into hospital for my kidney operation and the fear was that I would not be up to taking part in the swearing-in ceremony for a long time afterwards. This was more negotiable than Tanat.

I was sworn in on 10 June 1997 and Sarah's son, daughter, father and stepmother joined us for the ceremony. My sponsors were Baroness Hooper and Lord Renfrew of Kaimsthorn. I had known Gloria Hooper since the 1960s and she had been a very good friend. I spoke on her behalf in the European elections in 1979 when she became MEP for Liverpool. It was the last occasion that city ever elected a Conservative MP or MEP. She subsequently became a life peer in 1985 and held several posts as a junior minister. Colin Renfrew had been master at Jesus College although subsequent to my under-graduate days.

The introduction ceremony was very formal. We dressed in hired robes and paraded around the chamber. Garter King of Arms played a major role. It was almost the last occasion when this ceremony was used. Shortly afterwards it was replaced by a slimmed-down version, a precursor of the major reforms in membership which transformed the Lords.

Almost at once I was taken to the London Clinic where I had a major operation to remove my spleen and a cancerous cyst on my kidney. It was a success, but for many months I endured a slow convalescence and partial memory loss. I then had a few months getting used to the Lords and the opportunity of listening to the debates over hereditary peers. There was much anguish amongst hereditaries at their demise and great hostility towards Lady Jay, the Leader of the House. She handled the reform with clinical efficiency and I thought that her conduct of business was brisk but correct. It took quite a while for the new Labour life peers to settle in. They were appointed by Tony Blair to remedy the modest Labour membership. With the disappearance of the bulk of hereditaries the arithmetic changed. The Conservatives now had only a slight majority over Labour and were in a substantial minority overall, given the number of Liberal and crossbench peers.

I found the Lords procedures sufficiently unlike the Commons to be irritating. I missed having a Speaker who would call you for questions. In the Lords one had to stand up and shout to be heard. The place also had an exaggerated politeness. I was not a great reformer, although a permanent Conservative majority based upon hereditaries was indefensible. In the *House Magazine* I wrote, 'I have my own reform programme: cheap and effective. Introduce a dozen Dennis Skinners to liven things up.'

Initially I had no desk. It was a repeat of the poor Commons facilities I experienced in 1961. After a while I was allowed to share the desk of Geoffrey Howe. This was appropriate, as I had shared his cottage at Malpas from 1964 to 1996 when he was MP for Bebington. He was an understanding landlord. Eventually I was given a desk of my own in a Conservative room of nine members. This was an excellent arrangement. The room contained an eclectic and highly individual group. Amongst them was Lady Gardner of Parkes, who was shop steward: she got the air conditioning to work and a copy of *Dod's Parliamentary Companion* gratis for the room. I could talk about farming to the Earl of Shrewsbury, who exhibited at Oswestry Agricultural Show. Baroness Perry of Southward was our intellectual leader, an authority on human rights and a former civil servant and president of Lucy Cavendish College, Cambridge.

Lady Chalker had had a distinguished career in the Commons
and should have been in the Cabinet. She now did a lot of work
in South Africa and I valued her company. Altogether we were
a cheerful room and not politically motivated. I then found out
that I was just younger than the average of the room, a comfort-
ing discovery when you are in your seventies. It typified the
Lords' accumulated experience, political passion all but spent
and decidedly aged. There were two issues that seemed to preoc-
cupy their Lordships, hunting and homosexuality. The decision
of the Commons, on a free vote, to abolish hunting, inspired
opposition in the Lords that went beyond the rural enthusiasts
who marched with the Countryside Alliance. Some peers felt
it was an infringement of liberty, whatever their own views on
field sports, and others thought Parliament had more serious
matters to discuss. I never spoke on the subject, but I believed the
growth of gun packs after the abolition of hunting in Scotland
demonstrated that it was easier to abolish hunting than to
abolish cruelty.

I had supported the Leo Abse Private Member's Bill in the
mid-1960s which legalised private homosexual behaviour
between consenting adults. It was a free vote and about a third
of the Conservative MPs supported the Abse measure: the
remainder were opposed. There was no reaction in my constituency. Nearly thirty years later the atmosphere was different. The
move to align the law between homosexuals and heterosexuals
was strongly contested, as was the proposed removal of Section
28, which forbade the teaching of homosexuality in schools. In
the House of Lords Lady (Janet) Young led a powerfully argued
opposition to any relaxation of constraints on homosexuality.
She took the overwhelming majority of Conservatives with her
and I found myself in a modest minority of Tory peers who
voted otherwise. The figure was well down from the 30 per cent

who had supported the Abse Bill. I think age was a big factor in the Lords vote; and I found the atmosphere much more intolerant in the Lords than I had recollected from my days in the Commons.

I waited a year before making my maiden speech. That was even longer than I had postponed my maiden speech in the Commons, but this was largely on account of the protracted recovery from my kidney operation. I did not find speaking in the Lords as nerve-racking as had been my early days in the Commons. My speech, seven minutes long, was devoted to constitutional change and the need for devolution settlements in Scotland, Wales and London to give rise to certainty and durability and not to the harbingers of more change. The speech was reasonable enough and I got the customary praise from the succeeding speaker, the Earl of Longford. Thereafter I spoke only occasionally, but after preparation. My topics included the World Trade Organization, the enlargement of the European Union, September 11 and Iraq. Speaking in the Lords is a rather bland business and I miss the interruptions and sharpness of the Commons.

I took a keen interest in the all-party groups including Russia and all the former Warsaw Pact countries, effectively the nations seeking to enlarge the European Union. This gave me a chance to meet East European politicians at Westminster – the more welcome as dialysis treatment prevented me travelling to the continent.‡ I am afraid the membership of the groups was very modest and the level of discussion often not very demanding. We had a delegation from Mongolia. They were all dressed in smart city suits. Even worse was to follow when our talks turned upon whether or not they had the list system of proportional

---

‡ John underwent dialysis three times a week from 2001 – SB

representation. It seemed a far cry from Genghis Khan and the Gobi Desert.

It is easy to snipe at the relaxed style of the House of Lords but its advantages were considerable. Its select committee enquiries were of a high level and commanded general respect. Unfortunately the timings of my hospital treatment prevented me from membership. The general debates were well informed and the system of publishing the list of speakers and the indicated length of speeches was an improvement over the Commons practice when you patiently awaited 'catching the Speaker's eye' in order to be called. On the other hand the formalised situation of the Lords debates meant there were hardly any interruptions as they counted against the time allotted to speakers. I found Question Time a disappointment: about as much a farce of ministerial obfuscation as in the Commons. Business was started with prayers being said by a roster of bishops. Above all I valued the facilities of the library, which I used for reference and for the daily papers: *The Times* in the late morning and the *Evening Standard* in mid-afternoon. All maiden speakers praised the helpfulness of the staff – and rightly so. The attendants and the dining rooms were courteous and efficient, qualities that contrasted with the world outside.

As much as I enjoyed the Lords I never felt that it had remotely the same sense of history as the Commons. There I would get a thrill from going to the central lobby and meeting guests. I was constantly reminded of the chamber that was burned down in 1834 as I walked from St Stephen's Entrance to the central lobby flanked by statues from the eighteenth century, whose names such as William Pitt the Younger, Charles James Fox and Henry Grattan were the very stuff of history. I never tired of the sensation that I was immensely privileged to be working in a building where they too had placed the stamp of their day. Of course the Lords had the royal connections. The throne and the woolsack were magnificent. Missing was the clamour and struggle for power that was represented in the Commons by Lloyd George or Margaret Thatcher.

John Biffen died on 14 August 2007, three weeks after his last visit to the Lords.

APPENDIX

MICHAEL FOOT LETTER

Nov 5

Dear John,

Since you are the only member of the Government who has the skill to make its horrific policies appear even distantly appealing, I suppose it always had to be reckoned a possibility that some poor girl would be deluded by these charms. So I was not altogether surprised.

However, since your character is, as the wisest of us know, superior even to your intelligence (no insult to the latter is intended), I am sure your marriage will outlast your policies, the Government & the last spasms of mad monetarism, however lingering they may be.

In short, best wishes. It's been a good year for Somerset, if tragic for the rest of us.

Michael Foot

INDEX